LINEAR ALGEBRA

SECOND EDITION

LINEAR ALGEBRA

SECOND EDITION

SERGE LANG

Columbia University, New York, New York

ADDISON-WESLEY PUBLISHING COMPANY

Reading, Massachusetts · Menlo Park, California

London · Amsterdam · Don Mills, Ontario · Sydney

This book is in the

ADDISON-WESLEY SERIES IN MATHEMATICS

LYNN H. LOOMIS
Consulting Editor

Third printing, June 1972

ISBN 0-201-04211-8
DEFGHIJKLM-AL-7987

Foreword

The present book is meant as a text for a course in linear algebra, at the undergraduate level. Enough material has been included for a one-year course, but by suitable omissions, it will also be easy to use the book for one term.

During the past decade, the curriculum for algebra courses at the undergraduate level has shifted its emphasis towards linear algebra. The shift is partly due to the recognition that this part of algebra is easier to understand than some other parts (being less abstract, and in any case being directly motivated by spatial geometry), and partly because of the wide applications which exist for linear algebra. Consequently, I have started the book with the basic notion of vector in real Euclidean space, which sets the general pattern for much that follows. The chapters on groups and rings are included because of their important relation to the linear algebra, the group of invertible linear maps (or matrices) and the ring of linear maps of a vector space being perhaps the most striking examples of groups and rings. The fact that a vector space over a field can be viewed fruitfully as a module over its ring of endomorphisms is worth emphasizing as part of a linear algebra course. However, because of the general intent of the book, these chapters are not treated with quite the same degree of completeness which they might otherwise receive, and a short text on basic algebraic structures (groups, rings, fields, sets, etc.) will accompany this one to offer the opportunity of teaching a separate one-term course on these matters, principally intended for mathematics majors.

The tensor product, and especially the alternating product, are so important in courses in advanced calculus that it was imperative to insert a chapter on them, keeping the applications in mind. The limited purpose of the chapter here allows for concreteness and simplicity.

The appendix on convex sets pursues some of the geometric ideas of Chapter I, taking for granted some standard facts about continuous functions on compact sets, closures of sets, etc. It can essentially be read after Chapter I, and after knowing the definition of a linear map. Various odds and ends are given in a second appendix (including a proof of the algebraic closure of the complex numbers), which can be covered according to the judgement of the instructor.

The basic portion of this book, on vector spaces, matrices, linear maps, and determinants is now published separately as *Introduction to Linear Algebra*, with additional simplifications of language and text. For instance, we take vector spaces over the reals, we consider only the positive definite scalar product, we omit the dual space, etc., which are less worthy of emphasis for a first introduction, needed in immediate applications, e.g. in calculus. In the more complete text of a full course in linear algebra, these topics are of course included, as are many others, especially the structure theorems which form Part Two: spectral theorem, for symmetric, hermitian, unitary operators; triangulation theorems (including the Jordan normal form); primary decomposition; Schur's lemma; the Wedderburn-Rieffel theorem (with Rieffel's beautifully simple proof); etc. Of course, better students can handle the more complete book at once, but I hope that the separation will be pedagogically useful for others.

In this second edition, I have rewritten a few sections, and inserted a few new topics. I have also added many new exercises.

New York, 1970   SERGE LANG

Contents

Part One
Basic Theory

CHAPTER I

Vectors

CHAPTER II

Vector Spaces

CHAPTER III

Matrices

CONTENTS

Part Two
Structure Theorems

Part Three
Relations with Other Structures

Chapter XIII
Multilinear Products

Chapter XIV
Groups

Chapter XV
Rings

Appendix 1
Convex Sets

APPENDIX 2

Odds and Ends

APPENDIX 3

Angles

PART ONE
BASIC THEORY

CHAPTER I

Vectors

The concept of a vector is basic for the whole course. It provides geometric motivation for everything that follows. Hence the properties of vectors, both algebraic and geometric, will be discussed in full.

The cross product is included for the sake of completeness. It is almost never used in the rest of the book. It is the only aspect of the theory of vectors which is valid only in 3-dimensional space (not 2, nor 4, nor n-dimensional space). One significant feature of almost all the statements and proofs of this book (except for those concerning the cross product and determinants), is that they are neither easier nor harder to prove in 3- or n-space than they are in 2-space.

§1. Definition of points in n-space

We know that a number can be used to represent a point on a line, once a unit length is selected.

A pair of numbers (i.e. a couple of numbers) (x, y) can be used to represent a point in the plane.

These representations can be represented in a picture as follows.

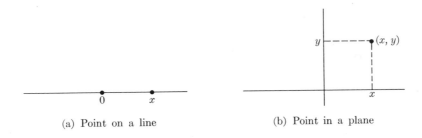

(a) Point on a line   (b) Point in a plane

Figure 1

We now observe that a triple of numbers (x, y, z) can be used to represent a point in space, that is 3-dimensional space, or 3-space. We simply introduce one more axis. The following picture illustrates this.

3

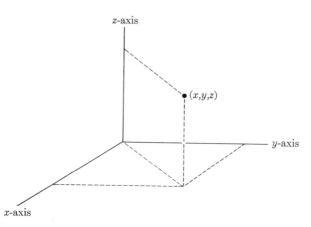

z-axis

(x,y,z)

y-axis

x-axis

Figure 2

Instead of using x, y, z we could also use (x_1, x_2, x_3). The line could be called 1-space, and the plane could be called 2-space.

Thus we can say that a single number represents a point in 1-space. A couple represents a point in 2-space. A triple represents a point in 3-space.

Although we cannot draw a picture to go further, there is nothing to prevent us from considering a quadruple of numbers

$$(x_1, x_2, x_3, x_4)$$

and decreeing that this is a point in 4-space. A quintuple would be a point in 5-space, then would come a sextuple, septuple, octuple, ...

We let ourselves be carried away and define a **point in n-space** to be an n-tuple of numbers

$$(x_1, x_2, \ldots, x_n),$$

if n is a positive integer. We shall denote such an n-tuple by a capital letter X, and try to keep small letters for numbers and capital letters for points. We call the numbers $x_1, \ldots, x_n$ the **coordinates** of the point X. For example, in 3-space, 2 is the first coordinate of the point $(2, 3, -4)$, and -4 is its third coordinate.

Most of our examples will take place when $n = 2$ or $n = 3$. Thus the reader may visualize either of these two cases throughout the book. However, two comments must be made: First, practically no formula or theorem is simpler by making such assumptions on n. Second, the case $n = 4$ does occur in physics, and the case $n = n$ occurs often enough in practice or theory to warrant its treatment here. Furthermore, part of our purpose is in fact to show that the general case is always similar to the case when $n = 2$ or $n = 3$.

Examples. One classical example of 3-space is of course the space we live in. After we have selected an origin and a coordinate system, we can describe the position of a point (body, particle, etc.) by 3 coordinates. Furthermore, as was known long ago, it is convenient to extend this space to a 4-dimensional space, with the fourth coordinate as time, the time origin being selected, say, as the birth of Christ—although this is purely arbitrary (it might be more convenient to select the birth of the solar system, or the birth of the earth as the origin, if we could determine these accurately). Then a point with negative time coordinate is a BC point, and a point with positive time coordinate is an AD point.

Don't get the idea that "time is *the* fourth dimension", however. The above 4-dimensional space is only one possible example. In economics, for instance, one uses a very different space, taking for coordinates, say, the number of dollars expended in an industry. For instance, we could deal with a 7-dimensional space with coordinates corresponding to the following industries:

1. Steel   2. Auto   3. Farm products   4. Fish
5. Chemicals   6. Clothing   7. Transportation

We agree that a megabuck per year is the unit of measurement. Then a point

$$(1{,}000, 800, 550, 300, 700, 200, 900)$$

in this 7-space would mean that the steel industry spent one billion dollars in the given year, and that the chemical industry spent 700 million dollars in that year.

We shall now define how to add points. If A, B are two points, say

$$A = (a_1, \ldots, a_n), \qquad B = (b_1, \ldots, b_n),$$

then we define $A + B$ to be the point whose coordinates are

$$(a_1 + b_1, \ldots, a_n + b_n).$$

For example, in the plane, if $A = (1, 2)$ and $B = (-3, 5)$, then

$$A + B = (-2, 7).$$

In 3-space, if $A = (-1, \pi, 3)$ and $B = (\sqrt{2}, 7, -2)$, then

$$A + B = (\sqrt{2} - 1, \pi + 7, 1).$$

Furthermore, if c is any number, we *define* cA to be the point whose coordinates are

$$(ca_1, \ldots, ca_n).$$

If $A = (2, -1, 5)$ and $c = 7$, then $cA = (14, -7, 35)$.

We observe that the following rules are satisfied:

(1) $(A + B) + C = A + (B + C)$.

(2) $A + B = B + A$.

(3) $c(A + B) = cA + cB$.

(4) If c_1, c_2 are numbers, then

$$(c_1 + c_2)A = c_1 A + c_2 A \qquad \text{and} \qquad (c_1 c_2)A = c_1(c_2 A).$$

(5) If we let $O = (0, \ldots, 0)$ be the point all of whose coordinates are 0, then $O + A = A + O = A$ for all A.

(6) $1 \cdot A = A$, and if we denote by $-A$ the n-tuple $(-1)A$, then

$$A + (-A) = O.$$

[Instead of writing $A + (-B)$, we shall frequently write $A - B$.] All these properties are very simple to prove, and we suggest that you verify them on some examples. We shall give in detail the proof of property (3). Let $A = (a_1, \ldots, a_n)$ and $B = (b_1, \ldots, b_n)$. Then

$$A + B = (a_1 + b_1, \ldots, a_n + b_n)$$

and

$$\begin{aligned} c(A + B) &= \big(c(a_1 + b_1), \ldots, c(a_n + b_n)\big) \\ &= (ca_1 + cb_1, \ldots, ca_n + cb_n) \\ &= cA + cB, \end{aligned}$$

this last step being true by definition of addition of n-tuples.

The other proofs are left as exercises.

Note. Do not confuse the number 0 and the n-tuple $(0, \ldots, 0)$. We usually denote this n-tuple by O, and also call it zero, because no difficulty can occur in practice.

We shall now interpret addition and multiplication by numbers geometrically in the plane (you can visualize simultaneously what happens in 3-space).

Take an example. Let $A = (2, 3)$ and $B = (-1, 1)$. Then

$$A + B = (1, 4).$$

The figure looks like a parallelogram (Fig. 3).

Take another example. Let $A = (3, 1)$ and $B = (1, 2)$. Then

$$A + B = (4, 3).$$

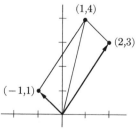

Figure 3

We see again that the geometric representation of our addition looks like a parallelogram (Fig. 4).

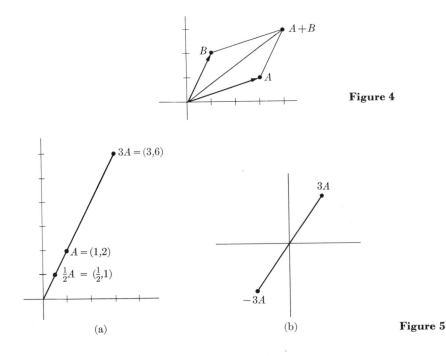

Figure 4

(a)   (b)   **Figure 5**

What is the representation of multiplication by a number?   Let $A = (1, 2)$ and $c = 3$. Then $cA = (3, 6)$ as in Fig. 5(a).

Multiplication by 3 amounts to stretching A by 3. Similarly, $\frac{1}{2}A$ amounts to stretching A by $\frac{1}{2}$, i.e. shrinking A to half its size. In general, if t is a number, $t > 0$, we interpret tA as a point in the same direction as A from the origin, but t times the distance.

Multiplication by a negative number reverses the direction. Thus $-3A$ would be represented as in Fig. 5(b).

EXERCISES

Find $A + B$, $A - B$, $3A$, $-2B$ in each of the following cases.

1. $A = (2, -1)$, $B = (-1, 1)$ 2. $A = (-1, 3)$, $B = (0, 4)$

3. $A = (2, -1, 5)$, $B = (-1, 1, 1)$ 4. $A = (-1, -2, 3)$, $B = (-1, 3, -4)$

5. $A = (\pi, 3, -1)$, $B = (2\pi, -3, 7)$ 6. $A = (15, -2, 4)$, $B = (\pi, 3, -1)$

7. Draw the points of Exercises 1 through 4 on a sheet of graph paper.

8. Let A, B be as in Exercise 1. Draw the points $A + 2B$, $A + 3B$, $A - 2B$, $A - 3B$, $A + \frac{1}{2}B$ on a sheet of graph paper.

§2. *Located vectors*

We define a **located vector** to be an ordered pair of points which we write $\overrightarrow{AB}$. (This is *not* a product.) We visualize this as an arrow between A and B. We call A the **beginning point** and B the **end point** of the located vector (Fig. 6).

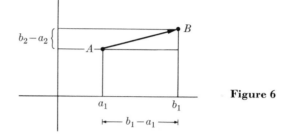

Figure 6

How are the coordinates of B obtained from those of A? We observe that in the plane,

$$b_1 = a_1 + (b_1 - a_1).$$

Similarly,

$$b_2 = a_2 + (b_2 - a_2).$$

This means that

$$B = A + (B - A).$$

Let $\overrightarrow{AB}$ and $\overrightarrow{CD}$ be two located vectors. We shall say that they are **equivalent** if $B - A = D - C$. Every located vector $\overrightarrow{AB}$ is equivalent to one whose beginning point is the origin, because $\overrightarrow{AB}$ is equivalent to $\overrightarrow{O(B - A)}$. Clearly this is the only located vector whose beginning point is the origin and which is equivalent to $\overrightarrow{AB}$. If you visualize the parallelogram law in the plane, then it is clear that equivalence of two located vectors can be interpreted geometrically by saying that the lengths of the line segments determined by the pair of points are equal, and that the "directions" in which they point are the same.

In the next figures, we have drawn the located vectors $\overrightarrow{O(B - A)}$, $\overrightarrow{AB}$, and $\overrightarrow{O(A - B)}$, $\overrightarrow{BA}$.

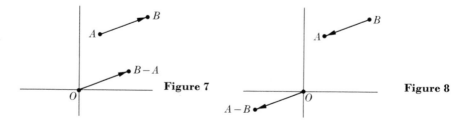

Figure 7

Figure 8

Given a located vector $\overrightarrow{OC}$ whose beginning point is the origin, we shall say that it is **located at the origin.** Given any located vector $\overrightarrow{AB}$, we shall say that it is **located at** A.

A located vector at the origin is entirely determined by its end point. In view of this, we shall call an n-tuple either a point or a **vector,** depending on the interpretation which we have in mind.

Two located vectors $\overrightarrow{AB}$ and $\overrightarrow{PQ}$ are said to be **parallel** if there is a number $c \neq 0$ such that $B - A = c(Q - P)$. They are said to have the **same direction** if there is a number $c > 0$ such that $B - A = c(Q - P)$, and to have **opposite direction** if there is a number $c < 0$ such that $B - A = c(Q - P)$. In the next pictures, we illustrate parallel located vectors.

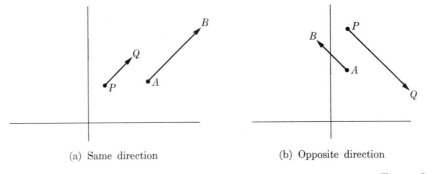

(a) Same direction   (b) Opposite direction

Figure 9

In a similar manner, any definition made concerning n-tuples can be carried over to located vectors. For instance, in the next section, we shall define what it means for n-tuples to be perpendicular. Then we can say that two located vectors $\overrightarrow{AB}$ and $\overrightarrow{PQ}$ are perpendicular if $B - A$ is perpendicular to $Q - P$. In the next figure, we have drawn a picture of such vectors in the plane.

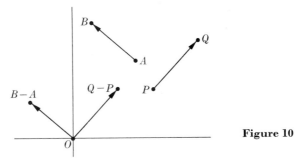

Figure 10

Example 1. Let $P = (1, -1, 3)$ and $Q = (2, 4, 1)$. Then $\overrightarrow{PQ}$ is equivalent to $\overrightarrow{OC}$, where $C = Q - P = (1, 5, -2)$. If $A = (4, -2, 5)$ and

$B = (5, 3, 3)$, then $\overrightarrow{PQ}$ is equivalent to $\overrightarrow{AB}$ because

$$Q - P = B - A = (1, 5, -2).$$

Example 2. Let $P = (3, 7)$ and $Q = (-4, 2)$. Let $A = (5, 1)$ and $B = (-16, -14)$. Then

$$Q - P = (-7, -5) \quad \text{and} \quad B - A = (-21, -15).$$

Hence $\overrightarrow{PQ}$ is parallel to $\overrightarrow{AB}$, because $B - A = 3(Q - P)$. Since $3 > 0$, we even see that $\overrightarrow{PQ}$ and $\overrightarrow{AB}$ have the same direction.

EXERCISES

In each case, determine which located vectors $\overrightarrow{PQ}$ and $\overrightarrow{AB}$ are equivalent.

1. $P = (1, -1), Q = (4, 3), A = (-1, 5), B = (5, 2)$.
2. $P = (1, 4), Q = (-3, 5), A = (5, 7), B = (1, 8)$.
3. $P = (1, -1, 5), Q = (-2, 3, -4), A = (3, 1, 1), B = (0, 5, 10)$.
4. $P = (2, 3, -4), Q = (-1, 3, 5), A = (-2, 3, -1), B = (-5, 3, 8)$.

In each case, determine which located vectors $\overrightarrow{PQ}$ and $\overrightarrow{AB}$ are parallel.

5. $P = (1, -1), Q = (4, 3), A = (-1, 5), B = (7, 1)$.
6. $P = (1, 4), Q = (-3, 5), A = (5, 7), B = (9, 6)$.
7. $P = (1, -1, 5), Q = (-2, 3, -4), A = (3, 1, 1), B = (-3, 9, -17)$.
8. $P = (2, 3, -4), Q = (-1, 3, 5), A = (-2, 3, -1), B = (-11, 3, -28)$.

9. Draw the located vectors of Exercises 1, 2, 5, and 6 on a sheet of paper to illustrate these exercises. Also draw the located vectors $\overrightarrow{QP}$ and $\overrightarrow{BA}$. Draw the points $Q - P, B - A, P - Q$, and $A - B$.

§3. *Scalar product*

It is understood that throughout a discussion we select vectors always in the same n-dimensional space.

Let $A = (a_1, \ldots, a_n)$ and $B = (b_1, \ldots, b_n)$ be two vectors. We define their **scalar** or **dot product** $A \cdot B$ to be

$$a_1 b_1 + \cdots + a_n b_n.$$

This product is a **number.** For instance, if

$$A = (1, 3, -2) \quad \text{and} \quad B = (-1, 4, -3),$$

then

$$A \cdot B = -1 + 12 + 6 = 17.$$

For the moment, we do not give a geometric interpretation to this scalar product. We shall do this later. We derive first some important properties. The basic ones are:

SP 1. *We have $A \cdot B = B \cdot A$.*

SP 2. *If A, B, C are three vectors, then*

$$A \cdot (B + C) = A \cdot B + A \cdot C = (B + C) \cdot A.$$

SP 3. *If x is a number, then*

$$(xA) \cdot B = x(A \cdot B) \qquad and \qquad A \cdot (xB) = x(A \cdot B).$$

SP 4. *If $A = O$ is the zero vector, then $A \cdot A = 0$, and otherwise $A \cdot A > 0$.*

We shall now prove these properties.
Concerning the first, we have

$$a_1 b_1 + \cdots + a_n b_n = b_1 a_1 + \cdots + b_n a_n,$$

because for any two numbers a, b, we have $ab = ba$. This proves the first property.

For SP 2, let $C = (c_1, \ldots, c_n)$. Then

$$B + C = (b_1 + c_1, \ldots, b_n + c_n)$$

and

$$A \cdot (B + C) = a_1(b_1 + c_1) + \cdots + a_n(b_n + c_n)$$
$$= a_1 b_1 + a_1 c_1 + \cdots + a_n b_n + a_n c_n.$$

Reordering the terms yields

$$a_1 b_1 + \cdots + a_n b_n + a_1 c_1 + \cdots + a_n c_n,$$

which is none other than $A \cdot B + A \cdot C$. This proves what we wanted.

We leave property SP 3 as an exercise.

Finally, for SP 4, we observe that if one coordinate a_i of A is not equal to 0, then there is a term $a_i^2 \neq 0$ and $a_i^2 > 0$ in the scalar product

$$A \cdot A = a_1^2 + \cdots + a_n^2.$$

Since every term is ≥ 0, it follows that the sum is > 0, as was to be shown.

In much of the work which we shall do concerning vectors, we shall use only the ordinary properties of addition, multiplication by numbers, and the four properties of the scalar product. We shall give a formal discussion of these later. For the moment, observe that there are other objects with which you are familiar and which can be added, subtracted, and multiplied by numbers, for instance the continuous functions on an interval $[a, b]$ (cf. Exercise 5).

Instead of writing $A \cdot A$ for the scalar product of a vector with itself, it will be convenient to write also A^2. (This is the only instance when we allow ourselves such a notation. Thus A^3 has no meaning.) As an exercise, verify the following identities:

$$(A + B)^2 = A^2 + 2A \cdot B + B^2,$$
$$(A - B)^2 = A^2 - 2A \cdot B + B^2.$$

A dot product $A \cdot B$ may very well be equal to 0 without either A or B being the zero vector. For instance, let $A = (1, 2, 3)$ and $B = (2, 1, -\frac{4}{3})$. Then $A \cdot B = 0$.

We define two vectors A, B to be **perpendicular** (or as we shall also say, **orthogonal**) if $A \cdot B = 0$. For the moment, it is not clear that in the plane, this definition coincides with our intuitive geometric notion of perpendicularity. We shall convince you that it does in the next section. Here we merely note an example. Say in $\mathbf{R}^3$, let

$$E_1 = (1, 0, 0), \qquad E_2 = (0, 1, 0), \qquad E_3 = (0, 0, 1)$$

be the three unit vectors, as shown on the diagram (Fig. 11).

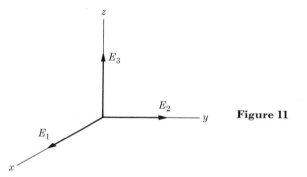

Figure 11

Then we see that $E_1 \cdot E_2 = 0$, and similarly $E_i \cdot E_j = 0$ if $i \neq j$. And these vectors look perpendicular. If $A = (a_1, a_2, a_3)$, then we observe that the i-th component of A, namely

$$a_i = A \cdot E_i$$

is the dot product of A with the i-th unit vector. We see that A is perpendicular to E_i (according to our definition of perpendicularity with the dot product) if and only if its i-th component is equal to 0.

EXERCISES

1. Find $A \cdot A$ for each one of the n-tuples of Exercises 1 through 6 of §1.

2. Find $A \cdot B$ for each one of the n-tuples as above.

3. Using only the four properties of the scalar product, verify in detail the identities given in the text for $(A + B)^2$ and $(A - B)^2$.

4. Which of the following pairs of vectors are perpendicular?

(a) $(1, -1, 1)$ and $(2, 1, 5)$ (b) $(1, -1, 1)$ and $(2, 3, 1)$
(c) $(-5, 2, 7)$ and $(3, -1, 2)$ (d) $(\pi, 2, 1)$ and $(2, -\pi, 0)$

5. Consider continuous functions on the interval $[-1, 1]$. Define the scalar product of two such functions f, g to be

$$\int_{-1}^{+1} f(x)g(x)\, dx.$$

We denote this integral also by $\langle f, g \rangle$. Verify that the four rules for a scalar product are satisfied, in other words, show that:

SP 1. $\langle f, g \rangle = \langle g, f \rangle$.

SP 2. $\langle f, g + h \rangle = \langle f, g \rangle + \langle f, h \rangle$.

SP 3. $\langle cf, g \rangle = c \langle f, g \rangle$.

SP 4. If $f = 0$, then $\langle f, f \rangle = 0$ and if $f \neq 0$, then $\langle f, f \rangle > 0$.

6. If $f(x) = x$ and $g(x) = x^2$, what are $\langle f, f \rangle$, $\langle g, g \rangle$, and $\langle f, g \rangle$?

7. Consider continuous functions on the interval $[-\pi, \pi]$. Define a scalar product similar to the above for this interval. Show that the functions $\sin nx$ and $\cos mx$ are orthogonal for this scalar product (m, n being integers).

8. Let A be a vector perpendicular to every vector X. Show that $A = O$.

§4. The norm of a vector

We define the **norm,** or **length,** of a vector A, and denote by $\|A\|$, the number

$$\|A\| = \sqrt{A \cdot A}.$$

Since $A \cdot A \geq 0$, we can take the square root.

In terms of coordinates, we see that

$$\|A\| = \sqrt{a_1^2 + \cdots + a_n^2},$$

and therefore that when $n = 2$ or $n = 3$, this coincides with our intuitive notion (derived from the Pythagoras theorem) of length. Indeed, when $n = 2$ and say $A = (a, b)$ then the norm of A is

$$\|A\| = \sqrt{a^2 + b^2},$$

as in the following picture.

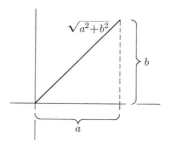

Figure 12

For example, if $A = (1, 2)$, then

$$\|A\| = \sqrt{1+4} = \sqrt{5}.$$

If $B = (-1, 2, 3)$, then

$$\|B\| = \sqrt{1+4+9} = \sqrt{14}.$$

If $n = 3$, then the picture looks like Fig. 13, with $A = (x, y, z)$.

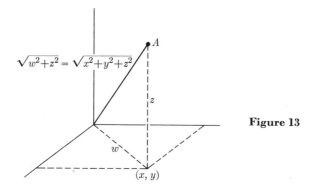

Figure 13

If we first look at the two components (x, y), then the length of the segment between $(0, 0)$ and (x, y) is equal to $w = \sqrt{x^2 + y^2}$, as indicated. Then again the length of A by the Pythagoras theorem would be

$$\sqrt{w^2 + z^2} = \sqrt{x^2 + y^2 + z^2}.$$

Thus when $n = 3$, our definition of length is compatible with the geometry of the Pythagoras theorem.

If $A = (a_1, \ldots, a_n)$ and $A \neq O$, then $\|A\| \neq 0$ because some coordinate $a_i \neq 0$, so that $a_i^2 > 0$, and hence $a_1^2 + \cdots + a_n^2 > 0$, so $\|A\| \neq 0$.

Observe that for any vector A we have

$$\|A\| = \|-A\|.$$

This is due to the fact that

$$(-a_1)^2 + \cdots + (-a_n)^2 = a_1^2 + \cdots + a_n^2,$$

because $(-1)^2 = 1$. Of course, this is as it should be from the picture:

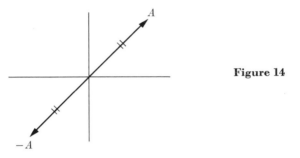

Figure 14

From the geometry of the situation, it is also reasonable to expect that if $c > 0$, then $\|cA\| = c\|A\|$, i.e. if we stretch a vector A by multiplying by a positive number c, then the length stretches also by that amount. We verify this formally using our definition of the length.

Theorem 1. *Let x be a number. Then*

$$\|xA\| = |x|\,\|A\|$$

(absolute value of x times the length of A).

Proof. By definition, we have

$$\|xA\|^2 = (xA) \cdot (xA),$$

which is equal to

$$x^2(A \cdot A)$$

by the properties of the scalar product. Taking the square root now yields what we want.

We shall say that a vector E is a **unit** vector if $\|E\| = 1$. Given any vector A, let $a = \|A\|$. If $a \neq 0$, then

$$\frac{1}{a} A$$

is a unit vector, because

$$\left\| \frac{1}{a} A \right\| = \frac{1}{a} a = 1.$$

We shall say that two vectors A, B (neither of which is O) have the **same direction** if there is a number $c > 0$ such that $cA = B$. In view of this definition, we see that the vector

$$\frac{1}{\|A\|} A$$

is a unit vector in the direction of A (provided $A \neq O$).

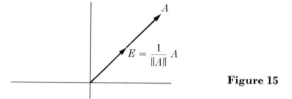

Figure 15

If E is the unit vector in the direction of A, and $\|A\| = a$, then

$$A = aE.$$

Example 1. Let $A = (1, 2, -3)$. Then $\|A\| = \sqrt{14}$. Hence the unit vector in the direction of A is the vector

$$E = \left(\frac{1}{\sqrt{14}}, \frac{2}{\sqrt{14}}, \frac{-3}{\sqrt{14}} \right).$$

We mention in passing that two vectors A, B (neither of which is O) have **opposite directions** if there is a number $c < 0$ such that $cA = B$.

Let A, B be two n-tuples. We define the **distance** between A and B to be

$$\|A - B\| = \sqrt{(A - B) \cdot (A - B)}.$$

This definition coincides with our geometric intuition when A, B are points in the plane (Fig. 16). It is the same thing as the length of the located vector $\overrightarrow{AB}$ or the located vector $\overrightarrow{BA}$.

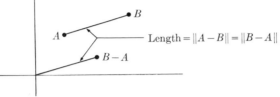

Figure 16

Example 2. Let $A = (-1, 2)$ and $B = (3, 4)$. Then the length of the located vector $\overrightarrow{AB}$ is $\|B - A\|$. But $B - A = (4, 2)$. Thus

$$\|B - A\| = \sqrt{16 + 4} = \sqrt{20}.$$

In the picture, we see that the horizontal side has length 4 and the vertical side has length 2. Thus our definitions reflect our geometric intuition derived from Pythagoras.

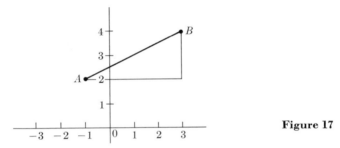

Figure 17

We are also in the position to justify our definition of perpendicularity. Given A, B in the plane, the condition that

$$\|A + B\| = \|A - B\|$$

(illustrated in Fig. 18(b)) coincides with the geometric property that A should be perpendicular to B.

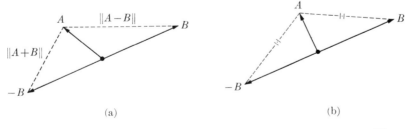

(a)   (b)

Figure 18

Taking the square of each side, we see that this condition is equivalent with

$$(A + B) \cdot (A + B) = (A - B) \cdot (A - B)$$

and expanding out, this equality is equivalent with

$$A \cdot A + 2A \cdot B + B \cdot B = A \cdot A - 2A \cdot B + B \cdot B.$$

Making cancellations, we obtain the equivalent condition

$$4A \cdot B = 0$$

or

$$A \cdot B = 0.$$

This achieves what we wanted to show, namely that

$$\|A - B\| = \|A + B\| \qquad \text{if and only if} \qquad A \cdot B = 0.$$

Observe that we have the general **Pythagoras theorem:** *If A, B are perpendicular, then*

$$\|A + B\|^2 = \|A\|^2 + \|B\|^2.$$

The theorem is illustrated on Fig. 19.

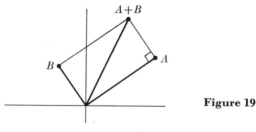

Figure 19

To prove this, we use the definitions, namely

$$\|A + B\|^2 = (A + B) \cdot (A + B) = A^2 + 2A \cdot B + B^2$$
$$= \|A\|^2 + \|B\|^2,$$

because $A \cdot B = 0$, and $A \cdot A = \|A\|^2$, $B \cdot B = \|B\|^2$ by definition.

Remark. If A is perpendicular to B, and x is any number, then A is also perpendicular to xB because

$$A \cdot xB = xA \cdot B = 0.$$

We shall now use the notion of perpendicularity to derive the notion of projection. Let A, B be two vectors and $B \neq O$. We wish to define the projection of A along B, which will be a vector P as shown in the picture.

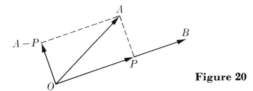

Figure 20

We seek a vector P such that $A - P$ is perpendicular to B, and such that P can be written in the form $P = cB$ for some number c. Suppose that we can find such a number c, namely one satisfying

$$(A - cB) \cdot B = 0.$$

We then obtain

$$A \cdot B = cB \cdot B,$$

and therefore

$$c = \frac{A \cdot B}{B \cdot B}.$$

We see that such a number c is uniquely determined by our condition of perpendicularity. Conversely, if we let c have the above value, then we have

$$(A - cB) \cdot B = A \cdot B - cB \cdot B = 0.$$

Thus this value of c satisfies our requirement.

We now define the vector cB to be the **projection** of A along B, if c is the number

$$c = \frac{A \cdot B}{B \cdot B},$$

and we define c to be the **component** of A along B. *If B is a unit vector, then we have simply*

$$c = A \cdot B.$$

Example. Let $A = (1, 2, -3)$ and $B = (1, 1, 2)$. Then the component of A along B is the *number*

$$c = \frac{A \cdot B}{B \cdot B} = \frac{-3}{6} = -\frac{1}{2}.$$

Hence the projection of A along B is the *vector*

$$cB = (-\tfrac{1}{2}, -\tfrac{1}{2}, -1).$$

Our construction has an immediate interpretation in the plane, which gives us a geometric interpretation for the scalar product. Namely, assume $A \neq O$ and look at the angle θ between A and B (Fig. 21).

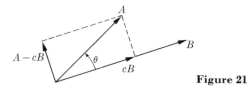

Figure 21

Then from plane geometry we see that

$$\cos \theta = \frac{c\|B\|}{\|A\|},$$

or substituting the value for c obtained above,

$$\boxed{A \cdot B = \|A\| \, \|B\| \cos \theta.}$$

In some treatments of vectors, one takes the relation

$$A \cdot B = \|A\| \, \|B\| \cos \theta$$

as definition of the scalar product. This is subject to the following disadvantages, not to say objections:

(a) The four properties of the scalar product SP 1 through SP 4 are then by no means obvious.

(b) Even in 3-space, one has to rely on geometric intuition to obtain the cosine of the angle between A and B, and this intuition is less clear than in the plane. In higher dimensional space, it fails even more.

(c) It is extremely hard to work with such a definition to obtain further properties of the scalar product.

Thus we prefer to lay obvious algebraic foundations, and then recover very simply all the properties. Aside from that, in analysis, one uses scalar products in the context of functions, where $\cos \theta$ becomes completely meaningless, for instance in Exercise 5 of §3, which is the starting point of the theory of Fourier series.

We shall prove further properties of the norm and scalar product using our results on perpendicularity. First note a special case. If

$$E_i = (0, \ldots, 0, 1, 0, \ldots, 0)$$

is the i-th unit vector of $\mathbf{R}^n$, and

$$A = (a_1, \ldots, a_n),$$

then

$$A \cdot E_i = a_i$$

is the i-th component of A, i.e. the component of A along E_i. We have

$$|a_i| = \sqrt{a_i^2} \leq \sqrt{a_1^2 + \cdots + a_n^2} = \|A\|,$$

so that the absolute value of each component of A is at most equal to the length of A.

We don't have to deal only with the special unit vector as above. Let E be any unit vector, that is a vector of length 1. Let c be the component of A along E. We saw that

$$c = A \cdot E.$$

Then $A - cE$ is perpendicular to E, and

$$A = A - cE + cE.$$

Then $A - cE$ is also perpendicular to cE, and by the Pythagoras theorem, we find

$$\|A\|^2 = \|A - cE\|^2 + \|cE\|^2 = \|A - cE\|^2 + c^2.$$

Thus we have the inequality $c^2 \leq \|A\|^2$, and

$$|c| \leq \|A\|.$$

In the next theorem, we generalize this inequality to a dot product $A \cdot B$ when B is not necessarily a unit vector.

Theorem 2. *Let A, B be two vectors in $\mathbf{R}^n$. Then*

$$|A \cdot B| \leq \|A\| \, \|B\|.$$

Proof. If $B = O$, then both sides of the inequality are equal to 0, and so our assertion is obvious. Suppose that $B \neq O$. Let E be the unit vector in the direction of B, so that

$$E = \frac{B}{\|B\|}.$$

We use the result just derived, namely $|A \cdot E| \leq \|A\|$, and find

$$\frac{|A \cdot B|}{\|B\|} \leq \|A\|.$$

Multiplying by $\|B\|$ yields the proof of our theorem.

In view of Theorem 2, we see that for vectors A, B in n-space, the number

$$\frac{A \cdot B}{\|A\| \, \|B\|}$$

has absolute value ≤ 1. Consequently,

$$-1 \leq \frac{A \cdot B}{\|A\| \, \|B\|} \leq 1,$$

and there exists a unique angle θ such that $0 \leq \theta \leq \pi$, and such that

$$\cos \theta = \frac{A \cdot B}{\|A\| \, \|B\|}.$$

We define this angle to be the **angle between A and B.**

Example. Let $A = (1, 2, -3)$ and $B = (2, 1, 5)$. Find the cosine of the angle θ between A and B.

By definition, we must have

$$\cos \theta = \frac{A \cdot B}{\|A\| \, \|B\|} = \frac{2 + 2 - 15}{\sqrt{14} \sqrt{30}} = \frac{-11}{\sqrt{420}}.$$

The inequality of Theorem 2 is known as the **Schwarz inequality.**

Theorem 3. *Let A, B be vectors. Then*

$$\|A + B\| \leq \|A\| + \|B\|.$$

Proof. Both sides of this inequality are positive or 0. Hence it will suffice to prove that their squares satisfy the desired inequality, in other words,

$$(A + B) \cdot (A + B) \leq (\|A\| + \|B\|)^2.$$

To do this, we consider

$$(A + B) \cdot (A + B) = A \cdot A + 2A \cdot B + B \cdot B.$$

In view of our previous result, this satisfies the inequality

$$\leqq \|A\|^2 + 2\|A\| \, \|B\| + \|B\|^2,$$

and the right-hand side is none other than

$$(\|A\| + \|B\|)^2.$$

Our theorem is proved.

Theorem 3 is known as the **triangle inequality.** The reason for this is that if we draw a triangle as in Fig. 22, then Theorem 3 expresses the fact that the length of one side is $\leqq$ the sum of the lengths of the other two sides (cf. Exercise 11).

Figure 22

EXERCISES

1. Find the length of the vector A in Exercises 1 through 6 of §1.

2. Find the length of the vector B in Exercises 1 through 6 of §1.

3. Find the projection of A along B in Exercises 1 through 6 of §1.

4. Find the projection of B along A in these exercises.

5. In Exercise 6 of §3, find the projection of f along g and the projection of g along f, using the same definition of projection that has been given in the text (and did not refer to coordinates).

6. Find the norm of the functions $\sin 3x$ and $\cos x$, with respect to the scalar product on the interval $[-\pi, \pi]$ given by the integral.

7. Find the norm of the constant function 1 on the interval $[-\pi, \pi]$.

8. Find the norm of the constant function 1 on the interval $[-1, 1]$.

9. Let $A_1, \ldots, A_r$ be non-zero vectors which are mutually perpendicular, in other words $A_i \cdot A_j = 0$ if $i \neq j$. Let $c_1, \ldots, c_r$ be numbers such that

$$c_1 A_1 + \cdots + c_r A_r = 0.$$

Show that all $c_i = 0$.

10. Let A, B be two non-zero vectors in n-space. Let θ be the angle between them. If $\cos \theta = 1$, show that A and B have the same direction. If $\cos \theta = -1$, show that A and B have opposite direction. [*Hint:* If c is the component of A along B, show that $(A - cB)^2 = O$.]

11. If A, B are two vectors in n-space, denote by $d(A, B)$ the distance between A and B, i.e. $d(A, B) = \|B - A\|$. Show that

$$d(A, B) = d(B, A),$$

and that for any three vectors A, B, C we have

$$d(A, B) \leq d(A, C) + d(B, C).$$

12. For any vectors A, B in n-space, prove the following relations:

(a) $\|A + B\|^2 + \|A - B\|^2 = 2\|A\|^2 + 2\|B\|^2$.
(b) $\|A + B\|^2 = \|A\|^2 + \|B\|^2 + 2A \cdot B$.
(c) $\|A + B\|^2 - \|A - B\|^2 = 4A \cdot B$.

Interpret (a) as a "parallelogram law".

13. Determine the cosine of the angles of the triangle whose vertices are

(a) $(2, -1, 1)$, $(1, -3, -5)$, $(3, -4, -4)$
(b) $(3, 1, 1)$, $(-1, 2, 1)$, $(2, -2, 5)$.

14. Show that if θ is the angle between A and B, then

$$\|A - B\|^2 = \|A\|^2 + \|B\|^2 - 2\|A\| \, \|B\| \cos \theta.$$

15. Let A, B, C be three non-zero vectors. If $A \cdot B = A \cdot C$, show by an example that we do not necessarily have $B = C$.

16. Let A, B be non-zero vectors, mutually perpendicular. Show that for any number c we have $\|A + cB\| \geq \|A\|$.

17. Let A, B be non-zero vectors. Assume that $\|A + cB\| \geq \|A\|$ for all numbers c. Show that A, B are perpendicular.

18. Let $B_1, \ldots, B_m$ be vectors of length 1 in n-space, and mutually perpendicular, that is $B_i \cdot B_j = 0$ if $i \neq j$. Let A be a vector in n-space, and let c_i be the component of A along B_i. Let $x_1, \ldots, x_m$ be numbers. Show that

$$\|A - (c_1 B_1 + \cdots + c_m B_m)\| \leq \|A - (x_1 B_1 + \cdots + x_m B_m)\|.$$

§5. *Lines and planes*

We define the parametric equation of a straight line passing through a point P in the direction of a vector $A \neq O$ to be

$$X = P + tA,$$

where t runs through all numbers (Fig. 23).

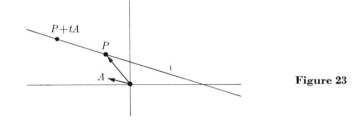

Figure 23

Suppose that we work in the plane, and write the coordinates of a point X as (x, y). Let $P = (p, q)$ and $A = (a, b)$. Then in terms of the coordinates, we can write

$$x = p + ta, \qquad y = q + tb.$$

We can then eliminate t and obtain the usual equation relating x and y.

For example, let $P = (2, 1)$ and $A = (-1, 5)$. Then the parametric equation of the line through P in the direction of A gives us

(∗) $$x = 2 - t, \qquad y = 1 + 5t.$$

Multiplying the first equation by 5 and adding yields

(∗∗) $$5x + y = 11,$$

which is familiar.

This elimination of t shows that every pair (x, y) which satisfies the parametric equation (∗) for some value of t also satisfies equation (∗∗). Conversely, suppose we have a pair of numbers (x, y) satisfying (∗∗). Let $t = 2 - x$. Then

$$y = 11 - 5x = 11 - 5(2 - t) = 1 + 5t.$$

Hence there exists some value of t which satisfies equation (∗). Thus we have proved that the pairs (x, y) which are solutions of (∗∗) are exactly the same pairs of numbers as those obtained by giving arbitrary values for t in (∗). Thus the straight line can be described parametrically as in (∗) or in terms of its usual equation (∗∗). Starting with the ordinary equation

$$5x + y = 11,$$

we let $t = 2 - x$ in order to recover the specific parametrization of (∗).

When we parametrize a straight line in the form

$$X = P + tA,$$

we have of course infinitely many choices for P on the line, and also infinitely many choices for A, differing by a scalar multiple. We can always select at least one. Namely, given an equation

$$ax + by = c$$

with numbers a, b, c, suppose that $a \neq 0$. We use y as parameter, and let

$$y = t.$$

Then we can solve for x, namely

$$x = \frac{c}{a} - \frac{b}{a} t.$$

Let $P = (c/a, 0)$ and $A = (-b/a, 1)$. We see that an arbitrary point (x, y) satisfying the equation

$$ax + by = c$$

can be expressed parametrically, namely

$$(x, y) = P + tA.$$

In higher dimension, starting with a parametric equation

$$X = P + tA,$$

we cannot eliminate t, and thus the parametric equation is the only one available to describe a straight line.

However, we can describe planes by an equation analogous to the single equation of the line. We proceed as follows.

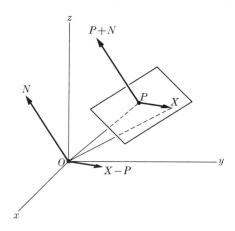

Figure 24

Let P be a point, and consider a located vector $\overrightarrow{ON}$. We define the **hyperplane** passing through P perpendicular to $\overrightarrow{ON}$ to be the collection of all points X such that the located vector $\overrightarrow{PX}$ is perpendicular to $\overrightarrow{ON}$. According to our definitions, this amounts to the condition

$$(X - P) \cdot N = 0,$$

which can also be written as

$$X \cdot N = P \cdot N.$$

We shall also say that this hyperplane is the one perpendicular to N, and consists of all vectors X such that $X - P$ is perpendicular to N. We have drawn a typical situation in 3-space in Fig. 24.

Instead of saying that N is perpendicular to the plane, one also says that N is **normal** to the plane.

Let t be a number $\neq 0$. Then the set of points X such that

$$(X - P) \cdot N = 0$$

coincides with the set of points X such that

$$(X - P) \cdot tN = 0.$$

Thus we may say that our plane is the plane passing through P and perpendicular to the *line* in the direction of N. To find the equation of the plane, we could use any vector tN (with $t \neq 0$) instead of N.

In 3-space, we get an ordinary plane. For example, let $P = (2, 1, -1)$ and $N = (-1, 1, 3)$. Then the equation of the plane passing through P and perpendicular to N is

$$-x + y + 3z = -2 + 1 - 3$$

or

$$-x + y + 3z = -4.$$

Observe that in 2-space, with $X = (x, y)$, we are led to the equation of the line in the ordinary sense. For example, the equation of the line passing through $(4, -3)$ and perpendicular to $(-5, 2)$ is

$$-5x + 2y = -20 - 6 = -26.$$

We are now in position to interpret the coefficients $(-5, 2)$ of x and y in this equation. They give rise to a vector perpendicular to the line. In any equation

$$ax + by = c$$

the vector (a, b) is perpendicular to the line determined by the equation. Similarly, in 3-space, the vector (a, b, c) is perpendicular to the plane determined by the equation

$$ax + by + cz = d.$$

For example, the plane determined by the equation

$$2x - y + 3z = 5$$

is perpendicular to the vector $(2, -1, 3)$. If we want to find a point in that plane, we of course have many choices. We can give arbitrary values to x and y, and then solve for z. To get a concrete point, let $x = 1$, $y = 1$. Then we solve for z, namely

$$3z = 5 - 2 + 1 = 4,$$

so that $z = \frac{4}{3}$. Thus

$$(1, 1, \tfrac{4}{3})$$

is a point in the plane.

Two vectors A, B are said to be **parallel** if there exists a number $c \neq 0$ such that $cA = B$. Two lines are said to be **parallel** if, given two distinct points P_1, Q_1 on the first line and P_2, Q_2 on the second, the vectors

$$P_1 - Q_1 \quad \text{and} \quad P_2 - Q_2$$

are parallel.

Two planes are said to be **parallel** (in 3-space) if their normal vectors are parallel. They are said to be **perpendicular** if their normal vectors are perpendicular. The **angle** between two planes is defined to be the angle between their normal vectors.

Example 1. Find the cosine of the angle between the planes

$$2x - y + z = 0,$$
$$x + 2y - z = 1.$$

This cosine is the cosine of the angle between the vectors

$$A = (2, -1, 1) \quad \text{and} \quad B = (1, 2, -1).$$

It is therefore equal to

$$\frac{A \cdot B}{\|A\| \, \|B\|} = -\frac{1}{6}.$$

Example 2. Let $Q = (1, 1, 1)$ and $P = (1, -1, 2)$. Let $N = (1, 2, 3)$. Find the point of intersection of the line through P in the direction of N, and the plane through Q perpendicular to N.

The parametric equation of the line through P in the direction of N is

(1) $X = P + tN.$

The equation of the plane through Q perpendicular to N is

(2) $(X - Q) \cdot N = 0.$

We visualize the line and plane as follows:

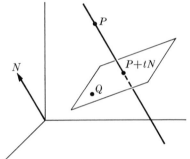

Figure 25

We must find the value of t such that the vector X in (1) also satisfies (2), that is

$$(P + tN - Q) \cdot N = 0,$$

or after using the rules of the dot product,

$$(P - Q) \cdot N + tN \cdot N = 0.$$

Solving for t yields

$$t = \frac{(Q - P) \cdot N}{N \cdot N} = \frac{1}{14}.$$

Thus the desired point of intersection is

$$P + tN = (1, -1, 2) + \tfrac{1}{14}(1, 2, 3) = (\tfrac{15}{14}, -\tfrac{12}{14}, \tfrac{31}{14}).$$

Example 3. Find the equation of the plane passing through the three points

$$P_1 = (1, 2, -1), \qquad P_2 = (-1, 1, 4), \qquad P_3 = (1, 3, -2).$$

We visualize schematically the three points as follows:

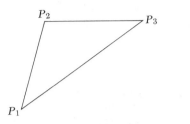

Figure 26

Then we find a vector N perpendicular to $\overrightarrow{P_1P_2}$ and $\overrightarrow{P_1P_3}$, or in other words, perpendicular to $P_2 - P_1$ and $P_3 - P_1$. We have

$$P_2 - P_1 = (-2, -1, +5),$$
$$P_3 - P_1 = (0, 1, -1).$$

Let $N = (a, b, c)$. We must solve:

$$-2a - b + 5c = 0,$$
$$b - c = 0.$$

We take $b = c = 1$ and solve for a, getting $a = 2$. Then

$$N = (2, 1, 1)$$

satisfies our requirements. The plane perpendicular to N, passing through P_1 is the desired plane. Its equation is therefore

$$2x + y + z = 2 + 2 - 1 = 3.$$

EXERCISES

Find a parametric equation for the line passing through the following points.

1. $(1, 1, -1)$ and $(-2, 1, 3)$
2. $(-1, 5, 2)$ and $(3, -4, 1)$

Find the equation of the line in 2-space, perpendicular to A and passing through P, for the following values of A and P.

3. $A = (1, -1)$, $P = (-5, 3)$
4. $A = (-5, 4)$, $P = (3, 2)$
5. Show that the lines

$$3x - 5y = 1, \qquad 2x + 3y = 5$$

are not perpendicular.

6. Which of the following pairs of lines are perpendicular?

(a) $3x - 5y = 1$ and $2x + y = 2$
(b) $2x + 7y = 1$ and $x - y = 5$
(c) $3x - 5y = 1$ and $5x + 3y = 7$
(d) $-x + y = 2$ and $x + y = 9$

7. Find the equation of the plane perpendicular to the given vector N and passing through the given point P.

(a) $N = (1, -1, 3)$, $P = (4, 2, -1)$
(b) $N = (-3, -2, 4)$, $P = (2, \pi, -5)$
(c) $N = (-1, 0, 5)$, $P = (2, 3, 7)$

8. Find the equation of the plane passing through the following three points.

(a) $(2, 1, 1)$, $(3, -1, 1)$, $(4, 1, -1)$
(b) $(-2, 3, -1)$, $(2, 2, 3)$, $(-4, -1, 1)$
(c) $(-5, -1, 2)$, $(1, 2, -1)$, $(3, -1, 2)$

9. Find a vector perpendicular to $(1, 2, -3)$ and $(2, -1, 3)$, and another vector perpendicular to $(-1, 3, 2)$ and $(2, 1, 1)$.

10. Let P be the point $(1, 2, 3, 4)$ and Q the point $(4, 3, 2, 1)$. Let A be the vector $(1, 1, 1, 1)$. Let L be the line passing through P and parallel to A.

(a) Given a point X on the line L, compute the distance between Q and X (as a function of the parameter t).

(b) Show that there is precisely one point X_0 on the line such that this distance achieves a minimum, and that this minimum is $2\sqrt{5}$.

(c) Show that $X_0 - Q$ is perpendicular to the line.

11. Let P be the point $(1, -1, 3, 1)$ and Q the point $(1, 1, -1, 2)$. Let A be the vector $(1, -3, 2, 1)$. Solve the same questions as in the preceding problem, except that in this case the minimum distance is $\sqrt{146/15}$.

12. Find a vector parallel to the line of intersection of the two planes

$$2x - y + z = 1,$$
$$3x + y + z = 2.$$

13. Same question for the planes,

$$2x + y + 5z = 2,$$
$$3x - 2y + z = 3.$$

14. Find a parametric equation for the line of intersection of the planes of Exercises 12 and 13.

15. Find the cosine of the angle between the following planes:

(a) $x + y + z = 1$ (b) $2x + 3y - z = 2$
    $x - y - z = 5$ $x - y + z = 1$
(c) $x + 2y - z = 1$ (d) $2x + y + z = 3$
    $-x + 3y + z = 2$ $-x - y + z = \pi$

16. Let $P = (1, 3, 5)$ and $A = (-2, 1, 1)$. Find the intersection of the line through P in the direction of A, and the plane $2x + 3y - z = 1$.

17. Let $Q = (1, -1, 2)$, $P = (1, 3, -2)$, and $N = (1, 2, 2)$. Find the point of the intersection of the line through P in the direction of N, and the plane through Q perpendicular to N.

18. Let P, Q be two points and N a vector in 3-space. Let P' be the point of intersection of the line through P, in the direction of N, and the plane through Q, perpendicular to N. We define the **distance** from P to that plane to be the distance between P and P'. Find this distance when

$$P = (1, 3, 5), \qquad Q = (-1, 1, 7), \qquad N = (-1, 1, -1).$$

19. In the notation of Exercise 18, show that the general formula for the distance is given by

$$\frac{|(Q - P) \cdot N|}{\|N\|}.$$

20. Find the distance between the indicated point and plane.
(a) $(1, 1, 2)$ and $3x + y - 5z = 2$.
(b) $(-1, 3, 2)$ and $2x - y + z = 1$.

21. Let $P = (1, 3, -1)$ and $Q = (-4, 5, 2)$. Determine the coordinates of the following points: (a) The midpoint of the line segment between P and Q. (b) The two points on this line segment lying one-third and two-thirds of the way from P to Q.

22. If P, Q are two arbitrary points in n-space, give the general formula for the midpoint of the line segment between P and Q.

§6. The cross product

This section applies only in 3-space!

Let $A = (a_1, a_2, a_3)$ and $B = (b_1, b_2, b_3)$ be two vectors in 3-space. We define their **cross product**

$$A \times B = (a_2 b_3 - a_3 b_2, \ a_3 b_1 - a_1 b_3, \ a_1 b_2 - a_2 b_1).$$

For instance, if $A = (2, 3, -1)$ and $B = (-1, 1, 5)$, then

$$A \times B = (16, -9, 5).$$

We leave the following assertions as exercises:

CP 1. $A \times B = -(B \times A)$.

CP 2. $A \times (B + C) = (A \times B) + (A \times C)$, *and*
$(B + C) \times A = B \times A + C \times A.$

CP 3. *For any number a, we have*

$$(aA) \times B = a(A \times B) = A \times (aB).$$

CP 4. $(A \times B) \times C = (A \cdot C)B - (B \cdot C)A.$

CP 5. $A \times B$ *is perpendicular to both A and B.*

As an example, we carry out this computation. We have

$$A \cdot (A \times B) = a_1(a_2b_3 - a_3b_2) + a_2(a_3b_1 - a_1b_3) + a_3(a_1b_2 - a_2b_1)$$
$$= 0$$

because all terms cancel. Similarly for $B \cdot (A \times B)$. This perpendicularity may be drawn as follows.

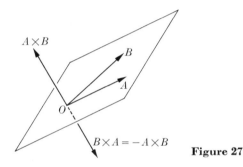

$A \times B$

B

A

O

$B \times A = -A \times B$

Figure 27

The vector $A \times B$ is perpendicular to the plane spanned by A and B. So is $B \times A$, but $B \times A$ points in the opposite direction.

Finally, as a last property, we have

CP 6. $(A \times B)^2 = (A \cdot A)(B \cdot B) - (A \cdot B)^2.$

Again, this can be verified by a computation on the coordinates. Namely, we have

$$(A \times B) \cdot (A \times B)$$
$$= (a_2b_3 - a_3b_2)^2 + (a_3b_1 - a_1b_3)^2 + (a_1b_2 - a_2b_1)^2,$$
$$(A \cdot A)(B \cdot B) - (A \cdot B)^2$$
$$= (a_1^2 + a_2^2 + a_3^2)(b_1^2 + b_2^2 + b_3^2) - (a_1b_1 + a_2b_2 + a_3b_3)^2.$$

Expanding everything out, we find that CP 6 drops out.

From our interpretation of the dot product, and the definition of the norm, we can rewrite CP 6 in the form

$$\|A \times B\|^2 = \|A\|^2\|B\|^2 - \|A\|^2\|B\|^2 \cos^2 \theta,$$

where θ is the angle between A and B. Hence we obtain

$$\|A \times B\|^2 = \|A\|^2 \|B\|^2 \sin^2 \theta$$

or

$$\|A \times B\| = \|A\| \, \|B\| \, |\sin \theta|.$$

This is analogous to the formula which gave us the absolute value of $A \cdot B$.

EXERCISES

Find $A \times B$ for the following vectors.

1. $A = (1, -1, 1)$ and $B = (-2, 3, 1)$
2. $A = (-1, 1, 2)$ and $B = (1, 0, -1)$
3. $A = (1, 1, -3)$ and $B = (-1, -2, -3)$
4. Find $A \times A$ and $B \times B$, in Exercises 1 through 3.
5. Let $E_1 = (1, 0, 0)$, $E_2 = (0, 1, 0)$, and $E_3 = (0, 0, 1)$. Find $E_1 \times E_2$, $E_2 \times E_3$, $E_3 \times E_1$.
6. Show that for any vector A in 3-space we have $A \times A = O$.
7. Compute $E_1 \times (E_1 \times E_2)$ and $(E_1 \times E_1) \times E_2$. Are these vectors equal to each other?

§7. *Complex numbers*

The complex numbers are a set of objects which can be added and multiplied, the sum and product of two complex numbers being also a complex number, and satisfy the following conditions.

(1) Every real number is a complex number, and if α, β are real numbers, then their sum and product as complex numbers are the same as their sum and product as real numbers.

(2) There is a complex number denoted by i such that $i^2 = -1$.

(3) Every complex number can be written uniquely in the form $a + bi$ where a, b are real numbers.

(4) The ordinary laws of arithmetic concerning addition and multiplication are satisfied. We list these laws:

If α, β, γ are complex numbers, then

$$(\alpha\beta)\gamma = \alpha(\beta\gamma) \qquad \text{and} \qquad (\alpha + \beta) + \gamma = \alpha + (\beta + \gamma).$$

We have $\alpha(\beta + \gamma) = \alpha\beta + \alpha\gamma$, and $(\beta + \gamma)\alpha = \beta\alpha + \gamma\alpha$.
We have $\alpha\beta = \beta\alpha$, and $\alpha + \beta = \beta + \alpha$.

If 1 is the real number one, then $1\alpha = \alpha$.

If 0 is the real number zero, then $0\alpha = 0$.

We have $\alpha + (-1)\alpha = 0$.

We shall now draw consequences of these properties. With each complex number $a + bi$, we associate the vector (a, b) in the plane. Let $\alpha = a_1 + a_2 i$ and $\beta = b_1 + b_2 i$ be two complex numbers. Then

$$\alpha + \beta = a_1 + b_1 + (a_2 + b_2)i.$$

Hence addition of complex numbers is carried out "componentwise" and corresponds to addition of vectors in the plane. For example,

$$(2 + 3i) + (-1 + 5i) = 1 + 8i.$$

In multiplying complex numbers, we use the rule $i^2 = -1$ to simplify a product and to put it in the form $a + bi$. For instance, let $\alpha = 2 + 3i$ and $\beta = 1 - i$. Then

$$\begin{aligned}
\alpha\beta = (2 + 3i)(1 - i) &= 2(1 - i) + 3i(1 - i) \\
&= 2 - 2i + 3i - 3i^2 \\
&= 2 + i - 3(-1) \\
&= 2 + 3 + i \\
&= 5 + i.
\end{aligned}$$

Let $\alpha = a + bi$ be a complex number. We define $\bar{\alpha}$ to be $a - bi$. Thus if $\alpha = 2 + 3i$, then $\bar{\alpha} = 2 - 3i$. The complex number $\bar{\alpha}$ is called the **conjugate** of α. We see at once that

$$\alpha\bar{\alpha} = a^2 + b^2.$$

With the vector interpretation of complex numbers, we see that $\alpha\bar{\alpha}$ is the square of the distance of the point (a, b) from the origin.

We now have one more important property of complex numbers, which will allow us to divide by complex numbers other than 0.

If $\alpha = a + bi$ is a complex number $\neq 0$, and if we let

$$\lambda = \frac{\bar{\alpha}}{a^2 + b^2}$$

then $\alpha\lambda = \lambda\alpha = 1$.

The proof of this property is an immediate consequence of the law of multiplication of complex numbers, because

$$\alpha\frac{\bar{\alpha}}{a^2 + b^2} = \frac{\alpha\bar{\alpha}}{a^2 + b^2} = 1.$$

The number λ above is called the **inverse** of α, and is denoted by α^{-1} or

$1/\alpha$. If α, β are complex numbers, we often write β/α instead of $\alpha^{-1}\beta$ (or $\beta\alpha^{-1}$), just as we did with real numbers. We see that we can divide by complex numbers $\neq 0$.

We define the **absolute value** of a complex number $\alpha = a_1 + ia_2$ to be

$$|\alpha| = \sqrt{a_1^2 + a_2^2}.$$

This absolute value is none other than the length of the vector (a_1, a_2). In terms of absolute values, we can write

$$\alpha^{-1} = \frac{\bar{\alpha}}{|\alpha|^2}$$

provided $\alpha \neq 0$.

The triangle inequality for the length of vectors can now be stated for complex numbers. If α, β are complex numbers, then

$$|\alpha + \beta| \leq |\alpha| + |\beta|.$$

Another property of the absolute value is given in Exercise 5.

EXERCISES

1. Express the following complex numbers in the form $x + iy$, where x, y are real numbers.

(a) $(-1 + 3i)^{-1}$
(b) $(1 + i)(1 - i)$
(c) $(1 + i)i(2 - i)$
(d) $(i - 1)(2 - i)$
(e) $(7 + \pi i)(\pi + i)$
(f) $(2i + 1)\pi i$
(g) $(\sqrt{2} + i)(\pi + 3i)$
(h) $(i + 1)(i - 2)(i + 3)$

2. Express the following complex numbers in the form $x + iy$, where x, y are real numbers.

(a) $(1 + i)^{-1}$
(b) $\dfrac{1}{3 + i}$
(c) $\dfrac{2 + i}{2 - i}$
(d) $\dfrac{1}{2 - i}$

(e) $\dfrac{1 + i}{i}$
(f) $\dfrac{i}{1 + i}$
(g) $\dfrac{2i}{3 - i}$
(h) $\dfrac{1}{-1 + i}$

3. Let α be a complex number $\neq 0$. What is the absolute value of $\alpha/\bar{\alpha}$? What is $\bar{\bar{\alpha}}$?

4. Let α, β be two complex numbers. Show that $\overline{\alpha\beta} = \bar{\alpha}\bar{\beta}$ and that

$$\overline{\alpha + \beta} = \bar{\alpha} + \bar{\beta}.$$

5. Show that $|\alpha\beta| = |\alpha|\,|\beta|$.

6. Define addition of n-tuples of complex numbers componentwise, and multiplication of n-tuples of complex numbers by complex numbers componentwise also. If $A = (\alpha_1, \ldots, \alpha_n)$ and $B = (\beta_1, \ldots, \beta_n)$ are n-tuples of complex

numbers, define their scalar product $\langle A, B \rangle$ to be

$$\alpha_1 \bar{\beta}_1 + \cdots + \alpha_n \bar{\beta}_n$$

(note the complex conjugation!). Prove the following rules:

HP 1. $\langle A, B \rangle = \overline{\langle B, A \rangle}$.

HP 2. $\langle A, B + C \rangle = \langle A, B \rangle + \langle A, C \rangle$.

HP 3. *If α is a complex number, then*

$$\langle \alpha A, B \rangle = \alpha \langle A, B \rangle \qquad and \qquad \langle A, \alpha B \rangle = \bar{\alpha} \langle A, B \rangle.$$

HP 4. *If $A = O$, then $\langle A, A \rangle = 0$, and otherwise, $\langle A, A \rangle > 0$.*

7. We assume that you know about the functions sine and cosine, and their addition formulas. Let θ be a real number.

(a) Define

$$e^{i\theta} = \cos\theta + i\sin\theta.$$

Show that if θ_1 and θ_2 are real numbers, then

$$e^{i(\theta_1 + \theta_2)} = e^{i\theta_1} e^{i\theta_2}.$$

Show that any complex number of absolute value 1 can be written in the form e^{it} for some real number t.

(b) Show that any complex number can be written in the form $re^{i\theta}$ for some real numbers r, θ with $r \geqq 0$.

(c) If $z_1 = r_1 e^{i\theta_1}$ and $z_2 = r_2 e^{i\theta_2}$ with real $r_1, r_2 \geqq 0$ and real θ_1, θ_2, show that

$$z_1 z_2 = r_1 r_2 e^{i(\theta_1 + \theta_2)}.$$

(d) If z is a complex number, and n an integer > 0, show that there exists a complex number w such that $w^n = z$. In fact, show that there exists n distinct such complex numbers w. [*Hint:* If $z = re^{i\theta}$, consider first $r^{1/n} e^{i\theta/n}$.]

CHAPTER II

Vector Spaces

As usual, a collection of objects will be called a **set.** A member of the collection is also called an **element** of the set. It is useful in practice to use short symbols to denote certain sets. For instance, we denote by **R** the set of all real numbers, and by **C** the set of all complex numbers. To say that "x is a real number" or that "x is an element of **R**" amounts to the same thing. The set of all n-tuples of real numbers will be denoted by $\mathbf{R}^n$. Thus "X is an element of $\mathbf{R}^n$" and "X is an n-tuple of real numbers" mean the same thing.

Instead of saying that u is an element of a set S, we shall also frequently say that u lies in S and write $u \in S$. If S and S' are sets, and if every element of S' is an element of S, then we say that S' is a **subset** of S. Thus the set of real numbers is a subset of the set of complex numbers. To say that S' is a subset of S is to say that S' is part of S. Observe that our definition of a subset does not exclude the possibility that $S' = S$. If S' is a subset of S, but $S' \neq S$, then we shall say that S' is a **proper** subset of S. Thus **C** is a subset of **C**, but **R** is a proper subset of **C**. To denote the fact that S' is a subset of S, we write $S' \subset S$, and also say that S' is **contained** in S.

If S_1, S_2 are sets, then the **intersection** of S_1 and S_2, denoted by $S_1 \cap S_2$, is the set of elements which lie in both S_1 and S_2. The **union** of S_1 and S_2, denoted by $S_1 \cup S_2$, is the set of elements which lie in S_1 or in S_2.

§1. Definitions

Let K be a subset of the complex numbers **C**. We shall say that K is a **field** if it satisfies the following conditions:

(a) If x, y are elements of K, then $x + y$ and xy are also elements of K.

(b) If $x \in K$, then $-x$ is also an element of K. If furthermore $x \neq 0$, then x^{-1} is an element of K.

(c) The elements 0 and 1 are elements of K.

39

We observe that both **R** and **C** are fields.

Let us denote by **Q** the set of rational numbers, i.e. the set of all fractions m/n, where m, n are integers, and $n \neq 0$. Then it is easily verified that **Q** is a field.

Let **Z** denote the set of all integers. Then **Z** is not a field, because condition (b) above is not satisfied. Indeed, if n is an integer $\neq 0$, then $n^{-1} = 1/n$ is not an integer (except in the trivial case that $n = 1$ or $n = -1$). For instance $\frac{1}{2}$ is not an integer.

The essential thing about a field is that it is a set of elements which can be added and multiplied, in such a way that addition and multiplication satisfy the ordinary rules of arithmetic, and in such a way that one can divide by non-zero elements. It is possible to axiomatize the notion further, but we shall do so only later, to avoid abstract discussions which become obvious anyhow when the reader has acquired the necessary mathematical maturity. Taking into account this possible generalization, we should say that a field as we defined it above is a field of (complex) numbers. However, we shall call such fields simply fields.

If the reader is so inclined, he may restrict himself to the fields of real and complex numbers for the entire linear algebra. Since, however, it is necessary to deal with each one of these fields, we are forced to choose a neutral letter K.

Let K, L be fields, and suppose that K is contained in L (i.e. that K is a subset of L). Then we shall say that K is a **subfield** of L. Thus every one of the fields which we are considering is a subfield of the complex numbers. In particular, we can say that **R** is a subfield of **C**, and **Q** is a subfield of **R**.

Let K be a field. Elements of K will also be called **numbers** (without specification) if the reference to K is made clear by the context, or they will be called **scalars.**

A **vector space** V **over the field** K is a set of objects which can be added and multiplied by elements of K, in such a way that the sum of two elements of V is again an element of V, the product of an element of V by an element of K is an element of V, and the following properties are satisfied:

VS 1. *Given elements u, v, w of V, we have*

$$(u + v) + w = u + (v + w).$$

VS 2. *There is an element of V, denoted by O, such that*

$$O + u = u + O = u$$

for all elements u of V.

VS 3. *Given an element u of V, there exists an element −u in V such that*

$$u + (-u) = O.$$

VS 4. *For all elements u, v of V, we have*

$$u + v = v + u.$$

VS 5. *If c is a number, then* $c(u + v) = cu + cv$.

VS 6. *If a, b are two numbers, then* $(a + b)v = av + bv$.

VS 7. *If a, b are two numbers, then* $(ab)v = a(bv)$.

VS 8. *For all elements u of V, we have* $1 \cdot u = u$ *(1 here is the number one).*

We have used all these rules when dealing with vectors, or with functions but we wish to be more systematic from now on, and hence have made a list of them. Further properties which can be easily deduced from these are given in the exercises and will be assumed from now on.

The algebraic properties of elements of an arbitrary vector space are very similar to those of elements of $\mathbf{R}^2$, $\mathbf{R}^3$, or $\mathbf{R}^n$. Consequently it is customary to call elements of an arbitrary vector space also **vectors**.

If u, v are vectors (i.e. elements of the arbitrary vector space V), then

$$u + (-v)$$

is usually written $u - v$.

We shall use 0 to denote the number zero, and O to denote the element of any vector space V satisfying property VS 2. We also call it zero, but there is never any possibility of confusion. We observe that this zero element O is uniquely determined by condition VS 2 (cf. Exercise 5).

Observe that for any element v in V we have

$$0v = O.$$

The proof is easy, namely

$$0v + v = 0v + 1v = (0 + 1)v = 1v = v.$$

Adding $-v$ to both sides shows that $0v = O$.

Other easy properties of a similar type will be used constantly and are given as exercises. For instance, prove that $(-1)v = -v$.

It is possible to add several elements of a vector space. Suppose we wish to add four elements, say u, v, w, z. We first add any two of them, then a third, and finally a fourth. Using the rules VS 1 and VS 4, we see that it does not matter in which order we perform the additions. This is exactly the same situation as we had with vectors. For example, we have

$$((u + v) + w) + z = (u + (v + w)) + z$$
$$= ((v + w) + u) + z$$
$$= (v + w) + (u + z), \text{ etc.}$$

Thus it is customary to leave out the parentheses, and write simply

$$u + v + w + z.$$

The same remark applies to the sum of any number n of elements of V, and a formal proof could easily be given by induction.

Let V be a vector space, and let W be a subset of V. Assume that W satisfies the following conditions.

(i) If v, w are elements of W, their sum $v + w$ is also an element of W.

(ii) If v is an element of W and c a number, then cv is an element of W.

(iii) The element O of V is also an element of W.

Then W itself is a vector space. Indeed, properties VS 1 through VS 8, being satisfied for all elements of V, are satisfied *a fortiori* for the elements of W. We shall call W a **subspace** of V.

Example 1. Let $V = \mathbf{R}^n$ and let W be the set of vectors in V whose last coordinate is equal to 0. Then W is a subspace of V, which we could identify with $\mathbf{R}^{n-1}$.

More generally, let K be a field. We let K^n be the set of all n-tuples of elements of K, i.e. the set of elements

$$X = (x_1, \ldots, x_n)$$

with $x_i \in K$ for $i = 1, \ldots, n$. We define addition of such n-tuples componentwise, just as we did for addition of n-tuples of real numbers. Thus if $Y = (y_1, \ldots, y_n)$ with $y_i \in K$, then

$$X + Y = (x_1 + y_1, \ldots, x_n + y_n).$$

If $c \in K$, we define cX to be $(cx_1, \ldots, cx_n)$. Then we verify immediately that the axioms for a vector space are satisfied by these operations, i.e. that K^n is a vector space over K.

Thus $\mathbf{C}^n$ is a vector space over $\mathbf{C}$, and $\mathbf{Q}^n$ is a vector space over $\mathbf{Q}$. We remark that $\mathbf{R}^n$ is not a vector space over $\mathbf{C}$. Thus when dealing with vector spaces, we shall always specify the field over which we take the vector space. When we write K^n, it will always be understood that it is meant as a vector space over K. Elements of K^n will also be called **vectors,** and it is also customary to call elements of an arbitrary vector space vectors.

We observe that the complex numbers form a vector space over the real numbers. This is immediate from the rules which we listed concerning the addition and multiplication of complex numbers in Chapter I, §7.

Example 2. Let V be an arbitrary vector space, and let $v_1, \ldots, v_n$ be elements of V. Let $x_1, \ldots, x_n$ be numbers. An expression of type

$$x_1 v_1 + \cdots + x_n v_n$$

is called a **linear combination** of $v_1, \ldots, v_n$. *The set of all linear combinations of $v_1, \ldots, v_n$ is a subspace of V.*

Proof. Let $y_1, \ldots, y_n$ be numbers. Then

$$(x_1 v_1 + \cdots + x_n v_n) + (y_1 v_1 + \cdots + y_n v_n)$$
$$= (x_1 + y_1)v_1 + \cdots + (x_n + y_n)v_n.$$

Thus the sum of two elements of W is again an element of W, i.e. a linear combination of $v_1, \ldots, v_n$. Furthermore, if c is a number, then

$$c(x_1 v_1 + \cdots + x_n v_n) = cx_1 v_1 + \cdots + cx_n v_n$$

is a linear combination of $v_1, \ldots, v_n$, and hence is an element of W. Finally,

$$O = 0v_1 + \cdots + 0v_n$$

is an element of W. This proves that W is a subspace of V.

In Example 2, the subspace W is called the subspace **generated** by $v_1, \ldots, v_n$. If $W = V$, i.e. if every element of V is a linear combination of $v_1, \ldots, v_n$, then we say that $v_1, \ldots, v_n$ **generate** V.

Example 3. Let A be a vector in $\mathbf{R}^3$. Let W be the set of all elements B in $\mathbf{R}^3$ such that $B \cdot A = 0$, i.e. such that B is perpendicular to A. Then W is a subspace of $\mathbf{R}^3$. To see this, note that $O \cdot A = 0$, so that O is in W. Next, suppose that B, C are perpendicular to A. Then

$$(B + C) \cdot A = B \cdot A + C \cdot A = 0,$$

so that $B + C$ is also perpendicular to A. Finally, if x is a number, then

$$(xB) \cdot A = x(B \cdot A) = 0,$$

so that xB is perpendicular to A. This proves that W is a subspace of $\mathbf{R}^3$.

More generally, if A is a vector in $\mathbf{R}^n$, then the set of all elements B in $\mathbf{R}^n$ such that $B \cdot A = 0$ is a subspace of $\mathbf{R}^n$. The proof is the same as when $n = 3$.

Example 4. **Function Spaces.** Let S be a set and K a field. By a **function** of S into K we shall mean a rule which to each element of S associates a unique element of K. Thus if f is a function of S into K, we express this by the symbols

$$f: S \to K.$$

We also say that f is a K**-valued** function. Let V be the set of all functions of S into K. If f, g are two such functions, then we can form their sum $f + g$. It is the function whose value at an element x of S is $f(x) + g(x)$. We write

$$(f + g)(x) = f(x) + g(x).$$

If $c \in K$, then we define cf to be the function such that

$$(cf)(x) = cf(x).$$

Thus the value of cf at x is $cf(x)$. It is then a very easy matter to verify that V is a vector space over K. We shall leave this to the reader. We observe merely that the zero element of V is the zero function, i.e. the function f such that $f(x) = 0$ for all $x \in S$. We shall denote this zero function by 0.

Let V be the set of all functions of $\mathbf{R}$ into $\mathbf{R}$. Then V is a vector space over $\mathbf{R}$. Let W be the subset of continuous functions. If f, g are continuous functions, then $f + g$ is continuous. If c is a real number, then cf is continuous. The zero function is continuous. Hence W is a subspace of the vector space of all functions of $\mathbf{R}$ into $\mathbf{R}$, i.e. W is a subspace of V.

Let U be the set of differentiable functions of $\mathbf{R}$ into $\mathbf{R}$. If f, g are differentiable functions, then their sum $f + g$ is also differentiable. If c is a real number, then cf is differentiable. The zero function is differentiable. Hence U is a subspace of V. In fact, U is a subspace of W, because every differentiable function is continuous.

Let V again be the vector space (over $\mathbf{R}$) of functions from $\mathbf{R}$ into $\mathbf{R}$. Consider the two functions e^t, e^{2t}. (Strictly speaking, we should say the two functions f, g such that $f(t) = e^t$ and $g(t) = e^{2t}$ for all $t \in \mathbf{R}$.) These functions generate a subspace of the space of all differentiable functions. The function $3e^t + 2e^{2t}$ is an element of this subspace. So is the function $2e^t + \pi e^{2t}$.

Example 5. Let V be a vector space and let U, W be subspaces. We denote by $U \cap W$ the intersection of U and W, i.e. the set of elements which lie both in U and W. Then $U \cap W$ is a subspace. For instance, if U, W are two planes in 3-space passing through the origin, then in general, their intersection will be a straight line passing through the origin, as shown in Fig. 1.

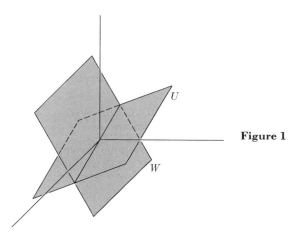

Figure 1

Example 6. Let U, W be subspaces of a vector space V. By

$$U + W$$

we denote the set of all elements $u + w$ with $u \in U$ and $w \in W$. Then we leave it to the reader to verify that $U + W$ is a subspace of V, said to be generated by U and W, and called the **sum** of U and W.

EXERCISES

1. Let V be a vector space. Using the properties VS 1 through VS 8, show that if c is a number, then $cO = O$.

2. Let c be a number $\neq 0$, and v an element of V. Prove that if $cv = O$, then $v = O$.

3. In the vector space of functions, what is the function satisfying the condition VS 2?

4. Let V be a vector space and v, w two elements of V. If $v + w = O$, show that $w = -v$.

5. Let V be a vector space, and v, w two elements of V such that $v + w = v$. Show that $w = O$.

6. Let A_1, A_2 be vectors in $\mathbf{R}^n$. Show that the set of all vectors B in $\mathbf{R}^n$ such that B is perpendicular to both A_1 and A_2 is a subspace.

7. Generalize Exercise 6, and prove: Let $A_1, \ldots, A_r$ be vectors in $\mathbf{R}^n$. Let W be the set of vectors B in $\mathbf{R}^n$ such that $B \cdot A_i = 0$ for every $i = 1, \ldots, r$. Show that W is a subspace of $\mathbf{R}^n$.

8. Show that the following sets of elements in $\mathbf{R}^2$ form subspaces.

(a) The set of all (x, y) such that $x = y$.
(b) The set of all (x, y) such that $x - y = 0$.
(c) The set of all (x, y) such that $x + 4y = 0$.

9. Show that the following sets of elements in $\mathbf{R}^3$ form subspaces.

(a) The set of all (x, y, z) such that $x + y + z = 0$.
(b) The set of all (x, y, z) such that $x = y$ and $2y = z$.
(c) The set of all (x, y, z) such that $x + y = 3z$.

10. If U, W are subspaces of a vector space V, show that $U \cap W$ and $U + W$ are subspaces.

11. Let K be a subfield of a field L. Show that L is a vector space over K. In particular, $\mathbf{C}$ and $\mathbf{R}$ are vector spaces over $\mathbf{Q}$.

12. Let K be the set of all numbers which can be written in the form $a + b\sqrt{2}$, where a, b are rational numbers. Show that K is a field.

13. Let K be the set of all numbers which can be written in the form $a + bi$, where a, b are rational numbers. Show that K is a field.

14. Let c be a rational number > 0, and let γ be a real number such that $\gamma^2 = c$. Show that the set of all numbers which can be written in the form $a + b\gamma$, where a, b are rational numbers, is a field.

§2. *Bases*

Let V be a vector space over the field K, and let $v_1, \ldots, v_n$ be elements of V. We shall say that $v_1, \ldots, v_n$ are **linearly dependent** over K if there exist elements $a_1, \ldots, a_n$ in K not all equal to 0 such that

$$a_1 v_1 + \cdots + a_n v_n = O.$$

If there do not exist such numbers, then we say that $v_1, \ldots, v_n$ are **linearly independent.** In other words, vectors $v_1, \ldots, v_n$ are linearly independent if and only if the following condition is satisfied:

Whenever $a_1, \ldots, a_n$ are numbers such that

$$a_1 v_1 + \cdots + a_n v_n = 0,$$

then $a_i = 0$ for all $i = 1, \ldots, n$.

Example 1. Let $V = \mathbf{R}^n$ and consider the vectors

$$E_1 = (1, 0, \ldots, 0)$$
$$\vdots$$
$$E_n = (0, 0, \ldots, 1).$$

Then $E_1, \ldots, E_n$ are linearly independent. Indeed, let $a_1, \ldots, a_n$ be numbers such that

$$a_1 E_1 + \cdots + a_n E_n = O.$$

Since

$$a_1 E_1 + \cdots + a_n E_n = (a_1, \ldots, a_n),$$

it follows that all $a_i = 0$.

Example 2. Let V be the vector space of all functions of a variable t. Let $f_1, \ldots, f_n$ be n functions. To say that they are linearly dependent is to say that there exist n numbers $a_1, \ldots, a_n$ not all equal to 0 such that

$$a_1 f_1(t) + \cdots + a_n f_n(t) = 0$$

for *all* values of t.

The two functions e^t, e^{2t} are linearly independent. To prove this, suppose that there are numbers a, b such that

$$ae^t + be^{2t} = 0$$

(for all values of t). Differentiate this relation. We obtain

$$ae^t + 2be^{2t} = 0.$$

Subtract the first from the second relation. We obtain $be^{2t} = 0$, and hence $b = 0$. From the first relation, it follows that $ae^t = 0$, and hence $a = 0$. Hence e^t, e^{2t} are linearly independent.

Consider again an arbitrary vector space V. Let $v_1, \ldots, v_n$ be linearly independent elements of V. Let $x_1, \ldots, x_n$ and $y_1, \ldots, y_n$ be numbers. Suppose that we have

$$x_1 v_1 + \cdots + x_n v_n = y_1 v_1 + \cdots + y_n v_n.$$

In other words, two linear combinations of $v_1, \ldots, v_n$ are equal. Then we must have $x_i = y_i$ for each $i = 1, \ldots, n$. Indeed, subtracting the right-hand side from the left-hand side, we get

$$x_1 v_1 - y_1 v_1 + \cdots + x_n v_n - y_n v_n = O.$$

We can write this relation also in the form

$$(x_1 - y_1) v_1 + \cdots + (x_n - y_n) v_n = O.$$

By definition, we must have $x_i - y_i = 0$ for all $i = 1, \ldots, n$, thereby proving our assertion.

If elements $v_1, \ldots, v_n$ of V generate V and in addition are linearly independent, then $\{v_1, \ldots, v_n\}$ is called a **basis** of V. We shall also say that the elements $v_1, \ldots, v_n$ **constitute** or **form** a basis of V.

The vectors $E_1, \ldots, E_n$ of Example 1 form a basis of $\mathbf{R}^n$.

Let W be the vector space of functions generated by the two functions e^t, e^{2t}. Then $\{e^t, e^{2t}\}$ is a basis of W.

Let V be a vector space, and let $\{v_1, \ldots, v_n\}$ be a basis of V. The elements of V can be represented by n-tuples relative to this basis, as follows. If an element v of V is written as a linear combination

$$v = x_1 v_1 + \cdots + x_n v_n$$

of the basis elements, then we call $(x_1, \ldots, x_n)$ the **coordinates** of v with respect to our basis, and we call x_i the i-th coordinate. The coordinates with respect to the usual basis $E_1, \ldots E_n$ of $\mathbf{R}^n$ are simply the coordinates as defined in Chapter I, §1. We say that the n-tuple $X = (x_1, \ldots, x_n)$ is the **coordinate vector** of v with respect to the basis $\{v_1, \ldots, v^n\}$.

For example, let V be the vector space of functions generated by the two functions e^t, e^{2t}. Then the coordinates of the function

$$3e^t + 5e^{2t}$$

with respect to the basis $\{e^t, e^{2t}\}$ are $(3, 5)$.

Example 3. Show that the vectors $(1, 1)$ and $(-3, 2)$ are linearly independent.

Let a, b be two numbers such that

$$a(1, 1) + b(-3, 2) = O.$$

Writing this equation in terms of components, we find

$$a - 3b = 0, \qquad a + 2b = 0.$$

This is a system of two equations which we solve for a and b. Subtracting the second from the first, we get $-5b = 0$, whence $b = 0$. Substituting in either equation, we find $a = 0$. Hence a, b are both 0, and our vectors are linearly independent.

Example 4. Find the coordinates of $(1, 0)$ with respect to the two vectors $(1, 1)$ and $(-1, 2)$.

We must find numbers a, b such that

$$a(1, 1) + b(-1, 2) = (1, 0).$$

Writing this equation in terms of coordinates, we find

$$a - b = 1, \qquad a + 2b = 0.$$

Solving for a and b in the usual manner yields $b = -\frac{1}{3}$ and $a = \frac{2}{3}$. Hence the coordinates of $(1, 0)$ with respect to $(1, 1)$ and $(-1, 2)$ are $(\frac{2}{3}, -\frac{1}{3})$.

Example 5. Show that the vectors $(1, 1)$ and $(-1, 2)$ form a basis of $\mathbf{R}^2$.

We have to show that they are linearly independent and that they generate $\mathbf{R}^2$. To prove linear independence, suppose that a, b are numbers such that

$$a(1, 1) + b(-1, 2) = (0, 0).$$

Then

$$a - b = 0, \qquad a + 2b = 0.$$

Subtracting the first equation from the second yields $3b = 0$, so that $b = 0$. But then from the first equation, $a = 0$, thus proving that our vectors are linearly independent. Next, let (a, b) be an arbitrary element of $\mathbf{R}^2$. We have to show that there exist numbers x, y such that

$$x(1, 1) + y(-1, 2) = (a, b).$$

In other words, we must solve the system of equations

$$x - y = a,$$
$$x + 2y = b.$$

Again subtract the first equation from the second. We find

$$3y = b - a,$$

whence

$$y = \frac{b - a}{3},$$

and finally

$$x = y + a = \frac{b - a}{3} + a.$$

This proves what we wanted. According to our definitions, (x, y) are the coordinates of (a, b) with respect to the basis $\{(1, 1), (-1, 2)\}$.

Let $\{v_1, \ldots, v_n\}$ be a set of elements of a vector space V. Let r be a positive integer $\leq n$. We shall say that $\{v_1, \ldots, v_r\}$ is a **maximal** subset of linearly independent elements if $v_1, \ldots, v_r$ are linearly independent, and if in addition, given any v_i with $i > r$, the elements $v_1, \ldots, v_r, v_i$ are linearly dependent.

The next theorem gives us a useful criterion to determine when a set of elements of a vector space is a basis.

Theorem 1. *Let $\{v_1, \ldots, v_n\}$ be a set of generators of a vector space V. Let $\{v_1, \ldots, v_r\}$ be a maximal subset of linearly independent elements. Then $\{v_1, \ldots, v_r\}$ is a basis of V.*

Proof. We must prove that $v_1, \ldots, v_r$ generate V. We shall first prove that each v_i (for $i > r$) is a linear combination of $v_1, \ldots, v_r$. By hypothesis, given v_i, there exist numbers $x_1, \ldots, x_r, y$ not all 0 such that

$$x_1 v_1 + \cdots + x_r v_r + y v_i = 0.$$

Furthermore, $y \neq 0$, because otherwise, we would have a relation of linear dependence for $v_1, \ldots, v_r$. Hence we can solve for v_i, namely

$$v_i = \frac{x_1}{-y} v_1 + \cdots + \frac{x_r}{-y} v_r,$$

thereby showing that v_i is a linear combination of $v_1, \ldots, v_r$.

Next, let v be any element of V. There exist numbers $c_1, \ldots, c_n$ such that

$$v = c_1 v_1 + \cdots + c_n v_n.$$

In this relation, we can replace each v_i $(i > r)$ by a linear combination of $v_1, \ldots, v_r$. If we do this, and then collect terms, we find that we have expressed v as a linear combination of $v_1, \ldots, v_r$. This proves that $v_1, \ldots, v_r$ generate V, and hence form a basis of V.

EXERCISES

1. Show that the following vectors are linearly independent (over **C** or **R**).

(a) $(1, 1, 1)$ and $(0, 1, -2)$ (b) $(1, 0)$ and $(1, 1)$
(c) $(-1, 1, 0)$ and $(0, 1, 2)$ (d) $(2, -1)$ and $(1, 0)$
(e) $(\pi, 0)$ and $(0, 1)$ (f) $(1, 2)$ and $(1, 3)$
(g) $(1, 1, 0)$, $(1, 1, 1)$, and $(0, 1, -1)$ (h) $(0, 1, 1)$, $(0, 2, 1)$, and $(1, 5, 3)$

2. Express the given vector X as a linear combination of the given vectors A, B, and find the coordinates of X with respect to A, B.

(a) $X = (1, 0)$, $A = (1, 1)$, $B = (0, 1)$
(b) $X = (2, 1)$, $A = (1, -1)$, $B = (1, 1)$
(c) $X = (1, 1)$, $A = (2, 1)$, $B = (-1, 0)$
(d) $X = (4, 3)$, $A = (2, 1)$, $B = (-1, 0)$

3. Find the coordinates of the vector X with respect to the vectors A, B, C.

(a) $X = (1, 0, 0)$, $A = (1, 1, 1)$, $B = (-1, 1, 0)$, $C = (1, 0, -1)$
(b) $X = (1, 1, 1)$, $A = (0, 1, -1)$, $B = (1, 1, 0)$, $C = (1, 0, 2)$
(c) $X = (0, 0, 1)$, $A = (1, 1, 1)$, $B = (-1, 1, 0)$, $C = (1, 0, -1)$

4. Let (a, b) and (c, d) be two vectors in the plane. If $ad - bc = 0$, show that they are linearly dependent. If $ad - bc \neq 0$, show that they are linearly independent.

5. Consider the vector space of all functions of a variable t. Show that the following pairs of functions are linearly independent.

(a) $1, t$ (b) t, t^2 (c) t, t^4 (d) e^t, t (e) te^t, e^{2t} (f) $\sin t, \cos t$ (g) $t, \sin t$
(h) $\sin t, \sin 2t$ (i) $\cos t, \cos 3t$

6. Consider the vector space of functions defined for $t > 0$. Show that the following pairs of functions are linearly independent.

(a) $t, 1/t$ (b) $e^t, \log t$

7. What are the coordinates of the function $3 \sin t + 5 \cos t = f(t)$ with respect to the basis $\{\sin t, \cos t\}$?

8. Let D be the derivative d/dt. Let $f(t)$ be as in Exercise 7. What are the coordinates of the function $Df(t)$ with respect to the basis of Exercise 7?

9. Let $A_1, \ldots, A_r$ be vectors in $\mathbf{R}^n$ and assume that they are mutually perpendicular (i.e. any two of them are perpendicular), and that none of them is equal to O. Prove that they are linearly independent.

10. Let V be the vector space of continuous functions on the interval $[-\pi, \pi]$. If f, g are two continuous functions on this interval, define their scalar product $\langle f, g \rangle$ to be

$$\langle f, g \rangle = \int_{-\pi}^{\pi} f(t)g(t) \, dt.$$

Show that the functions $\sin nt$ ($n = 1, 2, 3, \ldots$) are mutually perpendicular, i.e. that the scalar product of any two of them is equal to 0.

11. Show that the functions $\sin t, \sin 2t, \sin 3t, \ldots, \sin nt$ are linearly independent, for any integer $n \geqq 1$.

12. Let v, w be elements of a vector space and assume that $v \neq O$. If v, w are linearly dependent, show that there is a number a such that $w = av$.

§3. *Dimension of a vector space*

The main result of this section is that any two bases of a vector space have the same number of elements. To prove this, we first have an intermediate result.

Theorem 2. *Let V be a vector space over the field K. Let $\{v_1, \ldots, v_m\}$ be a basis of V over K. Let $w_1, \ldots, w_n$ be elements of V, and assume that $n > m$. Then $w_1, \ldots, w_n$ are linearly dependent.*

Proof. Assume that $w_1, \ldots, w_n$ are linearly independent. Since $\{v_1, \ldots, v_m\}$ is a basis, there exist elements $a_1, \ldots, a_m \in K$ such that

$$w_1 = a_1 v_1 + \cdots + a_m v_m.$$

By assumption, we know that $w_1 \neq O$, and hence some $a_i \neq 0$. After renumbering $v_1, \ldots, v_m$ if necessary, we may assume without loss of generality that say $a_1 \neq 0$. We can then solve for v_1, and get

$$a_1 v_1 = w_1 - a_2 v_2 - \cdots - a_m v_m,$$
$$v_1 = a_1^{-1} w_1 - a_1^{-1} a_2 v_2 - \cdots - a_1^{-1} a_m v_m.$$

The subspace of V generated by $w_1, v_2, \ldots, v_m$ contains v_1, and hence must be all of V since $v_1, v_2, \ldots, v_m$ generate V. The idea is now to continue our procedure stepwise, and to replace successively v_2, v_3, ... by w_2, w_3, ... until all the elements v_1, ..., v_m are exhausted, and w_1, ..., w_m generate V. Let us now assume by induction that there is an integer r with $1 \leqq r < m$ such that, after a suitable renumbering of v_1, ..., v_m, the elements w_1, ..., w_r, v_{r+1}, ..., v_m generate V. There exist elements b_1, ..., b_r, c_{r+1}, ..., c_m in K such that

$$w_{r+1} = b_1 w_1 + \cdots + b_r w_r + c_{r+1} v_{r+1} + \cdots + c_m v_m.$$

We cannot have $c_j = 0$ for $j = r + 1, \ldots, m$, for otherwise, we get a relation of linear dependence between w_1, ..., w_{r+1}, contradicting our assumption. After renumbering v_{r+1}, ..., v_m if necessary, we may assume without loss of generality that say $c_{r+1} \neq 0$. We then obtain

$$c_{r+1} v_{r+1} = w_{r+1} - b_1 w_1 - \cdots - b_r w_r - c_{r+2} v_{r+2} - \cdots - c_m v_m.$$

Dividing by c_{r+1}, we conclude that v_{r+1} is in the subspace generated by w_1, ..., w_{r+1}, v_{r+2}, ..., v_m. By our induction assumption, it follows that w_1, ..., w_{r+1}, v_{r+2}, ..., v_m generate V. Thus by induction, we have proved that w_1, ..., w_m generate V. If $n > m$, then there exist elements d_1, ..., $d_m \in K$ such that

$$w_n = d_1 w_1 + \cdots + d_m w_m,$$

thereby proving that w_1, ..., w_n are linearly dependent. This proves our theorem.

Theorem 3. *Let V be a vector space and suppose that one basis has n elements, and another basis has m elements. Then $m = n$.*

Proof. We apply Theorem 2 to the two bases. Theorem 2 implies that both alternatives $n > m$ and $m > n$ are impossible, and hence $m = n$.

Let V be a vector space having a basis consisting of n elements. We shall say that n is the **dimension** of V. If V consists of O alone, then V does not have a basis, and we shall say that V has dimension 0.

Example 1. The vector space $\mathbf{R}^n$ has dimension n over $\mathbf{R}$, the vector space $\mathbf{C}^n$ has dimension n over $\mathbf{C}$, and more generally for any field K, the vector space K^n has dimension n over K. Indeed, the n vectors

$$(1, 0, \ldots, 0), \quad (0, 1, \ldots, 0), \quad \ldots, \quad (0, \ldots, 0, 1)$$

form a basis of K^n over K.

The dimension of a vector space V over K will be denoted by $\dim_K V$, or simply $\dim V$.

A vector space which has a basis consisting of a finite number of elements, or the zero vector space, is called **finite dimensional.** Other vector spaces are called **infinite dimensional.** It is possible to give a definition for an infinite basis. The reader may look it up in a more advanced text. In this book, whenever we speak of the dimension of a vector space in the sequel, it is *assumed* that this vector space is finite dimensional.

Example 2. Let K be a field. Then K is a vector space over itself, and it is of dimension 1. In fact, the element 1 of K forms a basis of K over K, because any element $x \in K$ has a unique expression as $x = x \cdot 1$.

We shall now give criteria which allow us to tell when elements of a vector space constitute a basis.

Let $v_1, \ldots, v_n$ be linearly independent elements of a vector space V. We shall say that they form a **maximal set of linearly independent elements** of V if given any element w of V, the elements $w, v_1, \ldots, v_n$ are linearly dependent.

Theorem 4. *Let V be a vector space, and $\{v_1, \ldots, v_n\}$ a maximal set of linearly independent elements of V. Then $\{v_1, \ldots, v_n\}$ is a basis of V.*

Proof. We must show that $v_1, \ldots, v_n$ generate V, i.e. that every element of V can be expressed as a linear combination of $v_1, \ldots, v_n$. Let w be an element of V. The elements $w, v_1, \ldots, v_n$ of V must be linearly dependent by hypothesis, and hence there exist numbers $x_0, x_1, \ldots, x_n$ not all 0 such that

$$x_0 w + x_1 v_1 + \cdots + x_n v_n = O.$$

We cannot have $x_0 = 0$, because if that were the case, we would obtain a relation of linear dependence among $v_1, \ldots, v_n$. Therefore we can solve for w in terms of $v_1, \ldots, v_n$, namely

$$w = -\frac{x_1}{x_0} v_1 - \cdots - \frac{x_n}{x_0} v_n.$$

This proves that w is a linear combination of $v_1, \ldots, v_n$, and hence that $\{v_1, \ldots, v_n\}$ is a basis.

Theorem 5. *Let V be a vector space of dimension n, and let $v_1, \ldots, v_n$ be linearly independent elements of V. Then $v_1, \ldots, v_n$ constitute a basis of V.*

Proof. According to Theorem 2, $\{v_1, \ldots, v_n\}$ is a maximal set of linearly independent elements of V. Hence it is a basis by Theorem 4.

Corollary 1. *Let V be a vector space of dimension n and let W be a subspace, also of dimension n. Then $W = V$.*

Proof. A basis for W must also be a basis for V.

Corollary 2. *Let V be a vector space of dimension n. Let r be a positive integer with $r < n$, and let $v_1, \ldots, v_r$ be linearly independent elements of V. Then one can find elements $v_{r+1}, \ldots, v_n$ such that*

$$\{v_1, \ldots, v_n\}$$

is a basis of V.

Proof. Since $r < n$ we know that $\{v_1, \ldots, v_r\}$ cannot form a basis of V, and thus cannot be a maximal set of linearly independent elements of V. In particular, we can find v_{r+1} in V such that

$$v_1, \ldots, v_{r+1}$$

are linearly independent. If $r + 1 < n$, we can repeat the argument. We can thus proceed stepwise (by induction) until we obtain n linearly independent elements $\{v_1, \ldots, v_n\}$. These must be a basis by Theorem 5, and our corollary is proved.

Theorem 6. *Let V be a vector space having a basis consisting of n elements. Let W be a subspace which does not consist of O alone. Then W has a basis, and the dimension of W is $\leq n$.*

Proof. Let w_1 be a non-zero element of W. If $\{w_1\}$ is not a maximal set of linearly independent elements of W, we can find an element w_2 of W such that w_1, w_2 are linearly independent. Proceeding in this manner, one element at a time, there must be an integer $m \leq n$ such that we can find linearly independent elements $w_1, w_2, \ldots, w_m$, and such that

$$\{w_1, \ldots, w_m\}$$

is a maximal set of linearly independent elements of W (by Theorem 2, we cannot go on indefinitely finding linearly independent elements, and the number of such elements is at most n). If we now use Theorem 4, we conclude that $\{w_1, \ldots, w_m\}$ is a basis for W.

§4. *Sums and direct sums*

Let V be a vector space over the field K. Let U, W be subspaces of V. We define the **sum** of U and W to be the subset of V consisting of all sums $u + w$ with $u \in U$ and $w \in W$. We denote this sum by $U + W$. It is a subspace of V. Indeed, if $u_1, u_2 \in U$ and $w_1, w_2 \in W$ then

$$(u_1 + w_1) + (u_2 + w_2) = u_1 + u_2 + w_1 + w_2 \in U + W.$$

If $c \in K$, then

$$c(u_1 + w_1) = cu_1 + cw_1 \in U + W.$$

Finally, $O + O \in W$. This proves that $U + W$ is a subspace.

We shall say that V is a **direct sum** of U and W if for every element v of V there exist *unique* elements $u \in U$ and $w \in W$ such that $v = u + w$.

Theorem 7. *Let V be a vector space over the field K, and let U, W be subspaces. If $U + W = V$, and if $U \cap W = \{O\}$, then V is the direct sum of U and W.*

Proof. Given $v \in V$, by the first assumption, there exist elements $u \in U$ and $w \in W$ such that $v = u + w$. Thus V is the sum of U and W. To prove it is the direct sum, we must show that these elements u, w are uniquely determined. Suppose there exist elements $u' \in U$ and $w' \in W$ such that $v = u' + w'$. Thus

$$u + w = u' + w'.$$

Then

$$u - u' = w' - w.$$

But $u - u' \in U$ and $w' - w \in W$. By the second assumption, we conclude that $u - u' = O$ and $w' - w = O$, whence $u = u'$ and $w = w'$, thereby proving our theorem.

As a matter of notation, when V is the direct sum of subspaces U, W we write

$$V = U \oplus W.$$

Theorem 8. *Let V be a finite dimensional vector space over the field K. Let W be a subspace. Then there exists a subspace U such that V is the direct sum of W and U.*

Proof. We select a basis of W, and extend it to a basis of V, using Corollary 2 of Theorem 5 of §3. The assertion of our theorem is then clear. In the notation of that theorem, if $\{v_1, \ldots, v_r\}$ is a basis of W, then we let U be the space generated by $\{v_{r+1}, \ldots, v_n\}$.

We note that given the subspace W, there exist usually many subspaces U such that V is the direct sum of W and U. (For examples, see the exercises.) In the section when we discuss orthogonality later in this book, we shall use orthogonality to determine such a subspace.

Theorem 9. *If V is a finite dimensional vector space over K, and is the direct sum of subspaces U, W then*

$$\dim V = \dim U + \dim W.$$

Proof. Let $\{u_1, \ldots, u_r\}$ be a basis of U, and $\{w_1, \ldots, w_s\}$ a basis of W. Every element of U has a unique expression as a linear combination $x_1 u_1 + \cdots + x_r u_r$, with $x_i \in K$, and every element of W has a unique expression as a linear combination $y_1 w_1 + \cdots + y_s w_s$ with $y_j \in K$. Hence by definition, every element of V has a unique expression as a linear combination

$$x_1 u_1 + \cdots + x_r u_r + y_1 w_1 + \cdots + y_s w_s,$$

thereby proving that $u_1, \ldots, u_r, w_1, \ldots, w_s$ is a basis of V, and also proving our theorem.

Remark. We can also define V as a direct sum of more than two subspaces. Let $W_1, \ldots, W_r$ be subspaces of V. We shall say that V is their **direct sum** if every element of V can be expressed in a unique way as a sum

$$v = w_1 + \cdots + w_r$$

with w_i in W_i.

Suppose now that U, W are arbitrary vector spaces over the field K (i.e. not necessarily subspaces of some vector space). We let $U \times W$ be the set of all pairs (u, w) whose first component is an element u of U and whose second component is an element w of W. We define the addition of such pairs componentwise, namely, if $(u_1, w_1) \in U \times W$ and $(u_2, w_2) \in U \times W$ we define

$$(u_1, w_1) + (u_2, w_2) = (u_1 + u_2, w_1 + w_2).$$

If $c \in K$, we define the product $c(u_1, w_1)$ by

$$c(u_1, w_1) = (cu_1, cw_1).$$

It is then immediately verified that $U \times W$ is a vector space, called the **direct product** of U and W. When we discuss linear maps, we shall compare the direct product with the direct sum.

If n is a positive integer, written as a sum of two positive integers, $n = r + s$, then we see that K^n is the direct product $K^r \times K^s$.

We note that $\dim (U \times W) = \dim U + \dim W$. The proof is easy, and is left to the reader.

EXERCISES

1. Let $V = \mathbf{R}^2$, and let W be the subspace generated by $(2, 1)$. Let U be the subspace generated by $(0, 1)$. Show that V is the direct sum of W and U. If U' is the subspace generated by $(1, 1)$, show that V is also the direct sum of W and U'.

2. Let $V = K^3$ for some field K. Let W be the subspace generated by $(1, 0, 0)$, and let U be the subspace generated by $(1, 1, 0)$ and $(0, 1, 1)$. Show that V is the direct sum of W and U.

3. Let A, B be two vectors in $\mathbf{R}^2$, and assume neither of them is O. If there is no number c such that $cA = B$, show that A, B form a basis of $\mathbf{R}^2$, and that $\mathbf{R}^2$ is a direct sum of the subspaces generated by A and B respectively.

4. Prove the last assertion of the section concerning the dimension of $U \times W$.

CHAPTER III

Matrices

§1. The space of matrices

We consider a new kind of object, matrices. Let K be a field. Let n, m be two integers ≥ 1. An array of numbers in K

$$
\begin{pmatrix}
a_{11} & a_{12} & a_{13} & \cdots & a_{1n} \\
a_{21} & a_{22} & a_{23} & \cdots & a_{2n} \\
\vdots & \vdots & \vdots & & \vdots \\
a_{m1} & a_{m2} & a_{m3} & \cdots & a_{mn}
\end{pmatrix}
$$

is called a **matrix in** K. We can abbreviate the notation for this matrix by writing it (a_{ij}), $i = 1, \ldots, m$ and $j = 1, \ldots, n$. We say that it is an m by n matrix, or an $m \times n$ matrix. The matrix has m **rows** and n **columns.** For instance, the first column is

$$
\begin{pmatrix}
a_{11} \\
a_{21} \\
\vdots \\
a_{m1}
\end{pmatrix}
$$

and the second row is $(a_{21}, a_{22}, \ldots, a_{2n})$. We call a_{ij} the ij-**entry** or ij-**component** of the matrix. If we denote by A the above matrix, then the i-th row is denoted by A_i, and is defined to be

$$
A_i = (a_{i1}, a_{i2}, \ldots, a_{in}).
$$

The j-th column is denoted by A^j, and is defined to be

$$
A^j =
\begin{pmatrix}
a_{1j} \\
a_{2j} \\
\vdots \\
a_{mj}
\end{pmatrix}
$$

If you look back at Chapter I, §1, the example of 7-space taken from economics gives rise to a 7×7 matrix (a_{ij}) $(i, j = 1, .., 7)$, where a_{ij} is the amount spent by the i-th industry on the j-th industry. Thus keeping the notation of that example, if $a_{25} = 50$, this means that the auto industry bought 50 million dollars worth of stuff from the chemical industry during the given year.

Example 1. The following is a 2×3 matrix:

$$\begin{pmatrix} 1 & 1 & -2 \\ -1 & 4 & -5 \end{pmatrix}.$$

It has two rows and three columns.

The rows are $(1, 1, -2)$ and $(-1, 4, -5)$. The columns are

$$\begin{pmatrix} 1 \\ -1 \end{pmatrix}, \quad \begin{pmatrix} 1 \\ 4 \end{pmatrix}, \quad \begin{pmatrix} -2 \\ -5 \end{pmatrix}.$$

Thus the rows of a matrix may be viewed as n-tuples, and the columns may be viewed as vertical m-tuples. A vertical m-tuple is also called a **column vector**.

A vector $(x_1, \ldots, x_n)$ is a $1 \times n$ matrix. A column vector

$$\begin{pmatrix} x_1 \\ \vdots \\ x_n \end{pmatrix}$$

is an $n \times 1$ matrix.

When we write a matrix in the form (a_{ij}), then i denotes the row and j denotes the column. In Example 1, we have for instance $a_{11} = 1$, $a_{23} = -5$.

A single number (a) may be viewed as a 1×1 matrix.

Let (a_{ij}), $i = 1, \ldots, m$ and $j = 1, \ldots, n$ be a matrix. If $m = n$, then we say that it is a **square** matrix. Thus

$$\begin{pmatrix} 1 & 2 \\ -1 & 0 \end{pmatrix} \quad \text{and} \quad \begin{pmatrix} 1 & -1 & 5 \\ 2 & 1 & -1 \\ 3 & 1 & -1 \end{pmatrix}$$

are both square matrices.

We have a **zero matrix** in which $a_{ij} = 0$ for all i, j. It looks like this:

$$\begin{pmatrix} 0 & 0 & 0 & \cdots & 0 \\ 0 & 0 & 0 & \cdots & 0 \\ \vdots & \vdots & \vdots & & \vdots \\ 0 & 0 & 0 & \cdots & 0 \end{pmatrix}.$$

We shall write it O. We note that we have met so far with the zero number, zero vector, and zero matrix.

We shall now define addition of matrices and multiplication of matrices by numbers.

We define addition of matrices only when they have the same size. Thus let m, n be fixed integers ≥ 1. Let $A = (a_{ij})$ and $B = (b_{ij})$ be two $m \times n$ matrices. We define $A + B$ to be the matrix whose entry in the i-th row and j-th column is $a_{ij} + b_{ij}$. In other words, we add matrices of the same size componentwise.

Example 2. Let

$$A = \begin{pmatrix} 1 & -1 & 0 \\ 2 & 3 & 4 \end{pmatrix} \quad \text{and} \quad B = \begin{pmatrix} 5 & 1 & -1 \\ 2 & 1 & -1 \end{pmatrix}.$$

Then

$$A + B = \begin{pmatrix} 6 & 0 & -1 \\ 4 & 4 & 3 \end{pmatrix}.$$

If A, B are both $1 \times n$ matrices, i.e. n-tuples, then we note that our addition of matrices coincides with the addition which we defined in Chapter I for n-tuples.

If O is the zero matrix, then for any matrix A (of the same size, of course), we have $O + A = A + O = A$. This is trivially verified.

We shall now define the multiplication of a matrix by a number. Let c be a number, and $A = (a_{ij})$ be a matrix. We define cA to be the matrix whose ij-component is ca_{ij}. We write $cA = (ca_{ij})$. Thus we multiply each component of A by c.

Example 3. Let A, B be as in Example 2. Let $c = 2$. Then

$$2A = \begin{pmatrix} 2 & -2 & 0 \\ 4 & 6 & 8 \end{pmatrix} \quad \text{and} \quad 2B = \begin{pmatrix} 10 & 2 & -2 \\ 4 & 2 & -2 \end{pmatrix}.$$

We also have

$$(-1)A = -A = \begin{pmatrix} -1 & 1 & 0 \\ -2 & -3 & -4 \end{pmatrix}.$$

For all matrices A, we find that $A + (-1)A = O$.

We leave it as an exercise to verify that all properties VS 1 through VS 8 are satisfied by our rules for addition of matrices and multiplication of matrices by numbers. The main thing to observe here is that addition of matrices is defined in terms of the components, and for the addition of components, the conditions analogous to VS 1 through VS 4 are satisfied. They are standard properties of numbers. Similarly, VS 5 through VS 8 are true for multiplication of matrices by numbers, because the corresponding properties for the multiplication of numbers are true.

We see that the matrices (of a given size m × n) with components in a field K form a vector space over K which we may denote by $\mathrm{Mat}_{m \times n}(K)$.

We define one more notion related to a matrix. Let $A = (a_{ij})$ be an $m \times n$ matrix. The $n \times m$ matrix $B = (b_{ji})$ such that $b_{ji} = a_{ij}$ is called the **transpose** of A, and is also denoted by ^tA. Taking the transpose of a matrix amounts to changing rows into columns and vice versa. If A is the matrix which we wrote down at the beginning of this section, then ^tA is the matrix

$$\begin{pmatrix} a_{11} & a_{21} & a_{31} & \cdots & a_{m1} \\ a_{12} & a_{22} & a_{32} & \cdots & a_{m2} \\ \vdots & \vdots & \vdots & & \vdots \\ a_{1n} & a_{2n} & a_{3n} & \cdots & a_{mn} \end{pmatrix}$$

To take a special case:

$$\text{If } A = \begin{pmatrix} 2 & 1 & 0 \\ 1 & 3 & 5 \end{pmatrix} \quad \text{then} \quad {}^tA = \begin{pmatrix} 2 & 1 \\ 1 & 3 \\ 0 & 5 \end{pmatrix}.$$

If $A = (2, 1, -4)$ is a *row vector*, then

$$^tA = \begin{pmatrix} 2 \\ 1 \\ -4 \end{pmatrix}$$

is a *column vector*.

A matrix A is said to be **symmetric** if it is equal to its transpose, i.e. if $^tA = A$. A symmetric matrix is necessarily a square matrix. For instance, the matrix

$$\begin{pmatrix} 1 & -1 & 2 \\ -1 & 0 & 3 \\ 2 & 3 & 7 \end{pmatrix}$$

is symmetric.

Let $A = (a_{ij})$ be a *square* matrix. We call $a_{11}, \ldots, a_{nn}$ its **diagonal** components. A square matrix is said to be a **diagonal** matrix if all its components are zero except possibly for the diagonal components, i.e. if $a_{ij} = 0$ if $i \neq j$. Every diagonal matrix is a symmetric matrix. A diagonal matrix looks like this:

$$\begin{pmatrix} a_1 & 0 & \cdots & 0 \\ 0 & a_2 & \cdots & 0 \\ \vdots & \vdots & & \vdots \\ 0 & 0 & \cdots & a_n \end{pmatrix}$$

We define the **unit** $n \times n$ matrix to be the square matrix having all its components equal to 0 except the diagonal components, equal to 1. We denote this unit matrix by I_n, or I if there is no need to specify the n. Thus:

$$I_n = \begin{pmatrix} 1 & 0 & \cdots & 0 \\ 0 & 1 & \cdots & 0 \\ \vdots & \vdots & & \vdots \\ 0 & 0 & \cdots & 1 \end{pmatrix}.$$

EXERCISES ON MATRICES

1. Let

$$A = \begin{pmatrix} 1 & 2 & 3 \\ -1 & 0 & 2 \end{pmatrix} \quad \text{and} \quad B = \begin{pmatrix} -1 & 5 & -2 \\ 2 & 2 & -1 \end{pmatrix}.$$

Find $A + B$, $3B$, $-2B$, $A + 2B$, $2A + B$, $A - B$, $A - 2B$, $B - A$.

2. Let

$$A = \begin{pmatrix} 1 & -1 \\ 2 & 2 \end{pmatrix} \quad \text{and} \quad B = \begin{pmatrix} -1 & 1 \\ 0 & -3 \end{pmatrix}.$$

Find $A + B$, $3B$, $-2B$, $A + 2B$, $A - B$, $B - A$.

3. In Exercise 1, find ^tA and ^tB.

4. In Exercise 2, find ^tA and ^tB.

5. If A, B are arbitrary $m \times n$ matrices, show that

$$^t(A + B) = {}^tA + {}^tB.$$

6. If c is a number, show that

$$^t(cA) = c\,{}^tA.$$

7. If $A = (a_{ij})$ is a square matrix, then the elements a_{ii} are called the **diagonal** elements. How do the diagonal elements of A and ^tA differ?

8. Find $^t(A + B)$ and $^tA + {}^tB$ in Exercise 2.

9. Find $A + {}^tA$ and $B + {}^tB$ in Exercise 2.

10. Show that for any square matrix A, the matrix $A + {}^tA$ is symmetric.

11. Write down the row vectors and column vectors of the matrices A, B in Exercise 1.

12. Write down the row vectors and column vectors of the matrices A, B in Exercise 2.

EXERCISES ON DIMENSION

1. What is the dimension of the space of 2×2 matrices? Give a basis for this space.

2. What is the dimension of the space of $m \times n$ matrices? Give a basis for this space.

3. What is the dimension of the space of $n \times n$ matrices all of whose components are 0 except possibly the diagonal components?

4. What is the dimension of the space of $n \times n$ matrices which are **upper-triangular**, i.e. of the following type:

$$\begin{pmatrix} a_{11} & a_{12} & \cdots & a_{1n} \\ 0 & a_{22} & \cdots & a_{2n} \\ \vdots & \vdots & & \vdots \\ 0 & 0 & \cdots & a_{nn} \end{pmatrix}?$$

5. What is the dimension of the space of symmetric 2×2 matrices (i.e. 2×2 matrices A such that $A = {}^t A$)? Exhibit a basis for this space.

6. More generally, what is the dimension of the space of symmetric $n \times n$ matrices?

7. What is the dimension of the space of diagonal $n \times n$ matrices? What is a basis for this space?

8. Let V be a subspace of $\mathbf{R}^2$. What are the possible dimensions for V? Show that if $V \neq \mathbf{R}^2$, then either $V = \{O\}$, or V is a straight line passing through the origin.

9. Let V be a subspace of $\mathbf{R}^3$. What are the possible dimensions for V? Show that if $V \neq \mathbf{R}^3$, then either $V = \{O\}$, or V is a straight line passing through the origin, or V is a plane passing through the origin.

§2. *Linear equations*

We shall now give applications of the dimension theorems to the solution of linear equations.

Let K be a field. Let $A = (a_{ij})$, $i = 1, \ldots, m$ and $j = 1, \ldots, n$ be a matrix in K. Let $b_1, \ldots, b_m$ be elements of K. Equations like

$$\begin{aligned} a_{11}x_1 + \cdots + a_{1n}x_n &= b_1 \\ &\cdots \\ a_{m1}x_1 + \cdots + a_{mn}x_n &= b_m \end{aligned}$$

(*)

are called linear equations. We shall also say that (*) is a system of linear equations. The system is said to be **homogeneous** if all the numbers $b_1, \ldots, b_m$ are equal to 0. The number n is called the number of **unknowns,** and m is called the number of equations. We call (a_{ij}) the matrix of **coefficients.**

The system of equations

$$\begin{aligned} a_{11}x_1 + \cdots + a_{1n}x_n &= 0 \\ &\cdots \\ a_{m1}x_1 + \cdots + a_{mn}x_n &= 0 \end{aligned}$$

(**)

will be called the **homogeneous system** associated with (*).

The system (**) always has a solution, namely, the solution obtained by letting all $x_j = 0$. This solution will be called the **trivial** solution. A solution $(x_1, \ldots, x_n)$ such that some $x_i \neq 0$ is called **non-trivial.**

We consider first the homogeneous system (**). We can rewrite it in the following way:

$$x_1 \begin{pmatrix} a_{11} \\ \vdots \\ a_{m1} \end{pmatrix} + \cdots + x_n \begin{pmatrix} a_{1n} \\ \vdots \\ a_{mn} \end{pmatrix} = 0,$$

or in terms of the column vectors of the matrix $A = (a_{ij})$,

$$x_1 A^1 + \cdots + x_n A^n = O.$$

A non-trivial solution $X = (x_1, \ldots, x_n)$ of our system (**) is therefore nothing else than an n-tuple $X \neq O$ giving a relation of linear dependence between the columns $A^1, \ldots, A^n$. This way of rewriting the system gives us therefore a good interpretation, and allows us to apply Theorem 2 of Chapter II. The column vectors are elements of K^m, which has dimension m over K. Consequently:

Theorem 1. *Let*

$$a_{11}x_1 + \cdots + a_{1n}x_n = 0$$
$$\cdots$$
$$a_{m1}x_1 + \cdots + a_{mn}x_n = 0$$

be a homogeneous system of m linear equations in n unknowns, with coefficients in a field K. Assume that $n > m$. Then the system has a non-trivial solution in K.

Proof. By Theorem 2 of Chapter II, we know that the vectors $A^1, \ldots, A^n$ must be linearly dependent.

Of course, to solve explicitly a system of linear equations, we have so far no other method than the elementary method of elimination from elementary school. We give examples.

Example 1. Suppose that we have a single equation, like

$$2x + y - 4z = 0.$$

To find a non-trivial solution, we give all the variables except the first a special value $\neq 0$, say $y = 1$, $z = 1$. We then solve for x. We find $2x = -y + 4z = 3$, whence $x = \frac{3}{2}$.

Example 2. Consider a pair of equations, say

(1) $2x + 3y - z = 0,$

(2) $x + y + z = 0.$

We reduce the problem of solving these simultaneous equations to the preceding case of one equation, by eliminating one variable. Thus we multiply the second equation by 2 and subtract it from the first equation, getting

(3) $y - 3z = 0.$

Now we meet one equation in more than one variable. We give z any value $\neq 0$, say $z = 1$, and solve for y, namely $y = 3$. We then solve for x from the second equation, namely $x = -y - z$, and obtain $x = -4$. The values which we have obtained for x, y, z are also solutions of the first equation, because the first equation is (in an obvious sense) the sum of equation (2) multiplied by 2, and equation (3).

Example 3. We wish to find a solution for the system of equations

$$3x - 2y + z + 2w = 0,$$
$$x + y - z - w = 0,$$
$$2x - 2y + 3z = 0.$$

Again we use the elimination method. Multiply the second equation by 2 and subtract it from the third. We find

$$-4y + 5z + 2w = 0.$$

Multiply the second equation by 3 and subtract it from the first. We find

$$-5y + 4z + 5w = 0.$$

We have now eliminated x from our equations, and find two equations in three unknowns, y, z, w. We eliminate y from these two equations as follows: Multiply the top one by 5, multiply the bottom one by 4, and subtract them. We get

$$9z - 10w = 0.$$

Now give an arbitrary value $\neq 0$ to w, say $w = 1$. Then we can solve for z, namely

$$z = 10/9.$$

Going back to the equations before that, we solve for y, using

$$4y = 5z + 2w.$$

This yields

$$y = 68/9.$$

Finally we solve for x using say the second of the original set of three equations, so that

$$x = -y + z + w,$$

or numerically,

$$x = -49/9.$$

Thus we have found:

$$w = 1, \qquad z = 10/9,$$

$$y = 68/9, \qquad x = -49/9.$$

Note that we had three equations in four unknowns. By a successive elimination of variables, we reduced these equations to two equations in three unknowns, and then one equation in two unknowns.

Using precisely the same method, suppose that we start with three equations in five unknowns. Eliminating one variable will yield two equations in four unknowns. Eliminating another variable will yield one equation in three unknowns. We can then solve this equation, and proceed backwards to get values for the previous variables just as we have shown in the examples. A description of this procedure applying in general will be carried out in the appendix of this chapter, where we shall also give an alternative direct proof of Theorem 1.

We shall give later more efficient methods for finding solutions of linear equations.

We now consider the original system of equations (*). Let B be the column vector

$$B = \begin{pmatrix} b_1 \\ \vdots \\ b_m \end{pmatrix}.$$

Then we may rewrite (*) in the form

$$x_1 \begin{pmatrix} a_{11} \\ \vdots \\ a_{m1} \end{pmatrix} + \cdots + x_n \begin{pmatrix} a_{1n} \\ \vdots \\ a_{mn} \end{pmatrix} = \begin{pmatrix} b_1 \\ \vdots \\ b_m \end{pmatrix},$$

or abbreviated in terms of the column vectors of A,

$$x_1 A^1 + \cdots + x_n A^n = B.$$

Theorem 2. *Assume that $m = n$ in the system (*) above, and that the vectors $A^1, \ldots, A^n$ are linearly independent. Then the system (*) has a solution in K, and this solution is unique.*

Proof. The vectors $A^1, \ldots, A^n$ being linearly independent, they form a basis of K^n. Hence any vector B has a unique expression as a linear combination

$$B = x_1 A^1 + \cdots + x_n A^n,$$

with $x_i \in K$, and $X = (x_1, \ldots, x_n)$ is therefore the unique solution of the system.

EXERCISES

1. Let (**) be a system of homogeneous linear equations in a field K, and assume that $m = n$. Assume also that the column vectors of coefficients are linearly independent. Show that the only solution is the trivial solution.

2. Let (**) be a system of homogeneous linear equations in a field K, in n unknowns. Show that the set of solutions $X = (x_1, \ldots, x_n)$ is a vector space over K.

3. Solve the following systems of linear equations in **R**.

(a) $2x + 3y = 5$
    $4x - y = 7$

(b) $2x + 3y + z = 0$
    $x - 2y - z = 1$
    $x + 4y + z = 2$

4. Solve the following system of linear equations in **C**.

(a) $ix - 2y = 1$
    $x + iy = 2$

(b) $2x + iy - (1 + i)z = 1$
    $x - 2y + iz = 0$
    $-ix + y - (2 - i)z = 1$

(c) $(1 + i)x - y = 0$
    $ix + y = 3 - i$

(d) $ix - (2 + i)y = 1$
    $x + (2 - i)y = 1 + i$

5. Let $A^1, \ldots, A^n$ be column vectors of size m. Assume that they have coefficients in **R**, and that they are linearly independent over **R**. Show that they are linearly independent over **C**.

6. Find at least one non-trivial solution for each one of the following systems of equations.

(a) $3x + y + z = 0$

(b) $3x + y + z = 0$
    $x + y + z = 0$

(c) $2x - 3y + 4z = 0$
    $3x + y + z = 0$

(d) $2x + y + 4z + w = 0$
    $-3x + 2y - 3z + w = 0$
    $x + y + z = 0$

(e) $-x + 2y - 4z + w = 0$
    $x + 3y + z - w = 0$

(f) $-2x + 3y + z + 4w = 0$
    $x - y + 2z + 3w = 0$
    $2x + y + z - 2w = 0$

7. Show that the only solutions of the following systems of equations are trivial.

(a) $2x + 3y = 0$
$\qquad x - y = 0$

(b) $\quad 4x + 5y = 0$
$\qquad -6x + 7y = 0$

(c) $\quad 3x + 4y - 2z = 0$
$\qquad x + y + z = 0$
$\qquad -x - 3y + 5z = 0$

(d) $4x - 7y + 3z = 0$
$\qquad x + y = 0$
$\qquad y - 6z = 0$

(e) $7x - 2y + 5z + w = 0$
$\qquad x - y + z = 0$
$\qquad y - 2z + w = 0$
$\qquad x + z + w = 0$

(f) $\qquad -3x + y + z = 0$
$\qquad x - y + z - 2w = 0$
$\qquad x - z + w = 0$
$\qquad -x + y - 3w = 0$

8. Let (**) be a system of homogeneous linear equations with coefficients in **R**. If this system has a non-trivial solution in **C**, show that it has a non-trivial solution in **R**.

§3. *Multiplication of matrices*

We shall consider matrices over a fixed field K. We begin by noticing that the dot product defined in Chapter I for vectors with real coefficients works as well for vectors with components in K. Thus if $A = (a_1, \ldots, a_n)$ and $B = (b_1, \ldots, b_n)$ are in K^n, we define

$$A \cdot B = a_1 b_1 + \cdots + a_n b_n.$$

This is an element of K. We have the basic properties:

SP 1. *For all A, B in K^n, we have $A \cdot B = B \cdot A$.*

SP 2. *If A, B, C are in K^n, then*

$$A \cdot (B + C) = A \cdot B + A \cdot C = (B + C) \cdot A.$$

SP 3. *If $x \in K$, then*

$$(xA) \cdot B = x(A \cdot B) \qquad and \qquad A \cdot (xB) = x(A \cdot B).$$

Notice however that the positivity property does not hold in general. For instance, if $K = \mathbf{C}$, let $A = (1, i)$. Then $A \neq O$ but

$$A \cdot A = 1 + i^2 = 0.$$

For many applications, this positivity is not necessary, and one can use instead a property which we shall call **non-degeneracy,** namely:

If $A \in K^n$, and if $A \cdot X = 0$ for all $X \in K^n$ then $A = O$.

The proof is trivial, because we must have $A \cdot E_i = 0$ for each unit vector $E_i = (0, \ldots, 0, 1, 0, \ldots, 0)$ with 1 in the i-th component and 0 otherwise. But $A \cdot E_i = a_i$, and hence $a_i = 0$ for all i, so that $A = O$.

We shall now define the product of matrices.

Let $A = (a_{ij})$, $i = 1, \ldots, m$ and $j = 1, \ldots, n$, be an $m \times n$ matrix. Let $B = (b_{jk})$, $j = 1, \ldots, n$ and $k = 1, \ldots, s$, be an $n \times s$ matrix.

$$A = \begin{pmatrix} a_{11} & \cdots & a_{1n} \\ & \cdots & \\ a_{m1} & \cdots & a_{mn} \end{pmatrix},$$

$$B = \begin{pmatrix} b_{11} & \cdots & b_{1s} \\ & \cdots & \\ b_{n1} & \cdots & b_{ns} \end{pmatrix}.$$

We define the product AB to be the $m \times s$ matrix whose ik-coordinate is

$$\sum_{j=1}^{n} a_{ij}b_{jk} = a_{i1}b_{1k} + a_{i2}b_{2k} + \cdots + a_{in}b_{nk}.$$

If $A_1, \ldots, A_m$ are the row vectors of the matrix A, and if $B^1, \ldots, B^s$ are the column vectors of the matrix B, then the ik-coordinate of the product AB is equal to $A_i \cdot B^k$. Thus

$$AB = \begin{pmatrix} A_1 \cdot B^1 & \cdots & A_1 \cdot B^s \\ \vdots & & \vdots \\ A_m \cdot B^1 & \cdots & A_m \cdot B^s \end{pmatrix}.$$

Multiplication of matrices is therefore a generalization of the dot product.

Example 1. Let

$$A = \begin{pmatrix} 2 & 1 & 5 \\ 1 & 3 & 2 \end{pmatrix},$$

$$B = \begin{pmatrix} 3 & 4 \\ -1 & 2 \\ 2 & 1 \end{pmatrix}.$$

Then AB is a 2×2 matrix, and computations show that

$$AB = \begin{pmatrix} 2 & 1 & 5 \\ 1 & 3 & 2 \end{pmatrix} \begin{pmatrix} 3 & 4 \\ -1 & 2 \\ 2 & 1 \end{pmatrix} = \begin{pmatrix} 15 & 15 \\ 4 & 12 \end{pmatrix}.$$

Example 2. Let

$$C = \begin{pmatrix} 1 & 3 \\ -1 & -1 \end{pmatrix}.$$

Let A, B be as in Example 1. Then

$$BC = \begin{pmatrix} 3 & 4 \\ -1 & 2 \\ 2 & 1 \end{pmatrix} \begin{pmatrix} 1 & 3 \\ -1 & -1 \end{pmatrix} = \begin{pmatrix} -1 & 5 \\ -3 & -5 \\ 1 & 5 \end{pmatrix}$$

and

$$A(BC) = \begin{pmatrix} 2 & 1 & 5 \\ 1 & 3 & 2 \end{pmatrix} \begin{pmatrix} -1 & 5 \\ -3 & -5 \\ 1 & 5 \end{pmatrix} = \begin{pmatrix} 0 & 30 \\ -8 & 0 \end{pmatrix}.$$

Compute $(AB)C$. What do you find?

Let A be an $m \times n$ matrix and let B be an $n \times 1$ matrix, i.e. a column vector. Then AB is again a column vector. The product looks like this:

$$\begin{pmatrix} a_{11} & \cdots & a_{1n} \\ \vdots & & \vdots \\ a_{m1} & \cdots & a_{mn} \end{pmatrix} \begin{pmatrix} b_1 \\ \vdots \\ b_n \end{pmatrix} = \begin{pmatrix} c_1 \\ \vdots \\ c_m \end{pmatrix},$$

where

$$c_i = \sum_{j=1}^{n} a_{ij}b_j = a_{i1}b_1 + \cdots + a_{in}b_n.$$

If $X = (x_1, \ldots, x_m)$ is a row vector, i.e. a $1 \times m$ matrix, then we can form the product XA, which looks like this:

$$(x_1, \ldots, x_m) \begin{pmatrix} a_{11} & \cdots & a_{1n} \\ \vdots & & \vdots \\ a_{m1} & \cdots & a_{mn} \end{pmatrix} = (y_1, \ldots, y_n),$$

where

$$y_k = x_1 a_{1k} + \cdots + x_m a_{mk}.$$

In this case, XA is a $1 \times n$ matrix, i.e. a row vector.

Theorem 3. *Let A, B, C be matrices. Assume that A, B can be multiplied, and A, C can be multiplied, and B, C can be added. Then A, $B + C$ can be multiplied, and we have*

$$A(B + C) = AB + AC.$$

If x is a number, then

$$A(xB) = x(AB).$$

Proof. Let A_i be the i-th row of A and let B^k, C^k be the k-th column of B and C, respectively .... Then $B^k + C^k$ is the k-th column of $B + C$. By definition, the ik-component of AB is $A_i \cdot B^k$, the ik-component of AC is $A_i \cdot C^k$, and the ik-component of $A(B + C)$ is $A_i \cdot (B^k + C^k)$. Since

$$A_i \cdot (B^k + C^k) = A_i \cdot B^k + A_i \cdot C^k,$$

our first assertion follows. As for the second, observe that the k-th column of xB is xB^k. Since

$$A_i \cdot xB^k = x(A_i \cdot B^k),$$

our second assertion follows.

Theorem 4. *Let A, B, C be matrices such that A, B can be multiplied and B, C can be multiplied. Then A, BC can be multiplied. So can AB, C, and we have*

$$(AB)C = A(BC).$$

Proof. Let $A = (a_{ij})$ be an $m \times n$ matrix, let $B = (b_{jk})$ be an $n \times r$ matrix, and let $C = (c_{kl})$ be an $r \times s$ matrix. The product AB is an $m \times r$ matrix, whose ik-component is equal to the sum

$$a_{i1} b_{1k} + a_{i2} b_{2k} + \cdots + a_{in} b_{nk}.$$

We shall abbreviate this sum using our $\sum$ notation by writing

$$\sum_{j=1}^{n} a_{ij}b_{jk}.$$

By definition, the il-component of $(AB)C$ is equal to

$$\sum_{k=1}^{r}\left[\sum_{j=1}^{n} a_{ij}b_{jk}\right]c_{kl} = \sum_{k=1}^{r}\left[\sum_{j=1}^{n} a_{ij}b_{jk}c_{kl}\right].$$

The sum on the right can also be described as the sum of all terms

$$a_{ij}b_{jk}c_{kl},$$

where j, k range over all integers $1 \leqq j \leqq n$ and $1 \leqq k \leqq r$ respectively.

If we had started with the jl-component of BC and then computed the il-component of $A(BC)$ we would have found exactly the same sum, thereby proving the theorem.

Let A be a square $n \times n$ matrix. We shall say that A is **invertible** or **non-singular** if there exists an $n \times n$ matrix B such that

$$AB = BA = I_n.$$

Such a matrix B is uniquely determined by A, for if C is such that $AC = CA = I_n$, then

$$B = BI_n = B(AC) = (BA)C = I_nC = C.$$

(Cf. Exercise 1.) This matrix B will be called the **inverse** of A and will be denoted by A^{-1}. When we study determinants, we shall find an explicit way of finding it, whenever it exists.

Let A be a square matrix. Then we can form the product of A with itself, say AA, or repeated products,

$$A \cdots A$$

taken m times. By definition, if m is an integer ≥ 1, we define A^m to be the product $A \cdots A$ taken m times. We *define* $A^0 = I$ (the unit matrix of the same size as A). The usual rule $A^{r+s} = A^r A^s$ holds for integers $r, s \geqq 0$.

The next result relates the transpose with multiplication of matrices.

Theorem 5. *Let A, B be matrices which can be multiplied. Then ${}^tB$, ${}^tA$ can be multiplied, and*

$$^t(AB) = {}^tB\,{}^tA.$$

Proof. Let $A = (a_{ij})$ and $B = (b_{jk})$. Let $AB = C$. Then

$$c_{ik} = \sum_{j=1}^{n} a_{ij}b_{jk}.$$

Let ${}^tB = (b'_{kj})$ and ${}^tA = (a'_{ji})$. Then the ki-component of ${}^tB\,{}^tA$ is by definition

$$\sum_{j=1}^{n} b'_{kj}a'_{ji}.$$

Since $b'_{kj} = b_{jk}$ and $a'_{ji} = a_{ij}$ we see that this last expression is equal to

$$\sum_{j=1}^{n} b_{jk}a_{ij} = \sum_{j=1}^{n} a_{ij}b_{jk}.$$

By definition, this is the ki-component of ${}^tC$, as was to be shown.

In terms of multiplication of matrices, we can now write a system of linear equations in the form

$$AX = B,$$

where A is an $m \times n$ matrix, X is a column vector of size n, and B is a column vector of size m.

EXERCISES

1. Let I be the unit $n \times n$ matrix. Let A be an $n \times r$ matrix. What is IA? If A is an $m \times n$ matrix, what is AI?

2. Let O be the matrix all of whose coordinates are 0. Let A be a matrix of a size such that the product AO is defined. What is AO?

3. In each one of the following cases, find $(AB)C$ and $A(BC)$.

(a) $A = \begin{pmatrix} 2 & 1 \\ 3 & 1 \end{pmatrix}$, $B = \begin{pmatrix} -1 & 1 \\ 1 & 0 \end{pmatrix}$, $C = \begin{pmatrix} 1 & 4 \\ 2 & 3 \end{pmatrix}$

(b) $A = \begin{pmatrix} 2 & 1 & -1 \\ 3 & 1 & 2 \end{pmatrix}$, $B = \begin{pmatrix} 1 & 1 \\ 2 & 0 \\ 3 & -1 \end{pmatrix}$, $C = \begin{pmatrix} 1 \\ 3 \end{pmatrix}$

(c) $A = \begin{pmatrix} 2 & 4 & 1 \\ 3 & 0 & -1 \end{pmatrix}$, $B = \begin{pmatrix} 1 & 1 & 0 \\ 2 & 1 & -1 \\ 3 & 1 & 5 \end{pmatrix}$, $C = \begin{pmatrix} 1 & 2 \\ 3 & 1 \\ -1 & 4 \end{pmatrix}$

4. Let A, B be square matrices of the same size, and assume that $AB = BA$. Show that $(A + B)^2 = A^2 + 2AB + B^2$, and

$$(A + B)(A - B) = A^2 - B^2,$$

using the properties of matrices stated in Theorem 3.

5. Let

$$A = \begin{pmatrix} 1 & 2 \\ 3 & -1 \end{pmatrix}, \qquad B = \begin{pmatrix} 2 & 0 \\ 1 & 1 \end{pmatrix}.$$

Find AB and BA.

6. Let

$$C = \begin{pmatrix} 7 & 0 \\ 0 & 7 \end{pmatrix}.$$

Let A, B be as in Exercise 5. Find CA, AC, CB, and BC. State the general rule including this exercise as a special case.

7. Let $X = (1, 0, 0)$ and let

$$A = \begin{pmatrix} 3 & 1 & 5 \\ 2 & 0 & 1 \\ 1 & 1 & 7 \end{pmatrix}.$$

What is XA?

8. Let $X = (0, 1, 0)$, and let A be an arbitrary 3×3 matrix. How would you describe XA? What if $X = (0, 0, 1)$? Generalize to similar statements concerning $n \times n$ matrices, and their products with unit vectors.

9. Let A, B be the matrices of Exercise 3(a). Verify by computation that $^t(AB) = {}^tB{}^tA$. Do the same for 3(b) and 3(c). Prove the same rule for any two matrices A, B (which can be multiplied). If A, B, C are matrices which can be multiplied, show that $^t(ABC) = {}^tC{}^tB{}^tA$.

10. Let M be an $n \times n$ matrix such that $^tM = M$. Given two row vectors in n-space, say A and B define $\langle A, B \rangle$ to be AM^tB. (Identify a 1×1 matrix with a number.) Show that the conditions of a scalar product are satisfied, except possibly the condition concerning positivity. Give an example of a matrix M and vectors A, B such that AM^tB is negative (taking $n = 2$).

11. (a) Let A be the matrix

$$\begin{pmatrix} 0 & 1 & 1 \\ 0 & 0 & 1 \\ 0 & 0 & 0 \end{pmatrix}.$$

Find A^2, A^3. Generalize to 4×4 matrices.

(b) Let A be the matrix

$$\begin{pmatrix} 1 & 1 & 1 \\ 0 & 1 & 1 \\ 0 & 0 & 1 \end{pmatrix}.$$

Compute A^2, A^3, A^4.

12. Let X be the indicated column vector, and A the indicated matrix. Find AX as a column vector.

(a) $X = \begin{pmatrix} 3 \\ 2 \\ 1 \end{pmatrix}$, $A = \begin{pmatrix} 1 & 0 & 1 \\ 2 & 1 & 1 \\ 2 & 0 & -1 \end{pmatrix}$ (b) $X = \begin{pmatrix} 1 \\ 1 \\ 0 \end{pmatrix}$, $A = \begin{pmatrix} 2 & 1 & 5 \\ 0 & 1 & 1 \end{pmatrix}$

(c) $X = \begin{pmatrix} x_1 \\ x_2 \\ x_3 \end{pmatrix}$, $A = \begin{pmatrix} 0 & 1 & 0 \\ 0 & 0 & 0 \end{pmatrix}$ (d) $X = \begin{pmatrix} x_1 \\ x_2 \\ x_3 \end{pmatrix}$, $A = \begin{pmatrix} 0 & 0 & 0 \\ 1 & 0 & 0 \end{pmatrix}$

13. Let

$$A = \begin{pmatrix} 2 & 1 & 3 \\ 4 & 1 & 5 \end{pmatrix}.$$

Find AX for each of the following values of X.

(a) $X = \begin{pmatrix} 1 \\ 0 \\ 0 \end{pmatrix}$ (b) $X = \begin{pmatrix} 0 \\ 1 \\ 1 \end{pmatrix}$ (c) $X = \begin{pmatrix} 0 \\ 0 \\ 1 \end{pmatrix}$

14. Let

$$A = \begin{pmatrix} 3 & 7 & 5 \\ 1 & -1 & 4 \\ 2 & 1 & 8 \end{pmatrix}.$$

Find AX for each of the values of X given in Exercise 13.

15. Let

$$X = \begin{pmatrix} 0 \\ 1 \\ 0 \\ 0 \end{pmatrix} \quad \text{and} \quad A = \begin{pmatrix} a_{11} & \cdots & a_{14} \\ \vdots & & \vdots \\ a_{m1} & \cdots & a_{m4} \end{pmatrix}.$$

What is AX?

16. Let X be a column vector having all its components equal to 0 except the i-th component which is equal to 1. Let A be an arbitrary matrix, whose size is such that we can form the product AX. What is AX?

17. Let $A = (a_{ij})$, $i = 1, \ldots, m$ and $j = 1, \ldots, n$, be an $m \times n$ matrix. Let $B = (b_{jk})$, $j = 1, \ldots, n$ and $k = 1, \ldots, s$, be an $n \times s$ matrix. Let $AB = C$. Show that the k-th column C^k can be written

$$C^k = b_{1k}A^1 + \cdots + b_{nk}A^n.$$

(This will be useful in finding the determinant of a product.)

18. Let a, b be numbers, and let

$$A = \begin{pmatrix} 1 & a \\ 0 & 1 \end{pmatrix} \quad \text{and} \quad B = \begin{pmatrix} 1 & b \\ 0 & 1 \end{pmatrix}.$$

What is AB? What is A^n where n is a positive integer?

19. If A is a square $n \times n$ matrix, we call a square matrix B an **inverse** for A if $AB = BA = I_n$. Show that if B, C are inverses for A, then $B = C$.

20. Show that the matrix A in Exercise 18 has an inverse. What is this inverse?

21. Show that if A, B are $n \times n$ matrices which have inverses, then AB has an inverse.

22. Determine all 2×2 matrices A such that $A^2 = O$.

23. Let $A = \begin{pmatrix} \cos\theta & -\sin\theta \\ \sin\theta & \cos\theta \end{pmatrix}$. Show that $A^2 = \begin{pmatrix} \cos 2\theta & -\sin 2\theta \\ \sin 2\theta & \cos 2\theta \end{pmatrix}$.

Determine A^n by induction for any positive integer n.

24. Find a 2×2 matrix A such that $A^2 = -I = \begin{pmatrix} -1 & 0 \\ 0 & -1 \end{pmatrix}$.

25. Let A be an $n \times n$ matrix. Define the **trace** of A to be the sum of the diagonal elements. Thus if $A = (a_{ij})$, then

$$\operatorname{tr}(A) = \sum_{i=1}^{n} a_{ii}.$$

For instance, if

$$A = \begin{pmatrix} 1 & 2 \\ 3 & 4 \end{pmatrix},$$

then $\operatorname{tr}(A) = 1 + 4 = 5$. If

$$A = \begin{pmatrix} 1 & -1 & 5 \\ 2 & 1 & 3 \\ 1 & -4 & 7 \end{pmatrix},$$

then $\operatorname{tr}(A) = 9$. Compute the trace of the following matrices:

(a) $\begin{pmatrix} 1 & 7 & 3 \\ -1 & 5 & 2 \\ 2 & 3 & -4 \end{pmatrix}$ (b) $\begin{pmatrix} 3 & -2 & 4 \\ 1 & 4 & 1 \\ -7 & -3 & -3 \end{pmatrix}$ (c) $\begin{pmatrix} -2 & 1 & 1 \\ 3 & 4 & 4 \\ -5 & 2 & 6 \end{pmatrix}$.

26. Let A, B be the indicated matrices. Show that

$$\operatorname{tr}(AB) = \operatorname{tr}(BA).$$

(a) $A = \begin{pmatrix} 1 & -1 & 1 \\ 2 & 4 & 1 \\ 3 & 0 & 1 \end{pmatrix}$ $B = \begin{pmatrix} 3 & 1 & 2 \\ 1 & 1 & 0 \\ -1 & 2 & 1 \end{pmatrix}$

(b) $A = \begin{pmatrix} 1 & 7 & 3 \\ -1 & 5 & 2 \\ 2 & 3 & -4 \end{pmatrix}$ $B = \begin{pmatrix} 3 & -2 & 4 \\ 1 & 4 & 1 \\ -7 & -3 & 2 \end{pmatrix}$.

27. Prove in general that if A, B are square $n \times n$ matrices, then

$$\operatorname{tr}(AB) = \operatorname{tr}(BA).$$

28. For any square matrix A, show that $\operatorname{tr}(A) = \operatorname{tr}({}^t A)$.

29. Let

$$A = \begin{pmatrix} 1 & 0 & 0 \\ 0 & 2 & 0 \\ 0 & 0 & 3 \end{pmatrix}.$$

Find A^2, A^3, A^4.

30. Let A be a diagonal matrix, with diagonal elements $a_1, \ldots, a_n$. What is A^2, A^3, A^k for any positive integer k?

31. Let

$$A = \begin{pmatrix} 0 & 1 & 6 \\ 0 & 0 & 4 \\ 0 & 0 & 0 \end{pmatrix}.$$

Find A^3.

32. Let A be an invertible $n \times n$ matrix. Show that

$$^t(A^{-1}) = (^tA)^{-1}.$$

We may therefore write $^tA^{-1}$ without fear of confusion.

33. Let A be a complex matrix, $A = (a_{ij})$, and let $\overline{A} = (\overline{a}_{ij})$, where the bar means complex conjugate. Show that

$$^t(\overline{A}) = \overline{^tA}.$$

We then write simply $^t\overline{A}$.

34. Let A be a diagonal matrix:

$$A = \begin{pmatrix} a_1 & 0 & \cdots & 0 \\ 0 & a_2 & \cdots & 0 \\ \vdots & \vdots & & \vdots \\ 0 & 0 & \cdots & a_n \end{pmatrix}$$

If $a_i \neq 0$ for all i, show that A is invertible. What is its inverse?

35. Let A be a **strictly upper triangular matrix,** i.e. a square matrix (a_{ij}) having all its components below and on the diagonal equal to 0. We may express this by writing $a_{ij} = 0$ if $i \geq j$:

$$A = \begin{pmatrix} 0 & a_{12} & a_{13} & \cdots & a_{1n} \\ 0 & 0 & a_{23} & \cdots & a_{2n} \\ \vdots & \vdots & \vdots & & \vdots \\ & & & & a_{n-1,n} \\ 0 & 0 & 0 & \cdots & 0 \end{pmatrix}$$

Prove that $A^n = O$. (If you wish, you may do it only in case $n = 2, 3$ and 4. The general case can be done by induction.)

36. Let A be a triangular matrix with components 1 on the diagonal:

$$A = \begin{pmatrix} 1 & a_{12} & \cdots & & a_{1n} \\ 0 & 1 & \cdots & & a_{2n} \\ \vdots & \vdots & & & \vdots \\ 0 & 0 & \cdots & 1 & a_{n-1,n} \\ 0 & 0 & \cdots & 0 & 1 \end{pmatrix}$$

Let $N = A - I_n$. Show that $N^{n+1} = 0$. Note that $A = I + N$. Show that A is invertible, and that its inverse is

$$(I + N)^{-1} = I - N + N^2 - \cdots + (-1)^n N^n.$$

37. If N is a square matrix such that $N^{r+1} = 0$ for some positive integer r, show that $I - N$ is invertible and that its inverse is $I + N + \cdots + N^r$.

38. Let A be a triangular matrix:

$$A = \begin{pmatrix} a_{11} & a_{12} & \cdots & a_{1n} \\ 0 & a_{22} & \cdots & a_{2n} \\ \vdots & \vdots & & \vdots \\ 0 & 0 & \cdots & a_{nn} \end{pmatrix}$$

Assume that no diagonal element is 0, and let

$$B = \begin{pmatrix} a_{11}^{-1} & 0 & \cdots & 0 \\ 0 & a_{22}^{-1} & \cdots & 0 \\ \vdots & \vdots & & \vdots \\ 0 & 0 & \cdots & a_{nn}^{-1} \end{pmatrix}$$

Show that BA and AB are triangular matrices with components 1 on the diagonal.

39. A square matrix A is said to be **nilpotent** if $A^r = O$ for some integer $r \geq 1$. Let A, B be nilpotent matrices, of the same size, and assume $AB = BA$. Show that AB and $A + B$ are nilpotent.

Appendix. Elimination

To prove Theorem 1, concerning homogeneous linear equations, we used the theorem that n elements of a vector space of dimension m must be linearly dependent if $n > m$. Conversely, it is possible to give a direct proof by the elementary method of elimination for the theorem on homogeneous linear equations, and then prove the dimension theorem from it. We shall carry this out as an alternative procedure to the one given in the text.

Consider our system of homogeneous equations (**). Let $A_1, \ldots, A_m$ be the row vectors of the matrix (a_{ij}). Then we can rewrite our equations (**) in the form

$$A_1 \cdot X = 0$$

(**)
$$\vdots$$

$$A_m \cdot X = 0.$$

Using the notation of the dot product will make it easier to formulate the proof of our theorem, namely:

Theorem. *Let*

$$a_{11}x_1 + \cdots + a_{1n}x_n = 0$$

$$\vdots$$

$$a_{m1}x_1 + \cdots + a_{mn}x_n = 0$$

be a system of m linear equations in n unknowns, and assume that $n > m$. Then the system has a non-trivial solution.

Proof. The proof will be carried out by induction, i.e. a stepwise procedure.

Consider first the case of one equation in n unknowns, $n > 1$:

$$a_1x_1 + \cdots + a_nx_n = 0.$$

If all coefficients $a_1, \ldots, a_n$ are equal to 0, then any value of the variables will be a solution, and a non-trivial solution certainly exists. Suppose that some coefficient a_i is $\neq 0$. After renumbering the variables and the coefficients, we may assume that it is a_1. Then we give $x_2, \ldots, x_n$ arbitrary values, for instance we let

$$x_2 = \cdots = x_n = 1,$$

and solve for x_1, letting

$$x_1 = \frac{-1}{a_1} (a_2 + \cdots + a_n).$$

In the above manner, we obtain a non-trivial solution for our system of equations.

Let us now assume that our theorem is true for a system of $m - 1$ equations in more than $m - 1$ unknowns. We shall prove that it is true for m equations in n unknowns when $n > m$. We consider the system (**).

If all coefficients (a_{ij}) are equal to 0, we can give any non-zero value to our variables to get a solution. If some coefficient is not equal to 0, then after renumbering the equations and the variables, we may assume that it is a_{11}. We shall subtract a multiple of the first equation from the others to eliminate x_1. Namely, we consider the system of equations

$$\left(A_2 - \frac{a_{21}}{a_{11}} A_1\right) \cdot X = 0$$

$$\vdots$$

$$\left(A_m - \frac{a_{m1}}{a_{11}} A_1\right) \cdot X = 0,$$

which can also be written in the form

(***)
$$A_2 \cdot X - \frac{a_{21}}{a_{11}} A_1 \cdot X = 0$$

$$\vdots$$

$$A_m \cdot X - \frac{a_{m1}}{a_{11}} A_1 \cdot X = 0.$$

In this system, the coefficient of x_1 is equal to 0. Hence we may view (***) as a system of $m - 1$ equations in $n - 1$ unknowns, and $n - 1 > m - 1$.

According to our assumption, we can find a non-trivial solution $(x_2, \ldots, x_n)$ for this system. We can then solve for x_1 in the first equation, namely

$$x_1 = \frac{-1}{a_{11}} (a_{12}x_2 + \cdots + a_{1n}x_n).$$

In that way, we find a solution of $A_1 \cdot X = 0$. But according to (***), we have

$$A_i \cdot X = \frac{a_{i1}}{a_{11}} A_1 \cdot X$$

for $i = 2, \ldots, m$. Hence $A_i \cdot X = 0$ for $i = 2, \ldots, m$ and therefore we have found a non-trivial solution to our original system (**).

The argument we have just given allows us to proceed stepwise from one equation to two equations, then from two to three, and so forth. This concludes the proof.

Corollary. Let V be a vector space, and let $\{v_1, \ldots, v_m\}$ be a basis of V. Let $w_1, \ldots, w_n$ be elements of V and assume that $n > m$. Then $w_1, \ldots, w_n$ are linearly dependent.

Proof. Since $\{v_1, \ldots, v_m\}$ is a basis, there exist numbers (a_{ij}) such that we can write

$$w_1 = a_{11}v_1 + \cdots + a_{m1}v_m$$

$$\vdots$$

$$w_n = a_{1n}v_1 + \cdots + a_{mn}v_m.$$

If $x_1, \ldots, x_n$ are numbers, then

$$x_1 w_1 + \cdots + x_n w_n$$
$$= (x_1 a_{11} + \cdots + x_n a_{1n}) v_1 + \cdots + (x_1 a_{m1} + \cdots + x_n a_{mn}) v_n$$

(just add up the coefficients of $v_1, \ldots, v_n$ vertically downwards). According to the theorem, the system of equations

$$x_1 a_{11} + \cdots + x_n a_{1n} = 0$$
$$\vdots$$
$$x_1 a_{m1} + \cdots + x_n a_{mn} = 0$$

has a non-trivial solution, because $n > m$. In view of the preceding remark, such a solution $(x_1, \ldots, x_n)$ is such that

$$x_1 w_1 + \cdots + x_n w_n = 0,$$

as desired.

CHAPTER IV

Linear Mappings

We shall first define the general notion of a mapping, which generalizes the notion of a function. Among mappings, the linear mappings are the most important. A good deal of mathematics is devoted to reducing questions concerning arbitrary mappings to linear mappings. For one thing, they are interesting in themselves, and many mappings are linear. On the other hand, it is often possible to approximate an arbitrary mapping by a linear one, whose study is much easier than the study of the original mapping. This is done in the calculus of several variables.

§1. Mappings

Let S, S' be two sets. a **mapping** from S to S' is an association which to every element of S associates an element of S'. Instead of saying that F is a mapping from S into S', we shall often write the symbols $F: S \to S'$. A mapping will also be called a **map**, for the sake of brevity.

A function is a special type of mapping, namely it is a mapping from a set into the set of numbers, i.e. into $\mathbf{R}$, or $\mathbf{C}$.

We extend to mappings some of the terminology we have used for functions. For instance, if $T: S \to S'$ is a mapping, and if u is an element of S, then we denote by $T(u)$, or Tu, the element of S' associated to u by T. We call $T(u)$ the **value** of T at u, or also the **image** of u under T. The symbols $T(u)$ are read "T of u". The set of all elements $T(u)$, when u ranges over all elements of S, is called the **image** of T. If W is a subset of S, then the set of elements $T(w)$, when w ranges over all elements of W, is called the **image** of W under T, and is denoted by $T(W)$.

Let $F: S \to S'$ be a map from a set S into a set S'. If x is an element of S, we often write

$$x \mapsto F(x)$$

with a special arrow $\mapsto$ to denote the image of x under F. Thus, for instance, we would speak of the map F such that $F(x) = x^2$ as the map $x \mapsto x^2$.

Example 1. Let S and S' be both equal to $\mathbf{R}$. Let $f\colon \mathbf{R} \to \mathbf{R}$ be the function $f(x) = x^2$ (i.e. the function whose value at a number x is x^2). Then f is a mapping from $\mathbf{R}$ into $\mathbf{R}$. Its image is the set of numbers ≥ 0.

Example 2. Let S be the set of numbers ≥ 0, and let $S' = \mathbf{R}$. Let $g\colon S \to S'$ be the function such that $g(x) = x^{1/2}$. Then g is a mapping from S into $\mathbf{R}$.

Example 3. Let S be the set of functions having derivatives of all orders on the interval $0 < t < 1$, and let $S' = S$. Then the derivative $D = d/dt$ is a mapping from S into S. Indeed, our map D associates the function $df/dt = Df$ to the function f. According to our terminology, Df is the value of the mapping D at f.

Example 4. Let S be the set of continuous functions on the interval $[0, 1]$ and let S' be the set of differentiable functions on that interval. We shall define a mapping $\mathscr{s}\colon S \to S'$ by giving its value at any function f in S. Namely, we let $\mathscr{s}f$ (or $\mathscr{s}(f)$) be the function whose value at x is

$$(\mathscr{s}f)(x) = \int_0^x f(t)\, dt.$$

Then $\mathscr{s}(f)$ is a differentiable function.

Example 5. Let S be the set $\mathbf{R}^3$, i.e. the set of 3-tuples. Let $A = (2, 3, -1)$. Let $L\colon \mathbf{R}^3 \to \mathbf{R}$ be the mapping whose value at a vector $X = (x, y, z)$ is $A \cdot X$. Then $L(X) = A \cdot X$. If $X = (1, 1, -1)$, then the value of L at X is 6.

Just as we did with functions, we describe a mapping by giving its values. Thus, instead of making the statement in Example 5 describing the mapping L, we would also say: Let $L\colon \mathbf{R}^3 \to \mathbf{R}$ be the mapping $L(X) = A \cdot X$. This is somewhat incorrect, but is briefer, and does not usually give rise to confusion. More correctly, we can write $X \mapsto L(X)$ of $X \mapsto A \cdot X$ with the special arrow $\mapsto$ to denote the effect of the map L on the element X.

Example 6. Let $F\colon \mathbf{R}^2 \to \mathbf{R}^2$ be the mapping given by

$$F(x, y) = (2x, 2y).$$

Describe the image under F of the points lying on the circle $x^2 + y^2 = 1$.
    Let (x, y) be a point on the circle of radius 1.
    Let $u = 2x$ and $v = 2y$. Then u, v satisfy the relation

$$(u/2)^2 + (v/2)^2 = 1$$

or in other words,

$$\frac{u^2}{4} + \frac{v^2}{4} = 1.$$

Hence (u, v) is a point on the circle of radius 2. Therefore the image under F of the circle of radius 1 is a subset of the circle of radius 2. Conversely, given a point (u, v) such that

$$u^2 + v^2 = 4,$$

let $x = u/2$ and $y = v/2$. Then the point (x, y) satisfies the equation $x^2 + y^2 = 1$, and hence is a point on the circle of radius 1. Furthermore, $F(x, y) = (u, v)$. Hence every point on the circle of radius 2 is the image of some point on the circle of radius 1. We conclude finally that the image of the circle of radius 1 under F is precisely the circle of radius 2.

Note. In general, let S, S' be two sets. To prove that $S = S'$, one frequently proves that S is a subset of S' and that S' is a subset of S. This is what we did in the preceding argument.

Example 7. Let S be a set and let V be a vector space over the field K. Let F, G be mappings of S into V. We can define their sum $F + G$ as the map whose value at an element t of S if $F(t) + G(t)$. We also define the product of F by an element c of K to be the map whose value at an element t of S is $cF(t)$. It is easy to verify that conditions VS 1 through VS 8 are satisfied.

Example 8. Let S be a set. Let $F: S \to K^n$ be a mapping. For each element t of S, the value of F at t is a vector $F(t)$. The coordinates of $F(t)$ depend on t. Hence there are functions $f_1, \ldots, f_n$ of S into K such that

$$F(t) = (f_1(t), \ldots, f_n(t)).$$

These functions are called the **coordinate functions** of F. For instance, if $K = \mathbf{R}$ and if S is an interval of real numbers, which we denote by J, then a map

$$F: J \to \mathbf{R}^n$$

is also called a (parametric) **curve** in n-space.

Let S be an arbitrary set again, and let F, $G: S \to K^n$ be mappings of S into K^n. Let $f_1, \ldots, f_n$ be the coordinate functions of F, and $g_1, \ldots, g_n$ the coordinate functions of G. Then $G(t) = (g_1(t), \ldots, g_n(t))$ for all $t \in S$. Furthermore,

$$(F + G)(t) = F(t) + G(t) = (f_1(t) + g_1(t), \ldots, f_n(t) + g_n(t)),$$

and for any $c \in K$,

$$(cF)(t) = cF(t) = (cf_1(t), \ldots, cf_n(t)).$$

We see in particular that the coordinate functions of $F + G$ are

$$f_1 + g_1, \ldots, f_n + g_n.$$

Let U, V, W be sets. Let $F: U \to V$ and $G: V \to W$ be mappings. Then we can form the composite mapping from U into W, denoted by $G \circ F$. It is the mapping defined by the rule

$$(G \circ F)(t) = G(F(t))$$

for all $t \in U$.

Example 9. If $f: \mathbf{R} \to \mathbf{R}$ is a function and $g: \mathbf{R} \to \mathbf{R}$ is also a function, then $g \circ f$ is the composite function.

Let $G: \mathbf{R} \to \mathbf{R}^n$ be another mapping from $\mathbf{R}$ into $\mathbf{R}^n$, and let $g_1, \ldots, g_n$ be its coordinate functions. Then

$$G(t) = (g_1(t), \ldots, g_n(t)).$$

Then

$$(F + G)(t) = F(t) + G(t) = (f_1(t) + g_1(t), \ldots, f_n(t) + g_n(t)),$$

and for any number c,

$$(cF)(t) = cF(t) = (cf_1(t), \ldots, cf_n(t)).$$

Example 10. We can define a map $F: \mathbf{R} \to \mathbf{R}^n$ by the association

$$t \mapsto (2t, 10^t, t^3).$$

Thus $F(t) = (2t, 10^t, t^3)$, and $F(2) = (4, 100, 8)$. The coordinate functions of F are the functions f_1, f_2, f_3 such that

$$f_1(t) = 2t, \quad f_2(t) = 10^t \quad \text{and} \quad f_3(t) = t^3.$$

Let U, V, W be sets. Let $F: U \to V$ and $G: V \to W$ be mappings. Then we can form the composite mapping from U into W, denoted by $G \circ F$. It is by definition the mapping defined by

$$(G \circ F)(t) = G(F(t))$$

for all $t \in U$. If $f: \mathbf{R} \to \mathbf{R}$ is a function and $g: \mathbf{R} \to \mathbf{R}$ is also a function, then $g \circ f$ is the composite function.

The following statement is an important property of mappings.

Let U, V, W, S be sets. Let

$$F: U \to V, \qquad G: V \to W, \qquad and \qquad H: W \to S$$

be mappings. Then

$$H \circ (G \circ F) = (H \circ G) \circ F.$$

Proof. Here again, the proof is very simple. By definition, we have, for any element u of U:

$$(H \circ (G \circ F))(u) = H((G \circ F)(u)) = H(G(F(u))).$$

On the other hand,

$$((H \circ G) \circ F)(u) = (H \circ G)(F(u)) = H(G(F(u))).$$

By definition, this means that

$$(H \circ G) \circ F = H \circ (G \circ F).$$

We shall discuss inverse mappings, but before that, we need to mention two special properties which a mapping may have. Let

$$f: S \to S'$$

be a map. We say that f is **injective** if whenever x, $y \in S$ and $x \neq y$, then $f(x) \neq f(y)$. In other words, f is injective means that f takes on distinct values at distinct elements of S. For example, the map

$$f: \mathbf{R} \to \mathbf{R}$$

such that $f(x) = x^2$, is not injective, because $f(1) = f(-1) = 1$. Also the function $x \mapsto \sin x$ is not injective, because $\sin x = \sin (x + 2\pi)$. However, the map $f: \mathbf{R} \to \mathbf{R}$ such that $f(x) = x + 1$, is injective, because if $x + 1 = y + 1$ then $x = y$.

Again, let $f: S \to S'$ be a mapping. We shall say that f is **surjective** if the image of f is all of S'. Again, the map

$$f: \mathbf{R} \to \mathbf{R}$$

such that $f(x) = x^2$, is not surjective, because its image consists of all numbers ≥ 0, and this image is not equal to all of R. On the other hand, the map of $\mathbf{R}$ into $\mathbf{R}$ given by $x \mapsto x^3$ is surjective, because given a number y there exists a number x such that $y = x^3$ (the cube root of y). Thus every number is in the image of our map.

Let $\mathbf{R}^+$ be the set of real numbers $\geqq 0$. As a matter of convention, we agree to distinguish between the maps

$$\mathbf{R} \to \mathbf{R} \quad \text{and} \quad \mathbf{R}^+ \to \mathbf{R}^+$$

given by the same formula $x \mapsto x^2$. The point is that when we view the association $x \mapsto x^2$ as a map of $\mathbf{R}$ into $\mathbf{R}$, then it is not surjective, and it is not injective. But when we view this formula as defining a map from $\mathbf{R}^+$ into $\mathbf{R}^+$, then it gives both an injective and surjective map of $\mathbf{R}^+$ into itself, because every positive number has a positive square root, and such a positive square root is uniquely determined.

In general, when dealing with a map $f\colon S \to S'$, we must therefore always specify the sets S and S', to be able to say that f is injective, or surjective, or neither. To have a completely accurate notation, we should write

$$f_{S,S'}$$

or some such symbol which specifies S and S' into the notation, but this becomes too clumsy, and we prefer to use the context to make our meaning clear.

If S is any set, the **identity mapping** I_S is defined to be the map such that $I_S(x) = x$ for all $x \in S$. We note that the identity map is both injective and surjective. If we do not need to specify the reference to S (because it is made clear by the context), then we write I instead of I_S. Thus we have $I(x) = x$ for all $x \in S$. We sometimes denote I_S by id_S or simply id.

Finally, we define inverse mappings. Let $F\colon S \to S'$ be a mapping from one set into another set. We say that F has an **inverse** if there exists a mapping $G\colon S' \to S$ such that

$$G \circ F = I_S \quad \text{and} \quad F \circ G = I_{S'}.$$

By this we mean that the composite maps $G \circ F$ and $F \circ G$ are the identity mappings of S and S' respectively.

Example 11. Let $S = S'$ be the set of all numbers $\geqq 0$. Let

$$f\colon S \to S'$$

be the map such that $f(x) = x^2$. Then f has an inverse mapping, namely the map $g\colon S \to S$ such that $g(x) = \sqrt{x}$.

Example 12. Let $\mathbf{R}^+$ be the set of numbers > 0 and let $f\colon \mathbf{R} \to \mathbf{R}^+$ be the map such that $f(x) = e^x$. Then f has an inverse mapping which is nothing but the logarithm.

Example 13. This example is particularly important in geometric applications. Let V be a vector space, and let u be a fixed element of V. We let

$$T_u: V \to V$$

be the map such that $T_u(v) = v + u$. We call T_u the **translation** by u. If S is any subset of V, then $T_u(S)$ is called the translation of S by u, and consists of all vectors $v + u$, with $v \in S$. We often denote it by $S + u$. In the next picture, we draw a set S and its translation by a vector u.

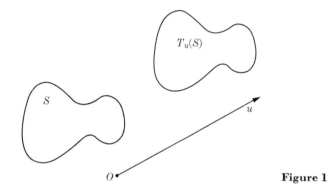

Figure 1

As exercises, we leave the proofs of the next two statements to the reader:

If u_1, u_2 are elements of V, then $T_{u_1+u_2} = T_{u_1} \circ T_{u_2}$.

If u is an element of V, then $T_u: V \to V$ has an inverse mapping which is nothing but the translation T_{-u}.

Let

$$f: S \to S'$$

be a map which has an inverse mapping g. Then f is both injective and surjective.

Proof. Let x, $y \in S$ and $x \neq y$. Let $g: S' \to S$ be the inverse mapping of f. If $f(x) = f(y)$, then we must have

$$x = g(f(x)) = g(f(y)) = y,$$

which is impossible. Hence $f(x) \neq f(y)$, and therefore f is injective. To prove that f is surjective, let $z \in S'$. Then

$$f(g(z)) = z$$

by definition of the inverse mapping, and hence $z = f(x)$, where $x = g(z)$. This proves that f is surjective.

The converse of the statement we just proved is also true, namely:

Let $f: S \rightarrow S'$ be a map which is both injective and surjective. Then f has an inverse mapping.

Proof. Given $z \in S'$, since f is surjective, there exists $x \in S$ such that $f(x) = z$. Since f is injective, this element x is uniquely determined by z, and we can therefore define

$$g(z) = x.$$

By definition of g, we find that $f(g(z)) = z$, and $g(f(x)) = x$, so that g is an inverse mapping for f.

Thus we can say that a map $f: S \rightarrow S'$ has an inverse mapping if and only if f is both injective and surjective.

EXERCISES

1. In Example 3, give Df as a function of x when f is the function:

(a) $f(x) = \sin x$ (b) $f(x) = e^x$ (c) $f(x) = \log x$

2. Prove the statement about translations in Example 13.

3. In Example 5, give $L(X)$ when X is the vector:

(a) $(1, 2, -3)$ (b) $(-1, 5, 0)$ (c) $(2, 1, 1)$

4. Let $F: \mathbf{R} \rightarrow \mathbf{R}^2$ be the mapping such that $F(t) = (e^t, t)$. What is $F(1)$, $F(0)$, $F(-1)$?

5. Let $G: \mathbf{R} \rightarrow \mathbf{R}^2$ be the mapping such that $G(t) = (t, 2t)$. Let F be as in Exercise 4. What is $(F + G)(1)$, $(F + G)(2)$, $(F + G)(0)$?

6. Let F be as in Exercise 4. What is $(2F)(0)$, $(\pi F)(1)$?

7. Let $A = (1, 1, -1, 3)$. Let $F: \mathbf{R}^4 \rightarrow \mathbf{R}$ be the mapping such that for any vector $X = (x_1, x_2, x_3, x_4)$ we have $F(X) = X \cdot A + 2$. What is the value of $F(X)$ when (a) $X = (1, 1, 0, -1)$ and (b) $X = (2, 3, -1, 1)$?

In Exercises 8 through 12, refer to Example 6. In each case, to prove that the image is equal to a certain set S, you must prove that the image is contained in S, and also that every element of S is in the image.

8. Let $F: \mathbf{R}^2 \rightarrow \mathbf{R}^2$ be the mapping defined by $F(x, y) = (2x, 3y)$. Describe the image of the points lying on the circle $x^2 + y^2 = 1$.

9. Let $F: \mathbf{R}^2 \rightarrow \mathbf{R}^2$ be the mapping defined by $F(x, y) = (xy, y)$. Describe the image under F of the straight line $x = 2$.

10. Let F be the mapping defined by $F(x, y) = (e^x \cos y, e^x \sin y)$. Describe the image under F of the line $x = 1$. Describe more generally the image under F of a line $x = c$, where c is a constant.

11. Let F be the mapping defined by $F(t, u) = (\cos t, \sin t, u)$. Describe geometrically the image of the (t, u)-plane under F.

12. Let F be the mapping defined by $F(x, y) = (x/3, y/4)$. What is the image under F of the ellipse

$$\frac{x^2}{9} + \frac{y^2}{16} = 1?$$

§2. Linear mappings

Let V, V' be vector spaces over the field K. A **linear mapping**

$$F: V \to V'$$

is a mapping which satisfies the following two properties.

LM 1. *For any elements u, v in V we have*

$$F(u + v) = F(u) + F(v).$$

LM 2. *For all c in K and v in V we have*

$$F(cv) = cF(v).$$

If we wish to specify the field K, we also say that F is K-**linear.** Since we usually deal with a fixed field K, we omit the prefix K, and say simply **linear.**

Example 1. Let V be a finite dimensional space over K, and let $\{v_1, \ldots, v_n\}$ be a basis of V. We define a map

$$F: V \to K^n$$

by associating to each element $v \in V$ its coordinate vector X with respect to the basis. Thus if

$$v = x_1 v_1 + \cdots + x_n v_n,$$

with $x_i \in K$, we let

$$F(v) = (x_1, \ldots, x_n).$$

We assert that F is a linear map. If

$$w = y_1 v_1 + \cdots + y_n v_n,$$

with coordinate vector $Y = (y_1, \ldots, y_n)$, then

$$v + w = (x_1 + y_1)v_1 + \cdots + (x_n + y_n)v_n,$$

whence $F(v + w) = X + Y = F(v) + F(w)$. If $c \in K$, then

$$cv = cx_1v_1 + \cdots + cx_nv_n,$$

and hence $F(cv) = cX = cF(v)$. This proves that F is linear.

Example 2. Let $V = \mathbf{R}^3$ be the vector space (over $\mathbf{R}$) of vectors in 3-space. Let $V' = \mathbf{R}^2$ be the vector space of vectors in 2-space. We can define a mapping

$$F: \mathbf{R}^3 \to \mathbf{R}^2$$

by the projection, namely $F(x, y, z) = (x, y)$. We leave it to you to check that the conditions LM 1 and LM 2 are satisfied.

More generally, let r, n be positive integers, $r < n$. Then we have a projection mapping

$$F: K^n \to K^r$$

defined by the rule

$$F(x_1, \ldots, x_n) = (x_1, \ldots, x_r).$$

It is trivially verified that this map is linear.

Example 3. Let $A = (1, 2, -1)$. Let $V = \mathbf{R}^3$ and $V' = \mathbf{R}$. We can define a mapping $L = L_A : \mathbf{R}^3 \to \mathbf{R}$ by the rule $X \mapsto X \cdot A$, i.e.

$$L(X) = X \cdot A$$

for any vector X in 3-space. The fact that L is linear summarize two known properties of the scalar product, namely, for any vectors X, Y in $\mathbf{R}^3$ we have

$$(X + Y) \cdot A = X \cdot A + Y \cdot A,$$

$$(cX) \cdot A = c(X \cdot A).$$

More generally, let K be a field, and A a fixed vector in K^n. We have a linear map (i.e. K-linear map)

$$L_A : K^n \to K$$

such that $L_A(X) = X \cdot A$ for all $X \in K^n$.

We can even generalize this to matrices. Let A be an $m \times n$ matrix in a field K. We obtain a linear map

$$L_A : K^n \to K^m$$

such that

$$L_A(X) = AX$$

for every column vector X in K^n. Again the linearity follows from properties of multiplication of matrices. If $A = (a_{ij})$ then AX looks like this:

$$\begin{pmatrix} a_{11} & \cdots & a_{1n} \\ & \cdots & \\ a_{m1} & \cdots & a_{mn} \end{pmatrix} \begin{pmatrix} x_1 \\ \vdots \\ x_n \end{pmatrix}$$

This type of multiplication will be met frequently in the sequel.

Example 4. Let V be any vector space. The mapping which associates to any element u of V this element itself is obviously a linear mapping, which is called the **identity** mapping. We denote it by id or simply I. Thus $id(u) = u$.

Example 5. Let V, V' be any vector spaces over the field K. The mapping which associates the element O in V' to any element u of V is called the **zero** mapping and is obviously linear.

Example 6. **The space of linear maps.** Let V, V' be two vector spaces over the field K. We consider the set of all linear mappings from V into V', and denote this set by $\mathcal{L}(V, V')$, or simply $\mathcal{L}$ if the reference to V, V' is clear. We shall define the addition of linear mappings and their multiplication by numbers in such a way as to make $\mathcal{L}$ into a vector space.

Let $T: V \to V'$ and $F: V \to V'$ be two linear mappings. We define their *sum* $T + F$ to be the map whose value at an element u of V is $T(u) + F(u)$. Thus we may write

$$(T + F)(u) = T(u) + F(u).$$

The map $T + F$ is then a linear map. Indeed, it is easy to verify that the two conditions which define a linear map are satisfied. For any elements u, v of V, we have

$$\begin{aligned} (T + F)(u + v) &= T(u + v) + F(u + v) \\ &= T(u) + T(v) + F(u) + F(v) \\ &= T(u) + F(u) + T(v) + F(v) \\ &= (T + F)(u) + (T + F)(v). \end{aligned}$$

Furthermore, if $c \in K$, then

$$\begin{aligned} (T + F)(cu) &= T(cu) + F(cu) \\ &= cT(u) + cF(u) \\ &= c[T(u) + F(u)] \\ &= c[(T + F)(u)]. \end{aligned}$$

Hence $T + F$ is a linear map.

If $a \in K$, and $T: V \to V'$ is a linear map, we define a map aT from V into V' by giving its value at an element u of V, namely $(aT)(u) = aT(u)$. Then it is easily verified that aT is a linear map. We leave this as an exercise.

We have just defined operations of addition and multiplication by numbers in our set $\mathfrak{L}$. Furthermore, if $T: V \to V'$ is a linear map, i.e. an element of $\mathfrak{L}$, then we can define $-T$ to be $(-1)T$, i.e. the product of the number -1 by T. Finally, we have the **zero-map**, which to every element of V associates the element O of V'. Then $\mathfrak{L}$ is a vector space. In other words, the set of linear maps from V into V' is itself a vector space. The verification that the rules VS 1 through VS 8 for a vector space are satisfied are easy and left to the reader.

Example 7. Let $V = V'$ be the vector space of real valued functions of a real variable which have derivatives of all orders. Let D be the derivative. Then $D: V \to V'$ is a linear map. This is merely a brief way of summarizing known properties of the derivative, namely

$$D(f + g) = Df + Dg, \quad \text{and} \quad D(cf) = cDf$$

for any differentiable functions f, g and constant c. If f is in V, and I is the identity map, then

$$(D + I)f = Df + f.$$

Thus when f is the function such that $f(x) = e^x$ then $(D + I)f$ is the function whose value at x is $e^x + e^x = 2e^x$.

If $f(x) = \sin x$, then $((D + I)f)(x) = \cos x + \sin x$.

Let $T: V \to V'$ be a linear mapping. Let u, v, w be elements of V. Then

$$T(u + v + w) = T(u) + T(v) + T(w).$$

This can be seen stepwise, using the definition of linear mappings. Thus

$$T(u + v + w) = T(u + v) + T(w) = T(u) + T(v) + T(w).$$

Similarly, given a sum of more than three elements, an analogous property is satisfied. For instance, let $u_1, \ldots, u_n$ be elements of V. Then

$$T(u_1 + \cdots + u_n) = T(u_1) + \cdots + T(u_n).$$

The sum on the right can be taken in any order. A formal proof can easily be given by induction, and we omit it.

If $a_1, \ldots, a_n$ are numbers, then

$$T(a_1 u_1 + \cdots + a_n u_n) = a_1 T(u_1) + \cdots + a_n T(u_n).$$

We show this for three elements.

$$T(a_1u + a_2v + a_3w) = T(a_1u) + T(a_2v) + T(a_3w)$$
$$= a_1T(u) + a_2T(v) + a_3T(w).$$

The next theorem will show us how a linear map is determined when we know its value on basis elements.

Theorem 1. *Let V and W be vector spaces. Let $\{v_1, \ldots, v_n\}$ be a basis of V, and let $w_1, \ldots, w_n$ be arbitrary elements of W. Then there exists a unique linear mapping $T: V \to W$ such that*

$$T(v_1) = w_1, \ldots, T(v_n) = w_n.$$

If $x_1, \ldots, x_n$ are numbers, then

$$T(x_1v_1 + \cdots + x_nv_n) = x_1w_1 + \cdots + x_nw_n.$$

Proof. We shall prove that a linear map T satisfying the required conditions exists. Let v be an element of V, and let $x_1, \ldots, x_n$ be the unique numbers such that $v = x_1v_1 + \cdots + x_nv_n$. We let

$$T(v) = x_1w_1 + \cdots + x_nw_n.$$

We then have defined a mapping T from V into W, and we contend that T is linear. If v' is an element of V, and if $v' = y_1v_1 + \cdots + y_nv_n$, then

$$v + v' = (x_1 + y_1)v_1 + \cdots + (x_n + y_n)v_n.$$

By definition, we obtain

$$T(v + v') = (x_1 + y_1)w_1 + \cdots + (x_n + y_n)w_n$$
$$= x_1w_1 + y_1w_1 + \cdots + x_nw_n + y_nw_n$$
$$= T(v) + T(v').$$

Let c be a number. Then $cv = cx_1v_1 + \cdots + cx_nv_n$, and hence

$$T(cv) = cx_1w_1 + \cdots + cx_nw_n = cT(v).$$

We have therefore proved that T is linear, and hence that there exists a linear map as asserted in the theorem.

Such a map is unique, because for any element $x_1v_1 + \cdots + x_nv_n$ of V, any linear map $F: V \to W$ such that $F(v_i) = w_i$ $(i = 1, \ldots, n)$ must also satisfy

$$F(x_1v_1 + \cdots + x_nv_n) = x_1F(v_1) + \cdots + x_nF(v_n)$$
$$= x_1w_1 + \cdots + x_nw_n.$$

This concludes the proof.

EXERCISES

1. Determine which of the following mappings F are linear.

(a) $F: \mathbf{R}^3 \to \mathbf{R}^2$ defined by $F(x, y, z) = (x, z)$.

(b) $F: \mathbf{R}^4 \to \mathbf{R}^4$ defined by $F(X) = -X$.

(c) $F: \mathbf{R}^3 \to \mathbf{R}^3$ defined by $F(X) = X + (0, -1, 0)$.

(d) $F: \mathbf{R}^2 \to \mathbf{R}^2$ defined by $F(x, y) = (2x + y, y)$.

(e) $F: \mathbf{R}^2 \to \mathbf{R}^2$ defined by $F(x, y) = (2x, y - x)$.

(f) $F: \mathbf{R}^2 \to \mathbf{R}^2$ defined by $F(x, y) = (y, x)$.

(g) $F: \mathbf{R}^2 \to \mathbf{R}$ defined by $F(x, y) = xy$.

(h) Let U be an open subset of $\mathbf{R}^3$, and let V be the vector space of differentiable functions on U. Let V' be the vector space of vector fields on U. Then grad: $V \to V'$ is a mapping. Is it linear?

2. Let $T: V \to W$ be a linear map from one vector space into another. Show that $T(O) = O$.

3. Let T be as in Exercise 2. Let u, v be elements of V, and let $Tu = w$. If $Tv = O$, show that $T(u + v)$ is also equal to w.

4. Determine all elements z of V such that $Tz = w$.

5. Let $T: V \to W$ be a linear map. Let v be an element of V. Show that $T(-v) = -T(v)$.

6. Let V be a vector space, and $f: V \to \mathbf{R}$, $g: V \to \mathbf{R}$ two linear mappings. Let $F: V \to \mathbf{R}^2$ be the mapping defined by $F(v) = (f(v), g(v))$. Show that F is linear. Generalize.

7. Let V, W be two vector spaces and let $F: V \to W$ be a linear map. Let U be the subset of V consisting of all elements v such that $F(v) = O$. Prove that U is a subspace of V.

8. Which of the mappings in Exercises 4, 7, 8, 9, of §1 are linear?

9. (a) Let $F: \mathbf{R}^3 \to \mathbf{R}^4$ be a linear map. Let P be a point of $\mathbf{R}^3$, and A a nonzero element of $\mathbf{R}^3$. Describe the image of the straight line $P + tA$ under F. [Distinguish the cases when $F(A) = O$ and $F(A) \neq O$.] (b) More generally, let $F: \mathbf{R}^n \to \mathbf{R}^m$ be a linear map. Let P be a point of $\mathbf{R}^n$ and A a non-zero element of $\mathbf{R}^n$. Show that the image under L of the straight line $P + tA$ ($t \in \mathbf{R}$) is a straight line, or a point. (c) Let V be a vector space, and v, w elements of V. The line segment between v and $v + w$ is defined to be the set of all points

$$v + tw, \qquad\qquad 0 \leq t \leq 1.$$

Let $L: V \to U$ be a linear map. Show that the image under L of a line segment in V is a line segment in U. Between what points?

Let V be a vector space, and let v_1, v_2 be two elements of V which are linearly independent. The set of elements of V which can be written in the form $t_1 v_1 + t_2 v_2$ with numbers t_1, t_2 satisfying

$$0 \leq t_1 \leq 1 \qquad \text{and} \qquad 0 \leq t_2 \leq 1,$$

is called a **parallelogram,** spanned by v_1, v_2.

10. Let V and W be vector spaces, and let $F: V \to W$ be a linear map. Let v_1, v_2 be linearly independent elements of V, and assume that $F(v_1)$, $F(v_2)$ are linearly independent. Show that the image under F of the parallelogram spanned by v_1 and v_2 is the parallelogram spanned by $F(v_1)$, $F(v_2)$.

11. Let F be a linear map from $\mathbf{R}^2$ into itself such that

$$F(E_1) = (1, 1) \qquad \text{and} \qquad F(E_2) = (-1, 2).$$

Let S be the square whose corners are at $(0, 0)$, $(1, 0)$, $(1, 1)$, and $(0, 1)$. Show that the image of this square under F is a parallelogram.

12. Let A, B be two non-zero vectors in the plane such that there is no constant $c \neq 0$ such that $B = cA$. Let T be a linear mapping of the plane into itself such that $T(E_1) = A$ and $T(E_2) = B$. Describe the image under T of the rectangle whose corners are $(0, 1)$, $(3, 0)$, $(0, 0)$, and $(3, 1)$.

13. Let A, B be two non-zero vectors in the plane such that there is no constant $c \neq 0$ such that $B = cA$. Describe geometrically the set of points $tA + uB$ for values of t and u such that $0 \leq t \leq 5$ and $0 \leq u \leq 2$.

14. Let $T_u: V \to V$ be the translation by a vector u. For which vectors u is T_u a linear map?

15. Let V, W be two vector spaces, and $F: V \to W$ a linear map. Let $w_1, \ldots, w_n$ be elements of W which are linearly independent, and let $v_1, \ldots, v_n$ be elements of V such that $F(v_i) = w_i$ for $i = 1, \ldots, n$. Show that $v_1, \ldots, v_n$ are linearly independent.

16. Let V be a vector space and $F: V \to \mathbf{R}$ a linear map. Let W be the subset of V consisting of all elements v such that $F(v) = O$. Assume that $W \neq V$, and let v_0 be an element of V which does not lie in W. Show that every element of V can be written as a sum $w + cv_0$, with some w in W and some number c.

17. In Exercise 16, show that W is a subspace of V. Let $\{v_1, \ldots, v_n\}$ be a basis of W. Show that $\{v_0, v_1, \ldots, v_n\}$ is a basis of V.

18. Let $L: \mathbf{R}^2 \to \mathbf{R}^2$ be a linear map, having the following effect on the indicated vectors:

(a) $L(3, 1) = (1, 2)$ and $L(-1, 0) = (1, 1)$
(b) $L(4, 1) = (1, 1)$ and $L(1, 1) = (3, -2)$
(c) $L(1, 1) = (2, 1)$ and $L(-1, 1) = (6, 3)$.

In each case compute $L(1, 0)$.

19. Let L be as in (a), (b), (c), of Exercise 18. Find $L(0, 1)$.

§3. *The kernel and image of a linear map*

Let V, W be vector spaces over K, and let $F\colon V \to W$ be a linear map. The set of elements $v \in V$ such that $F(v) = O$ is called the **kernel** of F.

Example 1. Let $L\colon \mathbf{R}^3 \to \mathbf{R}$ be the map such that

$$L(x, y, z) = 3x - 2y + z.$$

Thus if $A = (3, -2, 1)$, then we can write

$$L(X) = X \cdot A = A \cdot X.$$

Then the kernel of L is the set of solutions of the equation

$$3x - 2y + z = 0.$$

Of course, this generalizes to n-space. If A is an arbitrary vector in $\mathbf{R}^n$, we can define the linear map

$$L_A\colon \mathbf{R}^n \to \mathbf{R}$$

such that $L_A(X) = A \cdot X$. Its kernel can be interpreted as the set of all X which are perpendicular to A.

Example 2. Let $P\colon \mathbf{R}^3 \to \mathbf{R}^2$ be the projection, such that

$$P(x, y, z) = (x, y).$$

Then P is a linear map whose kernel consists of all vectors in $\mathbf{R}^3$ whose first two coordinates are equal to 0, i.e. all vectors

$$(0, 0, z)$$

with arbitrary component z.

We shall now prove that the kernel of a linear map $F\colon V \to W$ is a subspace of V. Since $F(O) = O$, we see that O is in the kernel. Let v, w be in the kernel. Then $F(v + w) = F(v) + F(w) = O + O = O$, so that $v + w$ is in the kernel. If c is a number, then $F(cv) = cF(v) = O$ so that cv is also in the kernel. Hence the kernel is a subspace.

The kernel of a linear map is useful to determine when the map is injective. Namely, let $F\colon V \to W$ be a linear map. We contend that the following two conditions are equivalent:

1. *The kernel of F is equal to $\{O\}$.*
2. *If v, w are elements of V such that $F(v) = F(w)$, then $v = w$. In other words, F is injective.*

To prove our contention, assume first that F satisfies the first condition, and suppose that v, w are such that $F(v) = F(w)$. Then

$$F(v - w) = F(v) - F(w) = O.$$

By assumption, $v - w = O$, and hence $v = w$.

Conversely, assume that F satisfies the second condition. If v is such that $F(v) = F(O) = O$, we conclude that $v = O$.

The kernel of F is also useful to describe the set of all elements of V which have a given image in W under F. We refer the reader to Exercise 5 for this.

Theorem 2. *Let $F: V \to W$ be a linear map whose kernel is $\{O\}$. If $v_1, \ldots, v_n$ are linearly independent elements of V, then $F(v_1), \ldots, F(v_n)$ are linearly independent elements of W.*

Proof. Let $x_1, \ldots, x_n$ be numbers such that

$$x_1 F(v_1) + \cdots + x_n F(v_n) = O.$$

By linearity, we get

$$F(x_1 v_1 + \cdots + x_n v_n) = O.$$

Hence $x_1 v_1 + \cdots + x_n v_n = O$. Since $v_1, \ldots, v_n$ are linearly independent it follows that $x_i = 0$ for $i = 1, \ldots, n$. This proves our theorem.

Let $F: V \to W$ be a linear map. The **image** of F is the set of elements w in W such that there exists an element v of V such that $F(v) = w$.

The image of F is a subspace of W. To prove this, observe first that $F(O) = O$, and hence O is in the image. Next, suppose that w_1, w_2 are in the image. Then there exist elements v_1, v_2 of V such that $F(v_1) = w_1$ and $F(v_2) = w_2$. Hence $F(v_1 + v_2) = F(v_1) + F(v_2) = w_1 + w_2$, thereby proving that $w_1 + w_2$ is in the image. If c is a number, then

$$F(cv_1) = cF(v_1) = cw_1.$$

Hence cw_1 is in the image. This proves that the image is a subspace of W.

We often abbreviate kernel and image by writing Ker and Im respectively. The next theorem relates the dimensions of the kernel and image of a linear map, with the dimension of the space on which the map is defined.

Theorem 3. *Let V be a vector space. Let $L: V \to W$ be a linear map of V into another space W. Let n be the dimension of V, q the dimension* *of the kernel of L, and s the dimension of the image of L. Then $n = q + s$. In other words,*

$$\dim V = \dim \operatorname{Ker} L + \dim \operatorname{Im} L.$$

Proof. If the image of L consists of O only, then our assertion is trivial. We may therefore assume that $s > 0$. Let $\{w_1, \ldots, w_s\}$ be a basis of the image of L. Let $v_1, \ldots, v_s$ be elements of V such that $L(v_i) = w_i$ for $i = 1, \ldots, s$. If the kernel of L is not $\{O\}$, let $\{u_1, \ldots, u_q\}$ be a basis of the kernel. If the kernel is $\{O\}$, it is understood that all reference to $\{u_1, \ldots, u_q\}$ is to be omitted in what follows. We contend that $\{v_1, \ldots, v_s, u_1, \ldots, u_q\}$ is a basis of V. This will suffice to prove our assertion. Let v be any element of V. Then there exist numbers $x_1, \ldots, x_s$ such that

$$L(v) = x_1 w_1 + \cdots + x_s w_s,$$

because $\{w_1, \ldots, w_s\}$ is a basis of the image of L. By linearity,

$$L(v) = L(x_1 v_1 + \cdots + x_s v_s),$$

and again by linearity, subtracting the right-hand side from the left-hand side, it follows that

$$L(v - x_1 v_1 - \cdots - x_s v_s) = O.$$

Hence $v - x_1 v_1 - \cdots - x_s v_s$ lies in the kernel of L, and there exist numbers $y_1, \ldots, y_q$ such that

$$v - x_1 v_1 - \cdots - x_s v_s = y_1 u_1 + \cdots + y_q u_q.$$

Hence

$$v = x_1 v_1 + \cdots + x_s v_s + y_1 u_1 + \cdots + y_q u_q$$

is a linear combination of $v_1, \ldots, v_s, u_1, \ldots, u_q$. This proves that these $s + q$ elements of V generate V.

We now show that they are linearly independent, and hence that they constitute a basis. Suppose that there exists a linear relation:

$$x_1 v_1 + \cdots + x_s v_s + y_1 u_1 + \cdots + y_q u_q = O.$$

Applying L to this relation, and using the fact that $L(u_j) = O$ for $j = 1, \ldots, q$, we obtain

$$x_1 L(v_1) + \cdots + x_s L(v_s) = O.$$

But $L(v_1), \ldots, L(v_s)$ are none other than $w_1, \ldots, w_s$, which have been assumed linearly independent. Hence $x_i = 0$ for $i = 1, \ldots, s$. Hence

$$y_1 u_1 + \cdots + y_q u_q = 0.$$

But $u_1, \ldots, u_q$ constitute a basis of the kernel of L, and in particular, are linearly independent. Hence all $y_j = 0$ for $j = 1, \ldots, q$. This concludes the proof of our assertion.

Example 1 (Cont.). The linear map $L: \mathbf{R}^3 \to \mathbf{R}$ of Example 1 is given by the formula

$$L(x, y, z) = 3x - 2y + z.$$

Its kernel consists of all solutions of the equation

$$3x - y + z = 0.$$

Its image is a subspace of $\mathbf{R}$, is not $\{O\}$, and hence consists of all of $\mathbf{R}$. Thus its image has dimension 1. Hence its kernel has dimension 2.

Example 2 (Cont.). The projection $P: \mathbf{R}^3 \to \mathbf{R}^2$ of Example 2 is obviously surjective, and its kernel has dimension 1.

In Chapter VI, §3 we shall investigate in general the dimension of the space of solutions of a system of homogeneous linear equations.

EXERCISES

1. Let A, B be two vectors in $\mathbf{R}^2$ forming a basis of $\mathbf{R}^2$. Let $F: \mathbf{R}^2 \to \mathbf{R}^n$ be a linear map. Show that either $F(A)$, $F(B)$ are linearly independent, or the image of F has dimension 1, or the image of F is $\{O\}$.

2. Let A be a non-zero vector in $\mathbf{R}^2$. Let $F: \mathbf{R}^2 \to W$ be a linear map such that $F(A) = O$. Show that the image of F is either a straight line or $\{O\}$.

3. Let $F: V \to W$ be a linear map, whose kernel is $\{O\}$. Assume that V and W have both the same dimension n. Show that the image of F is all of W.

4. Let $F: V \to W$ be a linear map and assume that the image of F is all of W. Assume that V and W have the same dimension n. Show that the kernel of F is $\{O\}$.

5. Let $L: V \to W$ be a linear map. Let w be an element of W. Let v_0 be an element of V such that $L(v_0) = w$. Show that any solution of the equation $L(X) = w$ is of type $v_0 + u$, where u is an element of the kernel of L.

6. Let V be the vector space of functions which have derivatives of all orders, and let $D: V \to V$ be the derivative. What is the kernel of D?

7. Let D^2 be the second derivative (i.e. the iteration of D taken twice). What is the kernel of D^2? In general, what is the kernel of D^n (n-th derivative)?

8. Let V be as in Exercise 6. We write the functions as functions of a variable t, and let $D = d/dt$. Let $a_1, \ldots, a_m$ be numbers. Let g be an element of V.

Describe how the problem of finding a solution of the differential equation

$$a_m \frac{d^m f}{dt^m} + a_{m-1} \frac{d^{m-1} f}{dt^{m-1}} + \cdots + a_0 f = g$$

can be interpreted as fitting the abstract situation described in Exercise 5.

9. (a) Let V, D be as in Exercise 6. Let $L = D - I$, where I is the identity mapping of V. What is the kernel of L? (b) Same question of $L = D - aI$, where a is a number.

10. (a) What is the dimension of the subspace of $\mathbf{R}^n$ consisting of those vectors $A = (a_1, \ldots, a_n)$ such that $a_1 + \cdots + a_n = 0$? (b) What is the dimension of the subspace of the space of $n \times n$ matrices (a_{ij}) such that

$$a_{11} + \cdots + a_{nn} = \sum_{i=1}^{n} a_{ii} = 0?$$

[For part (b), look at the next exercise.]

11. Let $A = (a_{ij})$ be an $n \times n$ matrix. Define the **trace** of A to be the sum of the diagonal elements, that is

$$\text{tr}(A) = \sum_{i=1}^{n} a_{ii}.$$

(a) Show that the trace is a linear map of the space of $n \times n$ matrices into $\mathbf{R}$.
(b) If A, B are $n \times n$ matrices, show that $\text{tr}(AB) = \text{tr}(BA)$.
(c) If B is invertible, show that $\text{tr}(B^{-1}AB) = \text{tr}(A)$.
(d) If A, B are $n \times n$ matrices, show that the association

$$(A, B) \mapsto \text{tr}(AB) = \langle A, B \rangle$$

satisfies the first three conditions of a scalar product. (For the general definition, cf. Chapter VI.)

12. Let S be the set of symmetric $n \times n$ matrices. Show that S is a vector space. What is the dimension of S? Exhibit a basis for S, when $n = 2$ and $n = 3$.

13. Let A be a symmetric $n \times n$ matrix. Show that

$$\text{tr}(AA) \geq 0,$$

and if $A \neq O$, then $\text{tr}(AA) > 0$.

14. An $n \times n$ matrix A is called **skew-symmetric** if ${}^t A = -A$. Show that any $n \times n$ matrix A can be written as a sum

$$A = B + C,$$

where B is symmetric and C is skew-symmetric. [*Hint:* Let $B = (A + {}^t A)/2$.] Show that if $A = B_1 + C_1$, where B_1 is symmetric and C_1 is skew-symmetric, then $B = B_1$ and $C = C_1$.

15. Let M be the space of all $n \times n$ matrices. Let

$$P: M \to M$$

be the map such that

$$P(A) = \frac{A + {}^t A}{2}.$$

(a) Show that P is linear. (b) Show that the kernel of P consists of the space of skew-symmetric matrices. (c) What is the dimension of the kernel of P?

16. Let M be the space of all $n \times n$ matrices. Let

$$F: M \to M$$

be the map such that

$$F(A) = \frac{A - {}^t A}{2}.$$

(a) Show that F is linear. (b) Describe the kernel of F, and determine its dimension.

17. (a) Let U, W be vector spaces. We let $U \times W$ be the set of all pairs (u, w) with $u \in U$ and $w \in W$. If (u_1, w_1), (u_2, w_2) are such pairs, define their sum

$$(u_1, w_1) + (u_2, w_2) = (u_1 + u_2, w_1 + w_2).$$

If c is a number, define $c(u, w) = (cu, cw)$. Show that $U \times W$ is a vector space with these definitions. What is the zero element? (b) If U has dimension n and W has dimension m, what is the dimension of $U \times W$? Exhibit a basis of $U \times W$ in terms of a basis for U and a basis for W. (c) If U is a subspace of a vector space V, show that the subset of $V \times V$ consisting of all elements (u, u) with $u \in U$ is a subspace.

18. (To be done after you have done Exercise 17.) Let U, W be subspaces of a vector space V. Show that

$$\dim U + \dim W = \dim (U + W) + \dim (U \cap W).$$

[*Hint:* Show that the map

$$L: U \times W \to V$$

given by

$$L(u, w) = u - w$$

is a linear map.]

§4. Composition and inverse of linear mappings

In §1 we have mentioned the fact that we can compose arbitrary maps. We can say something additional in the case of linear maps.

Theorem 4. *Let U, V, W be vector spaces over a field K. Let*

$$F: U \to V \quad and \quad G: V \to W$$

be linear maps. Then the composite map $G \circ F$ is also a linear map.

Proof. This is very easy to prove. Let u, v be elements of U. Since F is linear, we have $F(u + v) = F(u) + F(v)$. Hence

$$(G \circ F)(u + v) = G(F(u + v)) = G(F(u) + F(v)).$$

Since G is linear, we obtain

$$G(F(u) + F(v)) = G(F(u)) + G(F(v)).$$

Hence

$$(G \circ F)(u + v) = (G \circ F)(u) + (G \circ F)(v).$$

Next, let c be a number. Then

$$\begin{aligned}
(G \circ F)(cu) &= G(F(cu)) \\
&= G(cF(u)) \qquad \text{(because } F \text{ is linear)} \\
&= cG(F(u)) \qquad \text{(because } G \text{ is linear)}.
\end{aligned}$$

This proves that $G \circ F$ is a linear mapping.

The next theorem states that some of the rules of arithmetic concerning the product and sum of numbers also apply to the composition and sum of linear mappings

Theorem 5. *Let U, V, W be vector spaces over a field K. Let*

$$F : U \to V$$

be a linear mapping, and let G, H be two linear mappings of V into W. Then

$$(G + H) \circ F = G \circ F + H \circ F.$$

If c is a number, then

$$(cG) \circ F = c(G \circ F).$$

If $T : U \to V$ is a linear mapping from U into V, then

$$G \circ (F + T) = G \circ F + G \circ T.$$

The proofs are all simple. We shall just prove the first assertion and leave the others as exercises.

Let u be an element of U. We have:

$$\begin{aligned}
((G + H) \circ F)(u) = (G + H)(F(u)) &= G(F(u)) + H(F(u)) \\
&= (G \circ F)(u) + (H \circ F)(u).
\end{aligned}$$

By definition, it follows that $(G + H) \circ F = G \circ F + H \circ F$.

It may happen that $U = V = W$. Let $F: U \to U$ and $G: U \to U$ be two linear mappings. Then we may form $F \circ G$ and $G \circ F$. It is not always true that these two composite mappings are equal. As an example, let $U = \mathbf{R}^3$. Let F be the linear mapping given by

$$F(x, y, z) = (x, y, 0)$$

and let G be the linear mapping given by

$$G(x, y, z) = (x, z, 0).$$

Then

$$(G \circ F)(x, y, z) = (x, 0, 0),$$

but

$$(F \circ G)(x, y, z) = (x, z, 0).$$

Let $F: V \to V$ be a linear map of a vector space into itself. One sometimes calls F an **operator.** Then we can form the composite $F \circ F$, which is again a linear map of V into itself. Similarly, we can form the composite

$$F \circ F \circ \cdots \circ F$$

of F with itself n times for any integer $n \geqq 1$. We shall denote this composite by F^n. If $n = 0$, we define $F^0 = I$ (identity map). We have the rules

$$F^{r+s} = F^r \circ F^s$$

for integers $r, s \geqq 0$.

For simplicity of notation, we also often omit the small circle between linear mappings, and write FG instead of $F \circ G$.

Theorem 6. *Let $F: U \to V$ be a linear map, and assume that this map has an inverse mapping $G: V \to U$. Then G is a linear map.*

Proof. Let $v_1, v_2 \in V$. We must first show that

$$G(v_1 + v_2) = G(v_1) + G(v_2).$$

Let $u_1 = G(v_1)$ and $u_2 = G(v_2)$. By definition, this means that

$$F(u_1) = v_1 \quad \text{and} \quad F(u_2) = v_2.$$

Since F is linear, we find that

$$F(u_1 + u_2) = F(u_1) + F(u_2) = v_1 + v_2.$$

By definition of the inverse map, this means that $G(v_1 + v_2) = u_1 + u_2$, thus proving what we wanted. We leave the proof that $G(cv) = cG(v)$ as an exercise (Exercise 3).

Corollary. *Let* $F: U \to V$ *be a linear map whose kernel is* $\{O\}$, *and which is surjective. Then* F *has an inverse linear map.*

Proof. We had seen in §3 that if the kernel of F is $\{O\}$, then F is injective. Hence we conclude that F is both injective and surjective, so that an inverse mapping exists, and is linear by Theorem 6.

Example 1. Let $F: \mathbf{R}^2 \to \mathbf{R}^2$ be the linear map such that

$$F(x, y) = (3x - y, 4x + 2y).$$

We wish to show that F has an inverse. First note that the kernel of F is $\{O\}$, because if

$$3x - y = 0,$$
$$4x + 2y = 0,$$

then we can solve for x, y in the usual way: Multiply the first equation by 2 and add it to the second. We find $10x = 0$, whence $x = 0$, and then $y = 0$ because $y = 3x$. Hence F is injective, because its kernel is $\{O\}$. By Theorem 2 of §3, it follows that the image of F has dimension 2. But the image of F is a subspace of $\mathbf{R}^2$, which has also dimension 2, and hence this image is equal to all of $\mathbf{R}^2$, so that F is surjective. Hence F has an inverse, and this inverse is a linear map by Theorem 6.

A linear map $F: U \to V$ which has an inverse $G: V \to U$ (we also say **invertible**) is called an **isomorphism.**

Example 2. Let V be a vector space of dimension n. Let

$$\{v_1, \ldots, v_n\}$$

be a basis for V. Let

$$L: \mathbf{R}^n \to V$$

be the map such that

$$L(x_1, \ldots, x_n) = x_1 v_1 + \cdots + x_n v_n.$$

Then L is an isomorphism.

Proof. The kernel of L is $\{O\}$, because if

$$x_1 v_1 + \cdots + x_n v_n = 0,$$

then all $x_i = 0$ (since $v_1, \ldots, v_n$ are linearly independent). The image of L is all of V, because $v_1, \ldots, v_n$ generate V. By the corollary of Theorem 6, it follows that L is an isomorphism.

EXERCISES

1. Let $L: \mathbf{R}^2 \to \mathbf{R}^2$ be a linear map such that $L \neq O$ but $L^2 = L \circ L = O$. Show that there exists a basis $\{A, B\}$ of $\mathbf{R}^2$ such that

$$L(A) = B \text{ and } L(B) = O.$$

2. Let $\dim V > \dim W$. Let $L: V \to W$ be a linear map. Show that the kernel of L is not $\{O\}$.

3. Finish the proof of Theorem 6.

4. Let $\dim V = \dim W$. Let $L: V \to W$ be a linear map whose kernel is $\{O\}$. Show that L has an inverse linear map.

5. Let F, G be invertible linear maps of a vector space V onto itself. Show that

$$(F \circ G)^{-1} = G^{-1} \circ F^{-1}.$$

6. Let $L: \mathbf{R}^2 \to \mathbf{R}^2$ be the linear map defined by

$$L(x, y) = (x + y, x - y).$$

Show that L is invertible.

7. Let $L: \mathbf{R}^2 \to \mathbf{R}^2$ be the linear map defined by

$$L(x, y) = (2x + y, 3x - 5y).$$

Show that L is invertible.

8. Let $L: \mathbf{R}^3 \to \mathbf{R}^3$ be the linear maps as indicated. Show that L is invertible in each case.

(a) $L(x, y, z) = (x - y, x + z, x + y + 2z)$
(b) $L(x, y, z) = (2x - y + z, x + y, 3x + y + z)$.

9. Let $L: V \to V$ be a linear mapping such that $L^2 = O$. Show that $I - L$ is invertible. (I is the identity mapping on V.)

10. (a) Let $L: V \to V$ be a linear map such that $L^2 + 2L + I = O$. Show that L is invertible.

(b) Let $L: V \to V$ be a linear map such that $L^3 = O$. Show that $I - L$ is invertible.

11. Let V be a vector space. Let $P: V \to V$ be a linear map such that $P \circ P = P$. Let U be the image of P, and let W be the kernel of P. Show that V is the direct sum of U and W. [*Hint:* To show V is the sum, write an element of V in the form $v = v - Pv + Pv$.]

12. Let V be a vector space, and let P_1, P_2 be linear maps of V into itself. Assume that they satisfy the following conditions:

(a) $P_1 + P_2 = I$ (identity mapping),
(b) $P_1 \circ P_2 = O$ and $P_2 \circ P_1 = O$,
(c) $P_1 \circ P_1 = P_1$ and $P_2 \circ P_2 = P_2$.

Show that V is equal to the direct sum of the images of P_1 and P_2 respectively.

13. Notations being as in Exercise 12, show that the image of P_1 is equal to the kernel of P_2. [Prove the two statements:

Image of P_1 is contained in kernel of P_2;

Kernel of P_2 is contained in image of P_1.]

14. Let $F: V \to W$ and $G: W \to U$ be isomorphisms of vector spaces over K. Show that $G \circ F$ is invertible, and that

$$(G \circ F)^{-1} = F^{-1} \circ G^{-1}.$$

15. Let $F: V \to W$ and $G: W \to U$ be isomorphisms of vector spaces over K. Show that $G \circ F: V \to U$ is an isomorphism.

16. Let V, W be two vector spaces over K, of finite dimension n. Show that V and W are isomorphic.

17. Let A be a linear map of a vector space into itself, and assume that

$$A^2 - A + I = O$$

(where I is the identity map). Show that A^{-1} exists and is equal to $I - A$. Generalize (cf. Exercise 37 of Chapter III, §3).

18. Let A, B be linear maps of a vector space into itself. Assume that $AB = BA$. Show that

$$(A + B)^2 = A^2 + 2AB + B^2$$

and

$$(A + B)(A - B) = A^2 - B^2.$$

19. Let A, B be linear maps of a vector space into itself. If the kernel of A is $\{O\}$ and the kernel of B is $\{O\}$, show that the kernel of AB is also $\{O\}$.

20. More generally, let $A: V \to W$ and $B: W \to U$ be linear maps. Assume that the kernel of A is $\{O\}$ and the kernel of B is $\{O\}$. Show that the kernel of BA is $\{O\}$.

21. Let the notation be as in Exercise 20. Assume that A is surjective and that B is surjective. Show that BA is surjective.

§5. *Geometric applications*

Let V be a vector space and let v, u be elements of V. We define the **line segment** between v and $v + u$ to be the set of all points

$$v + tu, \qquad\qquad 0 \leqq t \leqq 1.$$

This line segment is illustrated in the following picture.

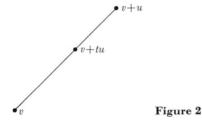

Figure 2

For instance, if $t = \frac{1}{2}$, then $v + \frac{1}{2}u$ is the point midway between v and $v + u$. Similarly, if $t = \frac{1}{3}$, then $v + \frac{1}{3}u$ is the point one third of the way between v and $v + u$ (Fig. 3).

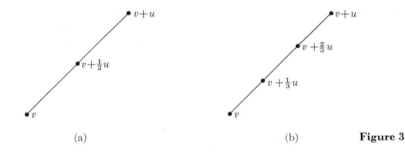

(a)   (b)   Figure 3

If v, w are elements of V, let $u = w - v$. Then the line segment between v and w is the set of all points $v + tu$, or

$$v + t(w - v), \qquad\qquad 0 \leqq t \leqq 1.$$

Figure 4

Observe that we can rewrite the expression for these points in the form

(1) $(1 - t)v + tw,$ $0 \leq t \leq 1,$

and letting $s = 1 - t$, $t = 1 - s$, we can also write it as

$$sv + (1 - s)w, \qquad 0 \leq s \leq 1.$$

Finally, we can write the points of our line segment in the form

(2) $t_1 v + t_2 w$

with t_1, $t_2 \geq 0$ and $t_1 + t_2 = 1$. Indeed, letting $t = t_2$, we see that every point which can be written in the form (2) satisfies (1). Conversely, we let $t_1 = 1 - t$ and $t_2 = t$ and see that every point of the form (1) can be written in the form (2).

Let $L: V \to V'$ be a linear map. Let S be the line segment in V between two points v, w. Then the image $L(S)$ of this line segment is the line segment in V' between the points $L(v)$ and $L(w)$. This is obvious from (2), because

$$L(t_1 v + t_2 w) = t_1 L(v) + t_2 L(w).$$

We shall now generalize this discussion to higher dimensional figures.

Let v, w be linearly independent elements of the vector space V. We define the **parallelogram** spanned by v, w to be the set of all points

$$t_1 v + t_2 w, \qquad 0 \leq t_i \leq 1 \quad \text{for} \quad i = 1, 2.$$

This definition is clearly justified since $t_1 v$ is a point of the segment between O and v (Fig. 5), and $t_2 w$ is a point of the segment between O and w. For all values of t_1, t_2 ranging independently between 0 and 1, we see geometrically that $t_1 v + t_2 w$ describes all points of the parallelogram.

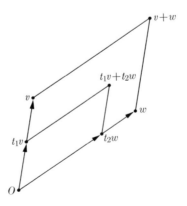

Figure 5

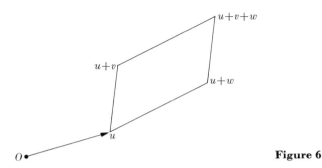

Figure 6

At the end of §1 we defined *translations*. We obtain the most general parallelogram (Fig. 6) by taking the translation of the parallelogram just described. Thus if u is an element of V, the translation by u of the parallelogram spanned by v and w consists of all points

$$u + t_1 v + t_2 w, \quad 0 \leq t_i \leq 1 \quad \text{for} \quad i = 1, 2.$$

As with line segments, we see that if $L \colon V \to V'$ is a linear map, then the image under L of a parallelogram is a parallelogram, because it is the set of points

$$L(u + t_1 v + t_2 w) = L(u) + t_1 L(v) + t_2 L(w)$$

with

$$0 \leq t_i \leq 1 \quad \text{for} \quad i = 1, 2.$$

We shall now describe triangles. We begin with triangles located at the origin. Let v, w again be linearly independent. We define the **triangle spanned** by O, v, w to be the set of all points

(3) $$\qquad\qquad t_1 v + t_2 w, \qquad 0 \leq t_i \quad \text{and} \quad t_1 + t_2 \leq 1.$$

We must convince ourselves that this is a reasonable definition. We do this by showing that the triangle defined above coincides with the set of points on all line segments between v and all the points of the segment between O and w. From Fig. 7, this second description of a triangle does coincide with our geometric intuition.

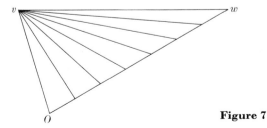

Figure 7

We denote the line segment between O and w by $\overline{Ow}$. A point on $\overline{Ow}$ can then be written tw with $0 \leq t \leq 1$. The set of points between v and tw is the set of points

$$(4) \qquad\qquad sv + (1 - s)tw, \qquad\qquad 0 \leq s \leq 1.$$

Let $t_1 = s$ and $t_2 = (1 - s)t$. Then

$$t_1 + t_2 = s + (1 - s)t \leq s + (1 - s) \leq 1.$$

Hence all points satisfying (4) also satisfy (3). Conversely, suppose given a point $t_1 v + t_2 w$ satisfying (3), so that

$$t_1 + t_2 \leq 1.$$

Then $t_2 \leq 1 - t_1$ and we let

$$s = t_1, \qquad t = t_2/(1 - t_1).$$

Then

$$t_1 v + t_2 w = t_1 v + (1 - t_1)\frac{t_2}{(1 - t_1)}w = sv + (1 - s)tw,$$

which shows that every point satisfying (3) also satisfies (4). This justifies our definition of a triangle.

As with parallelograms, an arbitrary triangle is obtained by translating a triangle located at the origin. In fact, we have the following description of a triangle.

Let v_1, v_2, v_3 be elements of V such that $v_1 - v_3$ and $v_2 - v_3$ are linearly independent. Let $v = v_1 - v_3$ and $w = v_2 - v_3$. Let S be the set of points

$$(5) \qquad\qquad t_1 v_1 + t_2 v_2 + t_3 v_3, \qquad 0 \leq t_i \quad \text{for} \quad i = 1, 2, 3$$
$$t_1 + t_2 + t_3 = 1.$$

Then S is the translation by v_3 of the triangle spanned by O, v, w. (Cf. Fig. 8.)

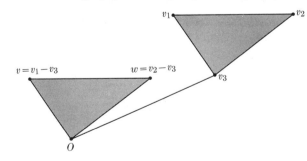

Figure 8

Proof. Let $P = t_1v_1 + t_2v_2 + t_3v_3$ be a point satisfying (5). Then

$$P = t_1(v_1 - v_3) + t_2(v_2 - v_3) + t_1v_3 + t_2v_3 + t_3v_3$$
$$= t_1v + t_2w + v_3,$$

and $t_1 + t_2 \leqq 1$. Hence our point P is a translation by v_3 of a point satisfying (3). Conversely, given a point satisfying (3), which we translate by v_3, we let $t_3 = 1 - t_2 - t_1$, and we can then reverse the steps we have just taken to see that

$$t_1v + t_2w + v_3 = t_1v_1 + t_2v_2 + t_3v_3.$$

This proves what we wanted.

Actually, it is (5) which is the most useful description of a triangle, because the vertices v_1, v_2, v_3 occupy a symmetric position in this definition.

One of the advantages of giving a definition of a triangle as we did it, is that it is then easy to see what happens to a triangle under a linear map. Let $L: V \to W$ be a linear map, and let v, w be elements of V which are linearly independent. Assume that $L(v)$ and $L(w)$ are also linearly independent. Let S be the triangle spanned by O, v, w. Then the image of S under L, namely $L(S)$, is the triangle spanned by O, $L(v)$, $L(w)$. Indeed, it is the set of all points

$$L(t_1v + t_2w) = t_1L(v) + t_2L(w)$$

with

$$0 \leqq t_i \qquad \text{and} \qquad t_1 + t_2 \leqq 1.$$

Similarly, let S be the triangle spanned by v_1, v_2, v_3. Then the image of S under L is the triangle spanned by $L(v_1)$, $L(v_2)$, $L(v_3)$ because it consists of the set of points

$$L(t_1v_1 + t_2v_2 + t_3v_3) = t_1L(v_1) + t_2L(v_2) + t_3L(v_3)$$

with $0 \leqq t_i$ and $t_1 + t_2 + t_3 = 1$.

The conditions of (5) are those which generalize to the fruitful concept of convex set which we now discuss.

Let S be a subset of a vector space V. We shall say that S is **convex** if given points P, Q in S the line segment between P and Q is contained in S. In Fig. 9, the set on the left is convex. The set on the right is not convex since the line segment between P and Q is not entirely contained in S.

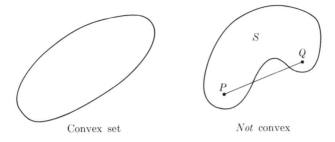

Figure 9

Convex set   *Not* convex

Theorem 7. *Let $P_1, \ldots, P_n$ be points of a vector space V. Let S be the set of all linear combinations*

$$t_1 P_1 + \cdots + t_n P_n$$

with $0 \leq t_i$ and $t_1 + \cdots + t_n = 1$. Then S is convex.

Proof. Let

$$P = t_1 P_1 + \cdots + t_n P_n$$

and

$$Q = s_1 P_1 + \cdots + s_n P_n$$

with $0 \leq t_i$, $0 \leq s_i$, and

$$t_1 + \cdots + t_n = 1,$$
$$s_1 + \cdots + s_n = 1.$$

Let $0 \leq t \leq 1$. Then:

$(1 - t)P + tQ$

$$= (1 - t)t_1 P_1 + \cdots + (1 - t)t_n P_n + ts_1 P_1 + \cdots + ts_n P_n$$
$$= [(1 - t)t_1 + ts_1]P_1 + \cdots + [(1 - t)t_n + ts_n]P_n.$$

We have $0 \leq (1 - t)t_i + ts_i$ for all i, and

$(1 - t)t_1 + ts_1 + \cdots + (1 - t)t_n + ts_n$

$$= (1 - t)(t_1 + \cdots + t_n) + t(s_1 + \cdots + s_n)$$
$$= (1 - t) + t$$
$$= 1.$$

This proves our theorem.

From Theorem 7, we see that a triangle, as we have defined it analytically, is convex. The convex set of Theorem 7 is therefore a natural generalization of a triangle (Fig. 10).

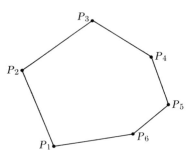

Figure 10

We shall call the convex set of Theorem 7 the convex set **spanned** by $P_1, \ldots, P_n$. Although we shall not need the next result, it shows that this convex set is the smallest convex set containing all the points $P_1, \ldots, P_n$.

Theorem 8. *Let $P_1, \ldots, P_n$ be points of a vector space V. Any convex set S' which contains $P_1, \ldots, P_n$ also contains all linear combinations*

$$t_1 P_1 + \cdots + t_n P_n$$

with $0 \leq t_i$ for all i and $t_1 + \cdots + t_n = 1$.

Proof. We prove this by induction. If $n = 1$, then $t_1 = 1$, and our assertion is obvious. Assume the theorem proved for some integer $n - 1 \geq 1$. We shall prove it for n. Let $t_1, \ldots, t_n$ be numbers satisfying the conditions of the theorem. If $t_n = 1$, then our assertion is trivial because $t_1 = \cdots = t_{n-1} = 0$. Suppose that $t_n \neq 1$. Then the linear combination $t_1 P_1 + \cdots + t_n P_n$ is equal to

$$(1 - t_n)\left(\frac{t_1}{1 - t_n} P_1 + \cdots + \frac{t_{n-1}}{1 - t_n} P_{n-1}\right) + t_n P_n.$$

Let

$$s_i = \frac{t_i}{1 - t_i} \qquad \text{for} \qquad i = 1, \ldots, n - 1.$$

Then $s_i \geq 0$ and $s_1 + \cdots + s_{n-1} = 1$ so that by induction, we conclude that the point

$$Q = s_1 P_1 + \cdots + s_{n-1} P_{n-1}$$

lies in S'. But then

$$(1 - t_n)Q + t_n P_n = t_1 P_1 + \cdots + t_n P_n$$

lies in S' by definition of a convex set, as was to be shown.

Example. Let V be a vector space, and let $L\colon V \to \mathbf{R}$ be a linear map. We contend that the set S of all elements v in V such that $L(v) < 0$ is convex.

Proof. Let $L(v) < 0$ and $L(w) < 0$. Let $0 < t < 1$. Then

$$L(tv + (1 - t)w) = tL(v) + (1 - t)L(w).$$

Then $tL(v) < 0$ and $(1 - t)L(w) < 0$ so $tL(v) + (1 - t)L(w) < 0$, whence $tv + (1 - t)w$ lies in S. If $t = 0$ or $t = 1$, then $tv + (1 - t)w$ is equal to v or w and thus also lies in S. This proves our assertion.

For a generalization of this example, see Exercise 6.

EXERCISES

1. Show that the image under a linear map of a convex set is convex.

2. Let S_1 and S_2 be convex sets in V. Show that the intersection $S_1 \cap S_2$ is convex.

3. Let $L\colon \mathbf{R}^n \to \mathbf{R}$ be a linear map. Let S be the set of all points A in $\mathbf{R}^n$ such that $L(A) \geqq 0$. Show that S is convex.

4. Let $L\colon \mathbf{R}^n \to \mathbf{R}$ be a linear map and c a number. Show that the set S consisting of all points A in $\mathbf{R}^n$ such that $L(A) > c$ is convex.

5. Let A be a non-zero vector in $\mathbf{R}^n$ and c a number. Show that the set of points X such that $X \cdot A \geqq c$ is convex.

6. Let $L\colon V \to W$ be a linear map. Let S' be a convex set in W. Let S be the set of all elements P in V such that $L(P)$ is in S'. Show that S is convex.

7. Show that a parallelogram is convex.

8. Let S be a convex set in V and let u be an element of V. Let $T_u\colon V \to V$ be the translation by u. Show that the image $T_u(S)$ is convex.

9. Let S be a convex set in the vector space V and let c be a number. Let cS denote the set of all elements cv with v in S. Show that cS is convex.

10. Let v, w be linearly independent elements of a vector space V. Let $F\colon V \to W$ be a linear map. Assume that $F(v)$, $F(w)$ are linearly dependent. Show that the image under F of the parallelogram spanned by v and w is either a point or a line segment.

CHAPTER V

Linear Maps and Matrices

§1. *The linear map associated with a matrix*

Let

$$A = \begin{pmatrix} a_{11} & \cdots & a_{1n} \\ \vdots & & \vdots \\ a_{m1} & \cdots & a_{mn} \end{pmatrix}$$

be an $m \times n$ matrix. We can then associate with A a map

$$L_A : K^n \rightarrow K^m$$

by letting

$$L_A(X) = AX$$

for every column vector X in K^n. Thus L_A is defined by the association $X \mapsto AX$, the product being the product of matrices. That L_A is linear is simply a special case of Theorem 3, Chapter III, §3, namely the theorem concerning properties of multiplication of matrices. Indeed, we have

$$A(X + Y) = AX + AY \qquad \text{and} \qquad A(cX) = cAX$$

for all vectors X, Y in K^n and all numbers c. We call L_A the linear map **associated** with the matrix A.

Example. If

$$A = \begin{pmatrix} 2 & 1 \\ -1 & 5 \end{pmatrix} \qquad \text{and} \qquad X = \begin{pmatrix} 3 \\ 7 \end{pmatrix},$$

then

$$L_A(X) = \begin{pmatrix} 2 & 1 \\ -1 & 5 \end{pmatrix}\begin{pmatrix} 3 \\ 7 \end{pmatrix} = \begin{pmatrix} 6 + 7 \\ -3 + 35 \end{pmatrix} = \begin{pmatrix} 13 \\ 32 \end{pmatrix}.$$

Theorem 1. *If A, B are $m \times n$ matrices and if $L_A = L_B$, then $A = B$. In other words, if matrices A, B give rise to the same linear map, then they are equal.*

Proof. By definition, we have $A_i \cdot X = B_i \cdot X$ for all i, if A_i is the i-th row of A and B_i is the i-th row of B. Hence $(A_i - B_i) \cdot X = 0$ for all i and all X. Hence $A_i - B_i = O$, and $A_i = B_i$ for all i. Hence $A = B$.

We can give a new interpretation for a system of homogeneous linear equations in terms of the linear map associated with a matrix. Indeed, such a system can be written

$$AX = O,$$

and hence we see that *the set of solutions is the kernel of the linear map L_A.*

EXERCISES

1. In each case, find the vector $L_A(X)$.

(a) $A = \begin{pmatrix} 2 & 1 \\ 1 & 0 \end{pmatrix}$, $X = \begin{pmatrix} 3 \\ -1 \end{pmatrix}$ ⠀⠀(b) $A = \begin{pmatrix} 1 & 0 \\ 0 & 0 \end{pmatrix}$, $X = \begin{pmatrix} 5 \\ 1 \end{pmatrix}$

(c) $A = \begin{pmatrix} 1 & 1 \\ 0 & 1 \end{pmatrix}$, $X = \begin{pmatrix} 4 \\ 1 \end{pmatrix}$ ⠀⠀(d) $A = \begin{pmatrix} 0 & 0 \\ 0 & 1 \end{pmatrix}$, $X = \begin{pmatrix} 7 \\ -3 \end{pmatrix}$

§2. The matrix associated with a linear map

We first consider a special case. *Let*

$$L: K^n \to K$$

be a linear map. We shall prove that there exists a vector A in K^n such that $L = L_A$, i.e. such that for all X we have

$$L(X) = A \cdot X.$$

Let $E_1, \ldots, E_n$ be the unit vectors in K^n. If $X = x_1 E_1 + \cdots + x_n E_n$ is any vector, then

$$L(X) = L(x_1 E_1 + \cdots + x_n E_n)$$
$$= x_1 L(E_1) + \cdots + x_n L(E_n).$$

If we now let

$$a_i = L(E_i),$$

we see that

$$L(X) = x_1 a_1 + \cdots + x_n a_n = X \cdot A.$$

This proves what we wanted. It also gives us an explicit determination of the vector A such that $L = L_A$, namely the components of A are precisely the values $L(E_1), \ldots, L(E_n)$, where E_i $(i = 1, \ldots, n)$ are the unit vectors of K^n.

We shall now generalize this to the case of an arbitrary linear map into K^m, not just into K.

Let $L: K^n \to K^m$ be a linear map. As usual, Let $E^1, \ldots, E^n$ be the unit column vectors in K^n, and let $e^1, \ldots, e^m$ be the unit column vectors in K^m. We can write any vector X in K^n as a linear combination

$$X = x_1 E^1 + \cdots + x_n E^n,$$

where x_j is the j-th component of X. We view $E^1, \ldots, E^n$ as column vectors. By linearity, we find that

$$L(X) = x_1 L(E^1) + \cdots + x_n L(E^n)$$

and we can write each $L(E^j)$ in terms of $e^1, \ldots, e^m$. In other words, there exist numbers a_{ij} such that

$$
\begin{aligned}
L(E^1) &= a_{11} e^1 + \cdots + a_{m1} e^m \\
&\ \ \vdots \qquad\quad \vdots \qquad\quad \vdots \\
L(E^n) &= a_{1n} e^1 + \cdots + a_{mn} e^m
\end{aligned}
$$

or in terms of the column vectors,

$$(*) \qquad L(E^1) = \begin{pmatrix} a_{11} \\ \vdots \\ a_{m1} \end{pmatrix}, \quad \ldots, \quad L(E^n) = \begin{pmatrix} a_{1n} \\ \vdots \\ a_{mn} \end{pmatrix}.$$

Hence

$$
\begin{aligned}
L(X) &= x_1(a_{11} e^1 + \cdots + a_{m1} e^m) + \cdots + x_n(a_{1n} e^1 + \cdots + a_{mn} e^m) \\
&= (a_{11} x_1 + \cdots + a_{1n} x_n) e^1 + \cdots + (a_{m1} x_1 + \cdots + a_{mn} x_n) e^m.
\end{aligned}
$$

Consequently, if we let $A = (a_{ij})$, then we see that

$$L(X) = AX.$$

Written out in full, this reads

$$
\begin{pmatrix} a_{11} & \cdots & a_{1n} \\ \vdots & & \vdots \\ a_{m1} & \cdots & a_{mn} \end{pmatrix}
\begin{pmatrix} x_1 \\ \vdots \\ x_n \end{pmatrix}
=
\begin{pmatrix} a_{11} x_1 + \cdots + a_{1n} x_n \\ \vdots \\ a_{m1} x_1 + \cdots + a_{mn} x_n \end{pmatrix}.
$$

Thus $L = L_A$ is the linear map associated with the matrix A. We also call A **the matrix associated with the linear map L.** We know that this matrix is uniquely determined by Theorem 1.

Example 1. Let $F: \mathbf{R}^3 \to \mathbf{R}^2$ be the projection, in other words the mapping such that $F(x_1, x_2, x_3) = (x_1, x_2)$. Then the matrix associated with F is

$$\begin{pmatrix} 1 & 0 & 0 \\ 0 & 1 & 0 \end{pmatrix}.$$

Example 2. Let $I: \mathbf{R}^n \to \mathbf{R}^n$ be the identity. Then the matrix associated with I is the matrix

$$\begin{pmatrix} 1 & 0 & 0 & \cdots & 0 \\ 0 & 1 & 0 & \cdots & 0 \\ \vdots & \vdots & \vdots & & \vdots \\ 0 & 0 & 0 & \cdots & 1 \end{pmatrix},$$

having components equal to 1 on the diagonal, and 0 otherwise.

Example 3. According to Theorem 1 of Chapter IV, §2, there exists a unique linear map $L: \mathbf{R}^4 \to \mathbf{R}^2$ such that

$$L(E^2) = \begin{pmatrix} 2 \\ 1 \end{pmatrix}, \quad L(E^2) = \begin{pmatrix} 3 \\ -1 \end{pmatrix},$$

$$L(E^3) = \begin{pmatrix} -5 \\ 4 \end{pmatrix}, \quad L(E^4) = \begin{pmatrix} 1 \\ 7 \end{pmatrix}.$$

According to the relations $(*)$, we see that the matrix associated with L is the matrix

$$\begin{pmatrix} 2 & 3 & -5 & 1 \\ 1 & -1 & 4 & 7 \end{pmatrix}.$$

Example 4. (Rotations). We can define a **rotation** in terms of matrices. Indeed, we call a linear map $L: \mathbf{R}^2 \to \mathbf{R}^2$ a **rotation** if its associated matrix can be written in the form

$$\begin{pmatrix} \cos \theta & -\sin \theta \\ \sin \theta & \cos \theta \end{pmatrix}.$$

The geometric justification for this definition comes from Fig. 1.

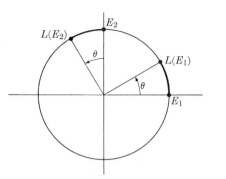

Figure 1

We see that

$$L(E_1) = (\cos \theta)E_1 + (\sin \theta)E_2,$$
$$L(E_2) = (-\sin \theta)E_1 + (\cos \theta)E_2.$$

Thus our definition corresponds precisely to the picture. When the matrix of the rotation is as above, we say that the rotation is by an angle θ. For example, the matrix associated with a rotation by an angle $\pi/2$ is

$$\begin{pmatrix} 0 & -1 \\ 1 & 0 \end{pmatrix}.$$

We observe finally that the operations on matrices correspond to the operations on the associated linear map. For instance, if A, B are $m \times n$ matrices, then

$$L_{A+B} = L_A + L_B$$

and if c is a number, then

$$L_{cA} = cL_A.$$

This is obvious, because

$$(A + B)X = AX + BX \qquad \text{and} \qquad (cA)X = c(AX).$$

Similarly for compositions of mappings. Indeed, let

$$F: K^n \rightarrow K^m \qquad \text{and} \qquad G: K^m \rightarrow K^s$$

be linear maps, and let A, B be the matrices associated with F and G respectively. Then for any vector X in K^n we have

$$(G \circ F)(X) = G(F(X)) = B(AX) = (BA)X.$$

Hence the product BA is the matrix associated with the composite linear map $G \circ F$.

EXERCISES

1. Find the matrix associated with the following linear maps. (Although the vectors are written horizontally, for typographical reasons, view them as column vectors.)

(a) $F: \mathbf{R}^4 \to \mathbf{R}^2$ given by $F(x_1, x_2, x_3, x_4) = (x_1, x_2)$ (the projection)

(b) The projection from $\mathbf{R}^4$ to $\mathbf{R}^3$

(c) $F: \mathbf{R}^2 \to \mathbf{R}^2$ given by $F(x, y) = (3x, 3y)$

(d) $F: \mathbf{R}^n \to \mathbf{R}^n$ given by $F(X) = 7X$

(e) $F: \mathbf{R}^n \to \mathbf{R}^n$ given by $F(X) = -X$

(f) $F: \mathbf{R}^4 \to \mathbf{R}^4$ given by $F(x_1, x_2, x_3, x_4) = (x_1, x_2, 0, 0)$

2. Find the matrix associated with the rotation for each of the following values of θ.

(a) $\pi/2$ (b) $\pi/4$ (c) π (d) $-\pi$ (e) $-\pi/3$

(f) $\pi/6$ (g) $5\pi/4$

3. In general, let $\theta > 0$. What is the matrix associated with the rotation by an angle $-\theta$ (i.e. clockwise rotation by θ)?

4. Let $X = (1, 2)$ be a point of the plane. Let F be the rotation through an angle of $\pi/4$. What are the coordinates of $F(X)$ relative to the usual basis $\{E_1, E_2\}$?

5. Same question when $X = (-1, 3)$, and F is the rotation through $\pi/2$.

6. Let $F: \mathbf{R}^n \to \mathbf{R}^n$ be a linear map which is invertible. Show that if A is the matrix associated with F, then A^{-1} is the matrix associated with the inverse of F.

7. Let F be a rotation through an angle θ. Show that for any vector X in $\mathbf{R}^2$ we have $\|X\| = \|F(X)\|$ (i.e. F preserves norms).

8. Let c be a number, and let $L: \mathbf{R}^n \to \mathbf{R}^n$ be the linear map such that $L(X) = cX$. What is the matrix associated with this linear map?

9. Let F_θ be rotation by an angle θ. If θ, φ are numbers, compute the matrix of the linear map $F_\theta \circ F_\varphi$ and show that it is the matrix of $F_{\theta+\varphi}$.

10. Let F_θ be rotation by an angle θ. Show that F_θ is invertible, and determine the matrix associated with F_θ^{-1}.

§3. Bases, matrices, and linear maps

In the first two sections we considered the relation between matrices and linear maps of K^n into K^m. Now let V, W be arbitrary finite dimensional vector spaces over K. Let

$$\mathcal{B} = \{v_1, \ldots, v_n\} \quad \text{and} \quad \mathcal{B}' = \{w_1, \ldots, w_m\}$$

be bases of V and W respectively. Then we know that elements of V and W have coordinate vectors with respect to these bases. In other words, if $v \in V$ we can express v uniquely as a linear combination

$$v = x_1 v_1 + \cdots + x_n v_n, \qquad\qquad x_i \in K.$$

Thus V is isomorphic to K^n under the map $K^n \to V$ given by

$$(x_1, \ldots, x_n) \mapsto x_1 v_1 + \cdots + x_n v_n.$$

Similarly for W. If $F: V \to W$ is a linear map, then using the above isomorphism, we can interpret F as a linear map of K^n into K^m, and thus associate a matrix with F, depending on our choice of bases, and denoted by

$$M_{\mathcal{B}'}^{\mathcal{B}}(F).$$

This matrix is the unique matrix A having the following property:

If X is the (column) coordinate vector of an element v of V, relative to the basis $\mathcal{B}$, then AX is the (column) coordinate vector of $F(v)$, relative to the basis $\mathcal{B}'$.

If $A = M_{\mathcal{B}'}^{\mathcal{B}}(F)$, and X is the coordinate vector of v with respect to $\mathcal{B}$, then by definition,

$$F(v) = (A_1 \cdot X) w_1 + \cdots + (A_m \cdot X) w_m.$$

This matrix A is determined by the effect of F on the basis elements as follows.

Let

$$F(v_1) = a_{11} w_1 + \cdots + a_{m1} w_m$$

(*)

$$F(v_n) = a_{1n} w_1 + \cdots + a_{mn} w_m.$$

Then A turns out to be the *transpose* of the matrix

$$\begin{pmatrix} a_{11} & a_{21} & \cdots & a_{m1} \\ a_{12} & a_{22} & \cdots & a_{m2} \\ & & \cdots & \\ a_{1n} & a_{2n} & \cdots & a_{mn} \end{pmatrix}.$$

Indeed, we have

$$F(v) = F(x_1 v_1 + \cdots + x_n v_n) = x_1 F(v_1) + \cdots + x_n F(v_n).$$

Using expression (*) for $F(v_1), \ldots, F(v_n)$ we find that

$$F(v) = x_1(a_{11} w_1 + \cdots + a_{m1} w_m) + \cdots + x_n(a_{1n} w_1 + \cdots + a_{mn} w_m),$$

and after collecting the coefficients of $w_1, \ldots, w_m$, we can rewrite this expression in the form

$$(a_{11}x_1 + \cdots + a_{1n}x_1)w_1 + \cdots + (a_{m1}x_1 + \cdots + a_{mn}x_n)w_m$$
$$= (A_1 \cdot X)w_1 + \cdots + (A_m \cdot X)w_m.$$

This proves our assertion.

Example 1. Let F be the linear map such that

$$F(v_1) = 3w_1 - w_2 + 17w_3,$$
$$F(v_2) = w_1 + w_2 - w_3,$$

assuming that dim $V = 2$ and dim $W = 3$. Then the matrix associated with F is the matrix

$$\begin{pmatrix} 3 & 1 \\ -1 & 1 \\ 17 & -1 \end{pmatrix}$$

equal to the transpose of

$$\begin{pmatrix} 3 & -1 & 17 \\ 1 & 1 & -1 \end{pmatrix}.$$

Example 2. Let $id\colon V \to V$ be the identity map. Then for any basis $\mathcal{B}$ of V we have

$$M_{\mathcal{B}}^{\mathcal{B}}(id) = I,$$

where I is the unit $n \times n$ matrix (if dim $V = n$). This is immediately verified.

Warning. Assume that $V = W$, but that we work with two bases $\mathcal{B}$ and $\mathcal{B}'$ of V which are distinct. Then the matrix associated with the identity mapping of V into itself relative to these two distinct bases will *not* be the unit matrix!

Example 3. **Rotations.** We shall encounter two situations. First, we shall pick two different coordinate systems differing by a rotation. The identity mapping will then have an associated matrix which is not the unit matrix. Second, we shall discuss the matrix associated with a rotation, with respect to a fixed basis.

Case 1. Let us start with our coordinate system in the plane as usual. Let $E_1 = (1, 0)$ and $E_2 = (0, 1)$ be the unit vectors. We consider another coordinate system obtained by rotating the given coordinate system counterclockwise by an angle θ. Then the unit vectors are moved into two new unit vectors E_1' and E_2' (Fig. 2).

From the picture, we see that

$$E'_1 = (\cos \theta)E_1 + (\sin \theta)E_2,$$
$$E'_2 = (-\sin \theta)E_1 + (\cos \theta)E_2.$$

If we multiply the first equation by $\cos \theta$, if we multiply the second by $-\sin \theta$, and add, we find:

$$E_1 = (\cos \theta)E'_1 - (\sin \theta)E'_2.$$

Similarly,

$$E_2 = (\sin \theta)E'_1 + (\cos \theta)E'_2.$$

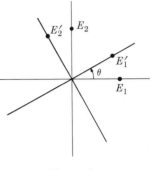

Figure 2

Let $id: \mathbf{R}^2 \to \mathbf{R}^2$ be the identity mapping. Let $\mathcal{B} = \{E_1, E_2\}$ and $\mathcal{B}' = \{E'_1, E'_2\}$. Then:

$$id(E_1) = E_1 = (\cos \theta)E'_1 + (-\sin \theta)E'_2,$$
$$id(E_2) = E_2 = (\sin \theta)E'_1 + (\cos \theta)E'_2.$$

Consequently, the matrix associated with the identity mapping relative to the bases $\mathcal{B}$ and $\mathcal{B}'$ is

$$\begin{pmatrix} \cos \theta & \sin \theta \\ -\sin \theta & \cos \theta \end{pmatrix}.$$

Case 2. Let us keep our standard coordinate system, with basis $\mathcal{B} = \{E_1, E_2\}$. Let $F: \mathbf{R}^2 \to \mathbf{R}^2$ be the mapping obtained by rotating the plane through an angle θ (counterclockwise). We can write $F = F_\theta$. Then

$$F(E_1) = E'_1 = (\cos \theta)E_1 + (\sin \theta)E_2,$$
$$F(E_2) = E'_2 = (-\sin \theta)E_1 + (\cos \theta)E_2.$$

Hence the matrix associated with F relative to the bases $\mathcal{B}, \mathcal{B}$ is the transpose of the matrix in Case 1, namely:

$$M^{\mathcal{B}}_{\mathcal{B}}(F_\theta) = \begin{pmatrix} \cos \theta & -\sin \theta \\ \sin \theta & \cos \theta \end{pmatrix}.$$

There is no avoiding the fact that the matrix in Case 1 turns out to be the transpose of the matrix in Case 2. Hence it is necessary always to be careful of the selection of bases to compute the matrix associated with a linear map.

Example 4. Let $\mathfrak{B} = \{v_1, \ldots, v_n\}$ and $\mathfrak{B}' = \{w_1, \ldots, w_n\}$ be bases of the same vector space V. There exists a matrix $A = (a_{ij})$ such that

$$
\begin{aligned}
w_1 &= a_{11}v_1 + \cdots + a_{1n}v_n, \\
&\vdots \qquad \vdots \qquad \cdots \qquad \vdots \\
w_n &= a_{n1}v_1 + \cdots + a_{nn}v_n.
\end{aligned}
$$

Then for each $i = 1, \ldots, n$ we see that $w_i = id(w_i)$. Hence by definition,

$$ M_{\mathfrak{B}}^{\mathfrak{B}'}(id) = {}^t A. $$

On the other hand, there exists a unique linear map $F \colon V \to V$ such that

$$ F(v_1) = w_1, \quad \ldots, \quad F(v_n) = w_n. $$

Again by definition, we have

$$ M_{\mathfrak{B}}^{\mathfrak{B}}(F) = {}^t A. $$

Theorem 2. *Let V, W be vector spaces. Let $\mathfrak{B}$ be a basis of V, and $\mathfrak{B}'$ a basis of W. Let f, g be two linear maps of V into W. Then*

$$ M(f + g) = M(f) + M(g). $$

If c is a number, then

$$ M(cf) = cM(f). $$

(The associated matrix is taken relative to the given bases $\mathfrak{B}$ and $\mathfrak{B}'$.)

The proof will be left as an exercise.

Theorem 2 means that the association

$$ f \mapsto M_{\mathfrak{B}'}^{\mathfrak{B}}(f) $$

is an isomorphism between the space of linear maps $\mathcal{L}(V, W)$ and the space of $m \times n$ matrices (if $\dim V = n$ and $\dim W = m$).

Let U, V, W be sets. Let $F \colon U \to V$ be a mapping, and let $G \colon V \to W$ be a mapping. Then we can form a composite mapping from U into W as discussed previously, namely $G \circ F$.

Theorem 3. *Let V, W, U be vector spaces. Let $\mathfrak{B}$, $\mathfrak{B}'$, $\mathfrak{B}''$ be bases for V, W, U respectively. Let*

$$ F \colon V \to W \qquad and \qquad G \colon W \to U $$

be linear maps. Then

$$M^{\mathfrak{B}'}_{\mathfrak{B}''}(G) M^{\mathfrak{B}}_{\mathfrak{B}'}(F) = M^{\mathfrak{B}}_{\mathfrak{B}''}(G \circ F).$$

(*Note.* Relative to our choice of bases, the theorem expresses the fact that composition of mappings corresponds to multiplication of matrices.)

Proof. Let A be the matrix associated with F relative to the bases $\mathfrak{B}$, $\mathfrak{B}'$ and let B be the matrix associated with G relative to the bases $\mathfrak{B}'$, $\mathfrak{B}''$. Let v be an element of V and let X be its (column) coordinate vector relative to $\mathfrak{B}$. Then the coordinate vector of $F(v)$ relative to $\mathfrak{B}'$ is AX. By definition, the coordinate vector of $G\big(F(v)\big)$ relative to $\mathfrak{B}'$ is $B(AX)$, which, by §2, is equal to $(BA)X$. But $G\big(F(v)\big) = (G \circ F)(v)$. Hence the coordinate vector of $(G \circ F)(v)$ relative to the basis $\mathfrak{B}''$ is $(BA)X$. By definition, this means that BA is the matrix associated with $G \circ F$, and proves our theorem.

Remark. In many applications, one deals with linear maps of a vector space V into itself. If a basis $\mathfrak{B}$ of V is selected, and $F: V \to V$ is a linear map, then the matrix

$$M^{\mathfrak{B}}_{\mathfrak{B}}(F)$$

is usually called the matrix associated with F relative to $\mathfrak{B}$ (instead of saying relative to $\mathfrak{B}$, $\mathfrak{B}$). From the definition, we see that

$$M^{\mathfrak{B}}_{\mathfrak{B}}(id) = I,$$

where I is the unit matrix. As a direct consequence of Theorem 5 we obtain

Corollary. *Let V be a vector space and $\mathfrak{B}$, $\mathfrak{B}'$ bases of V. Then*

$$M^{\mathfrak{B}}_{\mathfrak{B}'}(id) M^{\mathfrak{B}'}_{\mathfrak{B}}(id) = I = M^{\mathfrak{B}'}_{\mathfrak{B}}(id) M^{\mathfrak{B}}_{\mathfrak{B}'}(id).$$

In particular, $M^{\mathfrak{B}}_{\mathfrak{B}'}(id)$ is invertible.

Proof. Take $V = W = U$ in Theorem 3, and $F = G = id$. Our assertion then drops out.

The general formula of Theorem 5 will allow us to describe precisely how the matrix associated with a linear map changes when we change bases.

Theorem 4. *Let $F: V \to V$ be a linear map, and let $\mathfrak{B}$, $\mathfrak{B}'$ be bases of V. Then there exists an invertible matrix N such that*

$$M^{\mathfrak{B}'}_{\mathfrak{B}'}(F) = N^{-1} M^{\mathfrak{B}}_{\mathfrak{B}}(F) N.$$

In fact, we can take

$$N = M_{\mathfrak{B}}^{\mathfrak{B}'}(id).$$

Proof. Applying Theorem 3 step by step, we find that

$$M_{\mathfrak{B}'}^{\mathfrak{B}'}(F) = M_{\mathfrak{B}'}^{\mathfrak{B}}(id)M_{\mathfrak{B}}^{\mathfrak{B}}(F)M_{\mathfrak{B}}^{\mathfrak{B}'}(id).$$

The Corollary of Theorem 3 implies the assertion to be proved.

Let V be a finite dimensional vector space over K, and let $F: V \to V$ be a linear map. A basis $\mathfrak{B}$ of V is said to **diagonalize** F if the matrix associated with F relative to $\mathfrak{B}$ is a diagonal matrix. If there exists such a basis which diagonalizes F, then we say that F is **diagonalizable.** It is not always true that a linear map can be diagonalized. Later in this book, we shall find sufficient conditions under which it can. If A is an $n \times n$ matrix in K, we say that A can be **diagonalized** (in K) if the linear map on K^n represented by A can be diagonalized. From Theorem 4, we conclude at once:

Theorem 5. *Let V be a finite dimensional vector space over K, and let $F: V \to V$ be a linear map, and let M be its associated matrix relative to a basis $\mathfrak{B}$. Then F (or M) can be diagonalized (in K) if and only if there exists an invertible matrix N in K such that $N^{-1}MN$ is a diagonal matrix.*

In view of the importance of the map $M \mapsto N^{-1}MN$, we give it a special name. Two matrices, M, M' are called **similar** (in a field K) if there exists an invertible matrix N in K such that $M' = N^{-1}MN$.

We state one more formula describing changes of coordinates.

Theorem 6. *Let V, W be vector spaces over K, and let $F: V \to W$ be a linear map. Let $\mathfrak{B}$ be a basis of V and $\mathfrak{B}'$ a basis of W. If $v \in V$, denote by $M_{\mathfrak{B}}(v)$ the column vector of coordinates of v with respect to the basis $\mathfrak{B}$. Then*

$$M_{\mathfrak{B}'}\big(F(v)\big) = M_{\mathfrak{B}'}^{\mathfrak{B}}(F)M_{\mathfrak{B}}(v).$$

Proof. This is nothing but a reformulation of the definition of the matrix associated with a linear map.

Corollary. *Let V be a vector space, and let $\mathfrak{B}$, $\mathfrak{B}'$ be bases of V. Let $v \in V$. Then*

$$M_{\mathfrak{B}'}(v) = M_{\mathfrak{B}'}^{\mathfrak{B}}(id)M_{\mathfrak{B}}(v).$$

The corollary expresses in a succinct way the manner in which the coordinates of a vector change when we change the basis of the vector space.

The coordinates of a vector with respect to a given basis can be found by solving a system of linear equations, in a naive manner, as we saw in

Chapter II, §2. The matrix
$$M^{\mathcal{B}}_{\mathcal{B}'}(id)$$
can be found in exactly the same way.

EXERCISES

1. For each real number θ, let $F_\theta: \mathbf{R}^2 \to \mathbf{R}^2$ be the linear map represented by the matrix
$$\begin{pmatrix} \cos\theta & -\sin\theta \\ \sin\theta & \cos\theta \end{pmatrix}.$$
Show that if θ, θ' are real numbers, then $F_\theta F_{\theta'} = F_{\theta+\theta'}$. (You must use the addition formula for sine and cosine.) Also show that $F_\theta^{-1} = F_{-\theta}$.

2. In each one of the following cases, find $M^{\mathcal{B}}_{\mathcal{B}'}(id)$. The vector space in each case is $\mathbf{R}^3$.

(a) $\mathcal{B} = \{(1, 1, 0), (-1, 1, 1), (0, 1, 2)\}$
   $\mathcal{B}' = \{(2, 1, 1), (0, 0, 1), (-1, 1, 1)\}$
(b) $\mathcal{B} = \{(3, 2, 1), (0, -2, 5), (1, 1, 2)\}$
   $\mathcal{B}' = \{(1, 1, 0), (-1, 2, 4), (2, -1, 1)\}$

3. Let $\mathcal{B} = \{E_1, E_2\}$ be the usual basis of $\mathbf{R}^2$, and let $\mathcal{B}'$ be the basis obtained after rotating the coordinate system by an angle θ. Find the matrix associated with the identity relative to $\mathcal{B}$, $\mathcal{B}'$ for each of the following values of θ.

(a) $\pi/2$ (b) $\pi/4$ (c) π (d) $-\pi$
(e) $-\pi/3$ (f) $\pi/6$ (g) $5\pi/4$

4. In general, let $\theta > 0$. What is the matrix associated with the identity map, and rotation of bases by an angle $-\theta$ (i.e. clockwise rotation by θ)?

5. Let $X = (1, 2)$ be a point of the plane. Let F be the rotation through an angle of $\pi/4$. What are the coordinates of $F(X)$ relative to the usual basis $\{E_1, E_2\}$?

6. Same question when $X = (-1, 3)$, and F is the rotation through $\pi/2$.

7. In general, let F be the rotation through an angle θ. Let (x, y) be a point of the plane in the standard coordinate system. Let (x', y') be the coordinates of this point in the rotated system. Express x', y' in terms of x, y, and θ.

8. In each of the following cases, let $D = d/dt$ be the derivative. We give a set of linearly independent functions $\mathcal{B}$. These generate a vector space V, and D is a linear map from V into itself. Find the matrix associated with D relative to the bases $\mathcal{B}$, $\mathcal{B}$.

(a) $\{e^t, e^{2t}\}$
(b) $\{1, t\}$
(c) $\{e^t, te^t\}$
(d) $\{1, t, t^2\}$
(e) $\{1, t, e^t, e^{2t}, te^{2t}\}$
(f) $\{\sin t, \cos t\}$

9. (a) Let N be a square matrix. We say that N is nilpotent if there exists a positive integer r such that $N^r = 0$. Prove that if N is nilpotent, then $I - N$ is invertible. (b) State and prove the analogous statement for linear maps of a vector space into itself.

10. Let P_n be the vector space of polynomials of degree $\leqq n$. Then the derivative $D: P_n \to P_n$ is a linear map of P_n into itself. Let I be the identity mapping. Prove that the following linear maps are invertible: (a) $I - D^2$. (b) $D^m - I$ for any positive integer m. (c) $D^m - cI$ for any number $c \neq 0$.

CHAPTER VI

Scalar Products and Orthogonality

§1. Scalar products

Let V be a vector space over a field K. A **scalar product** on V is an association which to any pair of elements v, w of V associates a scalar, denoted by $\langle v, w \rangle$, or also $v \cdot w$, satisfying the following properties:

SP 1. *We have* $\langle v, w \rangle = \langle w, v \rangle$ *for all* $v, w \in V$.

SP 2. *If* u, v, w *are elements of* V, *then*

$$\langle u, v + w \rangle = \langle u, v \rangle + \langle u, w \rangle.$$

SP 3. *If* $x \in K$, *then*

$$\langle xu, v \rangle = x \langle u, v \rangle \qquad and \qquad \langle u, xv \rangle = x \langle u, v \rangle.$$

The scalar product is said to be **non-degenerate** if in addition it also satisfies the condition:

If v *is an element of* V, *and* $\langle v, w \rangle = 0$ *for all* $w \in V$, *then* $v = O$.

Example 1. Let $V = K^n$. Then the map

$$(X, Y) \mapsto X \cdot Y,$$

which to elements $X, Y \in K^n$ associates their dot product as we defined it previously, is a scalar product in the present sense.

Example 2. Let V be the space of continuous real-valued functions on the interval $[0, 1]$. If $f, g \in V$, we define

$$\langle f, g \rangle = \int_0^1 f(t)g(t)\, dt.$$

Simple properties of the integral show that this is a scalar product.

In both examples the scalar product is non-degenerate. We had pointed this out previously for the dot product of vectors in K^n. In the second example, it is also easily shown from simple properties of the integral.

In calculus, we study the second example, which gives rise to the theory of Fourier series. Here we discuss only general properties of scalar products and applications to Euclidean spaces. The notation $\langle \, , \, \rangle$ is used because in dealing with vector spaces of functions, a dot $f \cdot g$ may be confused with the ordinary product of functions.

Let V be a vector space with a scalar product. As always, we define elements v, w of V to be **orthogonal** or **perpendicular,** and write $v \perp w$, if $\langle v, w \rangle = 0$. If S is a subset of V, we denote by $S^\perp$ the set of all elements $w \in V$ which are perpendicular to all elements of S, i.e. $\langle w, v \rangle = 0$ for all $v \in S$. Then using SP 2 and SP 3, one verifies at once that $S^\perp$ is a subspace of V, called the **orthogonal space** of S. If w is perpendicular to S, we also write $w \perp S$. Let U be the subspace of V generated by the elements of S. If w is perpendicular to S, and if $v_1, v_2 \in S$, then

$$\langle w, v_1 + v_2 \rangle = \langle w, v_1 \rangle + \langle w, v_2 \rangle = 0.$$

If c is a scalar, then

$$\langle w, cv_1 \rangle = c\langle w, v_1 \rangle.$$

Hence w is perpendicular to linear combinations of elements of S, and hence w is perpendicular to U.

Example 3. Let (a_{ij}) be an $m \times n$ matrix in K, and let $A_1, \ldots, A_m$ be its row vectors. Let $X = (x_1, \ldots, x_n)$ as usual. The system of homogeneous linear equations

$$a_{11}x_1 + \cdots + a_{1n}x_n = 0$$
(**)
$$\cdots$$
$$a_{m1}x_1 + \cdots + a_{mn}x_n = 0$$

can also be written in an abbreviated form, namely

$$A_1 \cdot X = 0, \quad \ldots, \quad A_m \cdot X = 0.$$

The set of solutions X of this homogeneous system is a vector space over K. In fact, let W be the space generated by $A_1, \ldots, A_m$. Let U be the space consisting of all vectors in K^n perpendicular to $A_1, \ldots, A_m$. Then U is precisely the vector space of solutions of (**). The vectors $A_1, \ldots, A_m$ may not be linearly independent. We note that dim $W \leq m$, and we call

$$\dim U = \dim W^\perp$$

the *dimension of the space of solutions of the system of linear equations.* We shall discuss this dimension at greater length later.

Let V again be a vector space over the field K, with a scalar product.

Let $\{v_1, \ldots, v_n\}$ be a basis of V. We shall say that it is an **orthogonal basis** if $\langle v_i, v_j \rangle = 0$ for all $i \neq j$. We shall show later that if V is a finite dimensional vector space, with a scalar product, then there always exists an orthogonal basis. However, we shall first discuss important special cases over the real and complex numbers.

The real positive definite case

Let V be a vector space over $\mathbf{R}$, with a scalar product. We shall call this scalar product **positive definite** if $\langle v, v \rangle \geqq 0$ for all $v \in V$, and $\langle v, v \rangle > 0$ if $v \neq O$. The ordinary dot product of vectors in $\mathbf{R}^n$ is positive definite, and so is the scalar product of Example 2 above.

Let V be a vector space over $\mathbf{R}$, with a positive definite scalar product denoted by $\langle \ , \ \rangle$. Let W be a subspace. Then W has a scalar product defined by the same rule defining the scalar product in V. In other words, if w, w' are elements of W, we may form their product $\langle w, w' \rangle$. This scalar product on W is obviously positive definite.

For instance, if W is the subspace of $\mathbf{R}^3$ generated by the two vectors $(1, 1, 2)$ and $(\pi, -1, 0)$, then W is a vector space in its own right, and we can take the dot product of vectors lying in W to define a positive definite scalar product on W. We often have to deal with such subspaces, and this is one reason why we develop our theory on arbitrary (finite dimensional) spaces over $\mathbf{R}$ with a given positive definite scalar product, instead of working only on $\mathbf{R}^n$ with the dot product. Another reason is that we wish our theory to apply to situations as described in Example 2 of §1.

As in Chapter I, we define the **length,** or **norm** of an element $v \in V$ by

$$\|v\| = \sqrt{\langle v, v \rangle}.$$

If c is any number, then we immediately get

$$\|cv\| = |c| \, \|v\|,$$

because

$$\|cv\| = \sqrt{\langle cv, cv \rangle} = \sqrt{c^2 \langle v, v \rangle} = |c| \, \|v\|.$$

Thus we see the same type of arguments as in Chapter I apply here. In fact, any argument given in Chapter I which does not use coordinates applies to our more general situation. We shall see further examples as we go along.

As before, we say that an element $v \in V$ is a **unit vector** if $\|v\| = 1$. If $v \in V$ and $v \neq O$, then $v/\|v\|$ is a unit vector.

The following two identities follow directly from the definition of the length.

The Pythagoras theorem. *If v, w are perpendicular, then*

$$\|v + w\|^2 = \|v\|^2 + \|w\|^2.$$

The parallelogram law. *For any v, w we have*

$$\|v + w\|^2 + \|v - w\|^2 = 2\|v\|^2 + 2\|w\|^2.$$

The proofs are trivial. We give the first, and leave the second as an exercise. For the first, we have

$$\|v + w\|^2 = \langle v + w, v + w \rangle = \langle v, v \rangle + 2\langle v, w \rangle + \langle w, w \rangle$$
$$= \|v\|^2 + \|w\|^2.$$

Let w be an element of V such that $\|w\| \neq 0$. For any v there exists a unique number c such that $v - cw$ is perpendicular to w. Indeed, for $v - cw$ to be perpendicular to w we must have

$$\langle v - cw, w \rangle = 0,$$

whence $\langle v, w \rangle - \langle cw, w \rangle = 0$ and $\langle v, w \rangle = c\langle w, w \rangle$. Thus

$$c = \frac{\langle v, w \rangle}{\langle w, w \rangle}.$$

Conversely, letting c have this value shows that $v - cw$ is perpendicular to w. We call c the **component of v along** w, or the **Fourier coefficient** of v with respect to w. We call cw the **projection of v along** w.

In particular, if w is a unit vector, then the component of v along w is simply

$$c = \langle v, w \rangle.$$

Example 4. Let $V = \mathbf{R}^n$ with the usual scalar product, i.e., the dot product. If E_i is the i-th unit vector, and $X = (x_1, \ldots, x_n)$ then the component of X along E_i is simply

$$X \cdot E_i = x_i,$$

that is, the i-th component of X.

Example 5. Let V be the space of continuous functions on $[-\pi, \pi]$. Let f be the function given by $f(x) = \sin kx$, where k is some integer > 0. Then

$$\|f\| = \sqrt{\langle f, f \rangle} = \left(\int_{-\pi}^{\pi} \sin^2 kx \, dx \right)^{1/2}$$
$$= \sqrt{\pi}.$$

If g is any continuous function on $[-\pi, \pi]$, then the Fourier coefficient of g with respect to f is

$$\frac{\langle g, f \rangle}{\langle f, f \rangle} = \frac{1}{\pi} \int_{-\pi}^{\pi} g(x) \sin kx \, dx.$$

As with the case of n-space, we define the projection of v along w to be the vector cw, because of our usual picture:

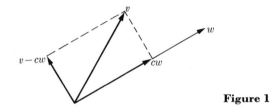

Figure 1

Exactly the same arguments which we gave in Chapter I can now be used to get the **Schwarz inequality,** namely:

Theorem 1. *For all v, $w \in V$ we have*

$$|\langle v, w \rangle| \leq \|v\| \, \|w\|.$$

Proof. If $w = O$, then both sides are equal to 0 and our inequality is obvious. Next, assume that $w = e$ is a unit vector, that is $e \in V$ and $\|e\| = 1$. If c is the component of v along e, then $v - ce$ is perpendicular to e, and also perpendicular to ce. Hence by the Pythagoras theorem, we find

$$\|v\|^2 = \|v - ce\|^2 + \|ce\|^2$$
$$= \|v - ce\|^2 + c^2.$$

Hence $c^2 \leq \|v\|^2$, so that $|c| \leq \|v\|$. Finally, if w is arbitrary $\neq O$, then $e = w/\|w\|$ is a unit vector, so that by what we just saw,

$$\left| \left\langle v, \frac{w}{\|w\|} \right\rangle \right| \leq \|v\|.$$

This yields

$$|\langle v, w \rangle| \leq \|v\| \, \|w\|,$$

as desired.

Theorem 2. *If v, $w \in V$, then*

$$\|v + w\| \leq \|v\| + \|w\|.$$

Proof. Exactly the same as that of the analogous theorem in Chapter I, §4.

Let $v_1, \ldots, v_n$ be non-zero elements of V which are mutually perpendicular, that is $\langle v_i, v_j \rangle = 0$ if $i \neq j$. Let c_i be the component of v along v_i. Then

$$v - c_1 v_1 - \cdots - c_n v_n$$

is perpendicular to $v_1, \ldots, v_n$. To see this, all we have to do is to take the product with v_j for any j. All the terms involving $\langle v_i, v_j \rangle$ will give 0 if $i \neq j$, and we shall have two remaining terms

$$\langle v, v_j \rangle - c_j \langle v_j, v_j \rangle$$

which cancel. Thus subtracting linear combinations as above orthogonalizes v with respect to $v_1, \ldots, v_n$. The next theorem shows that $c_1 v_1 + \cdots + c_n v_n$ gives the closest approximation to v as a linear combination of $v_1, \ldots, v_n$.

Theorem 3. *Let $v_1, \ldots, v_n$ be vectors which are mutually perpendicular, and such that $\|v_i\| \neq 0$ for all i. Let v be an element of V, and let c_i be the component of v along v_i. Let $a_1, \ldots, a_n$ be numbers. Then*

$$\left\| v - \sum_{k=1}^{n} c_k v_k \right\| \leq \left\| v - \sum_{k=1}^{n} a_k v_k \right\|.$$

Proof. We know that

$$v - \sum_{k=1}^{n} c_k v_k$$

is perpendicular to each v_i, $i = 1, \ldots, n$. Hence it is perpendicular to any linear combination of $v_1, \ldots, v_n$. Now we have:

$$\|v - \sum a_k v_k\|^2 = \|v - \sum c_k v_k + \sum (c_k - a_k) v_k\|^2$$

$$= \|v - \sum c_k v_k\|^2 + \|\sum (c_k - a_k) v_k\|^2$$

by the Pythagoras theorem. This proves that

$$\|v - \sum c_k v_k\|^2 \leq \|v - \sum a_k v_k\|^2,$$

and thus our theorem is proved.

The next theorem is known as the **Bessel inequality.**

Theorem 4. *If $v_1, \ldots, v_n$ are mutually perpendicular unit vectors, and if c_i is the Fourier coefficient of v with respect to v_i, then*

$$\sum_{i=1}^{n} c_i^2 \leq \|v\|^2.$$

Proof. We have

$$
\begin{aligned}
0 &\leq \langle v - \sum c_i v_i, v - \sum c_i v_i \rangle \\
&= \langle v, v \rangle - \sum 2c_i \langle v, v_i \rangle + \sum c_i^2 \\
&= \langle v, v \rangle - \sum c_i^2.
\end{aligned}
$$

From this our inequality follows.

EXERCISES

1. Let V be a vector space with a scalar product. Show that $\langle O, v \rangle = 0$ for all v in V.

2. Assume that the scalar product is positive definite. If $v_1, \ldots, v_n$ are non-zero elements which are mutually perpendicular, show that they are linearly independent.

3. Let M be a square $n \times n$ matrix which is equal to its transpose. If X, Y are column n-vectors, then

$$^t X M Y$$

is a 1×1 matrix, which we identify with a number. Show that the map

$$(X, Y) \mapsto {}^t X M Y$$

satisfies the three properties SP 1, SP 2, SP 3. Give an example of a 2×2 matrix M such that the fourth property is not satisfied.

§2. *Orthogonal bases, positive definite case*

Let V be a vector space with a positive definite scalar product throughout this section. A basis $\{v_1, \ldots, v_n\}$ of V is said to be **orthogonal** if its elements are mutually perpendicular, i.e. if $\langle v_i, v_j \rangle = 0$ whenever $i \neq j$.

If in addition each element of the basis has length 1, then the basis is called **orthonormal**.

The standard unit vectors of $\mathbf{R}^n$ form an orthonormal basis of $\mathbf{R}^n$, with respect to the ordinary dot product.

Theorem 5. *Let V be a finite dimensional vector space, with a positive definite scalar product. Let W be a subspace of V, and let $\{w_1, \ldots, w_m\}$ be an orthogonal basis of W. If $W \neq V$, then there exist elements $w_{m+1}, \ldots, w_n$ of V such that $\{w_1, \ldots, w_n\}$ is an orthogonal basis of V.*

Proof. The method of proof is as important as the theorem, and is called the **Gram-Schmidt orthogonalization process.** We know from Chapter III, §3 that we can find elements $v_{m+1}, \ldots, v_n$ of V such that

$$\{w_1, \ldots, w_m, v_{m+1}, \ldots, v_n\}$$

is a basis of V. Of course, it is not an orthogonal basis. Let W_{m+1} be the space generated by $w_1, \ldots, w_m, v_{m+1}$. We shall first obtain an orthogonal basis of W_{m+1}. The idea is to take v_{m+1} and subtract from it its projection along $w_1, \ldots, w_m$. Thus we let

$$c_1 = \frac{\langle v_{m+1}, w_1 \rangle}{\langle w_1, w_1 \rangle}, \quad \ldots, \quad c_m = \frac{\langle v_{m+1}, w_m \rangle}{\langle w_m, w_m \rangle}.$$

Let

$$w_{m+1} = v_{m+1} - c_1 w_1 - \cdots - c_m w_m.$$

Then w_{m+1} is perpendicular to $w_1, \ldots, w_m$. Furthermore, $w_{m+1} \neq O$ (otherwise v_{m+1} would be linearly dependent on $w_1, \ldots, w_m$), and v_{m+1} lies in the space generated by $w_1, \ldots, w_{m+1}$ because

$$v_{m+1} = w_{m+1} + c_1 w_1 + \cdots + c_m w_m.$$

Hence $\{w_1, \ldots, w_{m+1}\}$ is an orthogonal basis of W_{m+1}. We can now proceed by induction, showing that the space W_{m+s} generated by

$$w_1, \ldots, w_m, v_{m+1}, \ldots, v_{m+s}$$

has an orthogonal basis

$$\{w_1, \ldots, w_{m+1}, \ldots, w_{m+s}\}$$

with $s = 1, \ldots, n - m$. This concludes the proof.

Corollary. *Let V be a finite dimensional vector space with a positive definite scalar product. Assume that $V \neq \{O\}$. Then V has an orthogonal basis.*

Proof. By hypothesis, there exists an element v_1 of V such that $v_1 \neq O$. We let W be the subspace generated by v_1, and apply the theorem to get the desired basis.

We summarize the procedure by Theorem 5 once more. Suppose we are given an arbitrary basis $\{v_1, \ldots, v_n\}$ of V. We wish to orthogonalize it. We proceed as follows. We let

$$v_1' = v_1,$$

$$v_2' = v_2 - \frac{\langle v_2, v_1' \rangle}{\langle v_1', v_1' \rangle} v_1',$$

$$v_3' = v_3 - \frac{\langle v_3, v_2' \rangle}{\langle v_2', v_2' \rangle} v_2' - \frac{\langle v_3, v_1' \rangle}{\langle v_1', v_1' \rangle} v_1',$$

$$\vdots \qquad \vdots$$

$$v_n' = v_n - \frac{\langle v_n, v_{n-1}' \rangle}{\langle v_{n-1}', v_{n-1}' \rangle} v_{n-1}' - \cdots - \frac{\langle v_n, v_1' \rangle}{\langle v_1', v_1' \rangle} v_1'.$$

Then $\{v_1', \ldots, v_n'\}$ is an orthogonal basis.

Given an orthogonal basis, we can always obtain an orthonormal basis by dividing each vector by its length.

Example 1. Find an orthonormal basis for the vector space generated by the vectors $(1, 1, 0, 1)$, $(1, -2, 0, 0)$, and $(1, 0, -1, 2)$.

Let us denote these vectors by A, B, C. Let

$$B' = B - \frac{B \cdot A}{A \cdot A} A.$$

In other words, we subtract from B its projection along A. Then B' is perpendicular to A. We find

$$B' = \tfrac{1}{3}(4, -5, 0, 1).$$

Now we subtract from C its projection along A and B', and thus we let

$$C' = C - \frac{C \cdot A}{A \cdot A} A - \frac{C \cdot B'}{B' \cdot B'} B'.$$

Since A and B' are perpendicular, taking the scalar product of C' with A and B' shows that C' is perpendicular to both A and B'. We find

$$C' = \tfrac{1}{7}(-4, -2, -1, 6).$$

The vectors A, B', C' are non-zero and mutually perpendicular. They lie in the space generated by A, B, C. Hence they constitute an orthogonal basis for that space. If we wish an orthonormal basis, then we divide these vectors by their length, and thus obtain

$$\frac{A}{\|A\|} = \frac{1}{\sqrt{3}}\,(1, 1, 0, 1),$$

$$\frac{B'}{\|B'\|} = \frac{1}{\sqrt{42}}\,(4, -5, 0, 1),$$

$$\frac{C'}{\|C'\|} = \frac{1}{\sqrt{57}}\,(-4, -2, -1, 6),$$

as an orthonormal basis.

Theorem 6. *Let V be a vector space over $\mathbf{R}$ with a positive definite scalar product, of dimension n. Let W be a subspace of V of dimension r. Let $W^{\perp}$ be the subspace of V consisting of all elements which are perpendicular to W. Then V is the direct sum of W and $W^{\perp}$, and $W^{\perp}$ has dimension $n - r$. In other words,*

$$\dim W + \dim W^{\perp} = \dim V.$$

Proof. If W consists of O alone, or if $W = V$, then our assertion is obvious. We therefore assume that $W \neq V$ and that $W \neq \{O\}$. Let $\{w_1, \ldots, w_r\}$ be an orthonormal basis of W. By Theorem 5, there exist elements $u_{r+1}, \ldots, u_n$ of V such that

$$\{w_1, \ldots, w_r, u_{r+1}, \ldots, u_n\}$$

is an orthonormal basis of V. We shall prove that $\{u_{r+1}, \ldots, u_n\}$ is an orthonormal basis of $W^{\perp}$.

Let u be an element of $W^{\perp}$. Then there exist numbers $x_1, \ldots, x_n$ such that

$$u = x_1 w_1 + \cdots + x_r w_r + x_{r+1} u_{r+1} + \cdots + x_n u_n.$$

Since u is perpendicular to W, taking the product with any w_i ($i = 1, \ldots, r$), we find

$$0 = \langle u, w_i \rangle = x_i \langle w_i, w_i \rangle = x_i.$$

Hence all $x_i = 0$ ($i = 1, \ldots, r$). Therefore u is a linear combination of $u_{r+1}, \ldots, u_n$.

Conversely, let $u = x_{r+1} u_{r+1} + \cdots + x_n u_n$ be a linear combination of $u_{r+1}, \ldots, u_n$. Taking the product with any w_i yields 0. Hence u is perpendicular to all w_i $(i = 1, \ldots, r)$, and hence is perpendicular to W. This proves that $u_{r+1}, \ldots, u_n$ generate $W^{\perp}$. Since they are mutually perpendicular, and of norm 1, they form an orthonormal basis of $W^{\perp}$, whose dimension is therefore $n - r$. Furthermore, an element of $\overline{V}$ has a unique expression as a linear combination

$$x_1 w_1 + \cdots + x_r w_r + x_{r+1} u_{r+1} + \cdots + x_n u_n,$$

and hence a unique expression as a sum $w + u$ with $w \in \overline{W}$ and $u \in W^{\perp}$. Hence V is the direct sum of W and $W^{\perp}$

The space $W^{\perp}$ is called the **orthogonal complement** of W.

Example 2. Consider $\mathbf{R}^3$. Let A, B be two linearly independent vectors in $\mathbf{R}^3$. Then the space of vectors which are perpendicular to both A and B is a 1-dimensional space. If $\{N\}$ is a basis for this space, any other basis for this space is of type $\{tN\}$, where t is a number $\neq 0$.

Again in $\mathbf{R}^3$, let N be a non-zero vector. The space of vectors perpendicular to N is a 2-dimensional space, i.e. a plane, passing through the origin O.

Let V be a finite dimensional vector space over $\mathbf{R}$, with a positive definite scalar product. Let $\{e_1, \ldots, e_n\}$ be an orthonormal basis. Let $v, w \in V$. There exist numbers $x_1, \ldots, x_n \in \mathbf{R}$ and $y_1, \ldots, y_n \in \mathbf{R}$ such that

$$v = x_1 e_1 + \cdots + x_n e_n \quad \text{and} \quad w = y_1 e_1 + \cdots + y_n e_n.$$

Then

$$\langle v, w \rangle = \langle x_1 e_1 + \cdots + x_n e_n, y_1 e_1 + \cdots + y_n e_n \rangle$$

$$= \sum_{i,j=1}^{n} x_i y_j \langle e_i, e_j \rangle = x_1 y_1 + \cdots + x_n y_n.$$

Thus in terms of this orthonormal basis, if X, Y are the coordinate vectors of v and w respectively, the scalar product is given by the ordinary dot product $X \cdot Y$ of the coordinate vectors. This is definitely not the case if we deal with a basis which is not orthonormal. If $\{v_1, \ldots, v_n\}$ is any basis of V, and we write

$$v = x_1 v_1 + \cdots + x_n v_n,$$

$$w = y_1 v_1 + \cdots + y_n v_n$$

in terms of this basis, then

$$\langle v, w \rangle = \sum_{i,j=1}^{n} x_i y_j \langle v_i, v_j \rangle.$$

Each $\langle v_i, v_j \rangle$ is a number. If we let $a_{ij} = \langle v_i, v_j \rangle$, then

$$\langle v, w \rangle = \sum_{i,j=1}^{n} a_{ij} x_i x_j.$$

EXERCISES

1. What is the dimension of the subspace of $\mathbf{R}^6$ perpendicular to the two vectors $(1, 1, -2, 3, 4, 5)$ and $(0, 0, 1, 1, 0, 7)$?

2. Find orthonormal bases for the subspaces of $\mathbf{R}^3$ generated by the following vectors: (a) $(1, 1, -1)$ and $(1, 0, 1)$, (b) $(2, 1, 1)$ and $(1, 3, -1)$.

3. Find an orthonormal basis for the subspace of $\mathbf{R}^4$ generated by the vectors $(1, 2, 1, 0)$ and $(1, 2, 3, 1)$.

4. Find an orthonormal basis for the subspace of $\mathbf{R}^4$ generated by $(1, 1, 0, 0)$, $(1, -1, 1, 1)$, and $(-1, 0, 2, 1)$.

In the next exercises, we consider the vector space of continuous functions on the interval $[0, 1]$. We define the scalar product of two such functions f, g by the rule

$$\langle f, g \rangle = \int_0^1 f(t)g(t) \, dt.$$

5. Let V be the subspace of functions generated by the two functions $f(t) = t$ and $g(t) = t^2$. Find an orthonormal basis for V.

6. Let V be the subspace generated by the three functions $1, t, t^2$ (where 1 is the constant function). Find an orthonormal basis for V.

Hermitian products

We shall now describe the modification necessary to adapt the preceding results to vector spaces over the complex numbers. We wish to preserve the notion of a positive definite scalar product as far as possible. Since the dot product of vectors with complex coordinates may be equal to 0 without the vectors being equal to O, we must change something in the definition. It turns out that the needed change is very slight.

Let V be a vector space over the complex numbers. A **hermitian product** on V is a rule which to any pair of elements v, w of V associates a complex number, denoted again by $\langle v, w \rangle$, satisfying the following properties:

HP 1. *We have $\langle v, w \rangle = \overline{\langle w, v \rangle}$ for all v, $w \in V$. (Here the bar denotes complex conjugate.)*

HP 2. *If u, v, w are elements of V, then*

$$\langle u, v + w \rangle = \langle u, v \rangle + \langle u, w \rangle.$$

HP 3. *If $\alpha \in \mathbf{C}$, then*

$$\langle \alpha u, v \rangle = \alpha \langle u, v \rangle \qquad and \qquad \langle u, \alpha v \rangle = \bar{\alpha} \langle u, v \rangle.$$

The hermitian product is said to be **positive definite** if $\langle v, v \rangle \geq 0$ for all $v \in V$, and $\langle v, v \rangle > 0$ if $v \neq O$.

We define the words **orthogonal, perpendicular, orthogonal basis, orthogonal complement** as before. There is nothing to change either in our definition of **Fourier coefficient** and **projection of v along w**, or in the remarks which we made concerning these.

Example 3. Let $V = \mathbf{C}^n$. If $X = (x_1, \ldots, x_n)$ and $Y = (y_1, \ldots, y_n)$ are vectors in $\mathbf{C}^n$, we define their hermitian product to be

$$\langle X, Y \rangle = x_1 \bar{y}_1 + \cdots + x_n \bar{y}_n.$$

Conditions HP 1, 2 and 3 are immediately verified. This product is positive definite because if $X \neq O$, then some $x_i \neq 0$, and $x_i \bar{x}_i > 0$. Hence $\langle X, Y \rangle > 0$.

Example 4. Let V be the space of continuous complex-valued functions on the interval $[-\pi, \pi]$. If $f, g \in V$, we define

$$\langle f, g \rangle = \int_{-\pi}^{\pi} f(t)\overline{g(t)}\, dt.$$

Standard properties of the integral again show that this is a hermitian product which is positive definite. Let f_n be the function such that

$$f_n(t) = e^{int}.$$

A simple computation shows that f_n is orthogonal to f_m if n, m are distinct integers. Furthermore, we have

$$\langle f_n, f_n \rangle = \int_{-\pi}^{\pi} e^{int} e^{-int}\, dt = 2\pi.$$

If $f \in V$, then its Fourier coefficient with respect to f_n is therefore equal to

$$\frac{\langle f, f_n \rangle}{\langle f_n, f_n \rangle} = \frac{1}{2\pi} \int_{-\pi}^{\pi} f(t) e^{-int}\, dt,$$

which a reader acquainted with analysis will immediately recognize.

We return to our general discussion of hermitian products. We have the analogue of Theorem 5 and its corollary for positive definite hermitian products, namely:

Theorem 7. *Let V be a finite dimensional vector space over the complex numbers, with a positive definite hermitian product. Let W be a subspace of V, and let $\{w_1, \ldots, w_m\}$ be an orthogonal basis of W. If $W \neq V$, then there exist elements $w_{m+1}, \ldots, w_n$ of V such that $\{w_1, \ldots, w_n\}$ is an orthogonal basis of V.*

Corollary. *Let V be a finite dimensional vector space over the complex numbers, with a positive definite hermitian product. Assume that $V \neq \{O\}$. Then V has an orthogonal basis.*

The proofs are exactly the same as those given previously for the real case, and there is no need to repeat them.

We now come to the theory of the norm. Let V be a vector space over $\mathbf{C}$, with a positive definite hermitian product. If $v \in V$, we define its **norm** by letting

$$\|v\| = \sqrt{\langle v, v \rangle}.$$

Since $\langle v, v \rangle$ is real, ≥ 0, its square root is taken as usual to be the unique real number ≥ 0 whose square is $\langle v, v \rangle$.

We have the **Schwarz inequality,** namely

$$|\langle v, w \rangle| \leq \|v\| \, \|w\|.$$

The three properties of the norm hold as in the real case:

For all $v \in V$, we have $\|v\| \geq 0$, and $= 0$ if and only if $v = O$.

For any complex number α, we have $\|\alpha v\| = |\alpha| \, \|v\|$.

For any elements $v, w \in V$ we have $\|v + w\| \leq \|v\| + \|w\|$.

All these are again easily verified. We leave the first two as exercises, and carry out the third completely, using the Schwarz inequality.

It will suffice to prove that

$$\|v + w\|^2 \leq (\|v\| + \|w\|)^2.$$

To do this, we observe that

$$\|v + w\|^2 = \langle v + w, v + w \rangle = \langle v, v \rangle + \langle w, v \rangle + \langle v, w \rangle + \langle w, w \rangle.$$

But $\langle w, v \rangle + \langle v, w \rangle = \overline{\langle v, w \rangle} + \langle v, w \rangle \leq 2|\langle v, w \rangle|$. Hence by Schwarz,

$$\|v + w\|^2 \leq \|v\|^2 + 2|\langle v, w \rangle| + \|w\|^2$$

$$\leq \|v\|^2 + 2\|v\| \, \|w\| + \|w\|^2 = (\|v\| + \|w\|)^2.$$

Taking the square root of each side yields what we want.

An element v of V is said to be a **unit vector** as in the real case, if $\|v\| = 1$. An orthogonal basis $\{v_1, \ldots, v_n\}$ is said to be **orthonormal** if it consists of unit vectors. As before, we obtain an orthonormal basis from an orthogonal one by dividing each vector by its length.

Let $\{e_1, \ldots, e_n\}$ be an orthonormal basis of V. Let $v, w \in V$. There exist complex numbers $\alpha_1, \ldots, \alpha_n \in \mathbf{C}$ and $\beta_1, \ldots, \beta_n \in \mathbf{C}$ such that

$$v = \alpha_1 e_1 + \cdots + \alpha_n e_n$$

and

$$w = \beta_1 e_1 + \cdots + \beta_n e_n.$$

Then

$$\langle v, w \rangle = \langle \alpha_1 e_1 + \cdots + \alpha_n e_n, \beta_1 e_1 + \cdots + \beta_n e_n \rangle$$

$$= \sum_{i,j=1}^{n} \alpha_i \bar{\beta}_j \langle e_i, e_j \rangle$$

$$= \alpha_1 \bar{\beta}_1 + \cdots + \alpha_n \bar{\beta}_n.$$

Thus in terms of this orthonormal basis, if A, B are the coordinate vectors of v and w respectively, the hermitian product is given by the product described in Example 3, namely $A \cdot \bar{B}$.

We now have theorems which we state simultaneously for the real and complex cases. The proofs are word for word the same as the proof of Theorem 6, and so will not be reproduced.

Theorem 8   *Let V be either a vector space over $\mathbf{R}$ with a positive definite scalar product, or a vector space over $\mathbf{C}$ with a positive definite hermitian product. Assume that V has finite dimension n. Let W be a subspace of V of dimension r. Let $W^\perp$ be the subspace of V consisting of all elements of V which are perpendicular to W. Then $W^\perp$ has dimension $n - r$. In other words,*

$$\dim W + \dim W^\perp = \dim V.$$

Theorem 9.   *Let V be either a vector space over $\mathbf{R}$ with a positive definite scalar product, or a vector space over $\mathbf{C}$ with a positive definite hermitian product. Assume that V is finite dimensional. Let W be a subspace of V. Then V is the direct sum of W and $W^\perp$.*

EXERCISES

1. Find an orthonormal basis for the subspaces of $\mathbf{R}^3$ generated by the following vectors:
    (a) $(1, 1, -1)$ and $(1, 0, 1)$ (b) $(2, 1, 1)$ and $(1, 3, -1)$
2. Find an orthonormal basis for the subspace of $\mathbf{R}^4$ generated by the following vectors:
    (a) $(1, 2, 1, 0)$ and $(1, 2, 3, 1)$
    (b) $(1, 1, 0, 0)$, $(1, -1, 1, 1)$ and $(-1, 0, 2, 1)$

3. In the next exercises, we consider the vector space of continuous real-valued functions on the interval $[0, 1]$. We define the scalar product of two such functions f, g by the rule

$$\langle f, g \rangle = \int_0^1 f(t)g(t)\, dt.$$

Using standard properties of the integral, verify that this is a scalar product.

4. Let V be the subspace of functions generated by the two functions f, g such that $f(t) = t$ and $g(t) = t^2$. Find an orthonormal basis for V.

5. Let V be the subspace generated by the three functions 1, t, t^2 (where 1 is the constant function). Find an orthonormal basis for V.

6. Find an orthonormal basis for the subspace of $\mathbf{C}^3$ generated by the following vectors:

   (a) $(1, i, 0)$ and $(1, 1, 1)$ (b) $(1, -1, -i)$ and $(i, 1, 2)$

7. (a) Let V be the vector space of all $n \times n$ matrices over $\mathbf{R}$, and define the scalar product of two matrices A, B by

$$\langle A, B \rangle = \operatorname{tr}(AB),$$

where tr is the trace (sum of the diagonal elements). Show that this is a scalar product and that it is non-degenerate.

   (b) If A is a real symmetric matrix, show that $\operatorname{tr}(AA) \geqq 0$, and $\operatorname{tr}(AA) > 0$ if $A \neq 0$. Thus the trace defines a positive definite scalar product on the space of real symmetric matrices.

   (c) Let V be the vector space of real $n \times n$ symmetric matrices. What is dim V? What is the dimension of the subspace W consisting of those matrices A such that $\operatorname{tr}(A) = 0$? What is the dimension of the orthogonal complement $W^\perp$ relative to the positive definite scalar product of part (b)?

8. Notation as in Exercise 7, describe the orthogonal complement of the subspace of diagonal matrices   What is the dimension of this orthogonal complement?

9. Let V be a finite dimensional space over $\mathbf{R}$, with a positive definite scalar product. Let $\{v_1, \ldots, v_m\}$ be a set of elements of v, of norm 1, and mutually perpendicular (i.e. $\langle v_i, v_j \rangle = 0$ if $i \neq j$). Assume that for every $v \in V$ we have

$$\|v\|^2 = \sum_{i=1}^m \langle v, v_i \rangle^2.$$

Show that $\{v_1, \ldots, v_m\}$ is a basis of V.

10. Let V be a finite dimensional space over $\mathbf{R}$, with a positive definite scalar product. Prove the parallelogram law, for any elements v, $w \in V$,

$$\|u + v\|^2 + \|u - v\|^2 = 2(\|u\|^2 + \|v\|^2).$$

§3. *Application to linear equations*

Theorem 6 of the preceding section has an interesting application to the theory of linear equations. We consider such a system:

$$(**) \qquad \begin{aligned} a_{11}x_1 + \cdots + a_{1n}x_n &= 0 \\ &\;\vdots \\ a_{m1}x_1 + \cdots + a_{mn}x_n &= 0. \end{aligned}$$

We can interpret its space of solutions in three ways:

> (a) *It consists of those vectors X giving linear relations*
>
> $$x_1 A^1 + \cdots + x_n A^n = O$$
>
> *between the columns of A.*
> (b) *The solutions form the space orthogonal to the row vectors of the matrix A.*
> (c) *The solutions form the kernel of the linear map represented by A, i.e. are the solutions of the equation $AX = O$.*

We assume that these equations have coefficients a_{ij} in a field K. For the next theorem, we shall assume that if W is a subspace of K^n and $W^\perp$ is the subspace of K^n which is orthogonal to W, then

$$\dim W + \dim W^\perp = n.$$

This has been proved in the positive definite case, and will be proved in general in §5.

If $A = (a_{ij})$ is an $m \times n$ matrix, then the columns $A^1, \ldots, A^n$ generate a subspace, whose dimension is called the **column rank** of A. The rows $A_1, \ldots, A_m$ of A generate a subspace whose dimension is called the **row rank** of A. We may also say that the column rank of A is the maximum number of linearly independent columns, and the row rank is the maximum number of linearly independent rows of A.

Theorem 10. *Let $A = (a_{ij})$ be an $m \times n$ matrix. Then the row rank and the column rank of A are equal to the same number r. Furthermore, $n - r$ is the dimension of the space of solutions of the system of linear equations $(**)$.*

Proof. We shall prove all our statements simultaneously. We consider the map

$$L: K^n \to K^m$$

given by

$$L(X) = x_1 A^1 + \cdots + x_n A^n.$$

This map is obviously linear. Its image consists of the space generated by the column vectors of A. Its kernel is by definition the space of solutions of the system of linear equations. By Theorem 3 of Chapter IV, §3, we obtain

column rank + dim space of solutions = n.

On the other hand, interpreting the space of solutions as the orthogonal space to the row vectors, and using the theorem on the dimension of an orthogonal subspace, we obtain

row rank + dim space of solutions = n.

From this all our assertions follow at once, and Theorem 10 is proved.

In view of Theorem 10, the row rank, or the column rank, is also called the **rank.**

Let $b_1, \ldots, b_m$ be numbers, and consider the system of inhomogeneous equations

$$(*) \qquad \begin{aligned} A_1 \cdot X &= b_1 \\ &\vdots \\ A_m \cdot X &= b_m. \end{aligned}$$

It may happen that this system has no solution at all, i.e. that the equations are inconsistent. For instance, the system

$$2x + 3y - z = 1,$$
$$2x + 3y - z = 2$$

has no solution. However, if there is at least one solution, then all solutions are obtainable from this one by adding an arbitrary solution of the associated homogeneous system $(**)$ (cf. Exercise 7). Hence in this case again, we can speak of the dimension of the set of solutions. It is the dimension of the associated homogeneous system.

Example 1. Find the rank of the matrix

$$\begin{pmatrix} 2 & 1 & 1 \\ 0 & 1 & -1 \end{pmatrix}.$$

There are only two rows, so the rank is at most 2. On the other hand, the two columns

$$\begin{pmatrix} 2 \\ 0 \end{pmatrix} \quad \text{and} \quad \begin{pmatrix} 1 \\ 1 \end{pmatrix}$$

are linearly independent, for if a, b are numbers such that

$$a \begin{pmatrix} 2 \\ 0 \end{pmatrix} + b \begin{pmatrix} 1 \\ 1 \end{pmatrix} = \begin{pmatrix} 0 \\ 0 \end{pmatrix},$$

then

$$2a + b = 0,$$
$$b = 0,$$

so that $a = 0$. Therefore the two columns are linearly independent, and the rank is equal to 2.

Example 2. Find the dimension of the set of solutions of the following system of equations, and determine this set in $\mathbf{R}^3$:

$$2x + y + z = 1,$$
$$y - z = 0.$$

We see by inspection that there is at least one solution, namely $x = \frac{1}{2}$, $y = z = 0$. The rank of the matrix

$$\begin{pmatrix} 2 & 1 & 1 \\ 0 & 1 & -1 \end{pmatrix}$$

is 2. Hence the dimension of the set of solutions is 1. The vector space of solutions of the homogeneous system has dimension 1, and one solution is easily found to be

$$y = z = 1, \qquad x = -\tfrac{1}{2}.$$

Hence the set of solutions of the inhomogeneous system is the set of all vectors

$$(\tfrac{1}{2}, 0, 0) + t(-\tfrac{1}{2}, 1, 1),$$

where t ranges over all real numbers. We see that our set of solutions is a straight line.

Example 3. Find a basis for the space of solutions of the equation

$$3x - 2y + z = 0.$$

The space of solutions is the space orthogonal to the vector $(3, -2, 1)$ and hence has dimension 2. There are of course many bases for this space. To find one, we first extend $(3, -2, 1) = A$ to a basis of $\mathbf{R}^3$. We do this by selecting vectors B, C such that A, B, C are linearly independent. For instance, take

$$B = (0, 1, 0)$$

and

$$C = (0, 0, 1).$$

Then A, B, C are linearly independent. To see this, we proceed as usual. If a, b, c are numbers such that

$$aA + bB + cC = 0,$$

then

$$\begin{aligned} 3a \quad\quad\quad &= 0, \\ -2a + b \quad\quad &= 0, \\ a \quad\quad + c &= 0. \end{aligned}$$

This is easily solved to see that

$$a = b = c = 0,$$

so A, B, C are linearly independent. Now we must orthogonalize these vectors.

Let

$$B' = B - \frac{\langle B, A \rangle}{\langle A, A \rangle} A = (\tfrac{3}{7}, \tfrac{5}{7}, \tfrac{1}{7}),$$

$$C' = C - \frac{\langle C, A \rangle}{\langle A, A \rangle} A - \frac{\langle C, B' \rangle}{\langle B', B' \rangle} B'$$

$$= (0, 0, 1) - \tfrac{1}{14}(3, -2, 1) - \tfrac{1}{35}(3, 5, 1).$$

Then $\{B', C'\}$ is a basis for the space of solutions of the given equation.

EXERCISES

1. Find the rank of the following matrices.

(a) $\begin{pmatrix} 2 & 1 & 3 \\ 7 & 2 & 0 \end{pmatrix}$

(b) $\begin{pmatrix} -1 & 2 & -2 \\ 3 & 4 & -5 \end{pmatrix}$

(c) $\begin{pmatrix} 1 & 2 & 7 \\ 2 & 4 & -1 \end{pmatrix}$

(d) $\begin{pmatrix} 1 & 2 & -3 \\ -1 & -2 & 3 \\ 4 & 8 & -12 \\ 0 & 0 & 0 \end{pmatrix}$

(e) $\begin{pmatrix} 2 & 0 \\ 0 & -5 \end{pmatrix}$

(f) $\begin{pmatrix} -1 & 0 & 1 \\ 0 & 2 & 3 \\ 0 & 0 & 7 \end{pmatrix}$

(g) $\begin{pmatrix} 2 & 0 & 0 \\ -5 & 1 & 2 \\ 3 & 8 & -7 \end{pmatrix}$

(h) $\begin{pmatrix} 1 & 2 & -3 \\ -1 & -2 & 3 \\ 4 & 8 & -12 \\ 1 & -1 & 5 \end{pmatrix}$

2. Let A, B be two matrices which can be multiplied. Show that rank of $AB \leqq$ rank of A, and also rank of $AB \leqq$ rank of B.

3. Let A be a triangular matrix

$$\begin{pmatrix} a_{11} & a_{12} & \cdots & a_{1n} \\ 0 & a_{22} & \cdots & a_{2n} \\ \vdots & \vdots & \ddots & \vdots \\ 0 & 0 & \cdots & a_{nn} \end{pmatrix}.$$

Assume that none of the diagonal elements is equal to 0. What is the rank of A?

4. Find the dimension of the space of solutions of the following systems of equations. Also find a basis for this space of solutions.

(a) $2x + y - z = 0$
    $y + z = 0$

(b) $x - y + z = 0$

(c) $4x + 7y - \pi z = 0$
    $2x - y + z = 0$

(d) $x + y + z = 0$
    $x - y = 0$
    $y + z = 0$

5. What is the dimension of the space of solutions of the following systems of linear equations?

(a) $2x - 3y + z = 0$
    $x + y - z = 0$

(b) $\quad 2x + 7y = 0$
    $x - 2y + z = 0$

(c) $2x - 3y + z = 0$
    $x + y - z = 0$
    $3x + 4y = 0$
    $5x + y + z = 0$

(d) $\quad x + y + z = 0$
    $2x + 2y + 2z = 0$

6. Let A be a non-zero vector in n-space. Let P be a point in n-space. What is the dimension of the set of solutions of the equation

$$X \cdot A = P \cdot A?$$

7. Let $AX = B$ be a system of linear equations, where A is an $m \times n$ matrix, X is an n-vector, and B is an m-vector. Assume that there is one solution $X = X_0$. Show that every solution is of the form $X_0 + Y$, where Y is a solution of the homogeneous system $AY = O$, and conversely any vector of the form $X_0 + Y$ is a solution.

8. Let A be an $m \times n$ matrix of rank r. Let $L_A \colon \mathbf{R}^n \to \mathbf{R}^m$ be the usual linear map such that $L_A(X) = AX$ for $X \in \mathbf{R}^n$ (X is a column vector). Show that r is the dimension of the image of L_A.

§4. Bilinear maps and matrices

Let U, V, W be vector spaces over K, and let

$$\varphi \colon U \times V \to W$$

be a map. We say that φ is **bilinear** if for each fixed $u \in U$ the map

$$v \mapsto \varphi(u, v)$$

is linear, and for each fixed $v \in V$, the map

$$u \mapsto \varphi(u, v)$$

is linear. The first condition written out reads

$$\varphi(u, v_1 + v_2) = \varphi(u, v_1) + \varphi(u, v_2)$$
$$\varphi(u, cv) = c\varphi(u, v),$$

and similarly for the second condition on the other side.

Example. Let A be an $m \times n$ matrix, $A = (a_{ij})$. We can define a map

$$\varphi_A \colon K^m \times K^n \to K$$

by letting

$$\varphi_A(X, Y) = {}^t X A Y,$$

which written out looks like this:

$$(x_1, \ldots, x_m) \begin{pmatrix} a_{11} & \cdots & a_{1n} \\ \vdots & & \vdots \\ a_{m1} & \cdots & a_{mn} \end{pmatrix} \begin{pmatrix} y_1 \\ \vdots \\ y_n \end{pmatrix}.$$

Our vectors X and Y are supposed to be column vectors, so that ${}^t X$ is a row vector, as shown. Then ${}^t X A$ is a row vector, and ${}^t X A Y$ is a 1×1 matrix, i.e. a number. Thus φ_A maps pairs of vectors into K. Such a map φ_A satisfies properties similar to those of a scalar product. If we fix X, then the map $Y \mapsto {}^t X A Y$ is linear, and if we fix Y, then the map $X \mapsto {}^t X A Y$ is also linear. In other words, say fixing X, we have

$$\varphi_A(X, Y + Y') = \varphi_A(X, Y) + \varphi_A(X, Y'),$$
$$\varphi_A(X, cY) = c\varphi_A(X, Y),$$

and similarly on the other side. This is merely a reformulation of properties of multiplication of matrices, namely

$$^t X A(Y + Y') = {}^t X A Y + {}^t X A Y',$$
$$^t X A(cY) = c {}^t X A Y.$$

It is convenient to write out the multiplication ${}^t X A Y$ as a sum. Note that

$$^t X A = \sum_{i=1}^m x_i a_{ij},$$

and thus

$$^t X A Y = \sum_{j=1}^n \sum_{i=1}^m x_i a_{ij} y_j = \sum_{j=1}^n \sum_{i=1}^m a_{ij} x_i y_j.$$

Let us take a numerical example. Let

$$A = \begin{pmatrix} 1 & 2 \\ 3 & -1 \end{pmatrix}$$

If $X = \begin{pmatrix} x_1 \\ x_2 \end{pmatrix}$ and $Y = \begin{pmatrix} y_1 \\ y_2 \end{pmatrix}$ then

$$^t X A Y = x_1 y_1 + 2 x_1 y_2 + 3 x_2 y_1 - x_2 y_2.$$

Theorem 11.   *Given a bilinear map $\varphi \colon K^m \times K^n \to K$, there exists a unique matrix A such that $\varphi = \varphi_A$, i.e. such that*

$$\varphi(X, Y) = {}^t X A Y.$$

The set of bilinear maps of $K^n K^m$ into K is a vector space, denoted by $\mathrm{Bil}(K^n \times K^m, K)$, and the association

$$A \longmapsto \varphi_A$$

gives an isomorphism between $\mathrm{Mat}_{m \times n}(K)$ and $\mathrm{Bil}(K^n \times K^m, K)$.

Proof. We first prove the first statement, concerning the existence of a unique matrix A such that $\varphi = \varphi_A$. This statement is similar to the statement representing linear maps by matrices, and its proof is an extension of previous proofs. Remember that we used the standard bases for K^n to prove these previous results, and we used coordinates. We do the same here. Let $E^1, \ldots, E^m$ be the standard unit vectors for K^m, and let $U^1, \ldots, U^n$ be the standard unit vectors for K^n. We can then write any $X \in K^m$ as

$$X = \sum_{i=1}^{m} x_i E^i$$

and any $Y \in K^n$ as

$$Y = \sum_{j=1}^{n} y_j U^j.$$

Then

$$\varphi(X, Y) = \varphi(x_1 E^1 + \cdots + x_m E^m, y_1 U^1 + \cdots + y_n U^n).$$

Using the linearity on the left, we find

$$\varphi(X, Y) = \sum_{i=1}^{m} x_i \varphi(E^i, y_1 U^1 + \cdots + y_n U^n).$$

Using the linearity on the right, we find

$$\varphi(X, Y) = \sum_{i=1}^{m} \sum_{j=1}^{n} x_i y_j \varphi(E^i, U^j).$$

Let

$$a_{ij} = \varphi(E^i, U^j).$$

Then we see that

$$\varphi(X, Y) = \sum_{i=1}^{m} \sum_{j=1}^{n} a_{ij}x_i y_j,$$

which is precisely the expression we obtained for the product

$${}^t X A Y,$$

where A is the matrix (a_{ij}). This proves that $\varphi = \varphi_A$ for the choice of a_{ij} given above.

The uniqueness is also easy to see. Suppose that B is a matrix such that $\varphi = \varphi_B$. Then for *all* vectors X, Y we must have

$${}^t X A Y = {}^t X B Y.$$

Subtracting, we find

$${}^t X(A - B)Y = 0$$

for all X, Y. Let $C = A - B$, so that we can rewrite this last equality as

$${}^t X C Y = 0,$$

for all X, Y. Let $C = (c_{ij})$. We must prove that all $c_{ij} = 0$. The above equation being true for all X, Y, it is true in particular if we let $X = E^k$ and $Y = U^l$ (the unit vectors!). But then for this choice of X, we find

$$0 = {}^t E^k C U^l = c_{kl}.$$

This proves that $c_{kl} = 0$ for all k, l, and proves the first statement.

The second statement, concerning the isomorphism between the space of matrices and bilinear maps will be left as an exercise.

Exercises

1. Let A be $n \times n$ matrix, and assume that A is symmetric, i.e. $A = {}^t A$. Let $\varphi_A : K^n \times K^n \to K$ be its associated bilinear map. Show that

$$\varphi_A(X, Y) = \varphi_A(Y, X)$$

for all X, $Y \in K^n$, and thus that φ_A is a scalar product, i.e. satisfies conditions SP 1, SP 2, and SP 3.

2. Conversely, assume that A is an $n \times n$ matrix such that

$$\varphi_A(X, Y) = \varphi_A(Y, X)$$

for all X, Y. Show that A is symmetric.

3. Show that the bilinear maps of $K^n \times K^m$ into K form a vector space. More generally, let $\mathrm{Bil}(U \times V, W)$ be the set of bilinear maps of $U \times V$ into W. Show that $\mathrm{Bil}(U \times V, W)$ is a vector space.

4. Show that the association

$$A \mapsto \varphi_A$$

is an isomorphism between the space of $m \times n$ matrices, and the space of bilinear maps of $K^m \times K^n$ into K.

Note: In calculus, if f is a function of n variables, one associates with f a matrix of second partial derivatives.

$$\left(\frac{\partial^2 f}{\partial x_i \, \partial x_j} \right),$$

which is symmetric. This matrix represents the second derivative, which is a bilinear map.

5. Write out in full in terms of coordinates the expression for ${}^t X A Y$ when A is the following matrix, and X, Y are vectors of the corresponding dimension.

(a) $\begin{pmatrix} 2 & -3 \\ 4 & 1 \end{pmatrix}$

(b) $\begin{pmatrix} 4 & 1 \\ -2 & 5 \end{pmatrix}$

(c) $\begin{pmatrix} -5 & 2 \\ \pi & 7 \end{pmatrix}$

(d) $\begin{pmatrix} 1 & 2 & -1 \\ -3 & 1 & 4 \\ 2 & 5 & -1 \end{pmatrix}$

(e) $\begin{pmatrix} -4 & 2 & 1 \\ 3 & 1 & 1 \\ 2 & 5 & 7 \end{pmatrix}$

(f) $\begin{pmatrix} -\frac{1}{2} & 2 & -5 \\ 1 & \frac{2}{3} & 4 \\ -1 & 0 & 3 \end{pmatrix}$

§5. *General orthogonal bases*

Let V be a finite dimensional vector space over the field K, with a scalar product. This scalar product need not be positive definite, but there are interesting examples of such products nevertheless, even over the real numbers. For instance, one may define the product of two vectors $X = (x_1, x_2)$ and $Y = (y_1, y_2)$ to be $x_1 y_1 - x_2 y_2$. Thus

$$\langle X, X \rangle = x_1^2 - x_2^2.$$

Such products arise in many applications, in physics for instance, where one deals with a product of vectors in 4-space, such that if $X = (x, y, z, t)$, then

$$\langle X, X \rangle = x^2 + y^2 + z^2 - t^2.$$

In this section, we shall see what can be salvaged of the theorems concerning orthogonal bases.

Let V be a finite dimensional vector space over the field K, with a scalar product. If W is a subspace, it is not always true in general that V is the direct sum of W and $W^\perp$. This comes from the fact that there may be a non-zero vector v in V such that $\langle v, v \rangle = 0$. For instance, over the complex numbers, $(1, i)$ is such a vector. The theorem concerning the existence of an orthogonal basis is still true, however, and we shall prove it by a suitable modification of the arguments given in the preceding section.

We begin by some remarks. First, suppose that for every element u of V we have $\langle u, u \rangle = 0$. The scalar product is then said to be **null,** and V is called a **null space.** The reason for this is that we necessarily have $\langle v, w \rangle = 0$ for all v, w in V. Indeed, we can write

$$\langle v, w \rangle = \tfrac{1}{2}[\langle v + w, v + w \rangle - \langle v, v \rangle - \langle w, w \rangle].$$

By assumption, the right-hand side of this equation is equal to 0, as one sees trivially by expanding out the indicated scalar products. Any basis of V is then an orthogonal basis by definition.

Theorem 12. *Let V be a finite dimensional vector space over the field K, and assume that V has a scalar product. If $V \neq \{O\}$, then V has an orthogonal basis.*

Proof. We shall prove this by induction on the dimension of V. If V has dimension 1, then any non-zero element of V is an orthogonal basis of V, so our assertion is trivial.

Assume now that dim $V = n > 1$. Two cases arise.

Case 1. For every element $u \in V$, we have $\langle u, u \rangle = 0$. Then we already observed that any basis of V is an orthogonal basis.

Case 2. There exists an element v_1 of V such that $\langle v_1, v_1 \rangle \neq 0$. We can then apply the same method that was used in the positive definite case, i.e. the Gram-Schmidt orthogonalization. We shall in fact prove that *if v_1 is an element of V such that $\langle v_1, v_1 \rangle \neq 0$, and if V_1 is the 1-dimensional space generated by v_1, then V is the direct sum of V_1 and $V_1^\perp$.* Let $v \in V$ and let c be as always,

$$c = \frac{\langle v, v_1 \rangle}{\langle v_1, v_1 \rangle}.$$

Then $v - cv_1$ lies in $V_1^{\perp}$, and hence the expression

$$v = (v - cv_1) + cv_1$$

shows that V is the sum of V_1 and $V_1^{\perp}$. This sum is direct, because $V_1 \cap V_1^{\perp}$ is a subspace of V_1, which cannot be equal to V_1 (because $\langle v_1, v_1 \rangle \neq 0$), and hence must be O because V_1 has dimension 1. Since $\dim V_1^{\perp} < \dim V$, we can now repeat our entire procedure dealing with the space of $V_1^{\perp}$, in other words use induction. Thus we find an orthogonal basis of $V_1^{\perp}$, say $\{v_2, \ldots, v_n\}$. It then follows at once that $\{v_1, \ldots, v_n\}$ is an orthogonal basis of V.

Example 1. In $\mathbf{R}^2$, let $X = (x_1, x_2)$ and $Y = (y_1, y_2)$. Define their product

$$\langle X, Y \rangle = x_1 y_1 - x_2 y_2.$$

Then it happens that $(1, 0)$ and $(0, 1)$ are an orthogonal basis for this product also. However, $(1, 2)$ and $(2, 1)$ are an orthogonal basis for this product, but are not an orthogonal basis for the ordinary dot product.

Example 2. Let V be the subspace of $\mathbf{R}^3$ generated by the two vectors $A = (1, 2, 1)$ and $B = (1, 1, 1)$. If $X = (x_1, x_2, x_3)$ and $Y = (y_1, y_2, y_3)$ are vectors in $\mathbf{R}^3$, define their product to be

$$\langle X, Y \rangle = x_1 y_1 - x_2 y_2 - x_3 y_3.$$

We wish to find an orthogonal basis of V with respect to this product. We note that $\langle A, A \rangle = 1 - 4 - 1 = -4 \neq 0$. We let $v_1 = A$. We can then orthogonalize B, and we let

$$c = \frac{\langle B, A \rangle}{\langle A, A \rangle} = \frac{1}{2}.$$

We let $v_2 = B - \frac{1}{2}A$. Then $\{v_1, v_2\}$ is an orthogonal basis of V with respect to the given product.

EXERCISES

1. Find orthogonal bases of the subspace of $\mathbf{R}^3$ generated by the indicated vectors A, B, with respect to the indicated scalar product, written $X \cdot Y$.

   (a) $A = (1, 1, 1)$, $B = (1, -1, 2)$;
   $X \cdot Y = x_1 y_1 + 2 x_2 y_2 + x_3 y_3$
   (b) $A = (1, -1, 4)$, $B = (-1, 1, 3)$;
   $X \cdot Y = x_1 y_1 - 3 x_2 y_2 + x_1 y_3 + y_1 x_3 - x_3 y_2 - x_2 y_3$

2. Find an orthogonal base for the space $\mathbf{C}^2$ over $\mathbf{C}$, if the scalar product is given by $X \cdot Y = x_1 y_1 - i x_2 y_1 - i x_1 y_2 - 2 x_2 y_2$.

3. Same question as in Exercise 2, if the scalar product is given by

$$X \cdot Y = x_1 y_2 + x_2 y_1 + 4 x_1 y_1.$$

§6. *The dual space*

Let V be a vector space over a field K. We denote by V^* the set of all linear maps of V into K (viewed as a one-dimensional space over itself). We know that V^* itself is a vector space over K, since we can add linear maps, and multiply them by scalars. Elements of V^* will be called **functionals** (on V), and V^* is called the **dual space.**

Let φ be an element of V^* and v an element of V. It will be convenient to denote $\varphi(v)$ by the symbols $\langle \varphi, v \rangle$. The reason for this is that if $\varphi_1, \varphi_2 \in V^*$, then $(\varphi_1 + \varphi_2)(v) = \varphi_1(v) + \varphi_2(v)$, and if $c \in K$, then

$$(c\varphi)(v) = c\varphi(v).$$

In other words

$$\langle \varphi_1 + \varphi_2, v \rangle = \langle \varphi_1, v \rangle + \langle \varphi_2, v \rangle,$$
$$\langle c\varphi, v \rangle = c\langle \varphi, v \rangle.$$

Furthermore, if $v_1, v_2 \in V$, then

$$\langle \varphi, v_1 + v_2 \rangle = \langle \varphi, v_1 \rangle + \langle \varphi, v_2 \rangle,$$
$$\langle \varphi, cv \rangle = c\langle \varphi, v \rangle,$$

these last two properties being nothing else than the definition that φ is linear. Thus we have the same formalism as with scalar products, except for the fact that in the symbol $\langle \varphi, v \rangle$ the two components do not belong to the same space.

Example 1. Let $V = K^n$. Let $\varphi \colon K^n \to K$ be the projection on the first factor, i.e.

$$\varphi(x_1, \ldots, x_n) = x_1.$$

Then φ is a functional. Similarly, for each $i = 1, \ldots, n$ we have a functional φ_i such that

$$\varphi_i(x_1, \ldots, x_n) = x_i.$$

Example 2. Let V be a vector space over K, with a scalar product. Let v_0 be an element of V. The map

$$v \mapsto \langle v, v_0 \rangle, \qquad\qquad v \in V$$

is a functional, as follows at once from the definition of a scalar product.

Example 3. Let V be the vector space of continuous real-valued functions on the interval $[0, 1]$. We can define a functional on V by the formula

$$L(f) = \int_0^1 f(t)\, dt$$

for $f \in V$. Standard properties of the integral show that this is a linear map. If f_0 is a fixed element of V, then the map

$$f \mapsto \int_0^1 f_0(t)f(t)\, dt$$

is also a functional on V.

Example 4. Let V be as in Example 3. Let $\delta \colon V \to \mathbf{R}$ be the map such that $\delta(f) = f(0)$. Then δ is a functional, called the **Dirac functional.**

Let V be a vector space over the complex numbers, and suppose that V has a hermitian product. Let v_0 be an element of V. The map

$$v \mapsto \langle v, v_0 \rangle, \qquad\qquad v \in V$$

is a functional. However, it is not true that the map $v \mapsto \langle v_0, v \rangle$ is a functional! Indeed, we have for any $\alpha \in \mathbf{C}$,

$$\langle v_0, \alpha v \rangle = \bar{\alpha} \langle v_0, v \rangle.$$

Hence this last map is *not* linear. It is sometimes called **anti-linear** or **semi-linear.**

Theorem 13. *Let V be a finite dimensional vector space over the field K. Then the dual space V^* is also finite dimensional, and* $\dim V = \dim V^*$.

Proof. Let $\{v_1, \ldots, v_n\}$ be a basis of V. We shall find a basis of V^*. According to Theorem 1 of Chapter IV, §2 for each $i = 1, \ldots, n$ there exists a functional, which we denote by v_i^*, such that

$$\langle v_i^*, v_j \rangle = \begin{cases} 1 & \text{if } i = j, \\ 0 & \text{if } i \neq j. \end{cases}$$

(The theorem quoted is the one according to which we can find a linear map having prescribed values on basis elements.) We shall prove that $\{v_i^*, \ldots, v_n^*\}$ is a basis of V^*.

Let $\varphi \in V^*$. Let $c_i = \langle \varphi, v_i \rangle$. We contend that

$$\varphi = c_1 v_1^* + \cdots + c_n v_n^*.$$

For each i, we have

$$\langle c_1 v_1^* + \cdots + c_n v_n^*, v_i \rangle = c_i \langle v_i^*, v_i \rangle = c_i.$$

Since $c_i = \varphi(v_i)$, it follows that φ and $c_1 v_1^* + \cdots + c_n v_n^*$ have the same values on all elements of the basis $\{v_1, \ldots, v_n\}$. Hence they have the same values on linear combinations of these basis elements, and hence are equal on V. Therefore $v_1^*, \ldots, v_n^*$ generate V^*.

To prove that they are linearly independent, suppose that

$$x_1 v_1^* + \cdots + x_n v_n^* = 0,$$

with elements $x_i \in K$. Evaluate this expression on v_i. We find

$$0 = \langle x_1 v_1^* + \cdots + x_n v_n^*, v_i \rangle = x_i \langle v_i^*, v_i \rangle = x_i.$$

Hence all $x_i = 0$, and we have proved what we wanted.

The basis $\{v_1^*, \ldots, v_n^*\}$ of V^* described in the proof of the preceding theorem is called the **dual basis** of $\{v_1, \ldots, v_n\}$.

We shall use the same terminology of perpendicularity as with scalar products. Thus if S is a subset of V, and $\varphi \in V^*$, we say that φ is **orthogonal,** or **perpendicular** to S, if

$$\varphi(v) = \langle \varphi, v \rangle = 0$$

for all $v \in S$. The set of elements $\varphi \in V^*$ which are orthogonal to S is a subspace of V^*, which will be denoted again by $S^\perp$ (if the context makes it clear that there is no scalar product on V which might cause confusion). Every element of $S^\perp$ is perpendicular to the subspace of V generated by S.

Theorem 14. *Let V be a finite dimensional space over K. Let W be a subspace. Then*

$$\dim W + \dim W^\perp = \dim V.$$

Proof. Let $\{w_1, \ldots, w_r\}$ be a basis of W. We extend this basis to a basis $\{w_1, \ldots, w_n\}$ of V, using Corollary 1 of Theorem 5 of Chapter II, §3. Let $\{w_1^*, \ldots, w_n^*\}$ be the dual basis. We shall prove that $\{w_{r+1}^*, \ldots, w_n^*\}$ is a basis of $W^\perp$. This will imply our theorem. It will suffice to prove that $w_{r+1}^*, \ldots, w_n^*$ generate $W^\perp$ since they are linearly independent.

Let $\varphi \in W^\perp$. There exist elements $c_1, \ldots, c_n \in K$ such that

$$\varphi = c_1 w_1^* + \cdots + c_n w_n^*.$$

Since $\varphi \in W^\perp$, we have for each $i = 1, \ldots, r$:

$$0 = \varphi(w_i) = c_i \langle w_i^*, w_i \rangle = c_i$$

by definition of the dual basis. Hence

$$\varphi = c_{r+1} w_{r+1}^* + \cdots + c_n w_n^*.$$

This proves that $W^\perp$ is contained in the space generated by $w_{r+1}^*, \ldots, w_n^*$. Conversely, if $r + 1 \leqq j \leqq n$, then

$$\langle w_j^*, w_i \rangle = 0, \qquad\qquad i = 1, \ldots, r.$$

Hence w_j^* is contained in $W^\perp$. This proves that $W^\perp$ contains the space generated by $w_{r+1}^*, \ldots, w_n^*$, and finishes the proof of our theorem.

It is clear from the preceding argument that there is a strong relation between a scalar product on a vector space, and the dual space. We shall make this relation precise.

Let V be a vector space over the field K, and assume given a scalar product on V. To each element $v \in V$ we can associate a functional L_v in the dual space, namely the map such that

$$L_v(w) = \langle v, w \rangle$$

for all $w \in V$. If $v_1, v_2 \in V$, then $L_{v_1 + v_2} = L_{v_1} + L_{v_2}$. If $c \in K$ then $L_{cv} = c L_v$. These relations are essentially a rephrasing of the definition of scalar product. We may say that the map

$$v \mapsto L_v$$

is a linear map of V into the dual space V^*. The next theorem is very important.

Theorem 15. *Let V be a finite dimensional vector space over K, with a non-degenerate scalar product. Given a functional $L \colon V \to K$ there exists a unique element $v \in V$ such that*

$$L(w) = \langle v, w \rangle$$

for all $w \in V$.

Proof. Consider the set of all functionals on V which are of the type L_v, for some $v \in V$. This set is a subspace of V^*, because the zero functional is of this type, and we have the formulas

$$L_{v_1} + L_{v_2} = L_{v_1+v_2} \quad \text{and} \quad L_{cv} = cL_v.$$

Furthermore, if $\{v_1, \ldots, v_n\}$ is a basis of V, then $L_{v_1}, \ldots, L_{v_n}$ are linearly independent. Proof: If $x_1, \ldots, x_n \in K$ are such that

$$x_1 L_{v_1} + \cdots + x_n L_{v_n} = 0,$$

then

$$L_{x_1 v_1} + \cdots + L_{x_n v_n} = 0,$$

and hence

$$L_{x_1 v_1 + \cdots + x_n v_n} = 0.$$

However, if $v \in V$, and $L_v = 0$, then $v = O$ by the definition of non-degeneracy. Hence

$$x_1 v_1 + \cdots + x_n v_n = O,$$

and therefore $x_1 = \cdots = x_n = 0$, thereby proving our assertion. We conclude that the space of functionals of type L_v $(v \in V)$ is a subspace of V^*, of the same dimension as V^*, whence equal to V^*. This proves the theorem.

In the theorem, we say that the vector v **represents** the functional L, with respect to the non-degenerate scalar product.

We may give a shorter proof of Theorem 15. In fact, we prove:

Theorem 15'. *The map $v \mapsto L_v$ of V into V^* is an isomorphism.*

Proof. The kernel of the map is O by non-degeneracy, and since $\dim V = \dim V^*$, we can apply the Corollary of Theorem 6, Chapter IV, §4 to conclude the proof.

We gave the longer proof of Theorem 8 so that a similar argument can be applied later to a similar situation over the complex numbers.

Examples. We let $V = K^n$ with the usual dot product,

$$X \cdot Y = x_1 y_1 + \cdots + x_n y_n,$$

which we know is non-degenerate. If

$$\varphi \colon V \to K$$

is a linear map, then there exists a unique vector $A \in K^n$ such that for all $H \in K^n$ we have

$$\varphi(H) = A \cdot H.$$

This allows us to represent the *functional* φ by the *vector* A.

As a further example, let $V = \mathbf{R}^n$ with the usual dot product. Let $f \colon \mathbf{R}^n \to \mathbf{R}$ be a differentiable function. In calculus, one defines the derivative of f at X to be a linear map $\varphi \colon \mathbf{R}^n \to \mathbf{R}$. The vector which represents L with respect to the dot product is called the **gradient of f at X** and is denoted by $(\operatorname{grad} f)(X)$ or $\nabla f(X)$. Thus by definition we have

$$\varphi(H) = \nabla f(X) \cdot H$$

for all $H \in \mathbf{R}^n$.

As an application of our results concerning the dual space, we obtain the analogue of Theorem 3 for arbitrary non-degenerate scalar products, not only positive definite ones.

Theorem 16. *Let V be a finite dimensional vector space over a field K, with a non-degenerate scalar product. Let W be a subspace of V. Let $W^\perp$ be the subspace of V orthogonal to W. Then*

$$\dim V = \dim W + \dim W^\perp.$$

Proof. Since we shall deal with the scalar product on V and the dual space simultaneously, we shall denote by

$$\operatorname{Perp}_V(W)$$

the space of elements $v \in V$ such that $\langle v, w \rangle = 0$ for all $w \in W$, and by

$$\operatorname{Perp}_{V^*}(W)$$

the space of elements $\varphi \in V^*$ such that $\varphi(w) = 0$ for all $w \in W$. By definition, an element v of V is in $\operatorname{Perp}_V(W)$ if and only if the functional L_v lies in $\operatorname{Perp}_{V^*}(W)$. Hence the map $v \mapsto L_v$ induces an isomorphism between $\operatorname{Perp}_V(W)$ and $\operatorname{Perp}_{V^*}(W)$, which have therefore the same dimension. We apply Theorem 14 to conclude the proof.

Remark. We emphasize that Theorem 16 is true in spite of the fact that V is not necessarily the direct sum of W and $\operatorname{Perp}_V(W)$. For example, let $V = \mathbf{C}^2$ and let W be the subspace of dimension 1 generated by the vector $(1, i)$. We wish to determine $W^\perp$ in $\mathbf{C}^2$, where the perpendicularity is taken with respect to the ordinary dot product of vectors. Then certainly $W^\perp$ contains W since $(1, i) \cdot (1, i) = 0$. On the other hand, by our theorem, $\dim W^\perp = \dim \mathbf{C}^2 - \dim W = 1$. Hence $W^\perp = W$.

Theorem 16 proves the statement we needed for showing that the column rank is equal to the row rank (cf. Theorem 10, §3).

EXERCISES

1. Let A, B be two linearly independent vectors in $\mathbf{R}^n$. What is the dimension of the space perpendicular to both A and B?

2. Let A, B be two linearly independent vectors in $\mathbf{C}^n$. What is the dimension of the subspace of $\mathbf{C}^n$ perpendicular to both A and B? (Perpendicularity refers to the ordinary dot product of vectors in $\mathbf{C}^n$.)

3. Let V be a finite dimensional vector space over the field K. Let U, W be subspaces, and assume that V is the direct sum $U \oplus W$. Show that V^* is equal to the direct sum $U^\perp \oplus W^\perp$.

4. Let W be the subspace of $\mathbf{C}^3$ generated by the vector $(1, i, 0)$. Find a basis of $W^\perp$ in $\mathbf{C}^3$ (with respect to the ordinary dot product of vectors).

5. Let V be a vector space of finite dimension n over the field K. Let φ be a functional on V, and assume $\varphi \neq 0$. What is the dimension of the kernel of φ? Proof?

6. Let V be a vector space of dimension n over the field K. Let ψ, φ be two non-zero functionals on V. Assume that there is no element $c \in K$, $c \neq 0$ such that $\psi = c\varphi$. Show that

$$(\mathrm{Ker}\ \varphi) \cap (\mathrm{Ker}\ \psi)$$

has dimension $n - 2$.

7. Let V be a vector space of dimension n over the field K. Let V^{**} be the dual space of V^*. Show that each element $v \in V$ gives rise to an element λ_v in V^{**} and that the map $v \mapsto \lambda_v$ gives an isomorphism of V with V^{**}.

8. Let V be a finite dimensional vector space over the field K, with a non-degenerate scalar product. Let W be a subspace. Show that $W^{\perp\perp} = W$.

9. Show that the same conclusion as in the preceding exercise is valid if by $W^\perp$ we mean the orthogonal complement of W in the dual space V^*.

10. Let V be a finite dimensional vector space over the field K, and let W_1, W_2 be subspaces. Express $(W_1 + W_2)^\perp$ in terms of $W_1^\perp$ and $W_2^\perp$. Also, express $(W_1 \cap W_2)^\perp$ in terms of $W_1^\perp$ and $W_2^\perp$.

CHAPTER VII

Determinants

We have worked with vectors for some time, and we have often felt the need of a method to determine when vectors are linearly independent. Up to now, the only method available to us was to solve a system of linear equations by the elimination method. In this chapter, we shall exhibit a very efficient computational method to solve linear equations, and determine when vectors are linearly independent.

The cases of 2×2 and 3×3 determinants will be carried out separately in full, because the general case of $n \times n$ determinants involves notation which adds to the difficulties of understanding determinants. In a first reading, we suggest omitting the proofs in the general case.

§1. Determinants of order 2

Before stating the general properties of an arbitrary determinant, we shall consider a special case.

Let

$$A = \begin{pmatrix} a & b \\ c & d \end{pmatrix}$$

be a 2×2 matrix in a field K. We define its **determinant** to be $ad - bc$. Thus the determinant is an element of K. We denote it by

$$\begin{vmatrix} a & b \\ c & d \end{vmatrix} = ad - bc.$$

For example, the determinant of the matrix

$$\begin{pmatrix} 2 & 1 \\ 1 & 4 \end{pmatrix}$$

is equal to $2 \cdot 4 - 1 \cdot 1 = 7$. The determinant of

$$\begin{pmatrix} -2 & -3 \\ 4 & 5 \end{pmatrix}$$

is equal to $(-2) \cdot 5 - (-3) \cdot 4 = -10 + 12 = 2$.

167

The determinant can be viewed as a function of the matrix A. It can also be viewed as a function of its two columns. Let these be A^1 and A^2 as usual. Then we write the determinant as

$$D(A), \qquad \text{Det}(A), \qquad \text{or} \qquad D(A^1, A^2).$$

The following properties are easily verified by direct computation, which you should carry out completely.

As a function of the column vectors, the determinant is linear. This means: let b', d' be two numbers. Then

$$\text{Det}\begin{pmatrix} a & b+b' \\ c & d+d' \end{pmatrix} = \text{Det}\begin{pmatrix} a & b \\ c & d \end{pmatrix} + \text{Det}\begin{pmatrix} a & b' \\ c & d' \end{pmatrix}.$$

Furthermore, *if t is a number, then*

$$\text{Det}\begin{pmatrix} a & tb \\ c & td \end{pmatrix} = t\,\text{Det}\begin{pmatrix} a & b \\ c & d \end{pmatrix}.$$

The analogous properties also hold with respect to the first column. We give the proof for the additivity with respect to the second column to show how easy it is. Namely, we have

$$a(d+d') - c(b+b') = ad + ad' - cb - cb'$$
$$= ad - bc + ad' - b'c,$$

which is precisely the desired additivity. Thus in the terminology of Chapter VI, §4 we may say that the determinant is bilinear.

If the two columns are equal, then the determinant is equal to 0.

If A is the unit matrix,

$$A = \begin{pmatrix} 1 & 0 \\ 0 & 1 \end{pmatrix},$$

then $\text{Det}(A) = 1$.

The determinant also satisfies the following additional properties.

If one adds a multiple of one column to the other, then the value of the determinant does not change.

In other words, let t be a number. The determinant of the matrix

$$\begin{pmatrix} a+tb & b \\ c+td & d \end{pmatrix}$$

is the same as $D(A)$, and similarly when we add a multiple of the first column to the second.

If the two columns are interchanged, then the determinant changes by a sign.

In other words, we have

$$\mathrm{Det} \begin{pmatrix} a & b \\ c & d \end{pmatrix} = -\mathrm{Det} \begin{pmatrix} b & a \\ d & c \end{pmatrix}.$$

The determinant of A is equal to the determinant of its transpose, i.e. $D(A) = D({}^t A)$.

Explicitly, we have

$$\mathrm{Det} \begin{pmatrix} a & b \\ c & d \end{pmatrix} = \mathrm{Det} \begin{pmatrix} a & c \\ b & d \end{pmatrix}.$$

The vectors $\begin{pmatrix} a \\ c \end{pmatrix}$ *and* $\begin{pmatrix} b \\ d \end{pmatrix}$ *are linearly dependent if and only if the determinant* $ad - bc$ *is equal to* 0.

We give a direct proof for this property. Assume that there exist numbers x, y not both 0 such that

$$xa + yb = 0,$$
$$xc + yd = 0.$$

Say $x \neq 0$. Multiply the first equation by d, multiply the second by b, and subtract. We obtain

$$xad - xbc = 0,$$

whence $x(ad - bc) = 0$. It follows that $ad - bc = 0$. Conversely, assume that $ad - bc = 0$, and assume that not both vectors (a, c) and (b, d) are the zero vectors (otherwise, they are obviously linearly dependent). Say $a \neq 0$. Let $y = -a$ and $x = b$. Then we see at once that

$$xa + yb = 0,$$
$$xc + yd = 0,$$

so that (a, c) and (b, d) are linearly dependent, thus proving our assertion.

§2. *Existence of determinants*

We shall define determinants by induction, and give a formula for computing them at the same time. We first deal with the 3×3 case.

We have already defined 2×2 determinants. Let

$$A = (a_{ij}) = \begin{pmatrix} a_{11} & a_{12} & a_{13} \\ a_{21} & a_{22} & a_{23} \\ a_{31} & a_{32} & a_{33} \end{pmatrix}$$

be a 3×3 matrix. We define its determinant according to the formula known as the **expansion by a row**, say the first row. That is, we define

$$(*) \quad \mathrm{Det}(A) = a_{11} \begin{vmatrix} a_{22} & a_{23} \\ a_{32} & a_{33} \end{vmatrix} - a_{12} \begin{vmatrix} a_{21} & a_{23} \\ a_{31} & a_{33} \end{vmatrix} + a_{13} \begin{vmatrix} a_{21} & a_{22} \\ a_{31} & a_{32} \end{vmatrix}.$$

$$= \begin{vmatrix} a_{11} & a_{12} & a_{13} \\ a_{21} & a_{22} & a_{23} \\ a_{31} & a_{32} & a_{33} \end{vmatrix}.$$

We may describe this sum as follows. Let A_{ij} be the matrix obtained from A by deleting the i-th row and the j-th column. Then the sum expressing $\mathrm{Det}(A)$ can be written

$$a_{11} \, \mathrm{Det}(A_{11}) - a_{12} \, \mathrm{Det}(A_{12}) + a_{13} \, \mathrm{Det}(A_{13}).$$

In other words, each term consists of the product of an element of the first row and the determinant of the 2×2 matrix obtained by deleting the first row and the j-th column, and putting the appropriate sign to this term as shown.

Example 1. Let

$$A = \begin{pmatrix} 2 & 1 & 0 \\ 1 & 1 & 4 \\ -3 & 2 & 5 \end{pmatrix}.$$

Then

$$A_{11} = \begin{pmatrix} 1 & 4 \\ 2 & 5 \end{pmatrix}, \qquad A_{12} = \begin{pmatrix} 1 & 4 \\ -3 & 5 \end{pmatrix}, \qquad A_{13} = \begin{pmatrix} 1 & 1 \\ -3 & 2 \end{pmatrix}$$

and our formula for the determinant of A yields

$$\mathrm{Det}(A) = 2 \begin{vmatrix} 1 & 4 \\ 2 & 5 \end{vmatrix} - 1 \begin{vmatrix} 1 & 4 \\ -3 & 5 \end{vmatrix} + 0 \begin{vmatrix} 1 & 1 \\ -3 & 2 \end{vmatrix}$$
$$= 2(5 - 8) - 1(5 + 12) + 0$$
$$= -23.$$

The determinant of a 3×3 matrix can be written as

$$D(A) = \mathrm{Det}(A) = D(A^1, A^2, A^3).$$

We use this last expression if we wish to consider the determinant as a function of the columns of A.

Later we shall define the determinant of an $n \times n$ matrix, and we use the same notation

$$|A| = D(A) = \text{Det}(A) = D(A^1, \ldots, A^n).$$

Already in the 3×3 case we can prove the properties expressed in the next theorem, which we state, however, in the general case.

Theorem 1. *The determinant satisfies the following properties:*

1. *As a function of each column vector, the determinant is linear, i.e. if the j-th column A^j is equal to a sum of two column vectors, say $A^j = C + C'$, then*

$$D(A^1, \ldots, C + C', \ldots, A^n)$$
$$= D(A^1, \ldots, C, \ldots, A^n) + D(A^1, \ldots, C', \ldots, A^n).$$

Furthermore, if t is a number, then

$$D(A^1, \ldots, tA^j, \ldots, A^n) = tD(A^1, \ldots, A^j, \ldots, A^n).$$

2. *If two adjacent columns are equal, i.e. if $A^j = A^{j+1}$ for some $j = 1, \ldots, n - 1$, then the determinant $D(A)$ is equal to 0.*

3. *If I is the unit matrix, then $D(I) = 1$.*

Proof (in the 3 × 3 case). The proof is by direct computations. Suppose say that the first column is a sum of two columns:

$$A^1 = B + C, \quad \text{that is,} \quad \begin{pmatrix} a_{11} \\ a_{21} \\ a_{31} \end{pmatrix} = \begin{pmatrix} b_1 \\ b_2 \\ b_3 \end{pmatrix} + \begin{pmatrix} c_1 \\ c_2 \\ c_3 \end{pmatrix}.$$

Substituting in each term of $(*)$, we see that each term splits into a sum of two terms corresponding to B and C. For instance,

$$a_{11} \begin{vmatrix} a_{22} & a_{23} \\ a_{31} & a_{33} \end{vmatrix} = b_1 \begin{vmatrix} a_{22} & a_{23} \\ a_{31} & a_{33} \end{vmatrix} + c_1 \begin{vmatrix} a_{22} & a_{23} \\ a_{31} & a_{33} \end{vmatrix},$$

$$a_{12} \begin{vmatrix} b_2 + c_2 & a_{23} \\ b_3 + c_3 & a_{33} \end{vmatrix} = a_{12} \begin{vmatrix} b_2 & a_{23} \\ b_3 & a_{33} \end{vmatrix} + a_{12} \begin{vmatrix} c_2 & a_{23} \\ c_3 & a_{33} \end{vmatrix},$$

and similarly for the third term. The proof with respect to the other column is analogous. Furthermore, if t is a number, then

$$\text{Det}(tA^1, A^2, A^3) = ta_{11} \begin{vmatrix} a_{22} & a_{23} \\ a_{32} & a_{33} \end{vmatrix} - a_{12} \begin{vmatrix} ta_{21} & a_{23} \\ ta_{31} & a_{33} \end{vmatrix} + a_{13} \begin{vmatrix} ta_{21} & a_{22} \\ ta_{31} & a_{32} \end{vmatrix}$$
$$= t \, \text{Det}(A^1, A^2, A^3)$$

because each 2×2 determinant is linear in the first column, and we can take t outside each one of the second and third terms. Again the proof is similar with respect to the other columns. A direct substitution shows that if two adjacent columns are equal, then formula (*) yields 0 for the determinant. Finally, one sees at once that if A is the unit matrix, then $\text{Det}(A) = 1$. Thus the three properties are verified.

In the above proof, we see that the properties of 2×2 determinants are used to prove the properties of 3×3 determinants.

Furthermore, there is no particular reason why we selected the expansion according to the first row. We can also use the second row, and write a similar sum, namely:

$$-a_{21} \begin{vmatrix} a_{12} & a_{13} \\ a_{32} & a_{33} \end{vmatrix} + a_{22} \begin{vmatrix} a_{11} & a_{13} \\ a_{31} & a_{33} \end{vmatrix} - a_{23} \begin{vmatrix} a_{11} & a_{12} \\ a_{31} & a_{32} \end{vmatrix}$$
$$= -a_{21}\,\text{Det}(A_{21}) + a_{22}\,\text{Det}(A_{22}) - a_{23}\,\text{Det}(A_{23}).$$

Again, each term is the product of a_{2j}, the determinant of the 2×2 matrix obtained by deleting the second row and j-th column, and putting the appropriate sign in front of each term. This sign is determined according to the pattern:

$$\begin{pmatrix} + & - & + \\ - & + & - \\ + & - & + \end{pmatrix}.$$

One can see directly that the determinant can be expanded according to any row by multiplying out all the terms, and expanding the 2×2 determinants, thus obtaining the determinant as an alternating sum of six terms:

$$(**) \quad \text{Det}(A) = a_{11}a_{22}a_{33} - a_{11}a_{32}a_{23} - a_{12}a_{21}a_{33} + a_{12}a_{23}a_{31}$$
$$+ a_{13}a_{21}a_{32} - a_{13}a_{22}a_{31}.$$

Furthermore, we can also expand according to columns following the same principle. For instance, expanding out according to the first column:

$$a_{11} \begin{vmatrix} a_{22} & a_{23} \\ a_{32} & a_{33} \end{vmatrix} - a_{21} \begin{vmatrix} a_{12} & a_{13} \\ a_{32} & a_{33} \end{vmatrix} + a_{31} \begin{vmatrix} a_{12} & a_{13} \\ a_{22} & a_{23} \end{vmatrix}$$

yields precisely the same six terms as in (**).

The reader should now look at least at the general expression given for the expansion according to a row or column in Theorem 2_n, interpreting i, j to be 1, 2, or 3 for the 3×3 case.

Since the determinant of a 3×3 matrix is linear as a function of its columns, we may say that it is **trilinear**; just as a 2×2 determinant is bilinear. In the $n \times n$ case, we would say **n-linear**, or **multilinear**.

In the case of 3×3 determinants, we have the following result.

Theorem 2. *The determinant satisfies the rule for expansion according to rows and columns, and* $\mathrm{Det}(A) = \mathrm{Det}(^tA)$. *In other words, the determinant of a matrix is equal to the determinant of its transpose.*

This last assertion follows because taking the transpose of a matrix changes rows into columns and vice versa.

Example 1. Compute the determinant

$$\begin{vmatrix} 3 & 0 & 1 \\ 1 & 2 & 5 \\ -1 & 4 & 2 \end{vmatrix}$$

by expanding according to the second column.

The determinant is equal to

$$2 \begin{vmatrix} 3 & 1 \\ -1 & 2 \end{vmatrix} - 4 \begin{vmatrix} 3 & 1 \\ 1 & 5 \end{vmatrix} = 2(6 - (-1)) - 4(15 - 1) = -42.$$

Note that the presence of a 0 in the second column eliminates one term in the expansion, since this term would be 0.

We can also compute the above determinant by expanding according to the third column, namely the determinant is equal to

$$+1 \begin{vmatrix} 1 & 2 \\ -1 & 4 \end{vmatrix} - 5 \begin{vmatrix} 3 & 0 \\ -1 & 4 \end{vmatrix} + 2 \begin{vmatrix} 3 & 0 \\ 1 & 2 \end{vmatrix} = -42.$$

The $n \times n$ case

In the sequel, we deal mostly with 2×2 and 3×3 matrices, so that the reader may omit the discussion of the general case, or simply read the statement of the definitions and properties, and omit the proofs.

The general case of $n \times n$ determinants is done by induction. Suppose that we have been able to define determinants for $(n - 1) \times (n - 1)$ matrices. Let i, j be a pair of integers between 1 and n. If we cross out the i-th row and j-th column in the $n \times n$ matrix A, we obtain an $(n - 1) \times (n - 1)$ matrix, which we denote by A_{ij}. It looks like this:

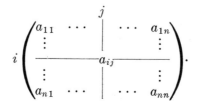

We give an expression for the determinant of an $n \times n$ matrix in terms of determinants of $(n-1) \times (n-1)$ matrices. Let i be an integer, $1 \leqq i \leqq n$. We define

$$D(A) = (-1)^{i+1} a_{i1} \operatorname{Det}(A_{i1}) + \cdots + (-1)^{i+n} a_{in} \operatorname{Det}(A_{in}).$$

Each A_{ij} is an $(n-1) \times (n-1)$ matrix.

This sum can be described in words. For each element of the i-th row, we have a contribution of one term in the sum. This term is equal to $+$ or $-$ the product of this element, times the determinant of the matrix obtained from A by deleting the i-th row and the corresponding column. The sign $+$ or $-$ is determined according to the chess-board pattern:

$$\begin{pmatrix} + & - & + & - & \cdots \\ - & + & - & + & \cdots \\ + & - & + & - & \cdots \\ & & \cdots & & \end{pmatrix}$$

This sum is called the **expansion of the determinant according to the i-th row**. We shall prove that this function D satisfies properties **1, 2,** and **3**.

Note that $D(A)$ is a sum of the terms

$$(-1)^{i+j} a_{ij} \operatorname{Det}(A_{ij})$$

as j ranges from 1 to n.

1. Consider D as a function of the k-th column, and consider any term

$$(-1)^{i+j} a_{ij} \operatorname{Det}(A_{ij}).$$

If $j \neq k$, then a_{ij} does not depend on the k-th column, and $\operatorname{Det}(A_{ij})$ depends linearly on the k-th column. If $j = k$, then a_{ij} depends linearly on the k-th column, and $\operatorname{Det}(A_{ij})$ does not depend on the k-th column. In any case, our term depends linearly on the k-th column. Since $D(A)$ is a sum of such terms, it depends linearly on the k-th column, and property **1** follows.

2. Suppose two adjacent columns of A are equal, namely $A^k = A^{k+1}$. Let j be an index $\neq k$ or $k+1$. Then the matrix A_{ij} has two adjacent equal columns, and hence its determinant is equal to 0. Thus the term corresponding to an index $j \neq k$ or $k+1$ gives a zero contribution to $D(A)$. The other two terms can be written

$$(-1)^{i+k} a_{ik} \operatorname{Det}(A_{ik}) + (-1)^{i+k+1} a_{i,k+1} \operatorname{Det}(A_{i,k+1}).$$

The two matrices A_{ik} and $A_{i,k+1}$ are equal because of our assumption that the k-th column of A is equal to the $(k+1)$-th column. Similarly, $a_{ik} = a_{i,k+1}$. Hence these two terms cancel since they occur with opposite signs. This proves property **2**.

3. Let A be the unit matrix. Then $a_{ij} = 0$ unless $i = j$, in which case $a_{ii} = 1$. Each A_{ij} is the unit $(n-1) \times (n-1)$ matrix. The only term in the sum which gives a non-zero contribution is

$$(-1)^{i+i} a_{ii} \operatorname{Det}(A_{ii}),$$

which is equal to 1. This proves property **3**.

Example 2. We wish to compute the determinant

$$\begin{vmatrix} 1 & 2 & 1 \\ -1 & 3 & 1 \\ 0 & 1 & 5 \end{vmatrix}.$$

We use the expansion according to the third row (because it has a zero in it), and only two non-zero terms occur:

$$(-1) \begin{vmatrix} 1 & 1 \\ -1 & 1 \end{vmatrix} + 5 \begin{vmatrix} 1 & 2 \\ -1 & 3 \end{vmatrix}.$$

We can compute explicitly the 2×2 determinants as in §1, and thus we get the value 23 for the determinant of our 3×3 matrix.

It will be shown in a subsequent section that the determinant of a matrix A is equal to the determinant of its transpose. When we have proved this result, we will obtain:

Theorem 2n. *Determinants satisfy the rule for expansion according to rows and columns. For any column A^j of the matrix $A = (a_{ij})$, we have*

$$\boxed{D(A) = (-1)^{1+j} a_{1j} D(A_{1j}) + \cdots + (-1)^{n+j} a_{nj} D(A_{nj}).}$$

In practice, the computation of a determinant is always done by using an expansion according to some row or column.

EXERCISES

1. Let c be a number and let A be a 3×3 matrix. Show that

$$D(cA) = c^3 D(A).$$

2. Let c be a number and let A be an $n \times n$ matrix. Show that

$$D(cA) = c^n D(A).$$

§3. *Additional properties of determinants*

To compute determinants efficiently, we need additional properties which will be deduced simply from properties **1, 2, 3** of Theorem **1**. There is no change here between the 3×3 and $n \times n$ case, so we write n. But again, the reader may read $n = 3$ if he wishes, the first time around.

4. *Let j be some integer, $1 \leq j < n$. If the j-th and $(j + 1)$-th columns are interchanged, then the determinant changes by a sign.*

Proof. In the matrix A, we replace the j-th and $(j + 1)$-th columns by $A^j + A^{j+1}$. We obtain a matrix with two equal adjacent columns and by property **2** we have:

$$0 = D(\ldots, A^j + A^{j+1}, A^j + A^{j+1}, \ldots).$$

Expanding out using property **1** repeatedly yields

$$0 = D(\ldots, A^j, A^j, \ldots) + D(\ldots, A^{j+1}, A^j, \ldots)$$
$$+ D(\ldots, A^j, A^{j+1}, \ldots) + D(\ldots, A^{j+1}, A^{j+1}, \ldots).$$

Using property **2**, we see that two of these four terms are equal to 0, and hence that

$$0 = D(\ldots, A^{j+1}, A^j, \ldots) + D(\ldots, A^j, A^{j+1}, \ldots).$$

In this last sum, one term must be equal to minus the other, as desired.

5. *If two columns A^j, A^i of A are equal, $j \neq i$, then the determinant of A is equal to 0.*

Proof. Assume that two columns of the matrix A are equal. We can change the matrix by a successive interchange of adjacent columns until we obtain a matrix with equal adjacent columns. (This could be proved formally by induction.) Each time that we make such an adjacent interchange, the determinant changes by a sign, which does not affect its being 0 or not. Hence we conclude by property **2** that $D(A) = 0$ if two columns are equal.

6. *If one adds a scalar multiple of one column to another then the value of the determinant does not change.*

Proof. Consider two distinct columns, say the k-th and j-th columns A^k and A^j with $k \neq j$. Let t be a scalar. We add tA^j to A^k. By property **1**, the determinant becomes

$$D(\ldots, A^k + tA^j, \ldots) = D(\ldots, A^k, \ldots) + D(\ldots, tA^j, \ldots)$$
$$ \uparrow \uparrow \uparrow$$
$$ k k k$$

(the k points to the k-th column). In both terms on the right, the indicated column occurs in the k-th place. But $D(\ldots, A^k, \ldots)$ is simply $D(A)$. Furthermore,

$$D(\ldots, tA^j, \ldots) = tD(\ldots, A^j, \ldots).$$
$$\quad\quad\uparrow \quad\quad\quad\quad\quad\quad\quad \uparrow$$
$$\quad\quad k \quad\quad\quad\quad\quad\quad\quad\quad k$$

Since $k \neq j$, the determinant on the right has two equal columns, because A^j occurs in the k-th place and also in the j-th place. Hence it is equal to 0. Hence

$$D(\ldots, A^k + tA^j, \ldots) = D(\ldots, A^k, \ldots),$$

thereby proving our property **6**.

With the above means at our disposal, we can now compute 3×3 determinants very efficiently. In doing so, we apply the operations described in property **6**, which we now see are valid for rows or columns, since $\mathrm{Det}(A) = \mathrm{Det}(^tA)$. We try to make as many entries in the matrix A equal to 0. We try especially to make all but one element of a column (or row) equal to 0, and then expand according to that column (or row). The expansion will contain only one term, and reduces our computation to a 2×2 determinant.

Example 1. Compute the determinant

$$\begin{vmatrix} 3 & 0 & 1 \\ 1 & 2 & 5 \\ -1 & 4 & 2 \end{vmatrix}.$$

We already have 0 in the first row. We subtract twice the second row from the third row. Our determinant is then equal to

$$\begin{vmatrix} 3 & 0 & 1 \\ 1 & 2 & 5 \\ -3 & 0 & -8 \end{vmatrix}.$$

We expand according to the second column. The expansion has only one term $\neq 0$, with a $+$ sign, and that is:

$$2\begin{vmatrix} 3 & 1 \\ -3 & -8 \end{vmatrix}.$$

The 2×2 determinant can be evaluated by our definition $ad - bc$, and we find $2(-24 - (-3)) = -42$.

Example 2. We wish to compute the determinant

$$\begin{vmatrix} 1 & 3 & 1 & 1 \\ 2 & 1 & 5 & 2 \\ 1 & -1 & 2 & 3 \\ 4 & 1 & -3 & 7 \end{vmatrix}.$$

We add the third row to the second row, and then add the third row to the fourth row. This yields

$$\begin{vmatrix} 1 & 3 & 1 & 1 \\ 3 & 0 & 7 & 5 \\ 1 & -1 & 2 & 3 \\ 4 & 1 & -3 & 7 \end{vmatrix} = \begin{vmatrix} 1 & 3 & 1 & 1 \\ 3 & 0 & 7 & 5 \\ 1 & -1 & 2 & 3 \\ 5 & 0 & -1 & 10 \end{vmatrix}.$$

We then add three times the third row to the first row and get

$$\begin{vmatrix} 4 & 0 & 7 & 10 \\ 3 & 0 & 7 & 5 \\ 1 & -1 & 2 & 3 \\ 5 & 0 & -1 & 10 \end{vmatrix},$$

which we expand according to the second column. There is only one term, namely

$$\begin{vmatrix} 4 & 7 & 10 \\ 3 & 7 & 5 \\ 5 & -1 & 10 \end{vmatrix}.$$

We subtract twice the second row from the first row, and then from the third row, yielding

$$\begin{vmatrix} -2 & -7 & 0 \\ 3 & 7 & 5 \\ -1 & -15 & 0 \end{vmatrix},$$

which we expand according to the third column, and get

$$-5(30 - 7) = -5(23) = -115.$$

EXERCISES

1. Compute the following determinants.

(a) $\begin{vmatrix} 2 & 1 & 2 \\ 0 & 3 & -1 \\ 4 & 1 & 1 \end{vmatrix}$ (b) $\begin{vmatrix} 3 & -1 & 5 \\ -1 & 2 & 1 \\ -2 & 4 & 3 \end{vmatrix}$ (c) $\begin{vmatrix} 2 & 4 & 3 \\ -1 & 3 & 0 \\ 0 & 2 & 1 \end{vmatrix}$

(d) $\begin{vmatrix} 1 & 2 & -1 \\ 0 & 1 & 1 \\ 0 & 2 & 7 \end{vmatrix}$ (e) $\begin{vmatrix} -1 & 5 & 3 \\ 4 & 0 & 0 \\ 2 & 7 & 8 \end{vmatrix}$ (f) $\begin{vmatrix} 3 & 1 & 2 \\ 4 & 5 & 1 \\ -1 & 2 & -3 \end{vmatrix}$

2. Compute the following determinants.

(a) $\begin{vmatrix} 1 & 1 & -2 & 4 \\ 0 & 1 & 1 & 3 \\ 2 & -1 & 1 & 0 \\ 3 & 1 & 2 & 5 \end{vmatrix}$ (b) $\begin{vmatrix} -1 & 1 & 2 & 0 \\ 0 & 3 & 2 & 1 \\ 0 & 4 & 1 & 2 \\ 3 & 1 & 5 & 7 \end{vmatrix}$ (c) $\begin{vmatrix} 3 & 1 & 1 \\ 2 & 5 & 5 \\ 8 & 7 & 7 \end{vmatrix}$

(d) $\begin{vmatrix} 4 & -9 & 2 \\ 4 & -9 & 2 \\ 3 & 1 & 0 \end{vmatrix}$ (e) $\begin{vmatrix} 4 & -1 & 1 \\ 2 & 0 & 0 \\ 1 & 5 & 7 \end{vmatrix}$ (f) $\begin{vmatrix} 2 & 0 & 0 \\ 1 & 1 & 0 \\ 8 & 5 & 7 \end{vmatrix}$

(g) $\begin{vmatrix} 4 & 0 & 0 \\ 0 & 1 & 0 \\ 0 & 0 & 27 \end{vmatrix}$ (h) $\begin{vmatrix} 5 & 0 & 0 \\ 0 & 3 & 0 \\ 0 & 0 & 9 \end{vmatrix}$ (i) $\begin{vmatrix} 2 & -1 & 4 \\ 3 & 1 & 5 \\ 1 & 2 & 3 \end{vmatrix}$

3. In general, what is the determinant of a diagonal matrix

$$\begin{vmatrix} a_{11} & 0 & 0 & \cdots & 0 \\ 0 & a_{22} & 0 & \cdots & 0 \\ \vdots & \vdots & & \ddots & \vdots \\ 0 & 0 & & & 0 \\ 0 & 0 & 0 & \cdots & a_{nn} \end{vmatrix} ?$$

4. Compute the determinant $\begin{vmatrix} \cos\theta & -\sin\theta \\ \sin\theta & \cos\theta \end{vmatrix}$.

5. (a) Let x_1, x_2, x_3 be numbers. Show that

$$\begin{vmatrix} 1 & x_1 & x_1^2 \\ 1 & x_2 & x_2^2 \\ 1 & x_3 & x_3^2 \end{vmatrix} = (x_2 - x_1)(x_3 - x_1)(x_3 - x_2).$$

(b) If $x_1, \ldots, x_n$ are numbers, then show by induction that

$$\begin{vmatrix} 1 & x_1 & \cdots & x_1^{n-1} \\ 1 & x_2 & \cdots & x_2^{n-1} \\ & & \cdots & \\ 1 & x_n & \cdots & x_n^{n-1} \end{vmatrix} = \prod_{i<j} (x_j - x_i),$$

the symbol on the right meaning that it is the product of all terms $x_j - x_i$ with $i < j$ and i, j integers from 1 to n. This determinant is called the **Vandermonde** determinant V_n. To do the induction easily, multiply each column by x_1 and subtract it from the next column on the right, starting from the right-hand side. You will find that

$$V_n = (x_n - x_1) \cdots (x_2 - x_1) V_{n-1}.$$

6. Find the determinants of the following matrices.

(a) $\begin{pmatrix} 1 & 2 & 5 \\ 0 & 1 & 7 \\ 0 & 0 & 3 \end{pmatrix}$ (b) $\begin{pmatrix} -1 & 5 & 20 \\ 0 & 4 & 8 \\ 0 & 0 & 6 \end{pmatrix}$

(c) $\begin{pmatrix} 2 & -6 & 9 \\ 0 & 1 & 4 \\ 0 & 0 & 8 \end{pmatrix}$ (d) $\begin{pmatrix} -7 & 98 & 54 \\ 0 & 2 & 46 \\ 0 & 0 & -1 \end{pmatrix}$

(e) $\begin{pmatrix} 1 & 4 & 6 \\ 0 & 0 & 1 \\ 0 & 0 & 8 \end{pmatrix}$ (f) $\begin{pmatrix} 4 & 0 & 0 \\ -5 & 2 & 0 \\ 79 & 54 & 1 \end{pmatrix}$

(g) $\begin{pmatrix} 1 & 5 & 2 & 3 \\ 0 & 2 & 7 & 6 \\ 0 & 0 & 4 & 1 \\ 0 & 0 & 0 & 5 \end{pmatrix}$ (h) $\begin{pmatrix} -5 & 0 & 0 & 0 \\ 7 & 2 & 0 & 0 \\ -9 & 4 & 1 & 0 \\ 96 & 2 & 3 & 1 \end{pmatrix}$

(i) Let A be a triangular $n \times n$ matrix, say a matrix such that all components below the diagonal are equal to 0.

$$A = \begin{pmatrix} a_{11} & & & & \\ 0 & a_{22} & & * & \\ 0 & 0 & \ddots & & \\ \vdots & \vdots & & \ddots & \\ 0 & 0 & \cdots & & a_{nn} \end{pmatrix}.$$

What is $D(A)$?

7. If $a(t)$, $b(t)$, $c(t)$, $d(t)$ are functions of t, one can form the determinant

$$\begin{vmatrix} a(t) & b(t) \\ c(t) & d(t) \end{vmatrix},$$

just as with numbers. Write out in full the determinant

$$\begin{vmatrix} \sin t & \cos t \\ -\cos t & \sin t \end{vmatrix}.$$

8. Write out in full the determinant

$$\begin{vmatrix} t+1 & t-1 \\ t & 2t+5 \end{vmatrix}.$$

9. Let $f(t)$, $g(t)$ be two functions having derivatives of all orders. Let $\varphi(t)$ be the function obtained by taking the determinant

$$\varphi(t) = \begin{vmatrix} f(t) & g(t) \\ f'(t) & g'(t) \end{vmatrix}.$$

Show that

$$\varphi'(t) = \begin{vmatrix} f(t) & g(t) \\ f''(t) & g''(t) \end{vmatrix},$$

i.e. the derivative is obtained by taking the derivative of the bottom row.

10. Let

$$A(t) = \begin{pmatrix} b_1(t) & c_1(t) \\ b_2(t) & c_2(t) \end{pmatrix}$$

be a 2×2 matrix of differentiable functions. Let $B(t)$ and $C(t)$ be its column vectors. Let

$$\varphi(t) = \mathrm{Det}(A(t)).$$

Show that

$$\varphi'(t) = D(B'(t), C(t)) + D(B(t), C'(t)).$$

11. Let $\alpha_1, \ldots, \alpha_n$ be distinct numbers, $\neq 0$. Show that the functions

$$e^{\alpha_1 t}, \ldots, e^{\alpha_n t}$$

are linearly independent over the complex numbers. [*Hint:* Suppose we have a linear relation

$$c_1 e^{\alpha_1 t} + \cdots + c_n e^{\alpha_n t} = 0$$

with constants c_i, valid for all t. If not all c_i are 0, without loss of generality, we may assume that none of them is 0. Differentiate the above relation $n - 1$ times. You get a system of linear equations. The determinant of its coefficients must be zero. (Why?) Get a contradiction from this.]

12. For this exercise, we assume that the reader is acquainted with polynomials.

(a) Let P_{ij} $(i, j = 1, \ldots, n)$ be polynomials. Assume that all polynomials in a given column in the matrix

$$\begin{pmatrix} P_{11} & \cdots & P_{1n} \\ \vdots & & \vdots \\ P_{n1} & \cdots & P_{nn} \end{pmatrix}$$

have the same degree, and let $d_1, \ldots, d_n$ be these degrees. Let c_{ij} $(\neq 0)$ be the leading coefficient of P_{ij}. Let Q be the determinant of the above matrix. Show that Q has an expression

$$Q(t) = ct^d + \text{terms of degree} < d$$

where $c = \mathrm{Det}(c_{ij})$. Hence if $\mathrm{Det}(c_{ij}) \neq 0$, we see that $Q \neq 0$. (If you wish, do this only for $n = 2$, and then $n = 3$ using the expansion according to a column. The general case can be done by induction. Similarly, you may assume $n = 2$ or 3 in the subsequent parts of the exercise.)

(b) Let D denote the derivative, $D = d/dt$. Let P be a polynomial, and α a number, $\alpha \neq 0$. Show that

$$D(P(t)e^{\alpha t}) = (D + \alpha)P(t)e^{\alpha t},$$

and by induction,

$$D^k(P(t)e^{\alpha t}) = (D + \alpha)^k P(t)e^{\alpha t}.$$

(c) Let $\alpha_1, \ldots, \alpha_n$ be distinct numbers $\neq 0$. Show that the functions $e^{\alpha_1 t}, \ldots, e^{\alpha_n t}$ are linearly independent over the polynomials, i.e. that if $P_1, \ldots, P_n$ are polynomials such that

$$P_1(t)e^{\alpha_1 t} + \cdots + P_n(t)e^{\alpha_n t} = 0$$

for all t, then $P_1, \ldots, P_n$ are the zero polynomials. [*Hint:* Differentiate the above expression $n - 1$ times. Prove that if $\alpha \neq 0$, then

$$\deg(D + \alpha)^k P = \deg P$$

for any polynomial P, and integer $k \geq 0$. You obtain a system of linear equations

$$P_{k1}(t)e^{\alpha_1 t} + \cdots + P_{kn}(t)e^{\alpha_n t} = 0$$

with $k = 0, \ldots, n - 1$. Hence the determinant $\text{Det}(P_{kj})$ must be 0. Apply part (a) to get a contradiction. You should recognize the determinant of leading coefficients as being a special kind of determinant.]

§4. Cramer's rule

The properties of the preceding section can be used to prove a well-known rule used in solving linear equations.

Theorem 3. *Let $A^1, \ldots, A^n$ be column vectors such that*

$$D(A^1, \ldots, A^n) \neq 0.$$

Let B be a column vector. If $x_1, \ldots, x_n$ are numbers such that

$$x_1 A^1 + \cdots + x_n A^n = B,$$

then for each $j = 1, \ldots, n$ we have

$$x_j = \frac{D(A^1, \ldots, B, \ldots, A^n)}{D(A^1, \ldots, A_n)},$$

where B occurs in the j-th column instead of A^j. In other words,

$$x_j = \frac{\begin{vmatrix} a_{11} & \cdots & b_1 & \cdots & a_{1n} \\ a_{21} & \cdots & b_2 & \cdots & a_{2n} \\ \vdots & & \vdots & & \vdots \\ a_{n1} & \cdots & b_n & \cdots & a_{nn} \end{vmatrix}}{\begin{vmatrix} a_{11} & \cdots & a_{1j} & \cdots & a_{1n} \\ a_{21} & \cdots & a_{2j} & \cdots & a_{2n} \\ \vdots & & \vdots & & \vdots \\ a_{n1} & \cdots & a_{nj} & \cdots & a_{nn} \end{vmatrix}}.$$

(The numerator is obtained from A by replacing the j-th column A^j by B. The denominator is the determinant of the matrix A.)

Theorem 3 gives us an explicit way of finding the coordinates of B with respect to $A^1, \ldots, A^n$. In the language of linear equations, Theorem 3 allows us to solve explicitly in terms of determinants the system of n linear equations in n unknowns:

$$x_1 a_{11} + \cdots + x_n a_{1n} = b_1,$$
$$\cdots$$
$$x_1 a_{n1} + \cdots + x_n a_{nn} = b_n.$$

We now prove Theorem 3.

Let B be written as in the statement of the theorem, and consider the determinant of the matrix obtained by replacing the j-th column of A by B. Then

$$D(A^1, \ldots, B, \ldots, A^n) = D(A^1, \ldots, x_1 A_1^1 + \cdots + x_n A_n^1, \ldots, A^n).$$

We use property **1** and obtain a sum:

$$D(A^1, \ldots, x_1 A^1, \ldots, A^n) + \cdots + D(A^1, \ldots, x_j A^j, \ldots, A^n)$$
$$+ \cdots + D(A^1, \ldots, x_n A^n, \ldots, A^n),$$

which by property **1** again, is equal to

$$x_1 D(A^1, \ldots, A^1, \ldots, A^n) + \cdots + x_j D(A^1, \ldots, A^n)$$
$$+ \cdots + x_n D(A^1, \ldots, A^n, \ldots, A^n).$$

In every term of this sum except the j-th term, two column vectors are equal. Hence every term except the j-th term is equal to 0, by property **5**. The j-th term is equal to

$$x_j D(A^1, \ldots, A^n),$$

and is therefore equal to the determinant we started with, namely $D(A^1, \ldots, B, \ldots, A^n)$. We can solve for x_j, and obtain precisely the expression given in the statement of the theorem.

The rule of Theorem 3, giving us the solution to the system of linear equations by means of determinants, is known as **Cramer's rule.**

Example. Solve the system of linear equations:

$$3x + 2y + 4z = 1,$$
$$2x - y + z = 0,$$
$$x + 2y + 3z = 1.$$

We have:

$$x = \frac{\begin{vmatrix} 1 & 2 & 4 \\ 0 & -1 & 1 \\ 1 & 2 & 3 \end{vmatrix}}{\begin{vmatrix} 3 & 2 & 4 \\ 2 & -1 & 1 \\ 1 & 2 & 3 \end{vmatrix}}, \quad y = \frac{\begin{vmatrix} 3 & 1 & 4 \\ 2 & 0 & 1 \\ 1 & 1 & 3 \end{vmatrix}}{\begin{vmatrix} 3 & 2 & 4 \\ 2 & -1 & 1 \\ 1 & 2 & 3 \end{vmatrix}}, \quad z = \frac{\begin{vmatrix} 3 & 2 & 1 \\ 2 & -1 & 0 \\ 1 & 2 & 1 \end{vmatrix}}{\begin{vmatrix} 3 & 2 & 4 \\ 2 & -1 & 1 \\ 1 & 2 & 3 \end{vmatrix}}.$$

Observe how the column

$$B = \begin{pmatrix} 1 \\ 0 \\ 1 \end{pmatrix}$$

shifts from the first column when solving for x, to the second column when solving for y, to the third column when solving for z. The denominator in all three expressions is the same, namely it is the determinant of the matrix of coefficients of the equations.

We know how to compute 3×3 determinants, and we then find $x = -\frac{1}{5}, y = 0, z = \frac{2}{5}$.

Determinants also allow us to determine when vectors are linearly independent.

Theorem 4. *Let $A^1, \ldots, A^n$ be column vectors (of dimension n). If they are linearly dependent, then*

$$D(A^1, \ldots, A^n) = 0.$$

If $D(A^1, \ldots, A^n) \neq 0$, then $A^1, \ldots, A^n$ are linearly independent.

Proof. The second assertion is merely an equivalent formulation of the first. It will therefore suffice to prove the first. Assume that $A^1, \ldots, A^n$ are linearly dependent. We can find numbers $x_1, \ldots, x_n$ not all 0 such that

$$x_1 A^1 + \cdots + x_n A^n = 0.$$

Suppose $x_j \neq 0$. Then

$$x_j A^j = -\sum_{k \neq j} x_k A^k.$$

We note that there is no j-th term on the right hand side. Dividing by x_j we obtain A^j as a linear combination of the vectors A^k with $k \neq j$.

In other words, there are numbers y_k $(k \neq j)$ such that

$$A^j = \sum_{k \neq j} y_k A^k,$$

namely $y_k = -x_k/x_j$. By linearity, we get

$$D(A^1, \ldots, A^n) = D(A^1, \ldots, \sum_{k \neq j} y_k A^k, \ldots, A^n)$$

$$= \sum_{k \neq j} y_k D(A^1, \ldots, A^k, \ldots, A^n)$$

with A^k in the j-th column, and $k \neq j$. In the sum on the right, each determinant has the k-th column equal to the j-th column and is therefore equal to 0 by property **5**. This proves Theorem 4.

Corollary. *If* $A^1, \ldots, A^n$ *are column vectors of* $\mathbf{R}^n$ *such that* $D(A^1, \ldots, A^n) \neq 0$, *and if B is a column vector of* $\mathbf{R}^n$, *then there exist numbers* $x_1, \ldots, x_n$ *such that*

$$x_1 A^1 + \cdots + x_n A^n = B.$$

Proof. According to the theorem, $A^1, \ldots, A^n$ are linearly independent, and hence form a basis of $\mathbf{R}^n$. Hence any vector of $\mathbf{R}^n$ can be written as a linear combination of $A^1, \ldots, A^n$.

In terms of linear equations, this corollary shows:

If a system of n homogeneous linear equations in n unknowns has a matrix of coefficients whose determinant is not 0, then this system has a solution, which can be determined by Cramer's rule.

EXERCISES

1. Solve the following systems of linear equations.

(a) $3x + y - z = 0$
$\quad\ \ x + y + z = 0$
$\quad\quad\quad y - z = 1$

(b) $\quad 2x - y + z = 1$
$\quad\ \ x + 3y - 2z = 0$
$\quad\ \ 4x - 3y + z = 2$

(c) $\quad 4x + y + z + w = 1$
$\quad\ \ x - y + 2z - 3w = 0$
$\quad\ \ 2x + y + 3z + 5w = 0$
$\quad\ \ x + y - z - w = 2$

(d) $x + 2y - 3z + 5w = 0$
$\quad\ 2x + y - 4z - w = 1$
$\quad\quad x + y + z + w = 0$
$\quad -x - y - z + w = 4$

§5. Permutations

(*Note.* The reader who is allergic to combinatorial arguments is advised to understand only the statements of the propositions, and to omit their proofs.)

We shall deal only with permutations of the set of integers $\{1, \ldots, n\}$, which we denote by J_n. By definition, a **permutation** of this set is a map

$$\sigma \colon \{1, \ldots, n\} \to \{1, \ldots, n\}$$

of J_n into itself such that, if $i, j \in J_n$ and $i \neq j$, then $\sigma(i) \neq \sigma(j)$. If σ is such a permutation, then the set of integers

$$\{\sigma(1), \ldots, \sigma(n)\}$$

has n distinct elements, and hence consists again of the integers $1, \ldots, n$ in a different arrangement. Thus to each integer $j \in J_n$ there exists a unique integer k such that $\sigma(k) = j$. We can define the **inverse permutation**, denoted by σ^{-1}, as the map

$$\sigma^{-1} \colon J_n \to J_n$$

such that $\sigma^{-1}(k) =$ unique integer $j \in J_n$ such that $\sigma(j) = k$. If σ, τ are permutations of J_n, then we can form their composite map

$$\sigma \circ \tau,$$

and this map will again be a permutation. We shall usually omit the small circle, and write $\sigma\tau$ for the composite map. Thus

$$(\sigma\tau)(i) = \sigma\big(\tau(i)\big).$$

By definition, for any permutation σ, we have

$$\sigma\sigma^{-1} = id \qquad \text{and} \qquad \sigma^{-1}\sigma = id,$$

where id is the identity permutation, that is, the permutation such that $id(i) = i$ for all $i = 1, \ldots, n$.

If $\sigma_1, \ldots, \sigma_r$ are permutations of J_n, then the inverse of the composite map

$$\sigma_1 \cdots \sigma_r$$

is the permutation

$$\sigma_r^{-1} \cdots \sigma_1^{-1}.$$

This is trivially seen by direct multiplication.

A **transposition** is a permutation which interchanges two numbers and leaves the others fixed. The inverse of a transposition τ is obviously equal to the transposition τ itself, so that $\tau^2 = id$.

Proposition 1. *Every permutation of J_n can be expressed as a product of transpositions.*

Proof. We shall prove our assertion by induction on n. For $n = 1$, there is nothing to prove. Let $n > 1$ and assume the assertion proved for $n - 1$. Let σ be a permutation of J_n. Let $\sigma(n) = k$. If $k \neq n$ let τ be the transposition of J_n such that $\tau(k) = n$, $\tau(n) = k$. If $k = n$, let $\tau = id$. Then $\tau\sigma$ is a permutation such that

$$\tau\sigma(n) = \tau(k) = n.$$

In other words, $\tau\sigma$ leaves n fixed. We may therefore view $\tau\sigma$ as a permutation of J_{n-1}, and by induction, there exist transpositions $\tau_1, \ldots, \tau_s$ of J_{n-1}, leaving n fixed, such that

$$\tau\sigma = \tau_1 \cdots \tau_s.$$

We can now write

$$\sigma = \tau^{-1}\tau_1 \cdots \tau_s = \tau\tau_1 \cdots \tau_s,$$

thereby proving our proposition.

Example 1. A permutation σ of the integers $\{1, \ldots, n\}$ is denoted by

$$\begin{bmatrix} 1 & \cdots & n \\ \sigma(1) & \cdots & \sigma(n) \end{bmatrix}.$$

Thus

$$\begin{bmatrix} 1 & 2 & 3 \\ 2 & 1 & 3 \end{bmatrix}$$

denotes the permutation σ such that $\sigma(1) = 2$, $\sigma(2) = 1$, and $\sigma(3) = 3$. This permutation is in fact a transposition. If σ' is the permutation

$$\begin{bmatrix} 1 & 2 & 3 \\ 3 & 1 & 2 \end{bmatrix},$$

then $\sigma\sigma' = \sigma \circ \sigma'$ is the permutation such that

$$\sigma\sigma'(1) = \sigma(\sigma'(1)) = \sigma(3) = 3,$$
$$\sigma\sigma'(2) = \sigma(\sigma'(2)) = \sigma(1) = 2,$$
$$\sigma\sigma'(3) = \sigma(\sigma'(3)) = \sigma(2) = 1,$$

so that we can write

$$\sigma\sigma' = \begin{bmatrix} 1 & 2 & 3 \\ 3 & 2 & 1 \end{bmatrix}.$$

Furthermore, the inverse of σ' is the permutation

$$\begin{bmatrix} 1 & 2 & 3 \\ 2 & 3 & 1 \end{bmatrix}$$

as is immediately determined from the definitions: Since $\sigma'(1) = 3$, we must have $\sigma'^{-1}(3) = 1$. Since $\sigma'(2) = 1$, we must have $\sigma'^{-1}(1) = 2$. Finally, since $\sigma'(3) = 2$, we must have $\sigma'^{-1}(2) = 3$.

Example 2. We wish to express the permutation

$$\sigma = \begin{bmatrix} 1 & 2 & 3 \\ 3 & 1 & 2 \end{bmatrix}$$

as a product of transpositions. Let τ be the transposition which interchanges 3 and 1, and leaves 2 fixed. Then using the definition, we find that

$$\tau\sigma = \begin{bmatrix} 1 & 2 & 3 \\ 1 & 3 & 2 \end{bmatrix}$$

so that $\tau\sigma$ is a transposition, which we denote by τ'. We can then write $\tau\sigma = \tau'$, so that

$$\sigma = \tau^{-1}\tau' = \tau\tau'$$

because $\tau^{-1} = \tau$. This is the desired product.

Example 3. Express the permutation

$$\sigma = \begin{bmatrix} 1 & 2 & 3 & 4 \\ 2 & 3 & 4 & 1 \end{bmatrix}$$

as a product of transpositions.

Let τ_1 be the transposition which interchanges 1 and 2, and leaves 3, 4 fixed. Then

$$\tau_1\sigma = \begin{bmatrix} 1 & 2 & 3 & 4 \\ 1 & 3 & 4 & 2 \end{bmatrix}.$$

Now let τ_2 be the transposition which interchanges 2 and 3, and leaves 1, 4 fixed. Then

$$\tau_2\tau_1\sigma = \begin{bmatrix} 1 & 2 & 3 & 4 \\ 1 & 2 & 4 & 3 \end{bmatrix},$$

and we see that $\tau_2\tau_1\sigma$ is a transposition, which we may denote by τ_3. Then we get $\tau_2\tau_1\sigma = \tau_3$ so that

$$\sigma = \tau_1\tau_2\tau_3.$$

Proposition 2. *To each permutation σ of J_n it is possible to assign a sign 1 or -1, denoted by $\epsilon(\sigma)$, satisfying the following conditions:*

(a) *If τ is a transposition, then $\epsilon(\tau) = -1$.*

(b) *If σ, σ' are permutations of J_n, then*

$$\epsilon(\sigma\sigma') = \epsilon(\sigma)\epsilon(\sigma').$$

In fact, if $A = (A^1, \ldots, A^n)$ is an $n \times n$ matrix, then $\epsilon(\sigma)$ can be defined by the condition

$$D(A^{\sigma(1)}, \ldots, A^{\sigma(n)}) = \epsilon(\sigma)D(A^1, \ldots, A^n).$$

Proof. Observe that $(A^{\sigma(1)}, \ldots, A^{\sigma(n)})$ is simply a different ordering from $(A^1, \ldots, A^n)$. Suppose first that we deal with a transposition τ, such that $\tau(i) = j$, $\tau(j) = i$ for $i \neq j$, and $\tau(k) = k$ if $k \neq i$, $k \neq j$. Say $i < j$. Consider the determinant

$$D(\ldots, A^j, \ldots, A^i, \ldots) = D(A^{\tau(1)}, \ldots, A^{\tau(n)}),$$

where A^j occurs in the i-th place, and A^i occurs in the j-th place. Making a succession of interchanges of adjacent columns, we move A^j one step to the right each time until it occurs in the $(j-1)$-th place. This involves $j - i - 1$ interchanges. We then interchange A^j with A^i, so that A^j is back to the j-th place, and we are faced with the determinant

$$D(\ldots\ldots, A^i, A^j, \ldots).$$

Finally we interchange adjacent columns, moving A^i back to the i-th place, thus involving $j - i - 1$ interchanges. We then obtain

$$D(A^{\tau(1)}, \ldots, A^{\tau(n)}) = (-1)^{j-i+j-i-1}D(A^1, \ldots, A^n)$$
$$= (-1)D(A^1, \ldots, A^n).$$

Therefore $\epsilon(\tau) = -1$.

Next, let σ be a permutation of J_n. Then

$$D(A^{\sigma(1)}, \ldots, A^{\sigma(n)}) = \pm D(A^1, \ldots, A^n),$$

and the sign $+$ or $-$ is determined by σ, and does not depend on $A^1, \ldots, A^n$. Indeed, by making a succession of transpositions, we can return $(A^{\sigma(1)}, \ldots, A^{\sigma(n)})$ to the standard ordering $(A^1, \ldots, A^n)$, and each transposition changes the determinant by a sign. Thus we may *define*

$$\epsilon(\sigma) = \frac{D(A^{\sigma(1)}, \ldots, A^{\sigma(n)})}{D(A^1, \ldots, A^n)}$$

for any choice of $A^1, \ldots, A^n$ whose determinant is not 0, say the unit vectors $E^1, \ldots, E^n$. There are of course many ways of applying a succession of transpositions to return $(A^{\sigma(1)}, \ldots, A^{\sigma(n)})$ to the standard ordering, but since the determinant is a well defined function, it follows that the sign $\epsilon(\sigma)$ is also well defined, and is the same, no matter which way we select. Thus we have

$$D(A^{\sigma(1)}, \ldots, A^{\sigma(n)}) = \epsilon(\sigma)D(A^1, \ldots, A^n),$$

and of course this holds even if $D(A^1, \ldots, A^n) = 0$ because in this case both sides are equal to 0.

Finally, let σ, σ' be permutations of J_n. Let $C^j = A^{\sigma'(j)}$ for $j = 1, \ldots, n$. Then on the one hand we have

$$(*) \qquad D(A^{\sigma'\sigma(1)}, \ldots, A^{\sigma'\sigma(n)}) = \epsilon(\sigma'\sigma)D(A^1, \ldots, A^n),$$

and on the other hand, we have

$$
\begin{aligned}
D(A^{\sigma'\sigma(1)}, \ldots, A^{\sigma'\sigma(n)}) &= D(C^{\sigma(1)}, \ldots, C^{\sigma(n)}) \\
&= \epsilon(\sigma)D(C^1, \ldots, C^n) \\
&= \epsilon(\sigma)D(A^{\sigma'(1)}, \ldots, A^{\sigma'(n)}) \\
(**) \qquad &= \epsilon(\sigma)\epsilon(\sigma')D(A^1, \ldots, A^n).
\end{aligned}
$$

Let $A^1, \ldots, A^n$ be the unit vectors $E^1, \ldots, E^n$. From the equality between $(*)$ and $(**)$, we conclude that $\epsilon(\sigma'\sigma) = \epsilon(\sigma')\epsilon(\sigma)$, thus proving our proposition.

Corollary 1. *If a permutation σ of J_n is expressed as a product of transpositions,*

$$\sigma = \tau_1 \cdots \tau_s,$$

where each τ_i is a transposition, then s is even or odd according as $\epsilon(\sigma) = 1$ or -1.

Proof. We have

$$\epsilon(\sigma) = \epsilon(\tau_1) \cdots \epsilon(\tau_s) = (-1)^s,$$

whence our assertion is clear.

Corollary 2. *If σ is a permutation of J_n, then*

$$\epsilon(\sigma) = \epsilon(\sigma^{-1}).$$

Proof. We have

$$1 = \epsilon(id) = \epsilon(\sigma\sigma^{-1}) = \epsilon(\sigma)\epsilon(\sigma^{-1}).$$

Hence either $\epsilon(\sigma)$ and $\epsilon(\sigma^{-1})$ are both equal to 1, or both equal to -1, as desired.

As a matter of terminology, a permutation is called **even** if its sign is 1, and it is called **odd** if its sign is -1. Thus every transposition is odd.

Example 4. The sign of the permutation σ in Example 2 is equal to 1 because $\sigma = \tau\tau'$. The sign of the permutation σ in Example 3 is equal to -1 because $\sigma = \tau_1\tau_2\tau_3$.

EXERCISES

1. Determine the sign of the following permutations.

(a) $\begin{bmatrix} 1 & 2 & 3 \\ 2 & 3 & 1 \end{bmatrix}$ (b) $\begin{bmatrix} 1 & 2 & 3 \\ 3 & 1 & 2 \end{bmatrix}$ (c) $\begin{bmatrix} 1 & 2 & 3 \\ 3 & 2 & 1 \end{bmatrix}$

(d) $\begin{bmatrix} 1 & 2 & 3 & 4 \\ 2 & 3 & 1 & 4 \end{bmatrix}$ (e) $\begin{bmatrix} 1 & 2 & 3 & 4 \\ 2 & 1 & 4 & 3 \end{bmatrix}$ (f) $\begin{bmatrix} 1 & 2 & 3 & 4 \\ 3 & 2 & 4 & 1 \end{bmatrix}$

(g) $\begin{bmatrix} 1 & 2 & 3 & 4 \\ 4 & 2 & 1 & 3 \end{bmatrix}$ (h) $\begin{bmatrix} 1 & 2 & 3 & 4 \\ 3 & 1 & 4 & 2 \end{bmatrix}$ (i) $\begin{bmatrix} 1 & 2 & 3 & 4 \\ 2 & 4 & 1 & 3 \end{bmatrix}$

2. In each one of the cases of Exercise 1, write the inverse of the permutation.

3. Show that the number of odd permutations of $\{1, \ldots, n\}$ for $n \geq 2$ is equal to the number of even permutations. [*Hint:* Let τ be a transposition. Show that the map $\sigma \mapsto \tau\sigma$ establishes an injective and surjective map between the even and the odd permutations.]

§6. *Uniqueness*

We make some remarks concerning an expansion of determinants. We shall generalize the formalism of bilinearity discussed in Chapter VI, §4 and first discuss the 3×3 case.

Let X^1, X^2, X^3 be three vectors in $\mathbf{R}^3$ and let (b_{ij}) $(i, j = 1, \ldots, 3)$ be a 3×3 matrix. Let

$$A^1 = b_{11}X^1 + b_{21}X^2 + b_{31}X^3 = \sum_{k=1}^{3} b_{k1}X^k$$

$$A^2 = b_{12}X^1 + b_{22}X^2 + b_{32}X^3 = \sum_{l=1}^{3} b_{l1}X^l$$

$$A^3 = b_{13}X^1 + b_{23}X^2 + b_{33}X^3 = \sum_{m=1}^{3} b_{m1}X^m.$$

Then we can expand using linearity,

$$D(A^1, A^2, A^3) = D\left(\sum_{k=1}^{3} b_{k1}X^k, \sum_{l=1}^{3} b_{l2}X, \sum_{m=1}^{3} b_{m3}X^m\right)$$

$$= \sum_{k=1}^{3} b_{k1}D\left(X^k, \sum_{l=1}^{3} b_{l2}X^l, \sum_{m=1}^{3} b_{m3}X^m\right)$$

$$= \sum_{k=1}^{3} \sum_{l=1}^{3} b_{k1}b_{l2}D\left(X^k, X^l, \sum_{m=1}^{3} b_{m3}X^m\right)$$

$$= \sum_{k=1}^{3} \sum_{l=1}^{3} \sum_{m=1}^{3} b_{k1}b_{l2}b_{m3}D(X^k, X^l, X^m).$$

Or rewriting just the result, we find the expansion

$$D(A^1, A^2, A^3) = \sum_{k=1}^{3} \sum_{l=1}^{3} \sum_{m=1}^{3} b_{k1} b_{l2} b_{m3} D(X^k, X^l, X^m)$$

If we wish to get a similar expansion for the $n \times n$ case, we must obviously adjust the notation, otherwise we run out of letters k, l, m. Thus instead of using k, l, m, we observe that these values k, l, m correspond to an arbitrary choice of an integer 1, or 2, or 3 for each one of the numbers 1, 2, 3 occurring as the second index in b_{ij}. Thus if we let σ denote such a choice, we can write

$$k = \sigma(1), \qquad l = \sigma(2), \qquad m = \sigma(3)$$

and

$$b_{k1} b_{l2} b_{m3} = b_{\sigma(1),1} b_{\sigma(2),2} b_{\sigma(3),3}.$$

Thus $\sigma: \{1, 2, 3\} \to \{1, 2, 3\}$ is nothing but an association, i.e. a function, from J_3 to J_3, and we can write

$$D(A^1, A^2, A^3) = \sum_{\sigma} b_{\sigma(1),1} b_{\sigma(2),2} b_{\sigma(3),3} D(X^{\sigma(1)}, X^{\sigma(2)}, X^{\sigma(3)}),$$

the sum being taken for all such possible σ.

We shall find an expression for the determinant which corresponds to the six-term expansion for the 3×3 case. At the same time, observe that the properties used in the proof are only properties **1**, **2**, **3**, and their consequences **4**, **5**, **6**, so that our proof applies to any function D satisfying these properties.

We first give the argument in the 2×2 case.

Let

$$A = \begin{pmatrix} a & b \\ c & d \end{pmatrix}$$

be a 2×2 matrix, and let

$$A^1 = \begin{pmatrix} a \\ c \end{pmatrix}, \qquad A^2 = \begin{pmatrix} b \\ d \end{pmatrix}$$

be its column vectors. We can write

$$A^1 = aE^1 + cE^2 \qquad \text{and} \qquad A^2 = bE^1 + dE^2,$$

where E^1, E^2 are the unit column vectors. Then

$$
\begin{aligned}
D(A) = D(A^1, A^2) &= D(aE^1 + cE^2, bE^1 + dE^2) \\
&= abD(E^1, E^1) + cbD(E^2, E^1) + adD(E^1, E^2) + cdD(E^2, E^2) \\
&= -bcD(E^1, E^2) + adD(E^1, E^2) \\
&= ad - bc.
\end{aligned}
$$

This proves that any function D satisfying the basic properties of a determinant is given by the formula of §1, namely $ad - bc$.

The proof in general is entirely similar, taking into account the n components. It is based on an expansion similar to the one we have just used in the 2×2 case. We can formulate it in a lemma.

Lemma. *Let $X^1, \ldots, X^n$ be n vectors in n-space. Let $B = (b_{ij})$ be an $n \times n$ matrix, and let*

$$
\begin{aligned}
A^1 &= b_{11}X^1 + \cdots + b_{n1}X^n \\
&\vdots \qquad \vdots \qquad\qquad \vdots \\
A^n &= b_{1n}X^1 + \cdots + b_{nn}X^n.
\end{aligned}
$$

Then

$$
D(A^1, \ldots, A^n) = \sum_\sigma \epsilon(\sigma) b_{\sigma(1),1} \cdots b_{\sigma(n),n} D(X^1, \ldots, X_n),
$$

where the sum is taken over all permutations σ of $\{1, \ldots, n\}$.

Proof. We must compute

$$
D(b_{11}X^1 + \cdots + b_{n1}X^n, \ldots, b_{1n}X^1 + \cdots + b_{nn}X^n).
$$

Using the linearity property with respect to each column, we can express this as a sum

$$
\sum_\sigma b_{\sigma(1),1} \cdots b_{\sigma(n),n} D(X^{\sigma(1)}, \ldots, X^{\sigma(n)}),
$$

where $\sigma(1), \ldots, \sigma(n)$ denote a choice of an integer between 1 and n for each value of $1, \ldots, n$. Thus each σ is a mapping of the set of integers $\{1, \ldots, n\}$ into itself, and the sum is taken over all such maps. If some σ assigns the same integer to distinct values i, j between 1 and n, then the determinant on the right has two equal columns, and hence is equal to 0. Consequently we can take our sum only for those σ which are such that $\sigma(i) \neq \sigma(j)$ whenever $i \neq j$, namely *permutations*. By Proposition 2 of §5, we have

$$D(X^{\sigma(1)}, \ldots, X^{\sigma(n)}) = \epsilon(\sigma)D(X^1, \ldots, X^n).$$

Substituting this for our expression of $D(A^1, \ldots, A^n)$ obtained above, we find the desired expression of the lemma.

Theorem 5. *Determinants are uniquely determined by properties* **1**, **2**, *and* **3**. *Let $A = (a_{ij})$. The determinant satisfies the expression*

$$D(A^1, \ldots, A^n) = \sum_\sigma \epsilon(\sigma)a_{\sigma(1),1} \cdots a_{\sigma(n),n},$$

where the sum is taken over all permutations of the integers $\{1, \ldots, n\}$.

Proof. We let $X^j = E^j$ be the unit vector having 1 in the j-th component, and we let $b_{ij} = a_{ij}$ in the Lemma. Since by hypothesis we have $D(E^1, \ldots, E^n) = 1$, we see that the formula of Theorem 5 drops out at once.

EXERCISES

1. Show that when $n = 3$, the expansion of Theorem 5 is the six term expression given in §2.

2. Let $A^1, \ldots, A^n$ be column vectors of dimension n and assume that they are linearly independent. Show that $D(A^1, \ldots, A^n) \neq 0$. [*Hint:* Express each one of the standard unit vectors $E^1, \ldots, E^n$ viewed as column vectors as linear combinations of $A^1, \ldots, A^n$. Using the fact that $D(E^1, \ldots, E^n) = 1$, and properties **1** and **2**, prove the assertion.] Thus in view of Theorem 3, we can now say that $A^1, \ldots, A^n$ are linearly dependent if and only if $D(A^1, \ldots, A^n) = 0$.

3. Let V, V' be vector spaces. Suppose that we have a product, defined between pairs of elements of V, and denoted by $v \wedge w$ for v, w elements of V. We assume that the values of the product lie in the space V', that is $v \wedge w$ is an element of V' for all v, w in V. Assume that the product satisfies the following conditions:

AP 1. *We have $(u + v) \wedge w = u \wedge w + v \wedge w$ and*

$$u \wedge (v + w) = u \wedge v + u \wedge w$$

for all u, v, w in V. Also for any number c,

$$(cu) \wedge v = c(u \wedge v) = u \wedge (cv).$$

AP 2. *We have $u \wedge u = 0$ for all u in V.*

Prove the following statements:

(a) We have $u \wedge v = -v \wedge u$.

(b) Let z be an element of V', and assume that $V = \mathbf{R}^2$. Let e^1, e^2 be the two unit vectors of $\mathbf{R}^2$. Show that a product satisfying AP 1, AP 2, and the condition that $e^1 \wedge e^2 = z$ is uniquely determined by these three conditions.

(c) Let z_1, z_2, z_3 be elements of V' and let $V = \mathbf{R}^3$. Let e^1, e^2, e^3 be the three unit vectors of $\mathbf{R}^3$. Show that a product satisfying AP 1, AP2, and the conditions

$$e^1 \wedge e^2 = z_1, \qquad e^1 \wedge e^3 = z_2, \qquad e^2 \wedge e^3 = z_3$$

is uniquely determined. [*Hint:* Write arbitrary elements of V in terms of the unit vectors and expand.]

Compare (c) with the formulas for the cross product given in Chapter I. Observe that the cross product satisfies AP 1 and AP 2. A product satisfying these conditions is called an **alternating product**.

4. Let V, V' be vector spaces, and consider a product as described in Exercise 2, satisfying conditions AP 1, and AP 2.

(a) Assume that dim $V = 2$. Show that the set of all elements $v \wedge w$ with v, w in V is a subspace of V', of dimension 0 or 1.

(b) Assume that dim $V = 3$. Let U' be the subspace of V' generated by all elements $v \wedge w$ with v, w in V. Show that U' has dimension ≤ 3.

§7. Determinant of a transpose

Theorem 6. *Let A be a square matrix. Then* $\mathrm{Det}(A) = \mathrm{Det}(^tA)$.

Proof. In Theorem 5, we had

$$(*) \qquad \mathrm{Det}(A) = \sum_\sigma \epsilon(\sigma) a_{\sigma(1),1} \cdots a_{\sigma(n),n}.$$

Let σ be a permutation of $\{1, \ldots, n\}$. If $\sigma(j) = k$, then $\sigma^{-1}(k) = j$. We can therefore write

$$a_{\sigma(j),j} = a_{k,\sigma^{-1}(k)}.$$

In a product

$$a_{\sigma(1),1} \cdots a_{\sigma(n),n}$$

each integer k from 1 to n occurs precisely once among the integers $\sigma(1), \ldots, \sigma(n)$. Hence this product can be written

$$a_{1,\sigma^{-1}(1)} \cdots a_{n,\sigma^{-1}(n)},$$

and our sum $(*)$ is equal to

$$\sum_\sigma \epsilon(\sigma^{-1}) a_{1,\sigma^{-1}(1)} \cdots a_{n,\sigma^{-1}(n)},$$

because $\epsilon(\sigma) = \epsilon(\sigma^{-1})$. In this sum, each term corresponds to a permutation σ. However, as σ ranges over all permutations, so does σ^{-1} because a permutation determines its inverse uniquely. Hence our sum is equal to

$$(**) \qquad \sum_\sigma \epsilon(\sigma) a_{1,\sigma(1)} \cdots a_{n,\sigma(n)}.$$

The sum $(**)$ is precisely the sum giving the expanded form of the determinant of the transpose of A. Hence we have proved what we wanted.

§8. Determinant of a product

We shall prove the important rule:

Theorem 7. *Let A, B be two $n \times n$ matrices. Then*

$$\mathrm{Det}(AB) = \mathrm{Det}(A)\,\mathrm{Det}(B).$$

The determinant of a product is equal to the product of the determinants.

Proof. Let $A = (a_{ij})$ and $B = (b_{jk})$:

$$\begin{pmatrix} a_{11} & \cdots & a_{1n} \\ \vdots & & \vdots \\ a_{n1} & \cdots & a_{nn} \end{pmatrix} \begin{pmatrix} b_{11} & \cdots & b_{1k} & \cdots & b_{1n} \\ \vdots & & \vdots & & \vdots \\ b_{n1} & \cdots & b_{nk} & \cdots & b_{nn} \end{pmatrix}.$$

Let $AB = C$, and let C^k be the k-th column of C. Then by definition,

$$C^k = b_{1k} A^1 + \cdots + b_{nk} A^n.$$

Thus

$$\begin{aligned} D(AB) &= D(C^1, \ldots, C^n) \\ &= D(b_{11} A^1 + \cdots + b_{n1} A^n, \ldots, b_{1n} A^1 + \cdots + b_{nn} A^n). \end{aligned}$$

If we expand this out using the Lemma before Theorem 5, we find a sum

$$\begin{aligned} D(AB) &= \sum_\sigma b_{\sigma(1),1} \cdots b_{\sigma(n),n} D(A^{\sigma(1)}, \ldots, A^{\sigma(n)}) \\ &= \sum_\sigma \epsilon(\sigma) b_{\sigma(1),1} \cdots b_{\sigma(n),n} D(A^1, \ldots, A^n). \end{aligned}$$

According to the formula for determinants which we found, this is equal to $D(B)D(A)$, as was to be shown.

Corollary. *Let A be an invertible $n \times n$ matrix. Then*

$$\mathrm{Det}(A^{-1}) = \mathrm{Det}(A)^{-1}.$$

Proof. We have $1 = D(I) = D(AA^{-1}) = D(A)D(A^{-1})$. This proves what we wanted.

§9. *Inverse of a matrix*

We consider first a special case. Let

$$A = \begin{pmatrix} a & b \\ c & d \end{pmatrix}$$

be a 2×2 matrix, and assume that its determinant $ad - bc \neq 0$. We wish to find an inverse for A, that is a 2×2 matrix

$$X = \begin{pmatrix} x & y \\ z & w \end{pmatrix}$$

such that

$$AX = XA = I.$$

Let us look at the first requirement, $AX = I$, which written out in full, looks like this:

$$\begin{pmatrix} a & b \\ c & d \end{pmatrix} \begin{pmatrix} x & y \\ z & w \end{pmatrix} = \begin{pmatrix} 1 & 0 \\ 0 & 1 \end{pmatrix}.$$

Let us look at the first column of AX. We must solve the equations

$$ax + bz = 1,$$
$$cx + dz = 0.$$

This is a system of two equations in two unknowns, x and z, which we know how to solve. Similarly, looking at the second column, we see that we must solve a system of two equations in the unknowns y, w, namely

$$ay + bw = 0,$$
$$cy + dw = 1.$$

Example. Let

$$A = \begin{pmatrix} 2 & 1 \\ 4 & 3 \end{pmatrix}.$$

We seek a matrix X such that $AX = I$. We must therefore solve the systems of linear equations

$$2x + z = 1, \qquad 2y + w = 0,$$
$$\text{and}$$
$$4x + 3z = 0, \qquad 4y + 3w = 1.$$

By the ordinary method of solving two equations in two unknowns, we find

$$x = 1, \qquad z = -1, \qquad \text{and} \qquad y = -\tfrac{1}{2}, \quad w = 1.$$

Thus the matrix

$$X = \begin{pmatrix} 1 & -\tfrac{1}{2} \\ -1 & 1 \end{pmatrix}$$

is such that $AX = I$. The reader will also verify by direct multiplication that $XA = I$. This solves for the desired inverse.

Similarly, in the 3×3 case, we would find three systems of linear equations, corresponding to the first column, the second column, and the third column. Each system could be solved to yield the inverse. We shall now give the general argument.

Let A be an $n \times n$ matrix. If B is a matrix such that $AB = I$ and $BA = I$ ($I =$ unit $n \times n$ matrix), then we called B an **inverse** of A, and we write $B = A^{-1}$. If there exists an inverse of A, then it is unique. Indeed, let C be an inverse of A. Then $CA = I$. Multiplying by B on the right, we obtain $CAB = B$. But $CAB = C(AB) = CI = C$. Hence $C = B$. A similar argument works for $AC = I$.

Theorem 8. Let $A = (a_{ij})$ be an $n \times n$ matrix, and assume that $D(A) \neq 0$. Then A is invertible. Let E^j be the j-th column unit vector, and let

$$b_{ij} = \frac{D(A^1, \ldots, E^j, \ldots, A^n)}{D(A)},$$

where E^j occurs in the i-th place. Then the matrix $B = (b_{ij})$ is an inverse for A.

Proof. Let $X = (X_{ij})$ be an unknown $n \times n$ matrix. We wish to solve for the components x_{ij}, so that they satisfy $AX = I$. From the definition of products of matrices, this means that for each j, we must solve

$$E^j = x_{1j}A^1 + \cdots + x_{nj}A^n.$$

This is a system of linear equations, which can be solved uniquely by Cramer's rule, and we obtain

$$x_{ij} = \frac{D(A^1, \ldots, E^j, \ldots, A^n)}{D(A)},$$

which is the formula given in the theorem.

We must still prove that $XA = I$. Note that $D({}^tA) \neq 0$. Hence by what we have already proved, we can find a matrix Y such that ${}^tAY = I$. Taking transposes, we obtain ${}^tYA = I$. Now we have

$$I = {}^tY(AX)A = {}^tYA(XA) = XA,$$

thereby proving what we want, namely that $X = B$ is an inverse for A.

We can write out the components of the matrix B in Theorem 8 as follows:

$$b_{ij} = \frac{\begin{vmatrix} a_{11} & \cdots & 0 & \cdots & a_{1n} \\ \vdots & & \vdots & & \vdots \\ a_{j1} & \cdots & 1 & \cdots & a_{jn} \\ \vdots & & \vdots & & \vdots \\ a_{n1} & \cdots & 0 & \cdots & a_{nn} \end{vmatrix}}{\mathrm{Det}(A)}.$$

If we expand the determinant in the numerator according to the i-th column, then all terms but one are equal to 0, and hence we obtain the numerator of b_{ij} as a subdeterminant of $\mathrm{Det}(A)$. Let A_{ij} be the matrix obtained from A by deleting the i-th row and the j-th column. Then

$$b_{ij} = \frac{(-1)^{i+j}\,\mathrm{Det}(A_{ji})}{\mathrm{Det}(A)}$$

(note the reversal of indices!) and thus we have the formula

$$A^{-1} = \text{transpose of } \left(\frac{(-1)^{i+j}\,\mathrm{Det}(A_{ij})}{\mathrm{Det}(A)} \right).$$

A square matrix whose determinant is $\neq 0$, or equivalently which admits an inverse, is called **non-singular**.

EXERCISES

1. Find the inverses of the matrices in Exercise 1, §3.

2. Using the fact that if A, B are two $n \times n$ matrices then

$$\mathrm{Det}(AB) = \mathrm{Det}(A)\,\mathrm{Det}(B),$$

prove that a matrix A such that $\mathrm{Det}(A) = 0$ does not have an inverse.

3. Write down explicitly the inverses of the 2×2 matrices:

(a) $\begin{pmatrix} 3 & -1 \\ 1 & 4 \end{pmatrix}$ (b) $\begin{pmatrix} -2 & 1 \\ 1 & 1 \end{pmatrix}$ (c) $\begin{pmatrix} a & b \\ c & d \end{pmatrix}$

4. If A is an $n \times n$ matrix whose determinant is $\neq 0$, and B is a given vector in n-space, show that the system of linear equations $AX = B$ has a unique solution. If $B = 0$, this solution is $X = 0$.

§10. *The rank of a matrix and subdeterminants*

Since determinants can be used to test linear independence, they can be used to determine the rank of a matrix.

Example 1. Let

$$A = \begin{pmatrix} 3 & 1 & 2 & 5 \\ 1 & 2 & -1 & 2 \\ 1 & 1 & 0 & 1 \end{pmatrix}.$$

This is a 3×4 matrix. Its rank is at most 3. If we can find three linearly independent columns, then we know that its rank is exactly 3. But the determinant

$$\begin{vmatrix} 3 & 1 & 2 \\ 1 & 2 & -1 \\ 1 & 1 & 0 \end{vmatrix}$$

is not equal to 0 (namely, it is equal to -3, as we see by subtracting the second column from the first, and then expanding according to the last row). Hence rank $A = 3$.

It may be that in a 3×4 matrix, some determinant of a 3×3 sub-matrix is 0, but the 3×4 matrix has rank 3. For instance, let

$$B = \begin{pmatrix} 3 & 1 & 2 & 5 \\ 1 & 2 & -1 & 2 \\ 4 & 3 & 1 & 1 \end{pmatrix}.$$

The determinant of the first three columns

$$\begin{vmatrix} 3 & 1 & 2 \\ 1 & 2 & -1 \\ 4 & 3 & 1 \end{vmatrix}$$

is equal to 0 (in fact, the last row is the sum of the first two rows). But the determinant

$$\begin{vmatrix} 1 & 2 & 5 \\ 2 & -1 & 2 \\ 3 & 1 & 1 \end{vmatrix}$$

is not zero (what is it?) so that again the rank of B is equal to 3.

If the rank of a 3×4 matrix

$$C = \begin{pmatrix} c_{11} & c_{12} & c_{13} & c_{14} \\ c_{21} & c_{22} & c_{23} & c_{24} \\ c_{31} & c_{32} & c_{33} & c_{34} \end{pmatrix}$$

is 2 or less, then the determinant of *every* 3×3 submatrix must be 0, otherwise we could argue as above to get three linearly independent columns. We note that there are four such subdeterminants, obtained by eliminating successively any one of the four columns. Conversely, if every such subdeterminant of every 3×3 submatrix is equal to 0, then it is easy to see that the rank is at most 2. Because if the rank were equal to 3, then there would be three linearly independent columns, and their determinant would not be 0. Thus we can compute such subdeterminants to get an estimate on the rank, and then use trial and error, and some judgment, to get the exact rank.

Example 2. Let

$$C = \begin{pmatrix} 3 & 1 & 2 & 5 \\ 1 & 2 & -1 & 2 \\ 4 & 3 & 1 & 7 \end{pmatrix}.$$

If we compute every 3×3 subdeterminant, we shall find 0. Hence the rank of C is at most equal to 2. However, the first two rows are linearly independent, for instance because the determinant

$$\begin{vmatrix} 3 & 1 \\ 1 & 2 \end{vmatrix}$$

is not equal to 0. It is the determinant of the first two columns of the 2×4 matrix

$$\begin{pmatrix} 3 & 1 & 2 & 5 \\ 1 & 2 & -1 & 2 \end{pmatrix}.$$

Hence the rank is equal to 2.

Of course, if we notice that the last row of C is equal to the sum of the first two, then we see at once that the rank is ≤ 2.

EXERCISES

Compute the ranks of the following matrices.

1. $\begin{pmatrix} 2 & 3 & 5 & 1 \\ 1 & -1 & 2 & 1 \end{pmatrix}$

2. $\begin{pmatrix} 3 & 5 & 1 & 4 \\ 2 & -1 & 1 & 1 \\ 5 & 4 & 2 & 5 \end{pmatrix}$

3. $\begin{pmatrix} 3 & 5 & 1 & 4 \\ 2 & -1 & 1 & 1 \\ 8 & 9 & 3 & 9 \end{pmatrix}$
4. $\begin{pmatrix} 3 & 5 & 1 & 4 \\ 2 & -1 & 1 & 1 \\ 7 & 1 & 2 & 5 \end{pmatrix}$

5. $\begin{pmatrix} -1 & 1 & 6 & 5 \\ 1 & 1 & 2 & 3 \\ -1 & 2 & 5 & 4 \\ 2 & 1 & 0 & 1 \end{pmatrix}$
6. $\begin{pmatrix} 2 & 1 & 6 & 6 \\ 3 & 1 & 1 & -1 \\ 5 & 2 & 7 & 5 \\ -2 & 4 & 3 & 2 \end{pmatrix}$

7. $\begin{pmatrix} 2 & 1 & 6 & 6 \\ 3 & 1 & 1 & -1 \\ 5 & 2 & 7 & 5 \\ 8 & 3 & 8 & 4 \end{pmatrix}$
8. $\begin{pmatrix} 3 & 1 & 1 & -1 \\ -2 & 4 & 3 & 2 \\ -1 & 9 & 7 & 3 \\ 7 & 4 & 2 & 1 \end{pmatrix}$

§11. Determinants as area and volume

It is remarkable that the determinant has an interpretation as a volume. We discuss first the 2-dimensional case, and thus speak of area, although we write Vol for the area of a 2-dimensional figure, to keep the terminology which generalizes to higher dimensions.

Consider the parallelogram spanned by two vectors v, w.

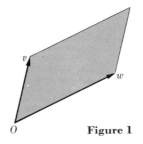

0 **Figure 1**

We view v, w as column vectors, and can thus form their determinant $D(v, w)$. This determinant may be positive or negative since

$$D(v, w) = -D(w, v).$$

Thus the determinant itself cannot be the area of this parallelogram, since area is always ≥ 0. However, we shall prove:

Theorem 9. *The area of the parallelogram spanned by v, w is equal to the absolute value of the determinant, namely $|D(v, w)|$.*

To prove Theorem 9, we introduce the notion of oriented area. Let $P(v, w)$ be the parallelogram spanned by v and w. We denote by $\text{Vol}_0(v, w)$ the area of $P(v, w)$ if the determinant $D(v, w) \geq 0$, and minus the area of $P(v, w)$ if the determinant $D(v, w) < 0$. Thus at least $\text{Vol}_0(v, w)$ has the same sign as the determinant, and we call $\text{Vol}_0(v,w)$ the **oriented area.**

We denote by $\mathrm{Vol}(v, w)$ the area of the parallelogram spanned by v, w. Hence $\mathrm{Vol}_0(v, w) = \pm \mathrm{Vol}(v, w)$.

To prove Theorem 9, it will suffice to prove:

The oriented area is equal to the determinant. In other words,

$$\mathrm{Vol}_0(v, w) = D(v, w).$$

Now to prove this, it will suffice to prove that Vol_0 satisfies the three properties characteristic of a determinant, namely:

1. Vol_0 is linear in each variable v and w.
2. $\mathrm{Vol}_0(v, v) = 0$ for all v.
3. $\mathrm{Vol}_0(E^1, E^2) = 1$ if E^1, E^2 are the standard unit vectors.

We know that these three properties characterize determinants, and this was proved in the section on uniqueness, §6. For the convenience of the reader, we repeat the argument here very briefly. We assume that we have a function g satisfying these three properties (with g replacing Vol_0). Then for any vectors

$$v = aE^1 + cE^2 \qquad \text{and} \qquad w = bE^1 + dE^2$$

we have

$$g(aE^1 + cE^2, bE^1 + dE^2) = abg(E^1, E^1) + adg(E^1, E^2)$$
$$+ cbg(E^2, E^1) + cdg(E^2, E^2).$$

The first and fourth term are equal to 0. By Exercise 1,

$$g(E^2, E^1) = -g(E^1, E^2)$$

and hence

$$g(v, w) = (ad - bc)g(E^1, E^2) = ad - bc.$$

This proves what we wanted.

In order to prove that Vol_0 satisfies the three properties, we shall use simple properties of area (or volume) like the following: The area of a line segment is equal to 0. If A is a certain region, then the area of A is the same as the area of a translation of A, i.e. the same as the area of the region A_w (consisting of all points $v + w$ with $v \in A$). If A, B are regions which are disjoint or such that their common points have area equal to 0, then

$$\mathrm{Vol}(A \cup B) = \mathrm{Vol}(A) + \mathrm{Vol}(B).$$

Consider now Vol_0. The last two properties are obvious. Indeed, the parallelogram spanned by v, v is simply a line segment, and its 2-dimensional area is therefore equal to 0. Thus property **2** is satisfied. As for the third property, the parallelogram spanned by the unit vectors E^1, E^2 is simply the unit square, whose area is 1. Hence in this case we have

$$\text{Vol}_0(E^1, E^2) = 1.$$

The harder property is the first. If the reader has not already done so, he should now read the geometric applications, §5 of Chapter IV, before reading the rest of this proof, which we shall base on geometric considerations concerning area.

We shall need a lemma.

Lemma 1. *If v, w are linearly dependent, then* $\text{Vol}_0(v, w) = 0$.

Proof. Suppose that we can write

$$av + bw = 0$$

with a or $b \neq 0$. Say $a \neq 0$. Then

$$v = -\frac{b}{a} w = cw$$

so that v, w lie on the same straight line, and the parallelogram spanned by v, w is a line segment (Fig. 2). Hence $\text{Vol}_0(v, w) = 0$, thus proving the lemma.

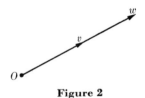

Figure 2

We also know that when v, w are linearly dependent, then $D(v, w) = 0$, so in this trivial case, our theorem is proved. In the subsequent lemmas, we assume that v, w are linearly independent.

Lemma 2. *Assume that v, w are linearly independent, and let n be a positive integer. Then*

$$\text{Vol}(nv, w) = n \, \text{Vol}(v, w).$$

Proof. The parallelogram spanned by nv and w consists of n parallelograms as shown in the following picture.

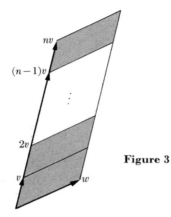

Figure 3

These n parallelograms are simply the translations of $P(v, w)$ by $v, 2v, \ldots, (n-1)v$, and each translation of $P(v, w)$ has the same area as $P(v, w)$. These translations have only line segments in common, and hence

$$\mathrm{Vol}(nv, w) = n\, \mathrm{Vol}(v, w)$$

as desired.

Corollary. *Assume that v, w are linearly independent and let n be a positive integer. Then*

$$\mathrm{Vol}\left(\frac{1}{n}v, w\right) = \frac{1}{n}\,\mathrm{Vol}(v, w).$$

If m, n are positive integers, then

$$\mathrm{Vol}\left(\frac{m}{n}v, w\right) = \frac{m}{n}\,\mathrm{Vol}(v, w).$$

Proof. Let $v_1 = (1/n)v$. By the lemma, we know that

$$\mathrm{Vol}(nv_1, w) = n\,\mathrm{Vol}(v_1, w).$$

This is merely a reformulation of our first assertion, since $nv_1 = v$. As for the second assertion, we write $m/n = m \cdot 1/n$ and apply the proved statements successively:

$$\mathrm{Vol}\left(m \cdot \frac{1}{n}v, w\right) = m\,\mathrm{Vol}\left(\frac{1}{n}v, w\right)$$

$$= m \cdot \frac{1}{n}\,\mathrm{Vol}(v, w)$$

$$= \frac{m}{n}\,\mathrm{Vol}(v, w).$$

Lemma 3. $\mathrm{Vol}(-v, w) = \mathrm{Vol}(v, w).$

Proof. The parallelogram spanned by $-v$ and w is a translation by $-v$ of the parallelogram $P(v, w)$. Hence $P(v, w)$ and $P(-v, w)$ have the same area. (Cf. Fig. 4.)

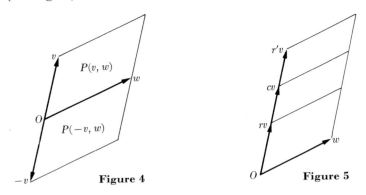

Figure 4   Figure 5

Lemma 4. *If c is any real number > 0, then*

$$\mathrm{Vol}(cv, w) = c\,\mathrm{Vol}(v, w).$$

Proof. Let r, r' be rational numbers such that $0 < r < c < r'$ (Fig. 5). Then

$$P(rv, w) \subset P(cv, w) \subset P(r'v, w).$$

Hence by Lemma 2,

$$
\begin{aligned}
r\,\mathrm{Vol}(v, w) &= \mathrm{Vol}(rv, w) \\
&\leq \mathrm{Vol}(cv, w) \\
&\leq \mathrm{Vol}(r'v, w) \\
&= r'\,\mathrm{Vol}(v, w).
\end{aligned}
$$

Letting r and r' approach c as a limit, we find that

$$\mathrm{Vol}(cv, w) = c\,\mathrm{Vol}(v, w),$$

as was to be shown.

From Lemmas 3 and 4 we can now prove that

$$\boxed{\mathrm{Vol}_0(cv, w) = c\,\mathrm{Vol}_0(v, w)}$$

for any real number c, and any vectors v, w. Indeed, if v, w are linearly dependent, then both sides are equal to 0. If v, w are linearly independent, we use the definition of Vol_0 and Lemmas 3, 4. Say $D(v, w) > 0$ and c is negative, $c = -d$. Then $D(cv, w) \leqq 0$ and consequently

$$
\begin{aligned}
\mathrm{Vol}_0(cv, w) = -\mathrm{Vol}(cv, w) &= -\mathrm{Vol}(-dv, w) \\
&= -\mathrm{Vol}(dv, w) \\
&= -d\,\mathrm{Vol}(v, w) \\
&= c\,\mathrm{Vol}(v, w) = c\,\mathrm{Vol}_0(v, w).
\end{aligned}
$$

A similar argument works when $D(v, w) \leqq 0$. We have therefore proved one of the conditions of linearity of the function Vol_0. The analogous property of course works on the other side, namely

$$
\boxed{\mathrm{Vol}_0(v, cw) = c\,\mathrm{Vol}_0(v, w).}
$$

For the other condition, we again have a lemma.

Lemma 5. *Assume that v, w are linearly independent. Then*

$$
\mathrm{Vol}(v + w, w) = \mathrm{Vol}(v, w).
$$

Proof. We have to prove that the parallelogram spanned by v, w has the same area as the parallelogram spanned by $v + w$, w.

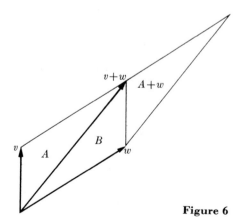

Figure 6

The parallelogram spanned by v, w consists of two triangles A and B as shown in the picture. The parallelogram spanned by $v + w$ and w consists of the triangles B and the translation of A by w. Since A and $A + w$ have the same area, we get:

$$\mathrm{Vol}(v, w) = \mathrm{Vol}(A) + \mathrm{Vol}(B) = \mathrm{Vol}(A + w) + \mathrm{Vol}(B) = \mathrm{Vol}(v + w, w),$$

as was to be shown.

We are now in a position to deal with the second property of linearity. Let w be a fixed non-zero vector in the plane, and let v be a vector such that $\{v, w\}$ is a basis of the plane. We shall prove that for any numbers c, d we have

$$(1) \qquad \mathrm{Vol}_0(cv + dw, w) = c\,\mathrm{Vol}_0(v, w).$$

Indeed, if $d = 0$, this is nothing but what we have shown previously. If $d \neq 0$, then again by what has been shown previously,

$$d\,\mathrm{Vol}_0(cv + dw, w) = \mathrm{Vol}_0(cv + dw, dw) = c\,\mathrm{Vol}_0(v, dw) = cd\,\mathrm{Vol}_0(v, w).$$

Canceling d yields relation (1).

From this last formula, the linearity now follows. Indeed, if

$$v_1 = c_1 v + d_1 w \qquad \text{and} \qquad v_2 = c_2 v + d_2 w,$$

then

$$
\begin{aligned}
\mathrm{Vol}_0(v_1 + v_2, w) &= \mathrm{Vol}_0((c_1 + c_2)v + (d_1 + d_2)w, w) \\
&= (c_1 + c_2)\,\mathrm{Vol}_0(v, w) \\
&= c_1\,\mathrm{Vol}_0(v, w) + c_2\,\mathrm{Vol}_0(v, w) \\
&= \mathrm{Vol}_0(v_1, w) + \mathrm{Vol}_0(v_2, w).
\end{aligned}
$$

This concludes the proof of the fact that

$$\mathrm{Vol}_0(v, w) = D(v, w),$$

and hence of Theorem 9.

Remark 1. The proof given above is slightly long, but each step is quite simple. Furthermore, when one wishes to generalize the proof to higher dimensional space (even 3-space), one can give an entirely similar proof. The reason for this is that the conditions characterizing a determinant involve only two coordinates at a time and thus always take place in some 2-dimensional plane. Keeping all but two coordinates fixed, the above proof then can be extended at once. Thus for instance in 3-space, let us denote by $P(u, v, w)$ the box spanned by vectors u, v, w (Fig. 7), namely all combinations

$$t_1 u + t_2 v + t_3 w \qquad \text{with} \qquad 0 \leq t_i \leq 1.$$

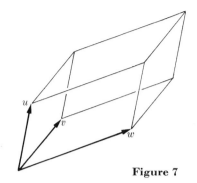

Figure 7

Let $\text{Vol}(u, v, w)$ be the volume of this box. Then

$$\text{Vol}(u, v, w) = |D(u, v, w)|$$

is again the absolute value of the determinant.

Remark 2. We have used geometric properties of area to carry out the above proof. One can lay foundations for all this purely analytically. If the reader is interested, cf. my book *Analysis I*.

Remark 3. In the special case of dimension 2, one could actually have given a simpler proof that the determinant is equal to the area. But we chose to give the slightly more complicated proof because it is the one which generalizes to the 3-dimensional, or n-dimensional case.

We interpret Theorem 9 in terms of linear maps. Given vectors v, w in the plane, we know that there exists a unique linear map

$$L: \mathbf{R}^2 \to \mathbf{R}^2$$

such that $L(E^1) = v$ and $L(E^2) = w$. In fact, if

$$v = aE^1 + cE^2, \qquad w = bE^1 + dE^2,$$

then the matrix associated with the linear map is

$$\begin{pmatrix} a & b \\ c & d \end{pmatrix}.$$

Furthermore, if we denote by C the unit cube spanned by E^1, E^2, and by P the parallelogram spanned by v, w, then P is the image under L of C, that is $L(C) = P$. Indeed, as we have seen, for $0 \leq t_i \leq 1$ we have

$$L(t_1 E^1 + t_2 E^2) = t_1 L(E^1) + t_2 L(E^2) = t_1 v + t_2 w.$$

If we define the determinant of a linear map to be the determinant of its associated matrix, we conclude that

(∗) (Area of P) = $|\text{Det}(L)|$.

To take a numerical example, the area of the parallelogram spanned by the vectors $(2, 1)$ and $(3, -1)$ (Fig. 8) is equal to the absolute value of

$$\begin{vmatrix} 2 & 1 \\ 3 & -1 \end{vmatrix} = -5$$

and hence is equal to 5.

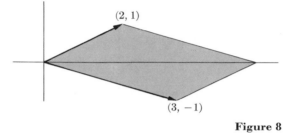

(2, 1)

(3, −1)

Figure 8

Theorem 10. *Let P be a parallelogram spanned by two vectors. Let $L: \mathbf{R}^2 \to \mathbf{R}^2$ be a linear map. Then*

$$\text{Area of } L(P) = |\text{Det } L| \ (\text{Area of } P).$$

Proof. Suppose that P is spanned by two vectors v, w. Then $L(P)$ is spanned by $L(v)$ and $L(w)$. (Cf. Fig. 9.) There is a linear map $L_1: \mathbf{R}^2 \to \mathbf{R}^2$ such that

$$L_1(E^1) = v \qquad \text{and} \qquad L_1(E^2) = w.$$

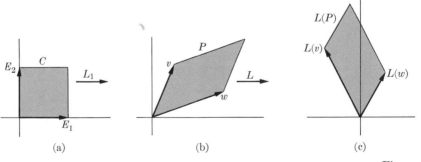

E_2 C L_1

E_1

(a)

P v L w

(b)

$L(P)$ $L(v)$ $L(w)$

(c)

Figure 9

Then $P = L_1(C)$, where C is the unit square, and

$$L(P) = L\big(L_1(C)\big) = (L \circ L_1)(C).$$

By what we proved above in $(*)$, we obtain

$$\text{Vol } L(P) = |\text{Det}(L \circ L_1)| = |\text{Det}(L)\,\text{Det}(L_1)| = |\text{Det}(L)|\,\text{Vol}(P),$$

thus proving our assertion.

Corollary. *For any rectangle R with sides parallel to the axes, and any linear map $L\colon \mathbf{R}^2 \to \mathbf{R}^2$ we have*

$$\text{Vol } L(R) = |\text{Det}(L)|\,\text{Vol}(R).$$

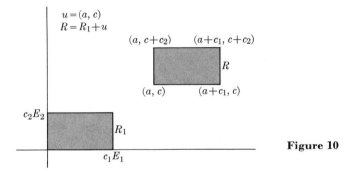

Figure 10

Proof. Let c_1, c_2 be the lengths of the sides of R. Let R_1 be the rectangle spanned by $c_1 E^1$ and $c_2 E^2$. Then R is the translation of R_1 by some vector, say $R = R_1 + u$. Then

$$L(R) = L(R_1 + u) = L(R_1) + L(u)$$

is the translation of $L(R_1)$ by $L(u)$. (Cf. Fig. 10.) Since area does not change under translation, we need only apply Theorem 8 to conclude the proof.

EXERCISES

1. If g satisfies the first two axioms of a determinant, prove that

$$g(v, w) = -g(w, v)$$

for all vectors v, w. This fact was used in the uniqueness proof. [*Hint:* Expand $g(v + w, v + w) = 0$.]

2. Find the area of the parallelogram spanned by the following vectors.

(a) $(2, 1)$ and $(-4, 5)$ (b) $(3, 4)$ and $(-2, -3)$

3. Find the area of the parallelogram such that three corners of the paralelogram are given by the following points.

(a) $(1, 1)$, $(2, -1)$, $(4, 6)$ (b) $(-3, 2)$, $(1, 4)$, $(-2, -7)$
(c) $(2, 5)$, $(-1, 4)$, $(1, 2)$ (d) $(1, 1)$, $(1, 0)$, $(2, 3)$

4. Find the volume of the parallelepiped spanned by the following vectors in 3-space.

(a) $(1, 1, 3)$, $(1, 2, -1)$, $(1, 4, 1)$ (b) $(1, -1, 4)$, $(1, 1, 0)$, $(-1, 2, 5)$
(c) $(-1, 2, 1)$, $(2, 0, 1)$, $(1, 3, 0)$ (d) $(-2, 2, 1)$, $(0, 1, 0)$, $(-4, 3, 2)$

PART TWO

STRUCTURE

THEOREMS

CHAPTER VIII

Bilinear Forms and the Standard Operators

§1. Bilinear forms

Let K be a field and V, W vector spaces over K. We recall that a map $g\colon V \times W \to K$ is said to be **bilinear** if it satisfies the following properties:

BI 1. *For all v_1, $v_2 \in V$ and $w \in W$ we have*

$$g(v_1 + v_2, w) = g(v_1, w) + g(v_2, w)$$

and for all $v \in V$ and w_1, $w_2 \in W$ we have

$$g(v, w_1 + w_2) = g(v, w_1) + g(v, w_2).$$

BI 2. *For all $c \in K$, $v \in V$ and $w \in W$,*

$$g(cv, w) = cg(v, w) = g(v, cw).$$

Thus we may say that a bilinear map is a map such that for all $v \in V$, the map $w \mapsto g(v, w)$ is linear, and for all $w \in W$, the map $v \mapsto g(v, w)$ is linear. If there is no need to refer to the map g explicitly, we shall usually write

$$g(v, w) = \langle v, w \rangle.$$

Our properties are thus similar to the analogous properties of the dot product.

If the spaces V, W are equal to the same space V, so that g maps $V \times V$ into K, then in that case, we say that g is a bilinear **form** on V. It is actually with such maps that we deal throughout this chapter.

If g, $g'\colon V \times V \to K$ are bilinear forms on V, then we can take their sum $g + g'$. It is again a bilinear form. If $c \in K$, then cg is a bilinear form. Thus the set of bilinear forms on V is a vector space over K, which we may denote by $\mathrm{Bil}(V \times V, K)$, or simply $\mathrm{Bil}(V)$ if the reference to K is clear.

In Chapter VI, §4 we related bilinear forms to matrices. Taking the two spaces to be equal to each other, and taking into account an obvious linearity property, we have as an immediate consequence of Theorem 11, Chapter VI, §4:

Theorem 1. *If $C = (c_{ij})$ is an $n \times n$ matrix, let g_C be the bilinear form on K^n given by*

$$g_C(X, Y) = {}^t XCY.$$

Then the association

$$C \mapsto g_C$$

is an isomorphism between $\mathrm{Bil}(K^n \times K^n, K)$ *and the space of* $n \times n$ *matrices in* K.

The matrix C in Theorem 1 is said to be the matrix **representing the bilinear form.**

A bilinear form, denoted by $\langle\,,\,\rangle$ thus gives rise to a certain kind of product between elements of V. We shall often take such products of sums. Let $v_1, \ldots, v_n$ and $w_1, \ldots, w_m$ be elements of V. Then we can expand out the product

$$\langle v_1 + \cdots + v_n, w_1, \ldots, w_m \rangle$$

$$= \langle v_1, w_1 + \cdots + w_m \rangle + \cdots + \langle v_n, w_1 + \cdots + w_m \rangle$$

$$= \langle v_1, w_1 \rangle + \cdots + \langle v_1, w_m \rangle + \cdots + \langle v_n, w_1 \rangle + \cdots + \langle v_n, w_m \rangle.$$

In this sum, each term is of type $\langle v_i, w_j \rangle$ with $i = 1, \ldots, n$ and $j = 1, \ldots, m$. Thus this sum may be abbreviated as

$$\sum_{i=1}^{n} \sum_{j=1}^{m} \langle v_i, w_j \rangle$$

or abbreviated still further as

$$\sum_{i,j} \langle v_i, w_j \rangle,$$

if the reference to the indices i, j is clear.

For instance,

$$\langle v + w, v + w \rangle = \langle v, v \rangle + \langle v, w \rangle + \langle w, v \rangle + \langle w, w \rangle.$$

It may happen that $\langle v, w \rangle \neq \langle w, v \rangle$, and so in general, we cannot further simplify.

A bilinear form $g \colon V \times V \to K$ is said to be **symmetric** if

$$g(v, w) = g(w, v)$$

for all v, $w \in V$. Thus a symmetric bilinear form is none other than a scalar product as defined in Chapter VI.

Corollary. *An $n \times n$ matrix C in K represents a symmetric bilinear form if and only if it is a symmetric matrix.*

Proof. Assume that C is symmetric, i.e. ${}^tC = C$. Since for all X, $Y \in K^n$ the matrix ${}^tXCY$ is a 1×1 matrix, i.e. an element of K, it is equal to its own transpose. Therefore

$$ {}^tXCY = {}^t({}^tXCY) = {}^tY{}^tC{}^{tt}X = {}^tYCX. $$

This shows that C represents a symmetric bilinear form.

Conversely, suppose that C represents a symmetric bilinear form, i.e. that ${}^tXCY = {}^tYCX$ for all X, $Y \in K^n$. Since

$$ {}^tYCX = {}^t({}^tYCX) = {}^tX{}^tC{}^{tt}Y = {}^tX{}^tCY, $$

we obtain ${}^tXCY = {}^tX{}^tCY$ for all X, $Y \in K^n$, and consequently $C = {}^tC$, in other words the matrix C is symmetric.

Example. The matrix

$$ C = \begin{pmatrix} 1 & -2 & 3 \\ -2 & 1 & 1 \\ 3 & 1 & 4 \end{pmatrix} $$

is a symmetric matrix. Let ${}^tX = (x_1, x_2, x_3)$ and ${}^tY = (y_1, y_2, y_3)$. If g is the associated bilinear form, then

$$ g(X, Y) = x_1y_1 - 2x_2y_1 + 3x_3y_1 - 2x_1y_2 + x_2y_2 + x_3y_2 $$
$$ + 3x_1y_3 + x_2y_3 + 4x_3y_3 $$
$$ = g(Y, X). $$

Let V be a finite dimensional vector space over K, and let $g: V \times V \to K$ be a bilinear form. Let $\{v_1, \ldots, v_n\}$ be a basis of V. Let v, w be elements of V, and write these elements in terms of the basis:

$$ v = x_1v_1 + \cdots + x_nv_n, $$
$$ w = y_1v_1 + \cdots + y_nv_n. $$

Then

$$ g(v, w) = \sum_{i,j=1}^n x_iy_jg(v_i, v_j). $$

If we let $c_{ij} = g(v_i, v_j)$, then

$$ g(v, w) = \sum_{i,j=1}^n c_{ij}x_iy_j. $$

Thus the bilinear form can be expressed in terms of the coordinate vectors X, Y and the matrix $C = (c_{ij})$.

Assume that the form g is symmetric.

If $\{v_1, \ldots, v_n\}$ is an *orthogonal* basis, then $g(v_i, v_j) = 0$ if $i \neq j$. Consequently the matrix (c_{ij}) is a diagonal matrix, say

$$\begin{pmatrix} c_1 & 0 & \cdots & 0 \\ 0 & c_2 & \cdots & 0 \\ \vdots & \vdots & & \vdots \\ 0 & 0 & \cdots & c_n \end{pmatrix},$$

and the form is then said to be **diagonalized.** The scalar product is then given in terms of the coordinate vectors with respect to the orthogonal basis by the simpler expression

$$g(v, w) = c_1 x_1 y_1 + \cdots + c_n x_n y_n.$$

Over the real numbers, if $\{v_1, \ldots, v_n\}$ is an *orthonormal* basis, with $g(v_i, v_i) = 1$ in addition, then in this case,

$$g(v, w) = x_1 y_1 + \cdots + x_n y_n$$

is simply the dot product.

We conclude this section by discussing changes of coordinates.

Let C be a square matrix representing a bilinear form g. Thus the bilinear form is given as

$$g(X, Y) = {}^t XCY$$

in terms of the coordinate vectors X and Y. Suppose that we change bases in our vector space. There exists a non-singular matrix N such that $X = NX'$ and $Y = NY'$, if X' and Y' are the coordinate vectors with respect to the other basis. In that case, we obtain

$$^t XCY = {}^t(NX')CNY' = {}^t X'\,{}^t NCNY'.$$

Consequently, with respect to the coordinate vectors X', Y', the matrix representing the form is

$$\boxed{{}^t NCN.}$$

Thus, unlike the change of matrix of a linear map (which changes by the *inverse*) the matrix of a bilinear map changes by the *transpose*. Following the notation of Chapter V, §3 we see that N is none other than

EXERCISES

1. Let g, written $\langle\ ,\ \rangle$, be the bilinear form on $\mathbf{R}^3$ whose associated matrix with respect to the standard basis is

$$\begin{pmatrix} 1 & 2 & 3 \\ -1 & 1 & 1 \\ 1 & 0 & 1 \end{pmatrix}.$$

Find two vectors X, Y in $\mathbf{R}^3$ such that $\langle X, Y \rangle \neq \langle Y, X \rangle$.

2. Find the matrix associated with g with respect to the basis $\{(1, 1, 0),$ $(0, 1, 0), (1, 1, 1)\}$, if g is the form of Exercise 1.

3. (a) Let V be a vector space over the field K, and suppose that V is a direct sum, $V = W_1 \oplus W_2$, of subspaces W_1, W_2. Let g_1 be a symmetric bilinear form on W_1, and let g_2 be a symmetric bilinear form on W_2. Show that there exists a unique bilinear form g on V such that, if $v = v_1 + v_2$ and $w = w_1 + w_2$ are elements of V, with $v_1, w_1 \in W_1$ and $v_2, w_2 \in W_2$, then $g(v, w) = g_1(v_1, w_1) + g_2(v_2, w_2)$.
   (b) If $\mathcal{B}_1$ is a basis for W_1 and $\mathcal{B}_2$ is a basis for W_2, what will the matrix of the form g look like, with respect to the basis $\mathcal{B}_1$, $\mathcal{B}_2$ of V?

4. Let V be the vector space over $\mathbf{R}$ consisting of all polynomials of degree $\leq n$. If $f, g \in V$, let

$$\langle f, g \rangle = \int_0^1 f(t)g(t)\, dt.$$

Find the matrix of this scalar product with respect to the basis $\{1, t, \ldots, t^n\}$.

5. Let V be the vector space over $\mathbf{R}$ whose basis is $\{\sin t, \cos t\}$. Let the scalar product be defined by

$$\langle f, g \rangle = \int_{-\pi}^{\pi} f(t)g(t)\, dt.$$

What is the matrix of this scalar product with respect to the given basis?

6. Let V be a finite dimensional vector space over the field K, and let g be a bilinear form on V, written $\langle\ ,\ \rangle$.
   (a) Show that for each $w \in V$, the map $v \mapsto \langle v, w \rangle$ is a functional L_w on V, and that the map $w \mapsto L_w$ is a linear map of V into the dual space V^*.
   (b) Show that the following conditions are equivalent:
       (i) The kernel of the map L above is $\{O\}$.
       (ii) The map L is an isomorphism between V and V^*.
       (iii) If C is the matrix representing the bilinear form with respect to a basis of V, then $\mathrm{Det}(C) \neq 0$.

   A bilinear form satisfying the preceding three conditions is said to be **non-degenerate**.

7. (a) Conversely, let V, W be finite dimensional vector spaces over K. Let $g: V \times W \to K$ be a bilinear map, written $g(v, w) = \langle v, w \rangle$. Show that to each pair of bases $\mathcal{B}$ of V and $\mathcal{B}'$ of W we can associate a matrix C, such that, if $v \in V$ and $w \in W$, and $X = M_{\mathcal{B}}(v)$, $Y = M_{\mathcal{B}'}(w)$, then

$$g(v, w) = {}^t XCY.$$

(b) Let $g: V \times W \to K$ be a bilinear map, written $\langle \, , \, \rangle$. For each $w \in W$, show that the map of V into K given by

$$L_w: v \longmapsto \langle v, w \rangle$$

is a functional on V, and that the map $w \longmapsto L_w$ is a linear map of W into the dual space V^*.

(c) Show that the following conditions are equivalent:

   (i) The map $L: W \to V^*$ is injective (its kernel is $\{O\}$).
   (ii) If C is a matrix associated with g as in (b), then C has rank n, where $n = \dim W$.

8. A square matrix C is said to be **skew-symmetric** if ${}^t C = -C$. A bilinear form g on K^n is said to be **alternating** if $g(X, X) = 0$ for all $X \in K^n$. Prove that a matrix C represents an alternating form if and only if it is skew-symmetric.

§2. *Quadratic forms*

Let V be a finite dimensional space over the field K. Let $g = \langle \, , \, \rangle$ be a symmetric bilinear form on V. By the **quadratic form** determined by g, we shall mean the function

$$f: V \to K$$

such that $f(v) = g(v, v) = \langle v, v \rangle$.

Example 1. If $V = K^n$, then $f(X) = X \cdot X = x_1^2 + \cdots + x_n^2$ is the quadratic form determined by the ordinary dot product.

In general, if $V = K^n$ and C is a symmetric matrix in K, representing a symmetric bilinear form, then the quadratic form is given as a function of X by

$$f(X) = {}^t XCX = \sum_{i,j=1}^{n} c_{ij}x_ix_j.$$

If C is a diagonal matrix, say

$$C = \begin{pmatrix} c_1 & 0 & \cdots & 0 \\ 0 & c_2 & \cdots & 0 \\ \vdots & \vdots & & \vdots \\ 0 & 0 & \cdots & c_n \end{pmatrix},$$

then the quadratic form has a simpler expression, namely

$$f(X) = c_1 x_1^2 + \cdots + c_n x_n^2.$$

Let V be again a finite dimensional vector space over the field K. Let g be a symmetric bilinear form, and f its quadratic form. Then we can recover the values of g entirely from those of f, because for $v, w \in V$,

$$\langle v, w \rangle = \tfrac{1}{4}[\langle v + w, v + w \rangle - \langle v - w, v - w \rangle]$$

or using g, f,

$$g(v, w) = \tfrac{1}{4}[f(v + w) - f(v - w)].$$

We also have the formula

$$\langle v, w \rangle = \tfrac{1}{2}[\langle v + w, v + w \rangle - \langle v, v \rangle - \langle w, w \rangle].$$

The proof is easy, expanding out using the bilinearity. For instance, for the second formula, we have

$$\langle v + w, v + w \rangle - \langle v, v \rangle - \langle w, w \rangle$$
$$= \langle v, v \rangle + 2\langle v, w \rangle + \langle w, w \rangle - \langle v, v \rangle - \langle w, w \rangle$$
$$= 2\langle v, w \rangle.$$

We leave the first as an exercise.

Example 2. Let $V = \mathbf{R}^2$ and let ${}^t X = (x, y)$ denote elements of $\mathbf{R}^2$. The function f such that

$$f(x, y) = 2x^2 + 3xy + y^2$$

is a quadratic form. Let us find the matrix of its bilinear symmetric form g. We write this matrix

$$C = \begin{pmatrix} a & b \\ b & d \end{pmatrix},$$

and we must have

$$f(x, y) = (x, y) \begin{pmatrix} a & b \\ b & d \end{pmatrix} \begin{pmatrix} x \\ y \end{pmatrix}$$

or in other words

$$2x^2 + 3xy + y^2 = ax^2 + 2bxy + dy^2.$$

Thus we obtain $a = 2$, $2b = 3$, and $d = 1$. The matrix is therefore

$$C = \begin{pmatrix} 2 & \frac{3}{2} \\ \frac{3}{2} & 1 \end{pmatrix}.$$

EXERCISES

1. Let V be a finite dimensional vector space over a field K. Let $f: V \to K$ be a function, and assume that the function g such that

$$g(v, w) = f(v + w) - f(v) - f(w)$$

is bilinear. Assume that $f(av) = a^2 f(v)$ for all $v \in V$ and $a \in K$. Show that f is a quadratic form, and determine a bilinear form from which it comes. Show that this bilinear form is unique.

2. What is the associated matrix of the quadratic form

$$f(X) = x^2 - 3xy + 4y^2$$

if $X = (x, y, z)$?

3. Let $f: \mathbf{R}^n \to \mathbf{R}$ be a twice continuously differentiable function, such that $f(tX) = t^2 f(X)$ for all $X \in \mathbf{R}^n$. Show that f is a quadratic form. (You need some formulas of calculus in several variables to do this.)

4. Let x_1, x_2, x_3, x_4 be the coordinates of a vector X, and y_1, y_2, y_3, y_4 the coordinates of a vector Y. Express in terms of these coordinates the bilinear form associated with the following quadratic forms.

   (a) $x_1 x_2$ (b) $x_1 x_3 + x_4^2$ (c) $2x_1 x_2 - x_3 x_4$ (d) $x_1^2 - 5x_2 x_3 + x_4^2$

5. Show that if f_1 is the quadratic form of the bilinear form g_1, and f_2 the quadratic form of the bilinear form g_2, then $f_1 + f_2$ is the quadratic form of the bilinear form $g_1 + g_2$.

§3. Symmetric operators

Let V be a finite dimensional vector space over a field K. We suppose that V has a *fixed* non-degenerate symmetric bilinear form, denoted by $\langle \ , \ \rangle$ throughout this section. If the reader wishes, he may take $V = K^n$, and he may take the fixed bilinear form to be the ordinary dot product

$$\langle X, Y \rangle = {}^t XY,$$

where X, Y are column vectors of K^n.

A linear map of V into itself will be called an **operator**. Let $A: V \to V$ be an operator. Then we can define by means of A a bilinear form on V, by the map

$$(v, w) \mapsto \langle Av, w \rangle$$

for v, $w \in V$. The verification that this is indeed a bilinear map is trivial. Conversely, every bilinear form can be so represented:

Theorem 2. *Let V be a finite dimensional vector space over the field K, with a non-degenerate symmetric bilinear form $\langle \ , \ \rangle$. Let g be any bilinear form on V. Then there exist unique operators A and B of V such that*

$$g(v, w) = \langle Av, w \rangle = \langle v, Bw \rangle$$

for all v, $w \in V$.

Proof. For each $w \in V$, the map

$$L_w : v \mapsto g(v, w)$$

is a linear map of V into K, i.e. a functional. We have seen in Theorem 15 of Chapter VI, §6 that every functional on V can be represented by a *unique* element of V, that is there exists a unique element w' of V such that, for all $v \in V$ we have

$$L_w(v) = \langle v, w' \rangle.$$

The association $w \mapsto w'$ is therefore a map of V into itself, which we denote by B. Thus $w' = Bw$, and we have the formula

$$g(v, w) = \langle v, Bw \rangle$$

for all v, $w \in V$. The map B is linear. To see this, suppose that w_1, $w_2 \in V$ and that w_1', $w_2' \in V$ are such that

$$g(v, w_1) = \langle v, w_1' \rangle \quad \text{and} \quad g(v, w_2) = \langle v, w_2' \rangle$$

for all $v \in V$. Then

$$\begin{aligned}
g(v, w_1 + w_2) &= g(v, w_1) + g(v, w_2) \\
&= \langle v, w_1' \rangle + \langle v, w_2' \rangle \\
&= \langle v, w_1' + w_2' \rangle.
\end{aligned}$$

Hence

$$B(w_1 + w_2) = Bw_1 + Bw_2.$$

Furthermore, if $c \in K$, then

$$g(v, cw_1) = cg(v, w_1) = c\langle v, w_1' \rangle = \langle v, cw_1' \rangle.$$

Hence $B(cw_1) = cB(w_1)$. This proves that B is linear. The fact that B is uniquely determined is due to the fact that for each w, we know that there is a *unique* element $w' = Bw$ such that $g(v, w) = \langle v, Bw \rangle$ for all $v \in V$.

Since our form $\langle\ ,\ \rangle$ is symmetric, we could have considered just as well the linear map $w \mapsto g(v, w)$ for each $v \in V$, and thus there exists a unique operator A such that

$$g(v, w) = \langle Av, w \rangle$$

for all $v, w \in V$. This proves our theorem.

In the theorem, we say that the operator A **represents** the form g.

By definition, the operator B in the preceding proof will be called the **transpose of** A and will be denoted by ^tA. The operator A is said to be **symmetric** (with respect to the fixed non-degenerate symmetric form $\langle\ ,\ \rangle$) if $^tA = A$.

For any operator A of V, we have by definition the formula

$$\langle Av, w \rangle = \langle v, {}^tAw \rangle$$

for all $v, w \in V$. If A is symmetric, then $\langle Av, w \rangle = \langle v, Aw \rangle$, and conversely.

Example 1. Let $V = K^n$ and let the symmetric form be the ordinary dot product. Then we may take A as a matrix in K, and elements of K^n as column vectors X, Y. Their dot product can be written as a matrix multiplication,

$$\langle X, Y \rangle = {}^tXY.$$

We have

$$\langle AX, Y \rangle = {}^t(AX)Y = {}^tX{}^tAY = \langle X, {}^tAY \rangle,$$

where ^tA now means the transpose of the matrix A. Thus when we deal with the ordinary dot product of n-tuples, the transpose of the operator is represented by the transpose of the associated matrix. This is the reason why we have used the same notation in both cases.

A symmetric operator A gives rise to a quadratic form f, such that

$$f(v) = \langle Av, v \rangle,$$

called the **quadratic form determined by** A.

Example 2. Let $V = \mathbf{R}^2$ and let A be the matrix

$$A = \begin{pmatrix} 3 & 5 \\ 5 & 13 \end{pmatrix}.$$

Then the quadratic form determined by A (viewed as a linear map of $\mathbf{R}^2$ into itself) is given by

$$f(x, y) = (x, y) \begin{pmatrix} 3 & 5 \\ 5 & 13 \end{pmatrix} \begin{pmatrix} x \\ y \end{pmatrix} = 3x^2 + 10xy + 13y^2.$$

Finally, the transpose satisfies the following formalism:

Theorem 3. *Let V be a finite dimensional vector space over the field K, with a non-degenerate symmetric bilinear form $\langle\ ,\ \rangle$. Let A, B be operators of V, and $c \in K$. Then:*

$$^t(A + B) = {}^tA + {}^tB \qquad\qquad ^t(AB) = {}^tB{}^tA$$
$$^t(cA) = c{}^tA \qquad\qquad ^{tt}A = A$$

Proof. We prove only the second formula. For all $v, w \in V$ we have

$$\langle ABv, w \rangle = \langle Bv, {}^tAw \rangle = \langle v, {}^tB{}^tAw \rangle.$$

By definition, this means that $^t(AB) = {}^tB{}^tA$. The other formulas are just as easy to prove.

EXERCISES

1. (a) A matrix A is called **skew-symmetric** if $^tA = -A$. Show that any matrix M can be expressed as a sum of a symmetric matrix and a skew-symmetric one, and that these latter are uniquely determined. [*Hint:* Let $A = \frac{1}{2}(M + {}^tM)$.]
   (b) If A is skew-symmetric then A^2 is symmetric.
   (c) Let A be skew-symmetric. Show that $\mathrm{Det}(A)$ is 0 if A is an $n \times n$ matrix and n is odd.

2. Let A be an invertible symmetric matrix. Show that A^{-1} is symmetric.

3. Show that a triangular symmetric matrix is diagonal.

4. Show that the diagonal elements of a skew-symmetric matrix are equal to 0.

5. Let V be a finite dimensional vector space over the field K, with a non-degenerate scalar product. Let v_0, w_0 be elements of V. Let $A : V \to V$ be the linear map such that $A(v) = \langle v_0, v \rangle w_0$. Describe ^tA.

6. Let V be the vector space over $\mathbf{R}$ of polynomials of degree ≤ 5. Let the scalar product be defined as usual by

$$\langle f, g \rangle = \int_0^1 f(t)g(t)\ dt.$$

Describe the transpose of the derivative D with respect to this scalar product.

7. Let V be a finite dimensional space over the field K, with a non-degenerate scalar product. Let $A : V \to V$ be a linear map. Show that the image of ^tA is the orthogonal space to the kernel of A.

8. Let V be a finite dimensional space over $\mathbf{R}$, with a positive definite scalar product. Let $P : V \to V$ be a linear map such that $PP = P$. Assume that $^tPP = P{}^tP$. Show that $P = {}^tP$.

9. A square $n \times n$ real symmetric matrix A is said to be **positive definite** if ${}^tXAX > 0$ for all $X \neq O$. If A, B are symmetric (of the same size) we define $A < B$ to mean that $B - A$ is positive. Show that if $A < B$ and $B < C$, then $A \overset{.}{<} C$.

10. Let V be a finite dimensional vector space over **R**, with a positive definite scalar product $\langle \, , \, \rangle$. An operator A of V is said to be **positive** if $\langle Av, v \rangle \geq 0$ for all $v \in V$, $v \neq O$. Suppose that $V = W + W^\perp$ is the direct sum of a subspace W and its orthogonal complement. Let P be the projection on W, and assume $W \neq \{O\}$. Show that P is symmetric and positive.

11. Let the notation be as in Exercise 10. Let c be a real number, and let A be the operator defined by

$$Av = cw$$

if we can write $v = w + w'$ with $w \in W$ and $w' \in W^\perp$. Show that A is symmetric.

12. Let the notation be as in Exercise 10. Let P again be the projection on W. Show that there is a symmetric operator A such that $A^2 = I + P$.

13. Let $A = (a_{ij})$ be an $m \times n$ real or complex matrix. Define a generalization of the absolute value, namely

$$|A| = mn \cdot \max |a_{ij}|.$$

(There will be no confusion with the determinant which does not occur in the present context.) If A, B are matrices which can be added, show that

$$|A + B| \leq |A| + |B|.$$

If they can be multiplied, show that

$$|AB| \leq |A| \, |B|.$$

If c is a number, show that

$$|cA| = |c| \, |A|.$$

14. Let A be a real symmetric matrix. Show that there exists a real number c so that $A + cI$ is positive.

15. Let V be a finite dimensional vector space over the field K, with a nondegenerate bilinear form $\langle \, , \, \rangle$. If $A : V \to V$ is a linear map such that

$$\langle Av, Aw \rangle = \langle v, w \rangle$$

for all $v, w \in V$, show that $\mathrm{Det}(A) = \pm 1$.

16. Let $Q = (q_{ij})$ $(i, j = 1, \ldots, n)$ be a square matrix of (infinitely differentiable real-valued) functions q_{ij} of a real variable. Let $Y = {}^t(y_1, \ldots, y_n)$ denote a column vector of functions. Let S_Q be the set of all Y such that

$$Y' = QY.$$

Show that S_Q is a vector space (over **R**). Let $\Phi = {}^t(\varphi_1, \ldots, \varphi_n)$ be a column vector of functions, and let

$$\langle \Phi, Y \rangle = \varphi_1 y_1 + \cdots + \varphi_n y_n.$$

Let D be the derivative. Define D applied to a matrix of functions to be the matrix obtained by applying D to each component. Show that

$$D\langle \Phi, Y \rangle = \langle D\Phi, Y \rangle + \langle \Phi, DY \rangle = \langle (D + {}^t Q)\Phi, Y \rangle.$$

By induction, prove that for any positive integer k,

$$D^k\langle \Phi, Y \rangle = \langle (D + {}^t Q)^k \Phi, Y \rangle.$$

17. Let A be a real symmetric matrix $\neq O$. Show that $\operatorname{tr}(AA) > 0$.

18. Let A, B be symmetric matrices of the same size over the field K. Show that AB is symmetric if and only if $AB = BA$.

§4. Hermitian operators

Let V be a finite dimensional vector space over the complex numbers. We suppose that V has a fixed positive definite hermitian product denoted by $\langle \, , \, \rangle$. A hermitian product is also called a **hermitian form.** *If the reader wishes, he may take $V = \mathbf{C}^n$, and he may take the fixed hermitian product to be the standard product*

$$\langle X, Y \rangle = {}^t X \bar{Y},$$

where X, Y are column vectors of $\mathbf{C}^n$.

Let $A: V \to V$ be an operator, i.e. a linear map of V into itself. For each $w \in V$, the map

$$L_w: V \to \mathbf{C}$$

such that

$$L_w(v) = \langle Av, w \rangle$$

for all $v \in V$ is a functional.

Theorem 4. *Let V be a finite dimensional vector space over $\mathbf{C}$ with a positive definite hermitian form $\langle \, , \, \rangle$. Given a functional L on V, there exists a unique $w' \in V$ such that $L(v) = \langle v, w' \rangle$ for all $v \in V$.*

Proof. The proof is similar to that given in the real case, say Theorem 15′ of Chapter VI, §6. We leave it to the reader.

From Theorem 4, we conclude that given w, there exists a unique w' such that

$$\langle Av, w \rangle = \langle v, w' \rangle$$

for all $v \in V$.

Remark. The association $w \mapsto L_w$ is *not* an isomorphism of V with the dual space! In fact, if $\alpha \in \mathbf{C}$, then $L_{\alpha w} = \bar{\alpha} L_w$. However, this is immaterial for the existence of the element w'.

The map $w \mapsto w'$ of V into itself will be denoted by A^*. By definition, we have the formula

$$\langle Av, w \rangle = \langle v, A^*w \rangle$$

for all $v, w \in V$. The map A^* is *linear*, and the reader is urged to write out all the details to check this. The proof is similar to the case of symmetric forms, and no bar appears to spoil the linearity of A^*. We call A^* the **adjoint** of A. It is the unique operator satisfying the preceding formula.

Example. Let $V = \mathbf{C}^n$ and let the form be the standard form given by

$$(X, Y) \mapsto {}^tX\overline{Y} = \langle X, Y \rangle,$$

for X, Y column vectors of $\mathbf{C}^n$. Then for any matrix A representing a linear map of V into itself, we have

$$\langle AX, Y \rangle = {}^t(AX)\overline{Y} = {}^tX^tA\overline{Y} = {}^tX(\overline{{}^t\overline{A}Y}).$$

Furthermore, by definition, the product $\langle AX, Y \rangle$ is equal to

$$\langle X, A^*Y \rangle = {}^tX\overline{(A^*Y)}.$$

This means that

$$\boxed{A^* = {}^t\overline{A}.}$$

We see that it would have been unreasonable to use the same symbol t for the adjoint of an operator over $\mathbf{C}$, as for the transpose over $\mathbf{R}$.

An operator A is called **hermitian** (or **self-adjoint**) if $A^* = A$. This means that for all $v, w \in V$ we have

$$\langle Av, w \rangle = \langle v, Aw \rangle.$$

In view of the preceding example, a square matrix A of complex numbers is called **hermitian** if ${}^t\overline{A} = A$, or equivalently, ${}^tA = \overline{A}$. If A is a hermitian matrix, then we can define on $\mathbf{C}^n$ a hermitian form by the rule

$$(X, Y) \mapsto {}^t(AX)\overline{Y}.$$

(Verify in detail that this map is a hermitian product.)

The $*$ operation satisfies rules analogous to those of the transpose, namely:

Theorem 5. *Let V be a finite dimensional vector space over $\mathbf{C}$, with a fixed positive definite hermitian form $\langle \,,\, \rangle$. Let A, B be operators of V, and* *let $\alpha \in \mathbf{C}$. Then*

$$(A + B)^* = A^* + B^* \qquad\qquad (AB)^* = B^*A^*$$
$$(\alpha A)^* = \bar{\alpha} A^* \qquad\qquad\quad A^{**} = A.$$

Proof. We shall prove the third rule, leaving the others to the reader. We have for all $v, w \in V$:

$$\langle \alpha Av, w \rangle = \alpha \langle Av, w \rangle = \alpha \langle v, A^*w \rangle = \langle v, \bar{\alpha} A^*w \rangle.$$

This last expression is also equal by definition to

$$\langle v, (\alpha A)^*w \rangle$$

and consequently $(\alpha A)^* = \bar{\alpha} A^*$, as contended.

We have the analogue of Theorem 2 for hermitian operators:

Theorem 6. *Let V be a finite dimensional vector space over the complex numbers, with a positive definite hermitian form $\langle \, , \, \rangle$. Let g be another hermitian form on V. Then there exists a unique hermitian operator A of V such that for all $v, w \in V$,*

$$g(v, w) = \langle Av, w \rangle.$$

Proof. The proof is entirely similar to that of Theorem 2 and will be left to the reader.

In Theorem 6 we say that the operator A **represents** the form g.

We have the analogue of quadratic forms for hermitian forms. Let g be a hermitian form, represented by the operator A. We define the analogue of the quadratic form to be the function f such that

$$f(v) = \langle Av, v \rangle.$$

We have the **polarization identity:**

$$\langle A(v + w), v + w \rangle - \langle A(v - w), v - w \rangle = 2[\langle Aw, v \rangle + \langle Av, w \rangle]$$

for all $v, w \in V$, or also

$$\langle A(v + w), v + w \rangle - \langle Av, v \rangle - \langle Aw, w \rangle = \langle Av, w \rangle + \langle Aw, v \rangle.$$

The verifications of these identities are trivial, just by expanding out the left-hand side.

Theorem 7. *Let V be as before. If A is an operator such that $\langle Av, v \rangle = 0$ for all $v \in V$, then $A = O$.*

Proof. The left-hand side of the polarization identity is equal to 0 for all $v, w \in V$. Hence we obtain

$$\langle Aw, v \rangle + \langle Av, w \rangle = 0$$

for all $v, w \in V$. Replace v by iv. Then by the rules for the hermitian product, we obtain

$$-i\langle Aw, v \rangle + i\langle Av, w \rangle = 0$$

whence

$$-\langle Aw, v \rangle + \langle Av, w \rangle = 0.$$

Adding this to the first relation obtained above yields

$$2\langle Av, w \rangle = 0$$

whence $\langle Av, w \rangle = 0$. Hence $A = O$, as was to be shown.

Theorem 8. *Let V be as before. Let A be an operator. Then A is hermitian if and only if $\langle Av, v \rangle$ is real for all $v \in V$.*

Proof. Suppose that A is hermitian. Then

$$\langle Av, v \rangle = \langle v, Av \rangle = \overline{\langle Av, v \rangle}.$$

Since a complex number equal to its complex conjugate must be a real number, we conclude that $\langle Av, v \rangle$ is real. Conversely, assume that $\langle Av, v \rangle$ is real for all $v \in V$. Then

$$\langle Av, v \rangle = \overline{\langle Av, v \rangle} = \langle v, Av \rangle = \langle A^*v, v \rangle.$$

Hence $\langle (A - A^*)v, v \rangle = 0$ for all $v \in V$, and by Theorem 7, we conclude that $A - A^* = O$ whence $A = A^*$, as was to be shown.

EXERCISES

1. Let A be an invertible hermitian matrix. Show that A^{-1} is hermitian.

2. Show that the analogue of Theorem 7 when V is a finite dimensional space over $\mathbf{R}$ is *false*. In other words, it may happen that Av is perpendicular to v for all $v \in V$ without A being the zero map!

3. Show that the analogue of Theorem 7 when V is a finite dimensional space over $\mathbf{R}$ is true if we assume in addition that A is symmetric.

4. Which of the following matrices are hermitian:

(a) $\begin{pmatrix} 2 & i \\ -i & 5 \end{pmatrix}$ (b) $\begin{pmatrix} 1+i & 2 \\ 2 & 5i \end{pmatrix}$ (c) $\begin{pmatrix} 1 & 1+i & 5 \\ 1-i & 2 & i \\ 5 & -i & 7 \end{pmatrix}$

5. Show that the diagonal elements of a hermitian matrix are real.

6. Show that a triangular hermitian matrix is diagonal.

7. Let A, B be hermitian matrices (of the same size). Show that $A + B$ is hermitian. If $AB = BA$, show that AB is hermitian.

8. Let V be a finite dimensional vector space over $\mathbf{C}$, with a positive definite hermitian form. Let $A: V \to V$ be a hermitian operator. Show that $I + iA$ and $I - iA$ are invertible. [*Hint:* If $v \neq O$, show that $\|(I + iA)v\| \neq 0$.]

9. Let A be a hermitian matrix. Show that ^tA and $\overline{A}$ are hermitian. If A is invertible, show that A^{-1} is hermitian.

10. Let V be a finite dimensional space over $\mathbf{C}$, with a positive definite hermitian form $\langle \, , \, \rangle$. Let $A: V \to V$ be a linear map. Show that the following conditions are equivalent:

  (i) We have $AA^* = A^*A$.
  (ii) For all $v \in V$, $\|Av\| = \|A^*v\|$ (where $\|v\| = \sqrt{\langle v, v \rangle}$).
  (iii) We can write $A = B + iC$, where B, C are Hermitian, and $BC = CB$.

11. Let A be a non-zero hermitian matrix. Show that $\operatorname{tr}(AA^*) > 0$.

§5. *Unitary operators*

Let V be a finite dimensional vector space over $\mathbf{R}$, with a positive definite scalar product. Let $A: V \to V$ be a linear map. We shall say that A is a *real unitary* map if

$$\langle Av, Aw \rangle = \langle v, w \rangle$$

for all v, $w \in V$. We may say that A is **unitary** means that A **preserves the product.** You will find that in the literature, a real unitary map is also called an **orthogonal** map. The reason why we use the terminology **unitary** is given by the next theorem.

Theorem 9. *Let V be as above. Let $A: V \to V$ be a linear map. The following conditions on A are equivalent:*

(1) *A is unitary.*

(2) *A preserves the length of vectors, i.e. for every $v \in V$, we have*

$$\|Av\| = \|v\|.$$

(3) *For every unit vector $v \in V$, the vector Av is also a unit vector.*

Proof. We leave the equivalence between (2) and (3) to the reader. It is trivial that (1) implies (2) since the square of the norm $\langle Av, Av \rangle$ is a special case of a product. Conversely, let us prove that (2) implies (1). We have

$$\langle A(v + w), A(v + w) \rangle - \langle A(v - w), A(v - w) \rangle = 4\langle Av, Aw \rangle.$$

Using the assumption (2), and noting that the left-hand side consists of squares of lengths, we see that the left-hand side of our equation is equal to

$$\langle v + w, v + w \rangle - \langle v - w, v - w \rangle$$

which is also equal to $4\langle v, w \rangle$. From this our theorem follows at once.

Theorem 9 shows why we called our maps unitary: They are *characterized* by the fact that they map unit vectors into unit vectors.

A unitary map U of course preserves perpendicularity, i.e. if v, w are perpendicular then Uv, Uw are also perpendicular, for

$$\langle Uv, Uw \rangle = \langle v, w \rangle = 0.$$

On the other hand, it does not follow that a map which preserves perpendicularity is necessarily unitary. For instance, over the real numbers, the map which sends a vector v on $2v$ preserves perpendicularity but is not unitary. Unfortunately, it is standard terminology to call real unitary maps orthogonal maps. We emphasize that such maps do more than preserve orthogonality: *They also preserve length.*

Theorem 10. *Let V be a finite dimensional vector space over $\mathbf{R}$, with a positive definite scalar product. A linear map $A: V \rightarrow V$ is unitary if and only if*

$$^t A A = I.$$

Proof. The operator A is unitary if and only if

$$\langle Av, Aw \rangle = \langle v, w \rangle$$

for all $v, w \in V$. This condition is equivalent with

$$\langle {}^t A A v, w \rangle = \langle v, w \rangle$$

for all $v, w \in V$, and hence is equivalent with $^t A A = I$.

There remains but to interpret in terms of matrices the condition that A be unitary. First we observe that a unitary map is invertible. Indeed, if A is unitary and $Av = O$, then $v = O$ because A preserves length.

If we take $V = \mathbf{R}^n$ in Theorem 10, and take the usual dot product as the scalar product, then we can represent A by a real matrix. Thus it is natural to define a real matrix A to be **unitary** (or orthogonal) if $^tAA = I_n$, or equivalently,

$$^tA = A^{-1}.$$

Example. The only unitary maps of the plane $\mathbf{R}^2$ into itself are the maps whose matrices are of the type

$$\begin{pmatrix} \cos\theta & -\sin\theta \\ \sin\theta & \cos\theta \end{pmatrix} \quad \text{or} \quad \begin{pmatrix} \cos\theta & \sin\theta \\ \sin\theta & -\cos\theta \end{pmatrix}$$

If the determinant of such a map is 1 then the matrix representing the map with respect to an orthonormal basis is necessarily of the first type, and the map is called a **rotation.** Drawing a picture shows immediately that this terminology is justified. A number of statements concerning the unitary maps of the plane will be given in the exercises. They are easy to work out, and provide good practice which it would be a pity to spoil in the text. These exercises are to be partly viewed as providing additional examples for this section.

The complex case. As usual, we have analogous notions in the complex case. *Let V be a finite dimensional vector space over $\mathbf{C}$, with a positive definite hermitian product.* Let $A: V \to V$ be a linear map. We define A to be *complex unitary* if

$$\langle Av, Aw \rangle = \langle v, w \rangle$$

for all $v, w \in V$. The analogue of Theorem 9 is true verbatim: The map A is unitary if and only if it preserves length, and also if and only if it preserves unit vectors. We leave the proof as an exercise.

The analogue of Theorem 10 is:

Theorem 11. *Let V be a finite dimensional vector space over $\mathbf{C}$, with a positive definite hermitian product. A linear map $A: V \to V$ is unitary if and only if*

$$A^*A = I.$$

We also leave the proof as an exercise.

Taking $V = \mathbf{C}^n$ with the usual hermitian form given by

$$\langle X, Y \rangle = x_1\bar{y}_1 + \cdots + x_n\bar{y}_n,$$

we can represent A by a complex matrix. Thus it is natural to define a complex matrix A to be **unitary** if $^t\bar{A}A = I_n$, or

$$^t\bar{A} = A^{-1}.$$

EXERCISES

1. (a) Let V be a finite dimensional space over $\mathbf{R}$, with a positive definite scalar product. Let $\{v_1, \ldots, v_n\}$ and $\{w_1, \ldots, w_n\}$ be orthonormal bases. Let $A: V \to V$ be an operator of V such that $Av_i = w_i$. Show that A is real unitary.

(b) State and prove the analogous result in the complex case.

2. Let V be as in Exercise 1. Let $\{v_1, \ldots, v_n\}$ be an orthonormal basis of V. Let A be a unitary operator of V. Show that $\{Av_1, \ldots, Av_n\}$ is an orthonormal basis.

3. Let A be a real unitary matrix. (a) Show that ^tA is unitary. (b) Show that A^{-1} exists and is unitary. (c) If B is real unitary, show that AB is unitary, and that $B^{-1}AB$ is unitary.

4. Let A be a complex unitary matrix. (a) Show that ^tA is unitary. (b) Show that A^{-1} exists and is unitary. (c) If B is complex unitary, show that AB is unitary, and that $B^{-1}AB$ is unitary.

5. (a) Let V be a finite dimensional space over $\mathbf{R}$, with a positive definite scalar product, and let $\{v_1, \ldots, v_n\} = \mathfrak{B}$ and $\{w_1, \ldots, w_n\} = \mathfrak{B}'$ be orthonormal bases of V. Show that the matrix $M_{\mathfrak{B}}^{\mathfrak{B}'}(id)$ is real unitary. [*Hint:* Use $\langle w_i, w_i \rangle = 1$ and $\langle w_i, w_j \rangle = 0$ if $i \neq j$, as well as the expression $w_i = \sum a_{ij}v_j$, for some $a_{ij} \in \mathbf{R}$.]

(b) Let $F: V \to V$ be such that $F(v_i) = w_i$ for all i. Show that $M_{\mathfrak{B}}^{\mathfrak{B}'}(F)$ is unitary.

6. Show that the absolute value of the determinant of a real unitary matrix is equal to 1. Conclude that if A is real unitary, then $\mathrm{Det}(A) = 1$ or -1.

7. If A is a complex square matrix, show that $\mathrm{Det}(\overline{A}) = \overline{\mathrm{Det}(A)}$. Conclude that the absolute value of the determinant of a complex unitary matrix is equal to 1.

8. Let A be a diagonal real unitary matrix. Show that the diagonal elements of A are equal to 1 or -1.

9. Let A be a diagonal complex unitary matrix. Show that each diagonal element has absolute value 1, and hence is of type $e^{i\theta}$, with real θ.

The following exercises describe various properties of real unitary maps of the plane $\mathbf{R}^2$.

10. Let V be a 2-dimensional vector space over $\mathbf{R}$, with a positive definite scalar product, and let A be a real unitary map of V into itself. Let $\{v_1, v_2\}$ and $\{w_1, w_2\}$ be orthonormal bases of V such that $Av_i = w_i$ for $i = 1, 2$. Let a, b, c, d be real numbers such that

$$w_1 = av_1 + bv_2,$$

$$w_2 = cv_1 + dv_2.$$

Show that $a^2 + b^2 = 1$, $c^2 + d^2 = 1$, $ac + bd = 0$, $a^2 = d^2$ and $c^2 = b^2$.

11. Show that the determinant $ad - bc$ is equal to 1 or -1. (Show that its square is equal to 1.)

12. Define a **rotation** of V to be a real unitary map A of V whose determinant is 1. Show that the matrix of A relative to an orthogonal basis of V is of type

$$\begin{pmatrix} a & -b \\ b & a \end{pmatrix}$$

for some real numbers a, b such that $a^2 + b^2 = 1$. Also prove the converse, that any linear map of V into itself represented by such a matrix on an orthogonal basis is unitary, and has determinant 1. Using calculus, one can then conclude that there exist a number θ such that $a = \cos\theta$ and $b = \sin\theta$.

13. Show that there exists a complex unitary matrix U such that, if

$$A = \begin{pmatrix} \cos\theta & -\sin\theta \\ \sin\theta & \cos\theta \end{pmatrix} \quad \text{and} \quad B = \begin{pmatrix} e^{i\theta} & 0 \\ 0 & e^{-i\theta} \end{pmatrix}$$

then $U^{-1}AU = B$.

14. Let $V = \mathbf{C}$ be viewed as a vector space of dimension 2 over $\mathbf{R}$. Let $\alpha \in \mathbf{C}$, and let $L_\alpha \colon \mathbf{C} \to \mathbf{C}$ be the map $z \mapsto \alpha z$. Show that L_α is an $\mathbf{R}$-linear map of V into itself. For which complex numbers α is L_α a unitary map with respect to the scalar product $\langle z, w \rangle = \mathrm{Re}(z\bar{w})$? What is the matrix of L_α with respect to the basis $\{1, i\}$ of $\mathbf{C}$ over $\mathbf{R}$?

§6. Sylvester's theorem

Let V be a finite dimensional vector space over the real numbers, of dimension > 0. Let $\langle\,,\,\rangle$ be a scalar product on V (i.e. a symmetric bilinear form). As we know, by Theorem 12 of Chapter VI, §5, we can always find an orthogonal basis. Our form need not be positive definite, and hence it may happen that there is a vector $v \in V$ such that $\langle v, v \rangle = 0$, or $\langle v, v \rangle = -1$.

Example. Let $V = \mathbf{R}^2$, and let the form be represented by the matrix

$$C = \begin{pmatrix} -1 & +1 \\ +1 & -1 \end{pmatrix}.$$

Then the vectors

$$v_1 = \begin{pmatrix} 1 \\ 0 \end{pmatrix} \quad \text{and} \quad v_2 = \begin{pmatrix} 1 \\ 1 \end{pmatrix}$$

form an orthogonal basis for the form, and we have

$$\langle v_1, v_1 \rangle = -1, \quad \text{as well as} \quad \langle v_2, v_2 \rangle = 0.$$

For instance, in term of coordinates, if $^tX = (1, 1)$ is the coordinate vector of say v_2 with respect to the standard basis of $\mathbf{R}^2$ given by $\{e^1, e^2\}$, then a trivial direct computation shows that

$$\langle X, X \rangle = {}^{t}XCX = 0.$$

Our purpose in this section is to analyse the general situation in arbitrary dimensions.

Let $\{v_1, \ldots, v_n\}$ be an orthogonal basis of V. Let

$$c_i = \langle v_i, v_i \rangle.$$

After renumbering the elements of our basis if necessary, we may assume that $\{v_1, \ldots, v_n\}$ are so ordered that:

$$c_1, \ldots, c_r > 0,$$

$$c_{r+1}, \ldots, c_s < 0,$$

$$c_{s+1}, \ldots, c_n = 0.$$

We are interested in the number of positive terms, negative terms, and zero terms, among the "squares" $\langle v_i, v_i \rangle$, in other words, in the numbers r and s. We shall see in this section that these numbers do not depend on the choice of orthogonal basis.

If X is the coordinate vector of an element of V with respect to our basis, and if f is the quadratic form associated with our scalar product, then in terms of the coordinate vector, we have

$$f(X) = c_1 x_1^2 + \cdots + c_r x_r^2 + c_{r+1} x_{r+1}^2 + \cdots + c_s x_s^2.$$

We see that in the expression of f in terms of coordinates, there are exactly r positive terms, and $s - r$ negative terms. Furthermore, $n - s$ variables have disappeared.

We can see this even more clearly by further normalizing our basis.

We generalize our notion of orthonormal basis. We recall that an orthogonal basis $\{v_1, \ldots, v_n\}$ is **orthonormal** if for each i we have

$$\langle v_i, v_i \rangle = 1 \quad \text{or} \quad \langle v_i, v_i \rangle = -1 \quad \text{or} \quad \langle v_i, v_i \rangle = 0.$$

If $\{v_1, \ldots, v_n\}$ is an orthogonal basis, then we can obtain an orthonormal basis from it just as in the positive definite case. We let $c_i = \langle v_i, v_i \rangle$. If $c_i = 0$, we let

$$v_i' = v_i.$$

If $c_i > 0$, we let

$$v_i' = \frac{v_i}{\sqrt{c_i}}.$$

If $c_i < 0$, we let

$$v_i' = \frac{v_i}{\sqrt{-c_i}}.$$

Then $\{v_1', \ldots, v_n'\}$ is an orthonormal basis.

Let $\{v_1, \ldots, v_n\}$ be an orthonormal basis of V, for our scalar product. If X is the coordinate vector of an element of V, then in terms of our orthonormal basis,

$$f(X) = x_1^2 + \cdots + x_r^2 - x_{r+1}^2 - \cdots - x_s^2.$$

Thus on an orthonormal basis, we see the number of positive and negative terms particularly clearly. In proving that the number of these does not depend on the orthonormal basis, we shall first deal with the number of terms which disappears, and we shall give a geometric interpretation for it.

Theorem 12. *Let V be a finite dimensional vector space over $\mathbf{R}$, with a scalar product. Assume $\dim V > 0$. Let V_0 be the subspace of V consisting of all vectors $v \in V$ such that $\langle v, w \rangle = 0$ for all $w \in V$. Let $\{v_1, \ldots, v_n\}$ be an orthogonal basis for V. Then the number of integers i such that $\langle v_i, v_i \rangle = 0$ is equal to the dimension of V_0.*

Proof. We suppose $\{v_1, \ldots, v_n\}$ so ordered that

$$\langle v_1, v_1 \rangle \neq 0, \quad \ldots, \quad \langle v_s, v_s \rangle \neq 0 \qquad \text{but} \qquad \langle v_i, v_i \rangle = 0 \quad \text{if} \quad i > s.$$

Since $\{v_1, \ldots, v_n\}$ is an orthogonal basis, it is then clear that $v_{s+1}, \ldots, v_n$ lie in V_0. Let v be an element of V_0, and write

$$v = x_1 v_1 + \cdots + x_s v_s + \cdots + x_n v_n$$

with $x_i \in \mathbf{R}$. Taking the scalar product with any v_j for $j \leq s$, we find

$$0 = \langle v, v_j \rangle = x_j \langle v_j, v_j \rangle.$$

Since $\langle v_j, v_j \rangle \neq 0$, it follows that $x_j = 0$. Hence v lies in the space generated by $v_{s+1}, \ldots, v_n$. We conclude that $v_{s+1}, \ldots, v_n$ form a basis of V_0.

In Theorem 12, the dimension of V_0 is called the **index of nullity of the form.** We see that the form is non-degenerate if and only if its index of nullity is 0.

Sylvester's Theorem. *Let V be a finite dimensional vector space over $\mathbf{R}$, with a scalar product. There exists an integer $r \geq 0$ having the following property. If $\{v_1, \ldots, v_n\}$ is an orthogonal basis of V, then there are precisely r integers i such that $\langle v_i, v_i \rangle > 0$.*

Proof. Let $\{v_1, \ldots, v_n\}$ and $\{w_1, \ldots, w_n\}$ be orthogonal bases. We suppose their elements so arranged that

$$\langle v_i, v_i \rangle > 0 \quad \text{if} \quad 1 \leqq i \leqq r$$

$$\langle v_i, v_i \rangle < 0 \quad \text{if} \quad r+1 \leqq i \leqq s$$

$$\langle v_i, v_i \rangle = 0 \quad \text{if} \quad s+1 \leqq i \leqq n.$$

Similarly,

$$\langle w_i, w_i \rangle > 0 \quad \text{if} \quad 1 \leqq i \leqq r'$$

$$\langle w_i, w_i \rangle < 0 \quad \text{if} \quad r'+1 \leqq i \leqq s'$$

$$\langle w_i, w_i \rangle = 0 \quad \text{if} \quad s'+1 \leqq i \leqq n.$$

We shall first prove that

$$v_1, \ldots, v_r, w_{r'+1}, \ldots, w_n$$

are linearly independent.

Suppose we have a relation

$$x_1 v_1 + \cdots + x_r v_r + y_{r'+1} w_{r'+1} + \cdots + y_n w_n = 0.$$

Then

$$x_1 v_1 + \cdots + x_r v_r = -(y_{r'+1} w_{r'+1} + \cdots + y_n w_n).$$

Let $c_i = \langle v_i, v_i \rangle$ and $d_i = \langle w_i, w_i \rangle$ for all i. Taking the scalar product of each side of the preceding equation with itself, we obtain

$$c_1 x_1^2 + \cdots + c_r x_r^2 = d_{r'+1} y_{r'+1}^2 + \cdots + d_{s'} y_{s'}^2.$$

The left-hand side is $\geqq 0$. The right-hand side is $\leqq 0$. The only way this can hold is that they are both equal to 0, and this holds only if

$$x_1 = \cdots = x_r = 0.$$

From the linear independence of $w_{r'+1}, \ldots, w_n$ it follows that all coefficients $y_{r'+1}, \ldots, y_n$ are also equal to 0.

Since dim $V = n$, we now conclude that

$$r + n - r' \leqq n$$

or in other words, $r \leqq r'$. But the situation holding with respect to our two bases is symmetric, and thus $r' \leqq r$. It follows that $r' = r$, and Sylvester's theorem is proved.

The integer r of Sylvester's theorem is called the **index of positivity** of the form.

EXERCISES

1. Determine the index of nullity and index of positivity for each form determined by the following symmetric matrices, on $\mathbf{R}^2$.

$$\text{(a)} \begin{pmatrix} 1 & 2 \\ 2 & -1 \end{pmatrix} \qquad \text{(b)} \begin{pmatrix} 1 & 1 \\ 1 & 1 \end{pmatrix} \qquad \text{(c)} \begin{pmatrix} 1 & -3 \\ -3 & 2 \end{pmatrix}$$

2. Let V be a finite dimensional space over $\mathbf{R}$, and let $\langle \ , \ \rangle$ be a scalar product on V. Show that V admits a direct sum decomposition

$$V = V^+ \oplus V^- \oplus V_0,$$

where V_0 is defined as in Theorem 12, and where the form is positive definite on V^+ and negative definite on V^-. (This means that

$$\langle v, v \rangle > 0 \qquad \text{for all} \qquad v \in V^+$$

$$\langle v, v \rangle < 0 \qquad \text{for all} \qquad v \in V^-.)$$

Show that the dimensions of the spaces V^+, V^- are the same in all such decompositions.

3. Let V be the vector space over $\mathbf{R}$ of 2×2 real symmetric matrices.
   (a) Show that the function f on V such that $f(A) = \text{Det}(A)$ is a quadratic form on V.
   (b) Let W be the subspace of V consisting of all A such that $\text{tr}(A) = 0$. Show that the bilinear form associated with the quadratic form f is negative definite on W.

CHAPTER IX

Polynomials and Matrices

§1. Polynomials

Let K be a field. By a **polynomial** over K we shall mean a function of K into itself such that there exist elements $a_0, \ldots, a_n \in K$ such that

$$f(t) = a_n t^n + \cdots + a_0$$

for all $t \in K$. Let

$$g(t) = b_m t^m + \cdots + b_0$$

be another polynomial with $b_j \in K$, then we can form the sum $f + g$. If, say, $n \geqq m$ we can write $b_j = 0$ if $j > m$,

$$g(t) = 0t^n + \cdots + b_m t^m + \cdots + b_0,$$

and then we can write the values of the sum $f + g$ as

$$(f + g)(t) = (a_n + b_n)t^n + \cdots + (a_0 + b_0).$$

Thus $f + g$ is again a polynomial. If $c \in K$, then

$$(cf)(t) = ca_n t^n + \cdots + ca_0,$$

and hence cf is a polynomial. Thus polynomials form a vector space over K. We can also take the product of the two polynomials, fg, and

$$(fg)(t) = (a_n b_m)t^{n+m} + \cdots + a_0 b_0,$$

so that fg is again a polynomial. In fact, if we write

$$(fg)(t) = c_{n+m} t^{n+m} + \cdots + c_0,$$

then

$$c_k = \sum_{i=0}^{k} a_i b_{k-i} = a_0 b_k + a_1 b_{k-1} + \cdots + a_k b_0.$$

All the preceding rules are probably familiar to you but we have recalled them to get in the right mood.

Theorem 1. *Let f, g be polynomials such that $f(t) = g(t)$ for all $t \in K$. Write*

$$f(t) = a_n t^n + \cdots + a_0,$$
$$g(t) = b_n t^n + \cdots + b_0.$$

Then $a_i = b_i$ for all i.

Proof. We give the proof here only when $K = \mathbf{R}$ or $\mathbf{C}$. We consider the polynomial $h = f - g$. Then $h(x) = 0$ for all x in K. We must show that $a_i - b_i = 0$ for all i. Suppose this is not the case. Let r be the largest integer such that $a_r \neq b_r$. Then we can write for all t,

$$0 = (a_r - b_r)t^r + \cdots + (a_0 - b_0).$$

Divide by t^r. Then

$$0 = a_r - b_r + \frac{a_{r-1} - b_{r-1}}{t} + \cdots + \frac{a_0 - b_0}{t^r}.$$

Now let t become very large (taking real values for t). Then all the terms to the right of $a_r - b_r$ approach 0. Hence $a_r - b_r = 0$, contradiction. We have proved our theorem.

Note. We have used the notion of limit. In Chapter XII, §1 we shall prove the same statement for more general fields, by a method which is completely algebraic. In this chapter, we are mainly concerned in discussing simple properties of polynomials for applications to the next two chapters, which take place over the real and complex numbers. Hence we do not shy away from a slight amount of analysis.

Theorem 1 shows that when we write a polynomial f in the form

$$f(t) = a_n t^n + \cdots + a_0$$

with $a_i \in K$, then the numbers $a_0, \ldots, a_n$ are uniquely determined. They are called the **coefficients** of the polynomial. If n is the largest integer such that $a_n \neq 0$, then we say that n is the **degree** of f and write $n = \deg f$. We also say that a_n is the **leading coefficient** of f. We say that a_0 is the **constant term** of f. If f is the zero polynomial, then we shall use the convention that $\deg f = -\infty$. We agree to the convention that

$$-\infty + -\infty = -\infty,$$
$$-\infty + a = -\infty, \qquad -\infty < a$$

for every integer a, and *no other operation with $-\infty$ is defined.*

The reason for our convention is that it makes the following theorem true without exception.

Theorem 2. *Let f, g be polynomials with coefficients in K. Then*

$$\deg (fg) = \deg f + \deg g.$$

Proof. Let

$$f(t) = a_n t^n + \cdots + a_0 \qquad \text{and} \qquad g(t) = b_m t^m + \cdots + b_0$$

with $a_n \neq 0$ and $b_m \neq 0$. Then from the multiplication rule for fg, we see that

$$f(t)g(t) = a_n b_m t^{n+m} + \text{terms of lower degree},$$

and $a_n b_m \neq 0$. Hence $\deg fg = n + m = \deg f + \deg g$. If f or g is 0, then our convention about $-\infty$ makes our assertion also come out.

A polynomial of degree 1 is also called a **linear** polynomial.

By a **root** α of f we shall mean a number such that $f(\alpha) = 0$. We admit without proof the following statement:

Theorem 3. *Let f be a polynomial with complex coefficients, of degree ≥ 1. Then f has a root in $\mathbf{C}$.*

We shall prove this theorem in an appendix, using some facts of analysis.

Theorem 4. *Let f be a polynomial with complex coefficients, leading coefficient 1, and $\deg f = n \geq 1$. Then there exist complex numbers $\alpha_1, \ldots, \alpha_n$ such that*

$$f(t) = (t - \alpha_1) \cdots (t - \alpha_n).$$

The numbers $\alpha_1, \ldots, \alpha_n$ are uniquely determined up to a permutation. Every root α of f is equal to some α_i, and conversely.

Proof. We shall give the proof of Theorem 4 (assuming Theorem 3) completely in Chapter XII. Since in this chapter, and the next two chapters, we do not need to know anything about polynomials except the simple statements of this section, we feel it is better to postpone the proof to this later chapter. Furthermore, the further theory of polynomials developed in Chapter XII will also have further applications to the theory of linear maps and matrices.

As a matter of terminology, let $\alpha_1, \ldots, \alpha_r$ be the distinct roots of the polynomial f in $\mathbf{C}$. Then we can write

$$f(t) = (t - \alpha_1)^{m_1} \cdots (t - \alpha_r)^{m_r},$$

with integers $m_1, \ldots, m_r > 0$, uniquely determined. We say that m_i is the **multiplicity** of α_i in f.

§2. Polynomials of matrices and linear maps

The set of polynomials with coefficients in K will be denoted by the symbols $K[t]$.

Let A be a square matrix with coefficients in K. Let $f \in K[t]$, and write

$$f(t) = a_n t^n + \cdots + a_0$$

with $a_i \in K$. We define

$$f(A) = a_n A^n + \cdots + a_0 I.$$

Example 1. Let $f(t) = 3t^2 - 2t + 5$. Let $A = \begin{pmatrix} 1 & -1 \\ 2 & 0 \end{pmatrix}$. Then

$$f(A) = 3 \begin{pmatrix} 1 & -1 \\ 2 & 0 \end{pmatrix}^2 - \begin{pmatrix} 2 & -2 \\ 4 & 0 \end{pmatrix} + \begin{pmatrix} 5 & 0 \\ 0 & 5 \end{pmatrix} = \begin{pmatrix} 4 & -5 \\ 0 & -1 \end{pmatrix}.$$

Theorem 5. *Let $f, g \in K[t]$. Let A be a square matrix with coefficients in K. Then*

$$(f + g)(A) = f(A) + g(A),$$

$$(fg)(A) = f(A)g(A).$$

If $c \in K$, then $(cf)(A) = cf(A)$.

Proof. Let $f(t)$ and $g(t)$ be written in the form

$$f(t) = a_n t^n + \cdots + a_0$$

and

$$g(t) = b_m t^m + \cdots + b_0$$

with $a_i, b_j \in K$. Then

$$(fg)(t) = c_{m+n} t^{m+n} + \cdots + c_0$$

where

$$c_k = \sum_{i=0}^{k} a_i b_{k-i}.$$

By definition,

$$(fg)(A) = c_{m+n} A^{m+n} + \cdots + c_0 I.$$

On the other hand,

$$f(A) = a_n A^n + \cdots + a_0 I$$

and

$$g(A) = b_m A^m + \cdots + b_0 I.$$

Hence

$$f(A)g(A) = \sum_{i=0}^{n} \sum_{j=0}^{m} a_i A^i b_j A^j = \sum_{i=0}^{n} \sum_{j=0}^{m} a_i b_j A^{i+j} = \sum_{k=0}^{m+n} c_k A^k.$$

Thus $f(A)g(A) = (fg)(A)$.

For the sum, suppose $n \geq m$, and let $b_j = 0$ if $j > m$. We have

$$(f + g)(A) = (a_n + b_n)A^n + \cdots + (a_0 + b_0)I$$
$$= a_n A^n + b_n A^n + \cdots + a_0 I + b_0 I$$
$$= f(A) + g(A).$$

If $c \in K$, then

$$(cf)(A) = ca_n A^n + \cdots + ca_0 I = cf(A).$$

This proves our theorem.

Example 2. Let $f(t) = (t - 1)(t + 3) = t^2 + 2t - 3$. Then

$$f(A) = A^2 + 2A - 3I = (A - I)(A + 3I).$$

If we multiply this last product directly using the rules for multiplication of matrices, we obtain in fact

$$A^2 - IA + 3AI - 3I^2 = A^2 + 2A - 3I.$$

Example 3. Let $\alpha_1, \ldots, \alpha_n$ be numbers. Let

$$f(t) = (t - \alpha_1) \cdots (t - \alpha_n).$$

Then

$$f(A) = (A - \alpha_1 I) \cdots (A - \alpha_n I).$$

Let V be a vector space over K, and let $A: V \to V$ be an operator (i.e. linear map of V into itself). Then we can form $A^2 = A \circ A = AA$, and in general $A^n = $ iteration of A taken n times for any positive integer n. We define $A^0 = I$ (where I now denotes the identity mapping). We have

$$A^{m+n} = A^m A^n$$

for all integers $m, n \geq 0$. If f is a polynomial in $K[t]$, then we can form $f(A)$ the same way that we did for matrices, and the same rules hold as stated in Theorem 5. The proofs are the same. The essential thing that we used was the ordinary laws of addition and multiplication, and these hold also for linear maps.

Theorem 6. *Let A be an $n \times n$ matrix in a field K. Then there exists a non-zero polynomial $f \in K[t]$ such that $f(A) = O$.*

Proof. The vector space of $n \times n$ matrices over K is finite dimensional, of dimension n^2. Hence the powers

$$I, A, A^2, \ldots, A^N$$

are linearly dependent for $N > n^2$. This means that there exist numbers $a_0, \ldots, a_N \in K$ such that not all $a_i = 0$, and

$$a_N A^N + \cdots + a_0 I = O.$$

We let $f(t) = a_N t^N + \cdots + a_0$ to get what we want.

As with Theorem 5, we note that Theorem 6 also holds for a linear map A of a finite dimensional vector space over K. The proof is again the same, and we shall use Theorem 6 indiscriminately for matrices or linear maps.

We shall determine later in Chapter X, §2 a polynomial $P(t)$ which can be constructed explicitly such that $P(A) = O$.

If we divide the polynomial f of Theorem 6 by its leading coefficient, then we obtain a polynomial g with leading coefficient 1 such that $g(A) = O$. It is usually convenient to deal with polynomials whose leading coefficient is 1, since it simplifies the notation.

EXERCISES

1. Compute $f(A)$ when $f(t) = t^3 - 2t + 1$ and $A = \begin{pmatrix} -1 & 1 \\ 2 & 4 \end{pmatrix}$.

2. Let A be a symmetric matrix, and let f be a polynomial with real coefficients. Show that $f(A)$ is also symmetric.

3. Let A be a hermitian matrix, and let f be a polynomial with real coefficients. Show that $f(A)$ is hermitian.

4. Let A, B be $n \times n$ matrices in a field K, and assume that B is invertible. Show that

$$(B^{-1}AB)^n = B^{-1}A^nB$$

for all positive integers n.

5. Let $f \in K[t]$. Let A, B be as in Exercise 4. Show that

$$f(B^{-1}AB) = B^{-1}f(A)B.$$

§3. *Eigenvectors and eigenvalues*

Let V be a vector space over the field K, and let

$$A : V \to V$$

be an operator of V (i.e. a linear map of V into itself). An element $v \in V$ is called an **eigenvector** of A if there exists $\lambda \in K$ such that $Av = \lambda v$. If

$v \neq O$ then λ is uniquely determined, because $\lambda_1 v = \lambda_2 v$ implies $\lambda_1 = \lambda_2$. In this case, we say that λ is an **eigenvalue** of A belonging to the eigenvector v. We also say that v is an eigenvector with the eigenvalue λ. Instead of eigenvector and eigenvalue, one also uses the terms **characteristic vector** and **characteristic value.**

If A is a square $n \times n$ matrix, with coefficients in K, then an **eigenvector** of A is by definition an eigenvector of the linear map of K^n into itself represented by this matrix, relative to the usual basis. Thus an eigenvector X of A is a (column) vector of K^n for which there exists $\lambda \in K$ such that $AX = \lambda X$.

Example 1. Let V be the vector space over $\mathbf{R}$ generated by all infinitely differentiable functions. Let $\lambda \in \mathbf{R}$. Then the function f such that $f(t) = e^{\lambda t}$ is an eigenvector of the derivative d/dt because $df/dt = \lambda e^{\lambda t}$.

Example 2. Let

$$A = \begin{pmatrix} a_1 & & 0 \\ & \ddots & \\ 0 & & a_n \end{pmatrix}$$

be a diagonal matrix in K. Then every unit vector e^i $(i = 1, \ldots, n)$ is an eigenvector of A. In fact, we have $Ae^i = a_i e^i$:

$$\begin{pmatrix} a_1 & 0 & \cdots & 0 \\ 0 & a_2 & \cdots & 0 \\ \vdots & \vdots & & \vdots \\ 0 & 0 & \cdots & a_n \end{pmatrix} \begin{pmatrix} 0 \\ \vdots \\ 1 \\ \vdots \\ 0 \end{pmatrix} = \begin{pmatrix} 0 \\ \vdots \\ a_i \\ \vdots \\ 0 \end{pmatrix}$$

Example 3. If $A : V \to V$ is a linear map, and v is an eigenvector of A, then for any non-zero scalar c, cv is also an eigenvector of A, with the same eigenvalue.

Theorem 7. *Let V be a vector space over the field K, and let $A : V \to V$ be a linear map. Let $\lambda \in K$. Let V_λ be the subspace of V generated by all eigenvectors of A having λ as eigenvalue. Then every non-zero element of V_λ is an eigenvector of A having λ as eigenvalue.*

Proof. Let $v_1, v_2 \in V$ be such that $Av_1 = \lambda v_1$ and $Av_2 = \lambda v_2$. Then

$$A(v_1 + v_2) = Av_1 + Av_2 = \lambda v_1 + \lambda v_2 = \lambda(v_1 + v_2).$$

If $c \in K$ then $A(cv_1) = cAv_1 = c\lambda v_1 = \lambda cv_1$. This proves our theorem.

The subspace V_λ in Theorem 7 is called the **eigenspace** of A belonging to λ.

Note. If v_1, v_2 are eigenvectors of A with different eigenvalues $\lambda_1 \neq \lambda_2$ then of course $v_1 + v_2$ is *not* an eigenvector of A. In fact, we have the following theorem:

Theorem 8. *Let V be a vector space over K, and let $A : V \to V$ be an operator. Let $v_1, \ldots, v_m$ be eigenvectors of A, with eigenvalues $\lambda_1, \ldots, \lambda_m$ respectively. Assume that these eigenvalues are distinct, i.e.*

$$\lambda_i \neq \lambda_j \qquad if \qquad i \neq j.$$

Then $v_1, \ldots, v_m$ are linearly independent.

Proof. By induction on m. For $m = 1$, an element $v_1 \in V$, $v_1 \neq O$ is linearly independent. Assume $m > 1$. Suppose that we have a relation

(*) $$c_1 v_1 + \cdots + c_m v_m = O$$

with $c_i \in K$. We must prove all $c_i = 0$. We multiply our relation (*) by λ_1 to obtain

$$c_1 \lambda_1 v_1 + \cdots + c_m \lambda_1 v_m = O.$$

We also apply A to our relation (*). By linearity, we obtain

$$c_1 \lambda_1 v_1 + \cdots + c_m \lambda_m v_m = O.$$

We now subtract these last two expressions, and obtain

$$c_2 (\lambda_2 - \lambda_1) v_1 + \cdots + c_m (\lambda_m - \lambda_1) v_m = O.$$

Since $\lambda_j - \lambda_1 \neq 0$ for $j = 2, \ldots, m$ we conclude by induction that $c_2 = \cdots = c_m = 0$. Going back to our original relation, we see that $c_1 v_1 = O$, whence $c_1 = 0$, and our theorem is proved.

Example 4. Let V be the vector space over $\mathbf{C}$ consisting of all complex valued differentiable functions of a real variable t. Let $\alpha_1, \ldots, \alpha_m$ be distinct complex numbers. The functions

$$e^{\alpha_1 t}, \ldots, e^{\alpha_m t}$$

are eigenvectors of the derivative, with distinct eigenvalues $\alpha_1, \ldots, \alpha_m$, and hence are linearly independent. Frequently in analysis, one considers the functions $e^{2\pi i n t}$ with $n = 1, 2, \ldots$

Theorem 9. *Let V be a finite dimensional vector space over K, and let $\lambda \in K$. Let $A : V \to V$ be a linear map. Then λ is an eigenvalue of A if and only if $A - \lambda I$ is not invertible.*

Proof. Assume that λ is an eigenvalue of A. Then there exists an element $v \in V$, $v \neq O$ such that $Av = \lambda v$. Hence $Av - \lambda v = O$, and

$(A - \lambda I)v = O$. Hence $A - \lambda I$ has a non-zero kernel, and $A - \lambda I$ cannot be invertible. Conversely, assume that $A - \lambda I$ is not invertible. By the Corollary of Theorem 6, Chapter IV, §4, we see that $A - \lambda I$ must have a non-zero kernel, meaning that there exists an element $v \in V$, $v \neq O$ such that $(A - \lambda I)v = O$. Hence $Av - \lambda v = O$, and $Av = \lambda v$. Thus λ is an eigenvalue of A. This proves our theorem.

Theorem 10. *Let V be a finite dimensional vector space over the complex numbers, and assume* dim $V \geq 1$. *Let $A : V \to V$ be a linear map. Then there exists a non-zero eigenvector of A.*

Proof. According to Theorem 6 of §2 there exists a non-zero polynomial $f \in \mathbf{C}[t]$ such that $f(A) = O$, and we may assume that f has leading coefficient 1. By Theorem 4 of §1, there exist complex numbers $\lambda_1, \ldots, \lambda_n$ such that

$$f(t) = (t - \lambda_1) \cdots (t - \lambda_n).$$

We conclude that

$$O = f(A) = (A - \lambda_1 I) \cdots (A - \lambda_n I).$$

Not every one of the linear maps $A - \lambda_i I$ is invertible, for otherwise, the composite

$$(A - \lambda_1 I) \cdots (A - \lambda_n I)$$

would also be invertible. Hence for some i, there exists an element $v \in V$, $v \neq O$ such that

$$(A - \lambda_i I)v = O.$$

But then $Av = \lambda_i v$, and we have found the desired eigenvector.

Remark. The assertion of Theorem 10 is false if our vector space V is over $\mathbf{R}$ instead of being over $\mathbf{C}$. For instance, a rotation by an angle θ in $\mathbf{R}^2$ does not have a real eigenvector if θ is not an integral multiple of π. (Cf. Exercise 3.)

Theorem 11. *Let V be a vector space over the field K, and let $A : V \to V$ be a linear map. Assume that there exists a basis $\{v_1, \ldots, v_n\}$ of V consisting of eigenvectors of A, with eigenvalues $\lambda_1, \ldots, \lambda_n$ respectively. Then the matrix associated with A with respect to this basis is the diagonal matrix*

$$\begin{pmatrix} \lambda_1 & 0 & \cdots & 0 \\ 0 & \lambda_2 & \cdots & 0 \\ \vdots & \vdots & & \vdots \\ 0 & 0 & \cdots & \lambda_n \end{pmatrix}$$

Proof. Obvious.

We already saw the converse of Theorem 11 in Example 2. Thus it is important to determine instances when a vector space has a basis consisting of eigenvectors for an operator. These instances are precisely those when the operator can be diagonalized. For example, Theorem 8 now yields:

Corollary 1. *Let V be a finite dimensional vector space over K, of dimension n. Let $A: V \to V$ be an operator. Assume that A has n distinct eigenvalues. Then V has a basis consisting of eigenvectors for A, and A can therefore be diagonalized.*

Or in terms of matrices:

Corollary 2. *Let A be an $n \times n$ matrix over a field K. Assume that A has n distinct eigenvalues in K. Then there exists a non-singular matrix B in K such that $B^{-1}AB$ is a diagonal matrix.*

In the exercises, we shall carry out the case of 2×2 matrices. We give an example.

Example 5. Find the eigenvalues and eigenvectors of the matrix

$$A = \begin{pmatrix} 1 & 2 \\ -1 & 1 \end{pmatrix}.$$

If there is an eigenvector $\begin{pmatrix} x \\ y \end{pmatrix}$ and an eigenvalue λ, then

$$x + 2y = \lambda x,$$
$$-x + y = \lambda y,$$

and consequently, subtracting the left-hand side from the right-hand side, we must have

$$x(\lambda - 1) - 2y = 0,$$
$$x + (\lambda - 1)y = 0.$$

Since not both x, y can be 0, the determinant

$$\begin{vmatrix} \lambda - 1 & -2 \\ 1 & \lambda - 1 \end{vmatrix}$$

is 0, and λ is a root of the polynomial

$$(\lambda - 1)^2 + 2 = 0,$$

or $\lambda^2 - 2\lambda + 3 = 0$. The roots are $1 + i\sqrt{2}$ and $1 - i\sqrt{2}$.

Conversely, if λ is a root of the preceding polynomial, then the preceding determinant is equal to 0, and there is a solution of the system of equations

$$x(\lambda - 1) - 2y = 0$$

$$x + (\lambda - 1)y = 0$$

with not both x, y equal to 0. In this way we find an eigenvalue λ and an eigenvector $\begin{pmatrix} x \\ y \end{pmatrix}$. We can do this explicitly. Let $\lambda_1 = 1 + i\sqrt{2}$ and $\lambda_2 = 1 - i\sqrt{2}$. Solving the system of linear equations with $\lambda = \lambda_1$ yields the eigenvector

$$v_1 = \begin{pmatrix} x_1 \\ y_1 \end{pmatrix} = \begin{pmatrix} 1 \\ \dfrac{i\sqrt{2}}{2} \end{pmatrix}.$$

Solving the system of linear equations with $\lambda = \lambda_2$ yields the eigenvector

$$v_2 = \begin{pmatrix} x_2 \\ y_2 \end{pmatrix} = \begin{pmatrix} 1 \\ \dfrac{-i\sqrt{2}}{2} \end{pmatrix}.$$

Remark. Any eigenvector with eigenvalue λ_1 is equal to cv_1 with some number $c \neq 0$. Any eigenvector with eigenvalue λ_2 is equal to $c'v_2$ with some number $c' \neq 0$. Observe that the eigenvalues and eigenvectors are *complex*, and that there are no real eigenvalues.

EXERCISES

1. Let

$$\begin{pmatrix} a & b \\ c & d \end{pmatrix}$$

be a 2×2 matrix in a field K. Show that any eigenvalue λ of this matrix is a root of the polynomial

$$\begin{vmatrix} t - a & -b \\ -c & t - d \end{vmatrix} = (t - a)(t - d) - bc.$$

2. Conversely, show that any root of the polynomial

$$\begin{vmatrix} t - a & -b \\ -c & t - d \end{vmatrix}$$

is an eigenvalue of the given matrix.

3. Show that if $\theta \in \mathbf{R}$ and θ is not an integral multiple of π, then the matrix

$$\begin{pmatrix} \cos\theta & -\sin\theta \\ \sin\theta & \cos\theta \end{pmatrix}$$

does not have a non-zero eigenvector in $\mathbf{R}^2$.

4. Show that if $\theta \in \mathbf{R}$, then the matrix

$$A = \begin{pmatrix} \cos\theta & \sin\theta \\ \sin\theta & -\cos\theta \end{pmatrix}$$

always has an eigenvector in $\mathbf{R}^2$, and in fact that there exists a vector v_1 such that $Av_1 = v_1$. [*Hint:* Let the first component of v_1 be

$$x = \frac{\sin\theta}{1 - \cos\theta}$$

if $\cos\theta \neq 1$. Then solve for y. What if $\cos\theta = 1$?]

5. In Exercise 4, let v_2 be a vector of $\mathbf{R}^2$ perpendicular to the vector v_1 found in that exercise. Show that $Av_2 = -v_2$. Define this to mean that A is a reflection.

6. Show that any 2×2 real unitary matrix whose determinant is -1 can be expressed as a product

$$\begin{pmatrix} 1 & 0 \\ 0 & -1 \end{pmatrix} \begin{pmatrix} \cos\theta & -\sin\theta \\ \sin\theta & \cos\theta \end{pmatrix}$$

for some real number θ.

7. Let V be a finite dimensional vector space over K, and let $A: V \to V$ be a linear map. Let $v \in V$ be an eigenvector of A, say $Av = \lambda v$. If f is a polynomial in $K[t]$, show that $f(A)v = f(\lambda)v$.

8. Let V be a finite dimensional vector space over a field K. Let A, B be linear maps of V into itself. Assume that $AB = BA$. Show that if v is an eigenvector of A, with eigenvalue λ, then Bv is an eigenvector of A, with eigenvalue λ also if $Bv \neq O$.

9. Let V be a finite dimensional vector space over the complex numbers. Let A, B be two linear maps of V into itself such that $AB = BA$. Show that A, B have a common eigenvector. [*Hint:* If λ is an eigenvalue of A, consider the space V_λ consisting of all vectors v such that $Av = \lambda v$, and show that B maps this space into itself. Then proceed on your own.]

10. Let V be a finite dimensional vector space over the field K. Let A, B be linear maps of V into itself, and assume that $AB = BA$. Assume that there exists a basis of V consisting of eigenvectors of A, and a basis of V consisting of eigenvectors of B. Show that there exists a basis all of whose elements are eigenvectors for both A and B (i.e. A and B can be simultaneously diagonalized).

§4. *The characteristic polynomial*

In the exercises of the preceding section, we determined a polynomial for any 2×2 matrix whose roots were the eigenvalues of the matrix. This was done by ordinary elimination. We shall now treat the general case, for arbitrary matrices.

Let A be an $n \times n$ matrix in a field K, $A = (a_{ij})$. We define the **characteristic polynomial** P_A of A to be the determinant

$$P_A(t) = \text{Det}(tI - A),$$

or written out in full,

$$P(t) = \begin{vmatrix} t - a_{11} & -a_{12} & \cdots & -a_{1n} \\ \vdots & \vdots & & \vdots \\ -a_{n1} & -a_{n2} & \cdots & t - a_{nn} \end{vmatrix} = \begin{vmatrix} t - a_{11} & & & \\ & \ddots & & -a_{ij} \\ -a_{ij} & & \ddots & \\ & & & t - a_{nn} \end{vmatrix}.$$

Example 1. The characteristic polynomial of the matrix

$$A = \begin{pmatrix} 1 & -1 & 3 \\ -2 & 1 & 1 \\ 0 & 1 & -1 \end{pmatrix}$$

is

$$\begin{vmatrix} t - 1 & 1 & -3 \\ 2 & t - 1 & -1 \\ 0 & -1 & t + 1 \end{vmatrix}$$

which we can expand according to the first column, to find

$$P_A(t) = t^3 - t^2 - 4t + 6.$$

For an arbitrary matrix $A = (a_{ij})$, the characteristic polynomial can be found by expanding according to the first column, and will always consist of a sum

$$(t - a_{11}) \cdots (t - a_{nn}) + \cdots$$

Each term other than the one we have written down will have degree $< n$. Hence the characteristic polynomial is of type

$$P_A(t) = t^n + \text{terms of lower degree.}$$

Theorem 12. *Let A be an $n \times n$ matrix in a field K. An element $\lambda \in K$ is an eigenvalue of A if and only if λ is a root of the characteristic polynomial of A.*

Proof. Assume that λ is an eigenvalue of A. Then $\lambda I - A$ is not invertible by Theorem 9, and hence $\text{Det}(\lambda I - A) = 0$, by Theorem 8 of Chapter VII, §9. Consequently λ is a root of the characteristic polynomial. Conversely, if λ is a root of the characteristic polynomial, then $\text{Det}(\lambda I - A) = 0$, and hence by the same Theorem 8 of Chapter VII, §9 we conclude that $\lambda I - A$ is not invertible. Hence λ is an eigenvalue of A by Theorem 9.

Theorem 12 gives us an explicit way of determining the eigenvalues of a matrix, *provided* that we can determine explicitly the roots of its characteristic polynomial. This is sometimes easy, especially in exercises at the end of chapters when the matrices are adjusted in such a way that one can determine the roots by inspection, or simple devices. It is considerably harder in other cases.

For instance, to determine the roots of the polynomial in Example 1, one would have to develop the theory of cubic polynomials. This can be done, but it involves formulas which are somewhat harder than the formula needed to solve a quadratic equation. One can also find methods to determine roots approximately. In any case, the determination of such methods belongs to another range of ideas than that studied in the present chapter.

Example 2. Find the eigenvalues of the matrix

$$A = \begin{pmatrix} 1 & 1 & -1 \\ 0 & 1 & 0 \\ 1 & 0 & 1 \end{pmatrix}.$$

We compute the characteristic polynomial, which is the determinant

$$\begin{vmatrix} t-1 & -1 & 1 \\ 0 & t-1 & 0 \\ -1 & 0 & t-1 \end{vmatrix}$$

easily computed to be

$$P(t) = (t-1)(t^2 - 2t + 2).$$

Its roots are $1, 1+i, 1-i$. These are the characteristic roots. We note that there is just one real characteristic root.

Example 3. The characteristic polynomial of the matrix

$$\begin{pmatrix} 1 & 1 & 2 \\ 0 & 5 & -1 \\ 0 & 0 & 7 \end{pmatrix}$$

is $(t-1)(t-5)(t-7)$. Can you generalize this?

Theorem 13. *Let A, B be two $n \times n$ matrices, and assume that B is invertible. Then the characteristic polynomial of A is equal to the characteristic polynomial of $B^{-1}AB$.*

Proof. By definition, and properties of the determinant,

$$\text{Det}(tI - A) = \text{Det}(B^{-1}(tI - A)B) = \text{Det}(tB^{-1}B - B^{-1}AB)$$

$$= \text{Det}(tI - B^{-1}AB).$$

This proves what we wanted.

We shall now define the characteristic polynomial of a linear map. We follow the usual pattern, and use its representation by matrices.

Let $A: V \rightarrow V$ be a linear map of a finite dimensional vector space over the field K. If $\mathfrak{B}$ is a basis of V, let M be the matrix representing A with respect to $\mathfrak{B}$. If $\mathfrak{B}'$ is another basis, there exists an invertible matrix N in K such that the matrix M' of A with respect to $\mathfrak{B}'$ is given by

$$M' = N^{-1}MN.$$

By Theorem 13, the characteristic polynomial of M is the same as that of M'. We define this characteristic polynomial to be the **characteristic polynomial of the linear map** A.

If λ is an eigenvalue of A, the **multiplicity** of λ is defined to be its multiplicity as a root of the characteristic polynomial of A.

EXERCISES

1. Let A be a diagonal matrix,

$$A = \begin{pmatrix} a_1 & 0 & \cdots & 0 \\ 0 & a_2 & \cdots & 0 \\ \vdots & \vdots & & \vdots \\ 0 & 0 & \cdots & a_n \end{pmatrix}.$$

   (a) What is the characteristic polynomial of A?
   (b) What are its eigenvalues?

2. Let A be a triangular matrix,

$$A = \begin{pmatrix} a_{11} & 0 & \cdots & 0 \\ a_{21} & a_{22} & \cdots & 0 \\ \vdots & \vdots & & \vdots \\ a_{n1} & a_{n2} & \cdots & a_{nn} \end{pmatrix}.$$

What is the characteristic polynomial of A, and what are its eigenvalues?

3. Find the characteristic polynomial of the following matrices, and also the eigenvalues in the complex numbers, as well as the eigenvectors.

(a) $\begin{pmatrix} 1 & i \\ i & -2 \end{pmatrix}$ (b) $\begin{pmatrix} 1 & i \\ -i & 1 \end{pmatrix}$ (c) $\begin{pmatrix} 1 & 2i \\ 0 & 2 \end{pmatrix}$

(d) $\begin{pmatrix} 2 & 4 \\ 5 & 3 \end{pmatrix}$ (e) $\begin{pmatrix} 1 & 2 \\ 2 & -2 \end{pmatrix}$ (f) $\begin{pmatrix} 3 & 2 \\ -2 & 3 \end{pmatrix}$

(g) $\begin{pmatrix} -1 & 2 & 2 \\ 2 & 2 & 2 \\ -3 & -6 & -6 \end{pmatrix}$ (h) $\begin{pmatrix} 3 & 2 & 1 \\ 0 & 1 & 2 \\ 0 & 1 & -1 \end{pmatrix}$

4. Let A be a 4×4 matrix whose characteristic polynomial is

$$(t - 2)(t + 1)(t + i)(t + 2i).$$

Prove that A can be diagonalized, over the complex numbers.

5. Let V be an n dimensional vector space over the complex numbers, and assume that the characteristic polynomial of a linear map $A : V \to V$ has n distinct roots. Show that V has a basis consisting of eigenvectors of A.

6. Let A be the matrix

$$\begin{pmatrix} 1 & a \\ 0 & 1 \end{pmatrix}$$

with some complex number $a \neq 0$. Show that A cannot be diagonalized.

7. Using the intermediate value theorem for continuous functions, prove that any real $n \times n$ matrix has a real non-zero eigenvector if n is odd.

8. Let A be a square matrix. Show that the eigenvalues of ${}^tA$ are the same as those of A. Are the eigenvectors of ${}^tA$ the same as those of A?

9. Show that the eigenvalues of the matrix

$$\begin{pmatrix} 0 & 1 & 0 & 0 \\ 0 & 0 & 1 & 0 \\ 0 & 0 & 0 & 1 \\ 1 & 0 & 0 & 0 \end{pmatrix}$$

in the complex numbers are ± 1 and $\pm i$.

10. Let V be the space generated over $\mathbf{R}$ by the two functions $\sin t$ and $\cos t$. Does the derivative (viewed as a linear map of V into itself) have any non-zero eigenvectors in V? If so, which?

11. Find the eigenvalues and eigenvectors of

$$\begin{pmatrix} 2 & -1 \\ 1 & 0 \end{pmatrix}$$

Show that the eigenvectors generate a 1-dimensional space.

12. Find the eigenvalues and eigenvectors of the following matrices.

(a) $\begin{pmatrix} 1 & 1 \\ 0 & 1 \end{pmatrix}$ (b) $\begin{pmatrix} 1 & 1 & 1 \\ 0 & 1 & 1 \\ 0 & 0 & 1 \end{pmatrix}$ (c) $\begin{pmatrix} 1 & 1 & 0 \\ 0 & 1 & 1 \\ 0 & 0 & 1 \end{pmatrix}$

CHAPTER X

Triangulation of Matrices and Linear Maps

§1. Existence of triangulation

Let V be a finite dimensional vector space over the field K, and assume $n = \dim V \geq 1$. Let $A: V \to V$ be a linear map. Let W be a subspace of V. We shall say that W is an **invariant** subspace of A, or is **A-invariant,** if A maps W into itself. This means that if $w \in W$, then Aw is also contained in W. We also express this property by writing $AW \subset W$. By a **fan** of A (in V) we shall mean a sequence of subspaces $\{V_1, \ldots, V_n\}$ such that V_i is contained in V_{i+1} for each $i = 1, \ldots, n-1$, such that $\dim V_i = i$, and finally such that each V_i is A-invariant. We see that the dimensions of the subspaces $V_1, \ldots, V_n$ increases by 1 from one subspace to the next. Furthermore, $V = V_n$.

We shall give an interpretation of fans by matrices. Let $\{V_1, \ldots, V_n\}$ be a fan for A. By a **fan basis** we shall mean a basis $\{v_1, \ldots, v_n\}$ of V such that $\{v_1, \ldots, v_i\}$ is a basis for V_i. One sees immediately that a fan basis exists. For instance, let v_1 be a basis for V_1. We extend v_1 to a basis $\{v_1, v_2\}$ of V_2 (possible by an old theorem), then to a basis $\{v_1, v_2, v_3\}$ of V_3, and so on inductively to a basis $\{v_1, \ldots, v_n\}$ of V_n.

Theorem 1. *Let $\{v_1, \ldots, v_n\}$ be a fan basis for A. Then the matrix associated with A relative to this basis is an upper triangular matrix.*

Proof. Since AV_i is contained in V_i for each $i = 1, \ldots, n$, there exist numbers a_{ij} such that

$$Av_1 = a_{11}v_1$$

$$Av_2 = a_{12}v_1 + a_{22}v_2$$

$$\vdots$$

$$Av_i = a_{1i}v_1 + a_{2i}v_2 + \cdots + a_{ii}v_i$$

$$\vdots$$

$$Av_n = a_{1n}v_1 + a_{2n}v_2 + \quad \cdots \quad + a_{nn}v_n.$$

This means that the matrix associated with A with respect to our basis is

257

the triangular matrix

$$\begin{pmatrix} a_{11} & a_{12} & \cdots & a_{1n} \\ 0 & a_{22} & \cdots & a_{2n} \\ \vdots & \vdots & & \vdots \\ 0 & 0 & \cdots & a_{nn} \end{pmatrix}$$

as was to be shown.

Remark. Let A be an upper triangular matrix as above. We view A as a linear map of K^n into itself. Then the column unit vectors $e^1, \ldots, e^n$ form a fan basis for A. If we let V_i be the space generated by $e^1, \ldots, e^i$, then $\{V_1, \ldots, V_n\}$ is the corresponding fan. Thus the converse of Theorem 1 is also obviously true.

We recall that it is not always the case that one can find an eigenvector (or eigenvalue) for a linear map if the given field K is not the complex numbers. Similarly, it is not always true that we can find a fan for a linear map when K is the real numbers. If $A : V \to V$ is a linear map, and if there exists a basis for V for which the associated matrix of A is triangular, then we say that A is **triangulable**. Similarly, if A is an $n \times n$ matrix, over the field K, we say that A is **triangulable over** K if it is triangulable as a linear map of K^n into itself. This is equivalent to saying that there exists a non-singular matrix B in K such that $B^{-1}AB$ is an upper triangular matrix.

Using the existence of eigenvectors over the complex numbers, we shall prove that any matrix or linear map can be triangulated over the complex numbers.

Theorem 2. *Let V be a finite dimensional vector space over the complex numbers, and assume that* $\dim V \geqq 1$. *Let $A : V \to V$ be a linear map. Then there exists a fan of A in V.*

Proof. We shall prove the theorem by induction. If $\dim V = 1$ then there is nothing more to prove. Assume that the theorem is true when $\dim V = n - 1$, $n > 1$. By Theorem 10 of Chapter IX, §3 there exists a non-zero eigenvector v_1 for A. We let V_1 be the subspace of dimension 1 generated by v_1. We can write V as a direct sum $V = V_1 \oplus W$ for some subspace W (by Theorem 8 of Chapter II, §4, asserting essentially that we can extend linearly independent vectors to a basis). The trouble now is that A does not map W into itself. Let P_1 be the projection of V on V_1, and let P_2 be the projection of V on W. Then P_2A is a linear map of V into V, which maps W into W (because P_2 maps any element of V into W). Thus we view P_2A as a linear map of W into itself. By induction, there exists a fan of P_2A in W, say $\{W_1, \ldots, W_{n-1}\}$. We let

$$V_i = V_1 + W_{i-1}$$

for $i = 2, \ldots, n$. Then V_i is contained in V_{i+1} for each $i = 1, \ldots, n$ and one verifies immediately that dim $V_i = i$.

(If $\{u_1, \ldots, u_{n-1}\}$ is a basis of W such that $\{u_1, \ldots, u_j\}$ is a basis of W_j, then $\{v_1, u_1, \ldots, u_{i-1}\}$ is a basis of V_i for $i = 2, \ldots, n$.)

To prove that $\{V_1, \ldots, V_n\}$ is a fan for A in V, it will suffice to prove that AV_i is contained in V_i. To do this, we note that

$$A = IA = (P_1 + P_2)A = P_1A + P_2A.$$

Let $v \in V_i$. We can write $v = cv_1 + w_i$, with $c \in \mathbf{C}$ and $w_i \in W_i$. Then $P_1Av = P_1(Av)$ is contained in V_1, and hence in V_i. Furthermore,

$$P_2Av = P_2A(cv_1) + P_2Aw_i.$$

Since $P_2A(cv_1) = cP_2Av_1$, and since v_1 is an eigenvector of A, say $Av_1 = \lambda_1v_1$, we find $P_2A(cv_1) = P_2(c\lambda_1v_1) = 0$. By induction hypothesis, P_2A maps W_i into itself, and hence P_2Aw_i lies in W_i. Hence P_2Av lies in $V_1 + W_i = V_i$. We conclude finally that $IAv = P_1Av + P_2Av$ lies in V_i, thereby proving our theorem.

Corollary 1. *Let V be a finite dimensional vector space over the complex numbers, and assume that* dim $V \geqq 1$. *Let $A : V \to V$ be a linear map. Then there exists a basis of V such that the matrix of A with respect to this basis is a triangular matrix.*

Proof. We had already given the arguments preceding Theorem 1.

Corollary 2. *Let M be a matrix of complex numbers. There exists a non-singular matrix B such that $B^{-1}MB$ is a triangular matrix.*

Proof. This is the standard interpretation of the change of matrices when we change bases, applied to the case covered by Corollary 1.

EXERCISES

1. Let A be an upper triangular matrix:

$$A = \begin{pmatrix} a_{11} & a_{12} & \cdots & a_{1n} \\ 0 & a_{22} & \cdots & a_{2n} \\ \vdots & \vdots & & \vdots \\ 0 & 0 & \cdots & a_{nn} \end{pmatrix}.$$

Viewing A as a linear map, what are the eigenvalues of A^2, A^3, in general of A^r where r is an integer $\geqq 1$?

2. Let A be a square matrix. We say that A is **nilpotent** if there exists an integer $r \geqq 1$ such that $A^r = 0$. Show that if A is nilpotent, then all eigenvalues of A are equal to 0.

3. Let V be a finite dimensional space over the complex numbers, and let $A: V \to V$ be a linear map. Assume that all eigenvalues of A are equal to 0. Show that A is nilpotent.

(In the two preceding exercises, try the 2×2 case explicitly first.)

4. Using fans, give a proof that the inverse of an invertible triangular matrix is also triangular. In fact, if V is a finite dimensional vector space, if $A: V \to V$ is a linear map which is invertible, and if $\{V_1, \ldots, V_n\}$ is a fan for A, show that it is also a fan for A^{-1}.

5. Let A be a square matrix of complex numbers such that $A^r = I$ for some positive integer r. If α is an eigenvalue of A, show that $\alpha^r = 1$.

6. Find a fan basis for the linear maps of $\mathbf{C}^2$ represented by the matrices

(a) $\begin{pmatrix} 1 & 1 \\ 1 & 1 \end{pmatrix}$ (b) $\begin{pmatrix} 1 & i \\ 1 & i \end{pmatrix}$ (c) $\begin{pmatrix} 1 & 2 \\ i & i \end{pmatrix}$

7. Prove that an operator $A: V \to V$ on a finite dimensional vector space can be written as a sum $A = D + N$, where D is diagonalizable and N is nilpotent.

§2. *Theorem of Hamilton-Cayley*

Let V be a finite dimensional vector space over a field K, and let $A: V \to V$ be a linear map. Assume that V has a basis consisting of eigenvectors of A, say $\{v_1, \ldots, v_n\}$. Let $\{\lambda_1, \ldots, \lambda_n\}$ be the corresponding eigenvalues. Then the characteristic polynomial of A is

$$P(t) = (t - \lambda_1) \cdots (t - \lambda_n),$$

and

$$P(A) = (A - \lambda_1 I) \cdots (A - \lambda_n I).$$

If we now apply $P(A)$ to any vector v_i, then the factor $A - \lambda_i I$ will kill v_i, in other words, $P(A)v_i = O$. Consequently, $P(A) = O$.

In general, we cannot find a basis as above. However, by using fans, we can construct a generalization of the argument just used in the diagonal case.

Theorem 3. *Let V be a finite dimensional vector space over the complex numbers, of dimension ≥ 1, and let $A: V \to V$ be a linear map. Let P be its characteristic polynomial. Then $P(A) = O$.*

Proof. By Theorem 2, we can find a fan for A, say $\{V_1, \ldots, V_n\}$. Let

$$\begin{pmatrix} a_{11} & \cdots & a_{1n} \\ 0 & \cdots & a_{2n} \\ \vdots & & \vdots \\ 0 & \cdots & a_{nn} \end{pmatrix}$$

be the matrix associated with A with respect to a fan basis, $\{v_1, \ldots, v_n\}$.

Then
$$Av_i = a_{ii}v_i + \text{an element of } V_{i-1}$$

or in other words, since $(A - a_{ii}I)v_i = Av_i - a_{ii}v_i$, we find that

$$(A - a_{ii}I)v_i \quad \text{lies in} \quad V_{i-1}.$$

Furthermore, the characteristic polynomial of A is given by

$$P(t) = (t - a_{11}) \cdots (t - a_{nn}),$$

so that

$$P(A) = (A - a_{11}I) \cdots (A - a_{nn}I).$$

We shall prove by induction that

$$(A - a_{11}I) \cdots (A - a_{ii}I)v = O$$

for all v in V_i, $i = 1, \ldots, n$. When $i = n$, this will yield our theorem.

Let $i = 1$. Then $(A - a_{11}I)v_1 = Av_1 - a_{11}v_1 = O$ and we are done.

Let $i > 1$, and assume our assertion proved for $i - 1$. Any element of V_i can be written as a sum $v' + cv_i$ with v' in V_{i-1}, and some scalar c. We note that $(A - a_{ii}I)v'$ lies in V_{i-1} because AV_{i-1} is contained in V_{i-1}, and so is $a_{ii}v'$. By induction,

$$(A - a_{11}I) \cdots (A - a_{i-1,i-1}I)(A - a_{ii}I)v' = O.$$

On the other hand, $(A - a_{ii}I)cv_i$ lies in V_{i-1}, and hence by induction,

$$(A - a_{11}I) \cdots (A - a_{i-1,i-1}I)(A - a_{ii}I)cv_i = O.$$

Hence for v in V_i, we have

$$(A - a_{11}I) \cdots (A - a_{ii}I)v = O,$$

thereby proving our theorem.

Corollary 1. *Let A be an $n \times n$ matrix of complex numbers, and let P be its characteristic polynomial. Then $P(A) = O$.*

Proof. We view A as a linear map of $\mathbf{C}^n$ into itself, and apply the theorem.

Corollary 2. *Let V be a finite dimensional vector space over the field K, and let $A : V \to V$ be a linear map. Let P be the characteristic polynomial of A. Then $P(A) = O$.*

Proof. Take a basis of V, and let M be the matrix representing A with respect to this basis. Then $P_M = P_A$, and it suffices to prove that $P_M(M) = O$. But we can apply Theorem 3 to conclude the proof.

Remark. One can base a proof of Theorem 3 on a continuity argument. Given a complex matrix A, one can, by various methods into which we don't go here, prove that there exist matrices Z of the same size as A, lying arbitrarily close to A (i.e. each component of Z is close to the corresponding component of A) such that P_Z has all its roots of multiplicity 1. In fact, the complex polynomials having roots of multiplicity > 1 are thinly distributed among all polynomials. Now, if Z is as above, then the linear map it represents is diagonalizable (because Z has distinct eigenvalues), and hence $P_Z(Z) = O$ trivially, as noted at the beginning of this section. However, $P_Z(Z)$ approaches $P_A(A)$ as Z approaches A. Hence $P_A(A) = O$.

§3. *Diagonalization of unitary maps*

Theorem 4. *Let V be a finite dimensional vector space over the complex numbers, and let* dim $V \geqq 1$. *Assume given a positive definite hermitian product on V. Let $A: V \to V$ be a unitary map. Then there exists an orthonormal basis of V consisting of eigenvectors of A.*

Proof. First observe that if w is an eigenvector for A, with eigenvalue λ, then $Aw = \lambda w$, and $\lambda \neq 0$ because A preserves length.

By Theorem 2, we can find a fan for A, say $\{V_1, \ldots, V_n\}$. Let $\{v_1, \ldots, v_n\}$ be a fan basis. We can use the Gram-Schmidt orthogonalization process to orthogonalize it. We recall the process:

$$v'_1 = v_1$$
$$v'_2 = v_2 - \frac{\langle v_2, v_1 \rangle}{\langle v_1, v_1 \rangle} v_1$$
$$\cdots$$

From this construction, we see that $\{v'_1, \ldots, v'_n\}$ is an orthogonal basis which is again a fan basis, because $\{v'_1, \ldots, v'_i\}$ is a basis of the same space V_i as $\{v_1, \ldots, v_i\}$. Dividing each v'_i by its length we obtain a fan basis $\{w_1, \ldots, w_n\}$ which is orthonormal. We contend that each w_i is an eigenvector for A. We proceed by induction. Since Aw_1 is contained in V_1, there exist a scalar λ_1 such that $Aw_1 = \lambda_1 w_1$, so that w_1 is an eigenvector, and $\lambda_1 \neq 0$. Assume that we have already proved that $w_1, \ldots, w_{i-1}$ are eigenvectors with non-zero eigenvalues. There exist scalars $c_1, \ldots, c_i$ such that

$$Aw_i = c_1 w_1 + \cdots + c_i w_i.$$

Since A preserves perpendicularity, Aw_i is perpendicular to Aw_k for every $k < i$. But $Aw_k = \lambda_k w_k$. Hence Aw_i is perpendicular to w_k itself, and hence $c_k = 0$.   Hence $Aw_i = c_i w_i$, and $c_i \neq 0$ because A preserves length. We can thus go from 1 to n to prove our theorem.

Corollary. *Let A be a complex unitary matrix. Then there exists a unitary matrix U such that $U^{-1}AU$ is a diagonal matrix.*

Proof.   Let $\{e^1, \ldots, e^n\} = \mathfrak{B}$ be the standard orthonormal basis of $\mathbf{C}^n$, and let $\{w_1, \ldots, w_n\} = \mathfrak{B}'$ be an orthonormal basis which diagonalizes A, viewed as a linear map of $\mathbf{C}^n$ into itself. Let

$$U = M_{\mathfrak{B}}^{\mathfrak{B}'}(id).$$

Then U is unitary (cf. Exercise 5 of Chapter VIII, §5), and if M' is the matrix of A relative to the basis $\mathfrak{B}'$, then

$$M' = U^{-1}AU.$$

It follows that M' is unitary.

For another (simpler) proof, cf. §4 of the next chapter.

EXERCISES

1. Let A be a complex unitary matrix. Show that each eigenvalue of A can be written $e^{i\theta}$ with some real θ.

2. Let A be a complex unitary matrix. Show that there exists a diagonal matrix B and a complex unitary matrix U such that $A = U^{-1}BU$.

CHAPTER XI

The Spectral Theorem

§1. *Eigenvectors of symmetric linear maps*

Throughout this chapter we are concerned with eigenvectors and eigenvalues for a special kind of operators, namely symmetric ones (or hermitian ones in the complex case). We begin with the symmetric case over the real numbers.

Let V be a finite dimensional vector space over the real numbers, of dimension ≥ 1. We assume that V has a fixed symmetric positive definite scalar product, denoted by $\langle \, , \, \rangle$. The reader may think of V as being $\mathbf{R}^n$, with its ordinary dot product, but we shall also consider subspaces of V, and then these subspaces have the scalar product given by that of V, but they are not equal to $\mathbf{R}^m$, and are isomorphic to $\mathbf{R}^m$ for some m, only when we have selected suitable bases. The whole point of this chapter will be to select bases subject to various conditions.

Let $A: V \to V$ be a linear map. We recall that A is said to be symmetric if

$$\langle Av, w \rangle = \langle v, Aw \rangle = \langle Aw, v \rangle$$

for all $v, w \in V$. If $V = \mathbf{R}^n$, and the scalar product is the ordinary dot product, and if we represent A by a matrix relative to the usual basis, then A is symmetric if and only if this matrix is symmetric. If V is given abstractly, but if we select an orthonormal basis of V, and if we represent A by a matrix with respect to this basis, then again A is symmetric if and only if the matrix is symmetric.

It will in fact be convenient to use $\mathbf{R}^n$ and $\mathbf{C}^n$ in some explicit arguments. For instance, we have the following theorem, which has essentially been proved before, but which we repeat here completely for the convenience of the reader.

Theorem 1. *Let A be an $n \times n$ real matrix which is symmetric. If λ is an eigenvalue of A in $\mathbf{C}$, then λ is real.*

Proof. We shall use the hermitian product in $\mathbf{C}^n$ such that if $Z, Z' \in \mathbf{C}^n$ then

$$\langle Z, Z' \rangle = {}^t Z \overline{Z}' = z_1 \overline{z}_1' + \cdots + z_n \overline{z}_n'.$$

Let Z be an eigenvector having λ as eigenvalue, so that $Z \neq O$ and $AZ = \lambda Z$. We have

$$\langle AZ, Z \rangle = \langle \lambda Z, Z \rangle = \lambda \langle Z, Z \rangle.$$

On the other hand, since A is symmetric and real, we have

$$\langle AZ, Z \rangle = \langle Z, {}^t AZ \rangle = \langle Z, AZ \rangle = \overline{\langle AZ, Z \rangle}.$$

Hence $\lambda \langle Z, Z \rangle$ is equal to its complex conjugate and is real. Since $\langle Z, Z \rangle$ is real and $\neq 0$, we conclude that λ is real.

Let Z be a vector in $\mathbf{C}^n$. We can write Z in a unique way as a sum $Z = X + iY$, where X, Y are real vectors in $\mathbf{R}^n$. This is true for each component of Z, and thus for Z itself. For instance,

$$\begin{pmatrix} 3 + 2i \\ 1 - i \end{pmatrix} = \begin{pmatrix} 3 \\ 1 \end{pmatrix} + i \begin{pmatrix} 2 \\ -1 \end{pmatrix}.$$

Theorem 2. *Let A be a real $n \times n$ symmetric matrix. Then A has a real non-zero eigenvector.*

Proof. We use the fact that if we view A as a linear map of $\mathbf{C}^n$ into $\mathbf{C}^n$, then A has a complex non-zero eigenvector Z. Thus there exists $\lambda \in \mathbf{C}$ such that $AZ = \lambda Z$, and by Theorem 1, λ is real. Write

$$Z = X + iY$$

with real vectors X, Y. Then

$$AZ = AX + iAY$$

and

$$AZ = \lambda Z = \lambda X + i\lambda Y.$$

Since λ is real, and since the real and imaginary parts of a complex vector are uniquely determined, we conclude that

$$AX = \lambda X \quad \text{and} \quad AY = \lambda Y.$$

Since at least one of X, Y is not the zero vector, one of them is a real non-zero eigenvector, as was to be shown.

Corollary. *Let V be a finite dimensional vector space over $\mathbf{R}$, of dimension ≥ 1, and with a positive definite scalar product. Let $A: V \to V$ be a symmetric linear map. Then A has a non-zero eigenvector in V.*

Proof. We select an orthonormal basis for V. Then A is represented by a symmetric real matrix, with respect to this basis. If X is a non-zero eigenvector of A in $\mathbf{R}^n$, then the element v of V having X as coordinate vector with respect to the basis is a non-zero eigenvector of A in V.

The preceding proof of Theorem 2 relied on a fact about complex numbers, namely the existence of a complex eigenvector for a complex matrix. Using another idea in calculus, it is amusing to give a different proof for Theorem 2, based on considerations of a maximum for a suitable function.

Let S denote the unit sphere in $\mathbf{R}^n$, i.e. the set of all vectors X in $\mathbf{R}^n$ such that $\|X\| = 1$.

With each symmetric real matrix A we associate the quadratic form $f: \mathbf{R}^n \to \mathbf{R}$ such that $f(X) = \langle AX, X \rangle$. We now look at values of f on the unit sphere.

Theorem 3. *Let A be a real symmetric $n \times n$ matrix. Let*

$$f(X) = \langle AX, X \rangle$$

for $X \in \mathbf{R}^n$. Let v be on the unit sphere, such that $f(v) \geq f(X)$ for all X on this sphere. Then v is an eigenvector of A.

Proof. Let w be a unit vector in $\mathbf{R}^n$ which is perpendicular to v. It is easily shown that there exists a differentiable curve

$$C: (a, b) \to \mathbf{R}^n$$

lying on the sphere, defined on an open interval containing 0, such that $C(0) = v$ and such that the tangent vector of C at 0 is w, namely $C'(0) = w$. [For instance, the curve

$$C(t) = (\cos t)v + (\sin t)w$$

is such a curve.] Since $f(v) = f(C(0))$ is a maximum for f on S, it is a maximum for $f \circ C$ on the interval (a, b), and hence $(f \circ C)'(0) = 0$. But by using the rule for differentiating a product,

$$\begin{aligned}
(f \circ C)'(t) &= \frac{d}{dt} \langle AC(t), C(t) \rangle \\
&= \langle AC'(t), C(t) \rangle + \langle AC(t), C'(t) \rangle \\
&= \langle C'(t), AC(t) \rangle + \langle C'(t), AC(t) \rangle \\
&= 2 \langle AC(t), C'(t) \rangle.
\end{aligned}$$

Hence

$$0 = (f \circ C)'(0) = 2 \langle AC(0), C'(0) \rangle = 2 \langle Av, w \rangle.$$

Hence Av is perpendicular to every vector w which is perpendicular to v, and it follows that Av lies in the space generated by v, in other words, there exists $\lambda \in \mathbf{R}$ such that $Av = \lambda v$. This proves our theorem.

Using the fact proved in analysis that the sphere is compact, and hence that any continuous function has a maximum, we conclude that there always exists a vector as in Theorem 3, and hence we have given another proof for the existence of an eigenvector of A.

EXERCISES

1. Let A be a real symmetric 3×3 matrix. Let $f(X) = \langle AX, X \rangle$ for all $X \in \mathbf{R}^n$. Let v be a vector on the ellipsoid defined by the equation

$$3x^2 + 4y^2 + 5z^2 = 1,$$

such that $f(v) \geq f(X)$ for all X on the ellipsoid. Show that v is an eigenvector of A.

2. More generally, let $\varphi : \mathbf{R}^3 \to \mathbf{R}$ be a continuously differentiable function. Let S be the surface defined by the equation $\varphi(X) = 0$. Assume that for each P in S, grad $\varphi(P) \neq 0$, and assume that S is closed and bounded. Let A be a real symmetric 3×3 matrix and let $f(X) = \langle AX, X \rangle$. Let v be a point of S such that $f(v) \geq f(X)$ for all X on S. Show that v is an eigenvector of A.

3. Let A be a real $n \times n$ matrix (not assumed to be symmetric). Assume however that all the eigenvalues of A are real. Show that A has a real non-zero eigenvector.

§2. The spectral theorem

We return to algebraic considerations.

Throughout this section, we assume that V is a finite dimensional vector space over $\mathbf{R}$, with a positive definite scalar product. We also assume $\dim V \geq 1$.

Theorem 4. *Let $A : V \to V$ be a symmetric linear map. Let v be a non-zero eigenvector of A. If w is an element of V, perpendicular to v, then Aw is also perpendicular to v.*

Proof. Absolutely trivial: We have

$$\langle Aw, v \rangle = \langle w, Av \rangle = \langle w, \lambda v \rangle = \lambda \langle w, v \rangle = 0.$$

Theorem 5. *Let $A : V \to V$ be a symmetric linear map. Then there exists an orthogonal basis of V consisting of eigenvectors of A.*

Proof. By induction on the dimension of V. If $\dim V = 1$, there is nothing further to prove. Assume $\dim V > 1$. By Theorem 2, there exists a non-zero eigenvector v_1 of A in V. Let $W = v_1^\perp$ be the orthogonal space of v_1. Then

$$\dim W = \dim V - 1.$$

By Theorem 4, A maps W into itself. Note that W has a positive definite scalar product, namely that induced by the scalar product of V, and that A, viewed as a linear map of W into itself is symmetric. By induction, there exists an orthogonal basis of W consisting of eigenvectors of A, say $\{v_2, \ldots, v_n\}$. Then v_i is perpendicular to v_1 for each $i > 1$, and hence $\{v_1, \ldots, v_n\}$ is the basis whose existence is asserted in the theorem.

Example. Let A be the matrix

$$\begin{pmatrix} 2 & 1 \\ 1 & 3 \end{pmatrix}.$$

Find an orthogonal basis of $\mathbf{R}^2$ consisting of eigenvectors of A.
  The eigenvalues of A are

$$\frac{5 \pm \sqrt{5}}{2}.$$

(One finds this by linear equations, or as roots of the characteristic polynomial, which is $t^2 - 5t + 5$.) Solving for an eigenvector, we must solve the equations

$$2x + y = \frac{5 + \sqrt{5}}{2}\, x,$$

$$x + 3y = \frac{5 + \sqrt{5}}{2}\, y.$$

We find $x = 2$, $y = 1 + \sqrt{5}$. Thus

$$v_1 = \begin{pmatrix} 2 \\ 1 + \sqrt{5} \end{pmatrix}$$

is an eigenvector. The orthogonal space to v_1 has dimension 1, hence consists of all real multiples of one vector perpendicular to v_1. We can take for instance

$$v_2 = \begin{pmatrix} 2 \\ 1 - \sqrt{5} \end{pmatrix}.$$

This is necessarily an eigenvector of A since A maps the orthogonal space to v_1 into itself. Then $\{v_1, v_2\}$ is the desired basis.

Corollary. *Let A be a symmetric real $n \times n$ matrix. Then there exists an $n \times n$ real unitary matrix U such that ${}^t U A U = U^{-1} A U$ is a diagonal matrix.*

Proof. We view A as the associated matrix of a linear map $F \colon \mathbf{R}^n \to \mathbf{R}^n$, relative to the standard basis $\mathfrak{B} = \{e^1, \dots, e^n\}$. By Theorem 5, we can find an orthonormal basis $\mathfrak{B}' = \{w_1, \dots, w_n\}$ of $\mathbf{R}^n$ such that $M_{\mathfrak{B}'}^{\mathfrak{B}'}(F)$ is diagonal. (Cf. Exercise 2 below.) Let $U = M_{\mathfrak{B}}^{\mathfrak{B}'}(id)$. Then $U^{-1} A U$ is diagonal. Furthermore, U is unitary. Indeed, let $U = (c_{ij})$. Then

$$w_i = \sum_{\nu=1}^{n} c_{\nu i} e_\nu, \qquad\qquad i = 1, \dots, n.$$

The conditions $w_i \cdot w_i = 1$ and $w_i \cdot w_j = 0$ if $i \neq j$ are immediately seen to mean that ${}^t U U = I$, that is ${}^t U = U^{-1}$. This proves our corollary.

Remark 1. In Theorem 5, we are dealing with two forms on the vector space V; first, the positive definite form $\langle \, , \, \rangle$ and second, the form g such that $g(v, w) = \langle Av, w \rangle$. We observe that an orthogonal basis $\{v_1, \dots, v_n\}$ of V consisting of eigenvectors of A is an orthogonal basis also for the second form.
  Proof.

$$g(v_i, v_j) = \langle Av_i, v_j \rangle = \langle \lambda_i v_i, v_j \rangle = \lambda_i \langle v_i, v_j \rangle.$$

This last expression is obviously equal to 0 if $i \neq j$, thereby proving that our basis is orthogonal also for the second form.

Remark 2. The given positive definite scalar product on V gives rise to a quadratic form $f_1 \colon V \to \mathbf{R}$ such that

$$f_1(v) = \langle v, v \rangle.$$

The operator A gives rise to a second quadratic form (not necessarily positive definite!), namely the form f_2 such that

$$f_2(v) = \langle Av, v \rangle.$$

Let $\{v_1, \dots, v_n\}$ be an orthogonal basis of V consisting of eigenvectors of A. Let $c_i = \langle v_i, v_i \rangle$. Let

$$v = x_1 v_1 + \cdots + x_n v_n, \qquad\qquad x_i \in \mathbf{R}$$

where X is the coordinate vector of v with respect to our basis. Then

$$Av = x_1 \lambda_1 v_1 + \cdots + x_n \lambda_n v_n,$$

if $\lambda_1, \ldots, \lambda_n$ are the eigenvalues of A corresponding to $v_1, \ldots, v_n$ respectively. Consequently

$$f_1(v) = c_1 x_1^2 + \cdots + c_n x_n^2 \qquad \text{and} \qquad f_2(v) = \lambda_1 c_1 x_1^2 + \cdots + \lambda_n c_n x_n^2.$$

We interpret this by saying that our two quadratic forms are **simultaneously diagonalized.** Theorem 5 may be stated by saying that *two real quadratic forms, one of which is positive definite, can be simultaneously diagonalized.*

A basis having the properties stated in Theorem 5 is called a **spectral basis for** A.

EXERCISES

1. Find an orthogonal basis of $\mathbf{R}^2$ consisting of eigenvectors of the given matrix.

(a) $\begin{pmatrix} 1 & 3 \\ 3 & 2 \end{pmatrix}$ (b) $\begin{pmatrix} -1 & 1 \\ 1 & 2 \end{pmatrix}$ (c) $\begin{pmatrix} 2 & 0 \\ 0 & 2 \end{pmatrix}$

(d) $\begin{pmatrix} 1 & 1 \\ 1 & 1 \end{pmatrix}$ (e) $\begin{pmatrix} 1 & -1 \\ -1 & 1 \end{pmatrix}$ (f) $\begin{pmatrix} 2 & -3 \\ -3 & 1 \end{pmatrix}$

2. Let A be a symmetric $n \times n$ real matrix. Show that one can find an *orthonormal* basis of $\mathbf{R}^n$ consisting of eigenvectors of A.

3. Let V be as in §2. Let $A: V \to V$ be a symmetric linear map. Let v_1, v_2 be eigenvectors of A with eigenvalues λ_1, λ_2 respectively. If $\lambda_1 \neq \lambda_2$, show that v_1 is perpendicular to v_2.

4. Let A be a symmetric 2×2 real matrix. Show that if the eigenvalues of A are distinct, then their eigenvectors form an orthogonal basis of $\mathbf{R}^2$.

5. Let V be as in §2. Let $A: V \to V$ be a symmetric linear map. If A has only one eigenvalue, show that *any* orthogonal basis of V consists of eigenvectors of A.

6. Let V be as in §2. Let $A: V \to V$ be a symmetric linear map. Let $\dim V = n$, and assume that there are n distinct eigenvalues of A. Show that their eigenvectors form an orthogonal basis of V.

7. Let V be as in §2. Let $A: V \to V$ be a symmetric linear map. If the kernel of A is $\{O\}$, then no eigenvalue of A is equal to 0, and conversely.

8. Show that every symmetric real matrix can be written in the form ${}^t U B U$, where B is diagonal, and U is real unitary.

9. Let V be as in §2, and let $A: V \to V$ be a symmetric linear map. Prove that the following conditions on A imply each other.
   (a) All eigenvalues of A are > 0.
   (b) For all elements $v \in V$, $v \neq O$, we have $\langle Av, v \rangle > 0$.

If the map A satisfies these conditions, it is said to be **positive definite**. The same of $\mathbf{R}^n$ into itself. Thus the second condition, in terms of coordinate vectors, reads:

(b′) For all vectors $X \in \mathbf{R}^n$, $X \neq O$, we have

$$^t X A X > 0.$$

10. Determine which of the following matrices are positive definite.

(a) $\begin{pmatrix} 1 & 2 \\ 2 & 1 \end{pmatrix}$ (b) $\begin{pmatrix} 1 & -1 \\ -1 & 2 \end{pmatrix}$ (c) $\begin{pmatrix} 3 & 2 \\ 2 & 1 \end{pmatrix}$

(d) $\begin{pmatrix} 1 & 2 & 3 \\ 2 & 0 & 1 \\ 3 & 1 & 1 \end{pmatrix}$ (e) $\begin{pmatrix} 1 & -1 & 0 \\ -1 & 0 & 1 \\ 0 & 1 & ? \end{pmatrix}$

11. Prove that the following conditions concerning a real symmetric matrix are equivalent. A matrix satisfying these conditions is called **negative definite.**

(a) All eigenvalues of A are < 0.

(b) For all vectors $X \in \mathbf{R}^n$, $X \neq O$, we have $^t X A X < 0$.

12. Let A be an $n \times n$ non-singular real symmetric matrix. Prove the following statements.

(a) If λ is an eigenvalue of A, then $\lambda \neq 0$.

(b) If λ is an eigenvalue of A, then λ^{-1} is an eigenvalue of A^{-1}.

(c) The matrices A and A^{-1} have the same set of eigenvectors.

13. Let A be a symmetric positive definite real matrix. Show that A^{-1} exists and is positive definite.

14. Let A be a real symmetric matrix all of whose eigenvalues are ≥ 0. Show that there exists a real symmetric matrix B such that $B^2 = A$, and $AB = BA$.

15. Prove that a symmetric real matrix A is positive definite if and only if there exists a non-singular real matrix N such that $A = {}^t N N$. [*Hint:* Use the corollary of Theorem 5, and write $^t U A U$ as the square of diagonal matrix, say B^2. Let $N = U B^{-1}$.]

16. Let V be as in §2. Let $A : V \to V$ be a symmetric linear map. Referring back to Sylvester's theorem, show that the index of nullity of the form

$$(v, w) \mapsto \langle Av, w \rangle$$

is equal to the dimension of the kernel of A. Show that the index of positivity is equal to the number of eigenvectors in a spectral basis having a positive eigenvalue.

17. Let V be as in §2. Let A and B be two symmetric operators of V such that $AB = BA$. Show that there exists an orthogonal basis of V which is a spectral basis simultaneously for A and B, i.e. consisting of eigenvectors for both

A and B. [*Hint.* If λ is an eigenvalue of A, and V_λ consists of all $v \in V$ such that $Av = \lambda v$, show that BV_λ is contained in V_λ. This reduces the problem to the case when $A = \lambda I$.]

18. Let V be as in §2, and let $A : V \to V$ be a symmetric operator. Let $\lambda_1, \ldots, \lambda_r$ be the distinct eigenvalues of A. If λ is an eigenvalue of A, let $V_\lambda(A)$ consist of the set of all $v \in V$ such that $Av = \lambda v$.

  (a) Show that $V_\lambda(A)$ is a subspace of V, and that A maps $V_\lambda(A)$ into itself.

  (b) Show that V is the direct sum of the spaces

$$V = V_{\lambda_1}(A) \oplus \cdots \oplus V_{\lambda_r}(A)$$

and that any two of these subspaces are mutually orthogonal.

We call $V_\lambda(A)$ the **eigenspace** of A belonging to λ.

19. Let the notation be as in the preceding exercise. Assume that A is positive definite. Show that there exists a symmetric positive definite operator B of V such that $B^2 = A$ and that B is uniquely determined. [*Hint:* Show first that the eigenspaces of B and A are the same, proceeding as follows. Let $\mu_1, \ldots, \mu_s$ be the distinct eigenvalues of B, and let

$$V = V_{\mu_1}(B) \oplus \cdots \oplus V_{\mu_s}(B)$$

be the decomposition of V into a direct sum of eigenspaces of B. Show that each $V_{\mu_i}(B)$ is an eigenspace of A, belonging to some eigenvalue λ_i of A, and that if $\mu_i \neq \mu_j$ then $\lambda_i \neq \lambda_j$. Conclude that $s = r$, $V_{\mu_i}(B) = V_{\lambda_i}(A)$, and hence that the effect of B is uniquely determined by A.

20. Let V be as in §2, and let $A : V \to V$ be an arbitrary invertible operator of V. Show that there exist a real unitary operator U and a symmetric positive definite operator P such that $A = UP$, and U, P are uniquely determined. [*Hint:* Let P be the symmetric positive definite operator such that $P^2 = {}^t A A$. Let $U = AP^{-1}$. Show that U is unitary. This gives the existence. To prove uniqueness, suppose $A = U_1 P_1$ with unitary U_1 and symmetric positive definite P_1. Let $U_2 = PP_1^{-1}$. Then $I = {}^t U_2 U_2$ (why?), and hence $P^2 = P_1^2$. Use Exercise 19 to conclude that $P = P_1$, and finally show that $U = U_1$.]

21. If P_1, P_2 are two symmetric positive definite real matrices (of the same size), and t, u are positive real numbers, show that $tP_1 + uP_2$ is symmetric positive definite.

22. Let V be as in §2, and let $A : V \to V$ be a symmetric operator. Let $\lambda_1, \ldots, \lambda_r$ be the distinct eigenvalues of A. Show that

$$(A - \lambda_1 I) \cdots (A - \lambda_r I) = 0.$$

23. Let V be as in §2, and let $A : V \to V$ be a symmetric operator. A subspace W of V is said to be **invariant** under A if $Aw \in W$ for all $w \in W$, i.e. $AW \subset W$. Prove that if A has no invariant subspace other than O and V, then $A = \lambda I$ for some number λ. [*Hint:* Show first that A has only one eigenvalue.]

§3. The complex case

As usual, we have an analogue of the spectral theorem in the complex case.

Theorem 6. *Let V be a finite dimensional vector space over the complex numbers, of dimension > 0. Let $\langle \, , \, \rangle$ be a positive definite hermitian form on V. Let $A : V \to V$ be a hermitian linear map. Then there exists an orthogonal basis of V consisting of eigenvectors of A.*

Proof. The same as the proof of Theorem 5.

As further exercises, make all the remarks concerning the hermitian case which are analogous to those made in the preceding section about the symmetric case. Also remark that if $\{v_1, \ldots, v_n\}$ is a basis as in the theorem, then the matrix of A relative to this basis is a *real* diagonal matrix. This means that the theory of hermitian maps (or matrices) can be handled just like the real case.

EXERCISES

Throughout these exercises, we assume that V is a finite dimensional vector space over $\mathbf{C}$, with a positive definite hermitian product. Also, we assume $\dim V > 0$.

1. An operator $A : V \to V$ is said to be **normal** if $AA^* = A^*A$. If A is normal, state and prove a spectral theorem for A. [*Hint for the proof:* Find a common eigenvector for A and A^*.]

2. If f is a polynomial with real coefficients and A is a hermitian operator, show that $f(A)$ is hermitian.

3. Define positive definiteness for hermitian operators, and prove the analogues of Exercises 9, 12 of §2.

4. If A is hermitian and positive definite, show that there exists an hermitian operator B such that $B^2 = A$ and $AB = BA$. Is B uniquely determined?

5. A hermitian operator A is called **positive** (not necessarily definite) if all its eigenvalues are ≥ 0. Show that this condition is equivalent to the condition $\langle Av, v \rangle \geq 0$ for all $v \in V$.

6. Show that a positive hermitian operator A has a square root, i.e. a positive hermitian operator B such that $B^2 = A$, and B is uniquely determined.

7. Show that the matrix

$$A = \begin{pmatrix} 1 & i \\ -i & 1 \end{pmatrix}$$

is positive, and find a square root.

8. Let A be a hermitian operator. Show that there exist positive hermitian operators P_1, P_2 such that $A = P_1 - P_2$.

9. Let A be an invertible operator. Show that there exist a complex unitary operator U and a hermitian positive definite operator P such that $A = UP$, and U, P are uniquely determined. [*Hint:* Proceed as in Exercise 20, §2.]

10. Let A, B be normal operators such that $AB = BA$. Show that AB is normal.

11. Let A be an $n \times n$ hermitian matrix. Show that there exists an $n \times n$ complex unitary matrix U such that U^*AU is a diagonal matrix. Find such a matrix U when A is equal to:

(a) $\begin{pmatrix} 2 & 1+i \\ 1-i & 1 \end{pmatrix}$ (b) $\begin{pmatrix} 1 & i \\ -i & 1 \end{pmatrix}$

12. Let A be a non-singular complex matrix. Show that A is hermitian positive definite if and only if there exists a non-singular matrix N such that $A = N^*N$.

§4. *Unitary operators*

In the spectral theorem of the preceding section we have found an orthogonal basis for the vector space, consisting of eigenvectors for an hermitian operator. We shall now treat the analogous case for a unitary operator.

Let V be a finite dimensional vector space over the reals, with a positive definite scalar product. We let

$$T: V \to V$$

be a unitary operator. This means that T satisfies any one of the following equivalent conditions:

T preserves length, i.e. $\|Tv\| = \|v\|$ for all $v \in V$.

T preserves scalar products, i.e. $\langle Tv, Tw \rangle = \langle v, w \rangle$ for $v, w \in V$.

T maps unit vectors on unit vectors.

We first treat two simple examples.

$$\boxed{\dim V = 1.}$$

Then V has a basis consisting of one element $\{v\}$, and $Tv = \pm v$ because T preserves length, and $Tv = cv$ for some $c \in \mathbf{R}$. Hence c must be ± 1.

$$\boxed{\dim V = 2.}$$

Let $\{v, w\}$ be an orthonormal basis of V. Write

$$Tv = av + bw,$$
$$Tw = cv + dw$$

with $a, b, c, d \in \mathbf{R}$. Then the matrix representing T with respect to this basis is

$$\begin{pmatrix} a & c \\ b & d \end{pmatrix}.$$

Since we are in the real case, we note that $T^* = {}^tT$ is the transpose of T, and

$$T^* = T^{-1}.$$

Since $\det(T) = \det({}^tT)$ and $\det(TT^*) = 1$, it follows that

$$\det T = 1 \quad \text{or} \quad \det T = -1.$$

We distinguish these two cases.

Case 1. **det $T = 1$.**

Since Tv has length 1, we have $av + bw$, $av + bw = 1$, and hence

$$(1) \qquad \qquad a^2 + b^2 = 1.$$

Similarly

$$(2) \qquad \qquad c^2 + d^2 = 1.$$

But T also preserves perpendicularity, and since $\langle v, w \rangle = 0$, we conclude from $\langle Tv, Tw \rangle = 0$ that

$$(3) \qquad \qquad ac + bd = 0.$$

Then $ac = -bd$ and $a^2c^2 = b^2d^2$. Multiply (1) above by c^2 and substitute this last value b^2d^2 for a^2c^2. We get $b^2 = c^2$ whence $b = \pm c$, and also $a^2 = d^2$, whence $a = \pm d$. We contend that $b = -c$. Otherwise, $b \neq -c$, so that $b \neq 0$ and $c \neq 0$ (because in this case, $b = c$). Then from (3) we find $a = -d$, and hence the determinant of T is

$$-a^2 - c^2$$

which is -1, contrary to the assumption of the present case. Hence in the present case, we have $b = -c$. We also have $a = d$, for otherwise $a = -d \neq 0$, and from (3) we would find $b = c$. *Hence the matrix of T*

is of type

$$\begin{pmatrix} a & -b \\ b & a \end{pmatrix}, \qquad a^2 + b^2 = 1.$$

We can then find a number θ such that $a = \cos\theta$ and $b = \sin\theta$, so that the matrix of T is of type

$$\begin{pmatrix} \cos\theta & -\sin\theta \\ \sin\theta & \cos\theta \end{pmatrix}$$

and we see that T is a rotation by θ.

Case 2. **det $T = -1$.**

We then multiply T by the linear map S whose matrix with respect to the given basis is

$$\begin{pmatrix} -1 & 0 \\ 0 & 1 \end{pmatrix}.$$

Note that $Sv = -v$ and $Sw = w$. Thus S may be interpreted as a reflection over w. Picture:

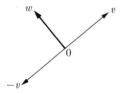

Observe that $\det S = -1$, and hence $\det TS = 1$. Thus TS can be analyzed by the preceding discussion, and is a rotation. Let $R = TS$. Multiplying both sides by S and noting that $S^2 = I$, we find

$$T = RS$$

so that T is equal to a reflection followed by a rotation.

We shall now reduce the general case to the previous ones.

Theorem 7. *Let V be a finite dimensional vector space over the reals, of dimension > 0, and with a positive definite scalar product. Let T be a unitary operator on V. Then V can be expressed as a direct sum*

$$V = V_1 \oplus \cdots \oplus V_r$$

of T-invariant subspaces, which are mutually orthogonal (i.e. V_i is orthogonal to V_j if $i \neq j$) and $\dim V_i$ is 1 or 2, for each i.

Proof. The proof will be very similar to that of the spectral theorem, but in the present case, we must take into account the possibility that $\dim V_i = 2$. We give the proof essentially in two lemmas.

Lemma 1. *There exists a T-invariant subspace W of V which has dimension 1 or 2.*

Proof. Let f be the characteristic polynomial of T, and factorize f into a product of irreducible factors over the reals, say

$$f(t) = p_1(t) \cdots p_s(t),$$

where p_j is irreducible, and has leading coefficient equal to 1. Then the degree of p_j is 1 or 2. We do not assume that the p_j are necessarily distinct. We know that $f(T) = O$. Hence for any $v \in V$, $v \neq O$ we have $f(T)v = O$, We consider the first index $j \geq 1$ such that

$$p_1(T) \ldots p_j(T)v = O.$$

Then $p_1(T) \ldots p_{j-1}(T)v \neq O$, and we let

$$w = p_1(T) \ldots p_{j-1}(T)v.$$

We have $p(T)w = O$ but $w \neq O$, where $p(t) = p_j(t)$. The degree of $p(t)$ is 1 or 2. If $\deg p = 1$, then we can write

$$p(t) = t + b$$

with some constant b, and hence $Tw + bw = O$, and $Tw = -bw$. Thus w is an eigenvector for T, and the space W generated by w satisfies our requirements. If $\deg p = 2$, then we can write

$$p(t) = t^2 + at + b$$

with real constants a, b, and $T^2w + aTw + bw = 0$. Hence

$$T^2w = -aTw - bw.$$

Let W be the space generated by w and Tw. Then $\dim W \leq 2$, and the formula just derived shows that W is T-invariant, thus proving our lemma.

Lemma 2. *Let W be a T-invariant subspace of V. Then $W^\perp$ is also T-invariant.*

Proof. Let $v \in W^\perp$ so that $\langle w, v \rangle = 0$ for all $w \in W$. Recall that $T^* = T^{-1}$. Since $T \mid W: W \to W$ maps W into itself and since T has kernel $\{0\}$, it follows that T^{-1} maps W into itself also. Now

$$\langle w, Tv \rangle = \langle T^*w, v \rangle = \langle T^{-1}w, v \rangle = 0,$$

thus proving our second lemma.

To conclude the proof of Theorem 7 is routine by induction. We first find a T-invariant subspace V_1 of dimension 1 or 2. Then $\dim V_1^\perp < \dim V$, and by induction we can write $V_1^\perp$ as a direct sum of mutually orthogonal T-invariant subspaces of dimension 1 or 2. This proves Theorem 7.

Theorem 7 gives us a good description of the effect of a unitary operator over the reals. We can always find a decomposition of the space V into an orthogonal sum such that on each summand, T is a rotation, a reflection, or a rotation followed by a reflection. In terms of a basis for the subspaces V_i in the theorem, we can then phrase a corollary.

Corollary. *Let V be a finite dimensional vector space over the reals, of dimension > 0 and with a positive definite scalar product. Let T be a unitary operator on V. Then there exists a basis of V such that the matrix of T with respect to this basis consists of blocks*

$$\begin{pmatrix} M_1 & O & \ldots & O \\ O & M_2 & \ldots & O \\ \vdots & \vdots & & \vdots \\ O & O & \ldots & M_r \end{pmatrix}$$

such that each M_i is a 1×1 matrix or a 2×2 matrix, of the following types:

$$(1), \quad (-1), \quad \begin{pmatrix} \cos\theta & -\sin\theta \\ \sin\theta & \cos\theta \end{pmatrix}, \quad \begin{pmatrix} -\cos\theta & \sin\theta \\ \sin\theta & \cos\theta \end{pmatrix}.$$

The Complex Case

Although we discussed the real case first, the complex case is in a sense even easier.

Theorem 8. *Let V be a non-zero finite dimensional vector space over the complex numbers, with a positive definite hermitian product. Let $T: V \to V$ be a unitary operator. Then V has an orthogonal basis consisting of eigenvectors of T.*

Proof. Let v_1 be a non-zero eigenvector, and let V_1 be the 1-dimensional space generated by v_1. Just as in Lemma 2, we see that the orthogonal complement $V_1^\perp$ is T-invariant, and by induction, we can find an orthogonal basis $\{v_2, \ldots, v_n\}$ of $V_1^{\perp}$ consisting of eigenvectors for T. Then $\{v_1, \ldots, v_n\}$ is the desired basis of V.

Remark. We had proved Theorem 8 already in the chapter on triangulation, namely in Theorem 4 of Chapter X, §3. The proof we have here, however, is in a sense more natural, fitting together with that of the spectral theorem for hermitian maps.

Since an eigenvalue of a unitary operator has absolute value 1, it can be written in the form $e^{i\theta}$ with real θ, and we see again that in this case, the unitary operator can be interpreted as a rotation on the 1-dimensional complex space (and therefore 2-dimensional real space) generated over **C** by a complex eigenvector.

Thus Theorems 7 and 8 combined show geometrically that a unitary operator can be obtained as a composition of rotations and reflections.

CHAPTER XII

Polynomials and Primary
Decomposition

§1. The Euclidean algorithm

We have already defined polynomials, and their degree, in Chapter IX. In this chapter, we deal with the other standard properties of polynomials. The basic one is the Euclidean algorithm, or long division, taught (presumably) in all elementary schools.

Theorem 1. *Let f, g be polynomials over the field K, i.e. polynomials in $K[t]$, and assume $\deg g \geqq 0$. Then there exist polynomials q, r in $K[t]$ such that*

$$f(t) = q(t)g(t) + r(t),$$

and $\deg r < \deg g$. The polynomials q, r are uniquely determined by these conditions.

Proof. Let $m = \deg g \geqq 0$. Write

$$f(t) = a_n t^n + \cdots + a_0,$$

$$g(t) = b_m t^m + \cdots + b_0,$$

with $b_m \neq 0$. If $n < m$, let $q = 0$, $r = f$. If $n \geqq m$, let

$$f_1(t) = f(t) - a_n b_m^{-1} t^{n-m} g(t).$$

(This is the first step in the process of long division.) Then $\deg f_1 < \deg f$. Continuing in this way, or more formally by induction on n, we can find polynomials q_1, r such that

$$f_1 = q_1 g + r,$$

with $\deg r < \deg g$. Then

$$
\begin{aligned}
f(t) &= a_n b_m^{-1} t^{n-m} g(t) + f_1(t) \\
&= a_n b_m^{-1} t^{n-m} g(t) + q_1(t)g(t) + r(t) \\
&= (a_n b_m^{-1} t^{n-m} + q_1)g(t) + r(t),
\end{aligned}
$$

and we have consequently expressed our polynomial in the desired form.

281

To prove the uniqueness, suppose that

$$f = q_1 g + r_1 = q_2 g + r_2,$$

with $\deg r_1 < \deg g$ and $\deg r_2 < \deg g$. Then

$$(q_1 - q_2)g = r_2 - r_1.$$

The degree of the left-hand side is either $\geq \deg g$, or the left-hand side is equal to 0. The degree of the right-hand side is either $< \deg g$, or the right-hand side is equal to 0. Hence the only possibility is that they are both 0, whence

$$q_1 = q_2 \qquad \text{and} \qquad r_1 = r_2,$$

as was to be shown.

Corollary 1. *Let f be a non-zero polynomial in $K[t]$. Let $\alpha \in K$ be such that $f(\alpha) = 0$. Then there exists a polynomial $q(t)$ in $K[t]$ such that*

$$f(t) = (t - \alpha)q(t).$$

Proof. We can write

$$f(t) = q(t)(t - \alpha) + r(t),$$

where $\deg r < \deg(t - \alpha)$. But $\deg(t - \alpha) = 1$. Hence r is constant. Since

$$0 = f(\alpha) = q(\alpha)(\alpha - \alpha) + r(\alpha) = r(\alpha),$$

it follows that $r = 0$, as desired.

Corollary 2. *Let K be a field such that every non-constant polynomial in $K[t]$ has a root in K. Let f be such a polynomial. Then there exist elements $\alpha_1, \ldots, \alpha_n \in K$ and $c \in K$ such that*

$$f(t) = c(t - \alpha_1) \cdots (t - \alpha_n).$$

Proof. In Corollary 1, observe that $\deg q = \deg f - 1$. Let $\alpha = \alpha_1$ in Corollary 1. By assumption, if q is not constant, we can find a root α_2 of q, and thus write

$$f(t) = q_2(t)(t - \alpha_1)(t - \alpha_2).$$

Proceeding inductively, we keep on going until q_{n+1} is constant.

Assuming as we do that the complex numbers satisfy the hypothesis of Corollary 2, we see that we have proved the existence of a factorization of a polynomial over the complex numbers into factors of degree 1. The uniqueness will be proved in the next section.

Corollary 3. *Let f be a polynomial of degree n in $K[t]$. There are at most n roots of f in K.*

Proof. Otherwise, if $m > n$, and $\alpha_1, \ldots, \alpha_m$ are distinct roots of f in K, then

$$f(t) = (t - \alpha_1) \cdots (t - \alpha_m)g(t)$$

for some polynomial g, whence $\deg f \geqq m$, contradiction.

EXERCISES

1. In each of the following cases, write $f = qg + r$ with $\deg r < \deg g$.
   (a) $f(t) = t^2 - 2g + 1$, $g(t) = t - 1$
   (b) $f(t) = t^3 + t - 1$, $g(t) = t^2 + 1$
   (c) $f(t) = t^3 + t$, $g(t) = t$
   (d) $f(t) = t^3 - 1$, $g(t) = t - 1$

2. If $f(t)$ has integer coefficients, and if $g(t)$ has integer coefficients and leading coefficient 1, show that when we express $f = qg + r$ with $\deg r < \deg g$, the polynomials q and r also have integer coefficients.

3. Using the intermediate value theorem of calculus, show that every polynomial of odd degree over the real numbers has a root in the real numbers.

4. Let $f(t) = t^n + \cdots + a_0$ be a polynomial with complex coefficients, of degree n, and let α be a root. Show that $|\alpha| \leqq n \cdot \max_i |a_i|$. [*Hint:* Write $-\alpha^n = a_{n-1}\alpha^{n-1} + \cdots + a_0$. If $|\alpha| > n \cdot \max_i |a_i|$, divide by α^n and take the absolute value, together with a simple estimate to get a contradiction.]

§2. Greatest common divisor

We shall define a notion which bears to the set of polynomials $K[t]$ the same relation as a subspace bears to a vector space.

By an **ideal of $K[t]$,** or a **polynomial ideal,** or more briefly an **ideal** we shall mean a subset J of $K[t]$ satisfying the following conditions.

The zero polynomial is in J. If f, g are in J, then $f + g$ is in J. If f is in J, and g is an arbitrary polynomial, then gf is in J.

From this last condition, we note that if $c \in K$, and f is in J, then cf is also in J. Thus an ideal may be viewed as a vector space over K. But it is more than that, in view of the fact that it can stand multiplication by arbitrary elements of $K[t]$, not only constants.

Example 1. Let $f_1, \ldots, f_n$ be polynomials in $K[t]$. Let J be the set of all polynomials which can be written in the form

$$g = g_1 f_1 + \cdots + g_n f_n$$

with some $g_i \in K[t]$. Then J is an ideal. Indeed, if

$$h = h_1 f_1 + \cdots + h_n f_n$$

with $h_j \in K[t]$, then

$$g + h = (g_1 + h_1)f_1 + \cdots + (g_n + h_n)f_n$$

also lies in J. Also, $0 = 0f_1 + \cdots + 0f_n$ lies in J. If f is an arbitrary polynomial in $K[t]$, then

$$fg = (fg_1)f_1 + \cdots + (fg_n)f_n$$

is also in J. Thus all our conditions are satisfied.

The ideal J in Example 1 is said to be generated by $f_1, \ldots, f_n$, and we say that $f_1, \ldots, f_n$ are a **set of generators.**

We note that each f_i lies in the ideal J of Example 1. For instance,

$$f_1 = 1 \cdot f_1 + 0f_2 + \cdots + 0f_n.$$

Example 2. The single element 0 is an ideal. Also, $K[t]$ itself is an ideal. We note that 1 is a generator for $K[t]$, which is called the **unit** ideal.

Example 3. Consider the ideal generated by the two polynomials $t - 1$ and $t - 2$. We contend that it is the unit ideal. Namely,

$$(t - 1) - (t - 2) = 1$$

is in it. Thus it may happen that we are given several generators for an ideal, and still we may find a single generator for it. We shall describe more precisely the situation in the subsequent theorems.

Theorem 2. *Let J be an ideal of $K[t]$. Then there exists a polynomial g which is a generator of J.*

Proof. Suppose that J is not the zero ideal. Let g be a polynomial in J which is not 0, and is of smallest degree. We assert that g is a generator for J. Let f be any element of J. By the Euclidean algorithm, we can find polynomials q, r such that

$$f = qg + r$$

with $\deg r < \deg g$. Then $r = f - qg$, and by the definition of an ideal, it follows that r also lies in J. Since $\deg r < \deg g$, we must have $r = 0$. Hence $f = qg$, and g is a generator for J, as desired.

Remark. Let g_1 be a non-zero generator for an ideal J, and let g_2 also be a generator. Then there exists a polynomial q such that $g_1 = qg_2$. Since

$$\deg g_1 = \deg q + \deg g_2,$$

it follows that $\deg g_2 \leqq \deg g_1$. By symmetry, we must have

$$\deg g_2 = \deg g_1.$$

Hence q is constant. We can write

$$g_1 = cg_2$$

with some constant c. Write

$$g_2(t) = a_n t^n + \cdots + a_0$$

with $a_n \neq 0$. Take $b = a_n^{-1}$. Then bg_2 is also a generator of J, and its leading coefficient is equal to 1. Thus we can always find a generator for an ideal ($\neq 0$) whose leading coefficient is 1. It is furthermore clear that this generator is uniquely determined.

Let f, g be non-zero polynomials. We shall say that g **divides** f, and write $g \mid f$, if there exists a polynomial q such that $f = gq$. Let f_1, f_2 be polynomials $\neq 0$. By a **greatest common divisor** of f_1, f_2 we shall mean a polynomial g such that g divides f_1 and f_2, and furthermore, if h divides f_1 and f_2, then h divides g.

Theorem 3. *Let f_1, f_2 be non-zero polynomials in $K[t]$. Let g be a generator for the ideal generated by f_1, f_2. Then g is a greatest common divisor of f_1 and f_2.*

Proof. Since f_1 lies in the ideal generated by f_1, f_2, there exists a polynomial q_1 such that

$$f_1 = q_1 g,$$

whence g divides f_1. Similarly, g divides f_2. Let h be a polynomial dividing both f_1 and f_2. Write

$$f_1 = h_1 h \qquad \text{and} \qquad f_2 = h_2 h$$

with some polynomials h_1 and h_2. Since g is in the ideal generated by f_1, f_2, there are polynomials g_1, g_2 such that $g = g_1 f_1 + g_2 f_2$, whence

$$g = g_1 h_1 h + g_2 h_2 h = (g_1 h_1 + g_2 h_2)h.$$

Consequently h divides g, and our theorem is proved.

Remark 1. The greatest common divisor is determined up to a non-zero constant multiple. If we select a greatest common divisor with leading coefficient 1, then it is uniquely determined.

Remark 2. Exactly the same proof applies when we have more than two polynomials. For instance, if $f_1, \ldots, f_n$ are non-zero polynomials, and if g is a generator for the ideal generated by $f_1, \ldots, f_n$, then g is a greatest common divisor of $f_1, \ldots, f_n$.

Polynomials $f_1, \ldots, f_n$ whose greatest common divisor is 1 are said to be **relatively prime.**

EXERCISES

1. Show that $t^n - 1$ is divisible by $t - 1$.

2. Show that $t^4 + 4$ can be factored as a product of polynomials of degree 2 with integer coefficients.

3. If n is odd, find the quotient of $t^n + 1$ by $t + 1$.

4. Let A be an $n \times n$ matrix over a field K, and let J be the set of all polynomials $f(t)$ in $K[t]$ such that $f(A) = O$. Show that J is an ideal.

§3. *Unique factorization*

A polynomial p in $K[t]$ will be said to be **irreducible** (over K) if it is of degree ≥ 1, and if, given a factorization $p = fg$ with f, $g \in K[t]$, then $\deg f$ or $\deg g = 0$ (i.e. one of f, g is constant). Thus, up to a non-zero constant factor, the only divisors of p are p itself, and 1.

Example 1. The only irreducible polynomials over the complex numbers are the polynomials of degree 1, i.e. non-zero constant multiples of polynomials of type $t - \alpha$, with $\alpha \in \mathbf{C}$.

Example 2. The polynomial $t^2 + 1$ is irreducible over **R**.

Theorem 4. *Every polynomial in $K[t]$ of degree ≥ 1 can be expressed as a product $p_1 \cdots p_m$ of irreducible polynomials. In such a product, the polynomials $p_1, \ldots, p_m$ are uniquely determined, up to a rearrangement, and up to non-zero constant factors.*

Proof. We first prove the existence of the factorization into a product of irreducible polynomials. Let f be in $K[t]$, of degree ≥ 1. If f is irreducible, we are done. Otherwise, we can write

$$f = gh$$

where $\deg g < \deg f$ and $\deg h < \deg f$. If g, h are irreducible, we are done. Otherwise, we further factor g and h into polynomials of lower degree. We cannot continue this process indefinitely, and hence find a factorization for f. (We can obviously phrase the proof as an induction.)

We must now prove uniqueness. We need a lemma.

Lemma. *Let p be irreducible in $K[t]$. Let f, $g \in K[t]$ be non-zero polynomials, and assume p divides fg. Then p divides f or p divides g.*

Proof. Assume that p does not divide f. Then the greatest common divisor of p and f is 1, and there exist polynomials h_1, h_2 in $K[t]$ such that

$$1 = h_1 p + h_2 f.$$

(We use Theorem 3.) Multiplying by g yields

$$g = gh_1p + h_2fg.$$

But $fg = ph_3$ for some h_3, whence

$$g = (gh_1 + h_2h_3)p,$$

and p divides g, as was to be shown.

The lemma will be applied when p divides a product of irreducible polynomials $q_1 \cdots q_s$. In that case, p divides q_1 or p divides $q_2 \cdots q_s$. Hence there exists a constant c such that $p = cq_1$, or p divides $q_2 \cdots q_s$. In the latter case, we can proceed inductively, and we conclude that in any case, there exists some i such that p and q_i differ by a constant factor.

Suppose now that we have two products of irreducible polynomials

$$p_1 \cdots p_r = q_1 \cdots q_s.$$

After renumbering the q_i, we may assume that $p_1 = c_1q_1$ for some constant c_1. Cancelling q_1, we obtain

$$c_1p_2 \cdots p_r = q_2 \cdots q_s.$$

Repeating our argument inductively, we conclude that there exist constants c_i such that $p_i = c_iq_i$ for all i, after making a possible permutation of $q_1, \ldots, q_s$. This proves the desired uniqueness.

Corollary 1. *Let f be a polynomial in $K[t]$ of degree ≥ 1. Then f has a factorization $f = cp_1 \cdots p_s$, where $p_1, \ldots, p_s$ are irreducible polynomials with leading coefficient 1, uniquely determined up to a permutation.*

Corollary 2. *Let f be a polynomial in $\mathbf{C}[t]$, of degree ≥ 1. Then f has a factorization*

$$f(t) = c(t - \alpha_1) \cdots (t - \alpha_n),$$

with $\alpha_i \in \mathbf{C}$ and $c \in \mathbf{C}$. The factors $t - \alpha_i$ are uniquely determined up to a permutation.

We shall deal mostly with polynomials having leading coefficient 1. Let f be such a polynomial of degree ≥ 1. Let $p_1, \ldots, p_r$ be the *distinct* irreducible polynomials (with leading coefficient 1) occurring in its factorization. Then we can express f as a product

$$f = p_1^{i_1} \cdots p_r^{i_r}$$

where $i_1, \ldots, i_r$ are positive integers, uniquely determined by $p_1, \ldots, p_r$.

This factorization will be called a normalized factorization for f. In particular, over the complex numbers, we can write

$$f(t) = (t - \alpha_1)^{i_1} \cdots (t - \alpha_r)^{i_r}.$$

A polynomial with leading coefficient 1 is sometimes called **monic.**

If p is irreducible, and $f = p^m g$, where p does not divide g, and m is an integer ≥ 0, then we say that m is the **multiplicity** of p in f. (We define p^0 to be 1.) We denote this multiplicity by $\mathrm{ord}_p f$, and also call it the **order** of f at p.

If α is a root of f, and

$$f(t) = (t - \alpha)^m g(t),$$

with $g(\alpha) \neq 0$, then $t - \alpha$ does not divide $g(t)$, and m is the multiplicity of $t - \alpha$ in f. We also say that m is the multiplicity of α in f.

There is an easy test for $m > 1$ in terms of the derivative.

Let $f(t) = a_n t^n + \cdots + a_0$ be a polynomial. Define its (formal) derivative to be

$$Df(t) = f'(t) = na_n t^n + (n - 1)a_{n-1} t^{n-2} + \cdots + a_1.$$

Then we have the following statements, whose proofs are left as exercises.

(a) If f, g are polynomials, then

$$(f + g)' = f' + g'.$$

Also

$$(fg)' = f'g + fg'.$$

If c is constant, then $(cf)' = cf'$.

(b) Let α be a root of f and assume $\deg f \geq 1$. Show that the multiplicity of α in f is > 1 if and only if $f'(\alpha) = 0$. Hence if $f'(\alpha) \neq 0$, show that the multiplicity of α is 1.

EXERCISES

1. Let f be a polynomial of degree 2 over a field K. Show that either f is irreducible over K, or f has a factorization into linear factors over K.

2. Let f be a polynomial of degree 3 over a field K. If f is not irreducible over K, show that f has a root in K.

3. Let $f(t)$ be an irreducible polynomial with leading coefficient 1 over the real numbers. Assume $\deg f = 2$. Show that $f(t)$ can be written in the form

$$f(t) = (t - a)^2 + b^2$$

with some $a, b \in \mathbf{R}$ and $b \neq 0$. Conversely, prove that any such polynomial is irreducible over $\mathbf{R}$.

4. Let f be a polynomial with complex coefficients, say

$$f(t) = \alpha_n t^n + \cdots + \alpha_0.$$

Define its complex conjugate,

$$\bar{f}(t) = \bar{\alpha}_n t^n + \cdots + \bar{\alpha}_0$$

by taking the complex conjugate of each coefficient. Show that if f, g are in $\mathbf{C}[t]$, then

$$\overline{(f+g)} = \bar{f} + \bar{g}, \quad \overline{(fg)} = \bar{f}\bar{g},$$

and if $\beta \in \mathbf{C}$, then $\overline{(\beta f)} = \bar{\beta}\bar{f}$.

5. Let $f(t)$ be a polynomial with real coefficients. Let α be a root of f, which is complex but not real. Show that $\bar{\alpha}$ is also a root of f.

6. Terminology being as in Exercise 5, show that the multiplicity of α in f is the same as that of $\bar{\alpha}$.

7. Let A be an $n \times n$ matrix in a field K. Let J be the set of polynomials f in $K[t]$ such that $f(A) = O$. Show that J is an ideal. The monic generator of J is called the **minimal** polynomial of A over K. A similar definition is made if A is a linear map of a finite dimensional vector space V into itself.

8. Let V be a finite dimensional space over K. Let $A: V \to V$ be a linear map. Let f be its minimal polynomial. If A can be diagonalized (i.e. if there exists a basis of V consisting of eigenvectors of A), show that the minimal polynomial is equal to the product

$$(t - \alpha_1) \cdots (t - \alpha_r),$$

where $\alpha_1, \ldots, \alpha_r$ are the distinct eigenvalues of A.

9. Show that the following polynomials have no multiple roots in $\mathbf{C}$.
   (a) $t^4 + t$ (b) $t^5 - 5t + 1$
   (c) any polynomial $t^2 + bt + c$ if b, c are numbers such that $b^2 - 4c$ is not 0.

10. Show that the polynomial $t^n - 1$ has no multiple roots in $\mathbf{C}$. Can you determine all the roots and give its factorization into factors of degree 1?

11. Let f, g be polynomials in $K[t]$, and assume that they are relatively prime. Show that one can find polynomials f_1, g_1 such that the determinant

$$\begin{vmatrix} f & g \\ f_1 & g_1 \end{vmatrix}$$

is equal to 1.

12. Let f_1, f_2, f_3 be polynomials in $K[t]$ and assume that they generate the unit ideal. Show that one can find polynomials f_{ij} in $K[t]$ such that the determinant

$$\begin{vmatrix} f_1 & f_2 & f_3 \\ f_{21} & f_{22} & f_{23} \\ f_{31} & f_{32} & f_{33} \end{vmatrix}$$

is equal to 1.

13. Let α be a complex number, and let J be the set of all polynomials $f(t)$ in $K[t]$ such that $f(\alpha) = 0$. Show that J is an ideal. Assume that J is not the zero ideal. Show that the monic generator of J is irreducible.

14. Let f, g be two polynomials, written in the form

$$f = p_1^{i_1} \cdots p_r^{i_r}$$

and

$$g = p_1^{j_1} \cdots p_r^{j_r}$$

where i_ν, j_ν are integers $\geqq 0$, and $p_1, \ldots, p_r$ are distinct irreducible polynomials.

(a) Show that the greatest common divisor of f and g can be expressed as a product $p_1^{k_1} \cdots p_r^{k_r}$ where $k_1, \ldots, k_r$ are integers $\geqq 0$. Express k_ν in terms of i_ν and j_ν.

(b) Define the least common multiple of polynomials, and express the least common multiple of f and g as a product $p_1^{k_1} \cdots p_r^{k_r}$ with integers $k_\nu \geqq 0$. Express k_ν in terms of i_ν and j_ν.

15. Give the greatest common divisor and least common multiple of the following pairs of polynomials:

(a) $(t - 2)^3(t - 3)^4(t - i)$ and $(t - 1)(t - 2)(t - 3)^3$

(b) $(t^2 + 1)(t^2 - 1)$ and $(t + i)^3(t^3 - 1)$

§4. The integers

The factorization theory of the integers follows closely the corresponding theory of polynomials over a field. Let $\mathbf{Z}$ denote the integers. We have the Euclidean algorithm.

Theorem 1'. *Let m, n be integers $\geqq 0$, and $m > 0$. Then there exist integers q, $r \geqq 0$ with $0 \leqq r < m$ such that*

$$n = qm + r.$$

The integers q, r are uniquely determined by these conditions.

Proof. If $n < m$, then we let $q = 0$ and $r = n$. If $n \geqq m$, then $0 \leqq n - m < n$. By induction, we can find integers q_1, $r \geqq 0$ and $r < m$ such that

$$n - m = q_1 m + r.$$

Then

$$n = m + q_1 m + r = (1 + q_1)m + r.$$

This proves the existence. We leave the uniqueness as an exercise.

We define an **ideal** J of integers to be a subset of $\mathbf{Z}$ having the following properties:

The integer 0 is in J. If m, n are in J, then $m + n$ is in J. If m is in J, and n is an arbitrary integer, then nm is in J.

As with polynomials, we define what it means for an ideal to be generated by integers $m_1, \ldots, m_n$. We have the zero ideal, and the unit ideal (namely $\mathbf{Z}$ itself). We have:

Theorem 2'. *Let J be an ideal of $\mathbf{Z}$. Then there exists an integer d which is a generator of J.*

Proof. Entirely similar to the proof of Theorem 2. We leave it to the reader as an easy exercise. [*Hint:* Instead of a polynomial of lowest degree, take the smallest positive integer in the ideal.]

We have the notion of divisibility, defined just as with polynomials.

Theorem 3'. *Let m_1, m_2 be positive integers. Let d be a positive generator for the ideal generated by m_1, m_2. Then d is a greatest common divisor of m_1, m_2.*

Proof. A pleasure for the reader to work out. Actually, it involves nothing more than copying *mutatis mutandis* the proof given for Theorem 3.

We define a **prime number** p to be an integer ≥ 2 such that, given a factorization $p = mn$ with positive integers m, n, then $m = 1$ or $n = 1$.

Theorem 4'. *Every positive integer $n \geq 2$ can be expressed as a product of prime numbers,*

$$n = p_1 \cdots p_r,$$

uniquely determined up to a permutation.

Proof. Copy the proof of Theorem 4, omitting irrelevant references to constants.

EXERCISES

1. Let $f(t) = t^n + a_{n-1}t^{n-1} + \cdots + a_0$, $a_0 \neq 0$, be a polynomial with integer coefficients. Show that if α is a root of f in $\mathbf{Z}$ then α divides a_0.

2. Let $f(t)$ be a polynomial of degree ≥ 1 with leading coefficient 1, and integer coefficients. Show that any root of f which is a rational number must in fact be an integer.

3. Show that the following polynomials are irreducible over the rational numbers.

    (a) $t^2 + 1$ (b) $t^2 - 2t + 2$ (c) $t^2 - t + 4$
    (d) $t^3 - t + 1$ (e) $t^3 + 3t - 1$ (f) $t^3 - 4t + 5$

4. Let a, b be relatively prime integers. Show that there exist integers c, d such that the determinant

$$\begin{vmatrix} a & b \\ c & d \end{vmatrix}$$

is equal to 1.

5. (Euclid) Show that there exist infinitely many prime numbers. [*Hint:* Given distinct prime numbers $p_1, \ldots, p_n$, construct a new one as follows. Let $a = p_1 \cdots p_n + 1$. Show that any prime number p dividing a cannot equal any one of the p_i.]

6. State and prove the analogue of Exercise 14 of the preceding section for positive integers.

7. Give the greatest common divisor and least common multiple of the following pairs of positive integers:

   (a) $5^3 2^6 3$ and $5^2 17$ (b) 248 and 28

§5. *Application to the decomposition of a vector space*

Let V be a vector space over the field K, and let $A: V \to V$ be an operator of V. Let W be a subspace of V. We shall say that W is an **invariant subspace** under A if Aw lies in W for each w in W, i.e. if AW is contained in W.

Example 1. Let v_1 be a non-zero eigenvector of A, and let V_1 be the 1-dimensional space generated by v_1. Then V_1 is an invariant subspace under A.

Example 2. Let λ be an eigenvalue of A, and let V_λ be the subspace of V consisting of all $v \in V$ such that $Av = \lambda v$. Then V_λ is an invariant subspace under A, called the **eigenspace** of λ.

Example 3. Let $f(t) \in K[t]$ be a polynomial, and let W be the kernel of $f(A)$. Then W is an invariant subspace under A.

Proof. Suppose that $f(A)w = O$. Since $tf(t) = f(t)t$, we get

$$Af(A) = f(A)A,$$

whence

$$f(A)(Aw) = f(A)Aw = Af(A)w = O.$$

Thus Aw is also in the kernel of $f(A)$, thereby proving our assertion.

Remark in general that for any two polynomials f, g we have

$$f(A)g(A) = g(A)f(A)$$

because $f(t)g(t) = g(t)f(t)$. We use this frequently in the sequel.

We shall now describe how the factorization of a polynomial into two factors whose greatest common divisor is 1, gives rise to a decomposition of the vector space V into a direct sum of invariant subspaces.

Theorem 5. *Let $f(t) \in K[t]$ be a polynomial, and suppose that $f = f_1 f_2$, where f_1, f_2 are polynomials of degree ≥ 1, and greatest common divisor equal to 1. Let $A : V \to V$ be an operator. Assume that $f(A) = O$. Let*

$$W_1 = \text{kernel of } f_1(A) \qquad and \qquad W_2 = \text{kernel of } f_2(A).$$

Then V is the direct sum of W_1 and W_2.

Proof. By assumption, there exist polynomials g_1, g_2 such that

$$g_1(t)f_1(t) + g_2(t)f_2(t) = 1.$$

Hence

(*) $$g_1(A)f_1(A) + g_2(A)f_2(A) = I.$$

Let $v \in V$. Then

$$v = g_1(A)f_1(A)v + g_2(A)f_2(A)v.$$

The first term in this sum belongs to W_2, because

$$f_2(A)g_1(A)f_1(A)v = g_1(A)f_1(A)f_2(A)v = g_1(A)f(A)v = O.$$

Similarly, the second term in this sum belongs to W_2. Thus V is the sum of W_1 and W_2.

To show that this sum is direct, we must prove that an expression

$$v = w_1 + w_2$$

with $w_1 \in W_1$ and $w_2 \in W_2$, is uniquely determined by v. Applying $g_1(A)f_1(A)$ to this sum, we find

$$g_1(A)f_1(A)v = g_1(A)f_1(A)w_2,$$

because $f_1(A)w_1 = O$. Applying the expression (*) to w_2 itself, we find

$$w_2 = g_1(A)f_1(A)w_2$$

because $f_2(A)w_2 = O$. Consequently

$$w_2 = g_1(A)f_1(A)v,$$

and hence w_2 is uniquely determined. Similarly, $w_1 = g_2(A)f_2(A)v$ is uniquely determined, and the sum is therefore direct. This proves our theorem.

Theorem 5 applies as well when f is expressed as a product of several factors. We state the result over the complex numbers.

Theorem 6. *Let V be a vector space over* **C**, *and let $A: V \to V$ be an operator. Let $P(t)$ be a polynomial such that $P(A) = O$, and let*

$$P(t) = (t - \alpha_1)^{m_1} \cdots (t - \alpha_r)^{m_r}$$

be its factorization, the $\alpha_1, \ldots, \alpha_r$ being the distinct roots. Let U_i be the kernel of $(A - \alpha_i I)^{m_i}$. Then V is the direct sum of the subspaces $U_1, \ldots, U_r$.

Proof. The proof can be done by induction, splitting off the factors $(t - \alpha_1)^{m_1}, (t - \alpha_2)^{m_2}, \ldots$ one by one. Thus we first obtain a direct sum decomposition into the kernel U_1 of $(A - \alpha_1 I)^{m_1}$, and the kernel W of

$$(A - \alpha_2 I)^{m_2} \cdots (A - \alpha_r I)^{m_r}.$$

Now, inductively, we can assume that W is expressed as a direct sum

$$W = U_2 \oplus \cdots \oplus U_r$$

where U_j $(j = 2, \ldots, r)$ is the kernel of $(A - \alpha_j I)^{m_j}$ in W. Then

$$V = U_1 \oplus U_2 \oplus \cdots \oplus U_r$$

is a direct sum. We still have to prove that U_j $(j = 2, \ldots, r)$ is the kernel of $(A - \alpha_j I)^{m_j}$ in V. Let

$$v = u_1 + u_2 + \cdots + u_r$$

be an element of V, with $u_i \in U_i$, and such that v is in the kernel of $(A - \alpha_j I)^{m_j}$. Then in particular, v is in the kernel of

$$(A - \alpha_2 I)^{m_2} \cdots (A - \alpha_r I)^{m_r},$$

whence v must be in W, and consequently $u_1 = 0$. Since v lies in W, we can now conclude that $v = u_j$ because W is the direct sum of $U_2, \ldots, U_r$.

Example 4. Let V be the space of (infinitely differentiable) solutions of the differential equation

$$D^n f + a_{n-1} D^{n-1} f + \cdots + a_0 f = 0,$$

with constant complex coefficients a_i. Let

$$P(t) = t^n + a_{n-1} t^{n-1} + \cdots + a_0.$$

Factor $P(t)$ as in Theorem 6,

$$P(t) = (t - \alpha_1)^{m_1} \cdots (t - \alpha_r)^{m_r}.$$

Then V is the direct sum of the spaces of solutions of the differential equations

$$(D - \alpha_i I)^{m_i} f = 0,$$

for $i = 1, \ldots, r$. Thus the study of the original differential equation is reduced to the study of the much simpler equation

$$(D - \alpha I)^m f = 0.$$

The solutions of this equation are easily found. For any complex α, we have

$$(D - \alpha I)^m f = e^{\alpha t} D^m (e^{-\alpha t} f).$$

(The proof is a simple induction.) Consequently, f lies in the kernel of $(D - \alpha I)^m$ if and only if

$$D^m (e^{-\alpha t} f) = 0.$$

The only functions whose m-th derivative is 0 are the polynomials of degree $\leqq m - 1$. Hence the space of solutions of $(D - \alpha I)^m f = 0$ is the space generated by the functions

$$e^{\alpha t}, te^{\alpha t}, \ldots, t^{m-1} e^{\alpha t}.$$

These functions are easily verified to be linearly independent, and consequently, the space of solutions is finite dimensional, of dimension m.

EXERCISE

1. In Theorem 5, show that image of $f_1(A)$ = kernel of $f_2(A)$.

§6. *Schur's lemma*

Let V be a vector space over K, and let S be a set of operators of V. Let W be a subspace of V. We shall say that W is an S-**invariant** subspace if BW is contained in W for all B in S. We shall say that V is a **simple S-space** if $V \neq \{O\}$ and if the only S-invariant subspaces are V itself and the zero subspace.

Remark 1. Let $A: V \to V$ be an operator such that $AB = BA$ for all $B \in S$. Then the image and kernel of A are S-invariant subspaces of V.

Proof. Let w be in the image of A, say $w = Av$ with some $v \in V$. Then $Bw = BAv = ABv$. This shows that Bw is also in the image of A, and hence that the image of A is S-invariant. Let u be in the kernel of A. Then $ABu = BAu = O$. Hence Bu is also in the kernel, which is therefore an S-invariant subspace.

Remark 2. Let S be as above, and let $A: V \to V$ be an operator. Assume that $AB = BA$ for all $B \in S$. If f is a polynomial in $K[t]$, then $f(A)B = Bf(A)$ for all $B \in S$. Prove this as a simple exercise.

Theorem 7. *Let V be a vector space over K, and let S be a set of operators of V. Assume that V is a simple S-space. Let $A: V \to V$ be a linear map such that $AB = BA$ for all B in S. Then either A is invertible, or A is the zero map.*

Proof. Assume $A \neq O$. By Remark 1, the kernel of A is $\{O\}$, and its image is all of V. Hence A is invertible.

Theorem 8. *Let V be a finite dimensional vector space over the complex numbers. Let S be a set of operators of V, and assume that V is a simple S-space. Let $A: V \to V$ be a linear map such that $AB = BA$ for all B in S. Then there exists a number λ such that $A = \lambda I$.*

Proof. Let J be the ideal of polynomials f in $\mathbf{C}[t]$ such that $f(A) = O$. Let g be a generator for this ideal, with leading coefficient 1. Then $g \neq 0$. We contend that g is irreducible. Otherwise, we can write $g = h_1 h_2$ with polynomials h_1, h_2 of degrees $< \deg g$. Consequently $h_1(A) \neq O$. By Theorem 7, and Remarks 1, 2 we conclude that $h_1(A)$ is invertible. Similarly, $h_2(A)$ is invertible. Hence $h_1(A)h_2(A)$ is invertible, an impossibility which proves that g must be irreducible. But the only irreducible polynomials over the complex numbers are of degree 1, and hence $g(t) = t - \lambda$ for some $\lambda \in \mathbf{C}$. Since $g(A) = O$, we conclude that $A - \lambda I = O$, whence $A = \lambda I$, as was to be shown.

EXERCISES

1. Let V be a finite dimensional vector space over the field K, and let S be the set of all linear maps of V into itself. Show that V is a simple S-space.

2. Let $V = \mathbf{R}^2$, let S consist of the matrix $\begin{pmatrix} 1 & a \\ 0 & 1 \end{pmatrix}$ viewed as linear map of V into itself. Here, a is a fixed non-zero real number. Determine all S-invariant subspaces of V.

3. Let V be a vector space over the field K, and let $\{v_1, \ldots, v_n\}$ be a basis of V. For each permutation σ of $\{1, \ldots, n\}$ let $A_\sigma: V \to V$ be the linear map such that

$$A_\sigma(v_i) = v_{\sigma(i)}.$$

(a) Show that for any two permutations σ, τ we have

$$A_\sigma A_\tau = A_{\sigma\tau},$$

and $A_{id} = I$.

(b) Show that the subspace generated by $v = v_1 + \cdots + v_n$ is an in-variant subspace for the set S_n consisting of all A_σ.

(c) Show that the element v of part (b) is an eigenvector of each A_σ. What is the eigenvalue of A_σ belonging to v?

(d) Let $n = 2$, and let σ be the permutation which is not the identity. Show that $v_1 - v_2$ generates a 1-dimensional subspace which is in-variant under A_σ. Show that $v_1 - v_2$ is an eigenvector of A_σ. What is the eigenvalue?

4. Let V be a vector space over the field K, and let $A : V \to V$ be an operator. Assume that $A^r = I$ for some integer $r \geq 1$. Let $T = I + A + \cdots + A^{r-1}$. Let v_0 be an element of V. Show that the space generated by Tv_0 is an invariant subspace of A, and that Tv_0 is an eigenvector of A. If $Tv_0 \neq O$, what is the eigenvalue?

5. Let V be a vector space over the field K, and let S be a set of operators of V. Let U, W be S-invariant subspaces of V. Show that $U + W$ and $U \cap W$ are S-invariant subspaces.

§7. *The Jordan normal form*

In Chapter X, §1 we proved that a linear map over the complex num-bers can always be triangularized. This result suffices for many appli-cations, but it is possible to improve it and find a basis such that the matrix of the linear map has an exceptionally simple triangular form. We do this now, using the primary decomposition.

We first consider a special case, which turns out to be rather typical afterwards. Let V be a vector space over the complex numbers. Let $A : V \to V$ be a linear map. Let $\alpha \in \mathbf{C}$ and let $v \in V$, $v \neq 0$. We shall say that v is $(A - \alpha I)$-**cyclic** if there exists an integer $r \geq 1$ such that $(A - \alpha I)^r v = 0$. The smallest positive integer r having this property will then be called a **period** of v relative to $A - \alpha I$. If r is such a period, then we have $(A - \alpha I)^k v \neq 0$ for any integer k such that $0 \leq k < r$.

Lemma 1. *If $v \neq 0$ is $(A - \alpha I)$-cyclic, with period r, then the elements*

$$v, (A - \alpha I)v, \ldots, (A - \alpha I)^{r-1}v$$

are linearly independent.

Proof. Let $B = A - \alpha I$ for simplicity. A relation of linear dependence between the above elements can be written

$$f(B)v = 0$$

where f is a polynomial $\neq 0$ of degree $\leq r - 1$, namely

$$c_0 v + c_1 B v + \cdots + c_s B^s v = 0,$$

with $f(t) = c_0 + c_1 t + \cdots + c_s t^s$, and $s \leq r - 1$. We also have $B^r v = 0$ by hypothesis. Let $g(t) = t^r$. If h is the greatest common divisor of f and g, then we can write

$$h = f_1 f + g_1 g,$$

where f_1, g_1 are polynomials, and thus $h(B) = f_1(B)f(B) + g_1(B)g(B)$. It follows that $h(B)v = 0$. But $h(t)$ divides t^r and is of degree $\leq r - 1$, so that $h(t) = t^d$ with $d < r$. This contradicts the hypothesis that r is a period of v, and proves the lemma.

The vector space V will be called **cyclic** if there exists some number α and an element $v \in V$ which is $(A - \alpha I)$-cyclic. If this is the case, then Lemma 1 implies that

(*) $$\{(A - \alpha I)^{r-1}v, \ldots, (A - \alpha I)v, v\}$$

is a basis for V. With respect to this basis, the matrix of A is then particularly simple. Indeed, for each k we have

$$A(A - \alpha I)^k v = (A - \alpha I)^{k+1}v + \alpha(A - \alpha I)^k v.$$

By definition, it follows that the associated matrix for A with respect to this basis is equal to the triangular matrix

$$\begin{pmatrix} \alpha & 1 & 0 & \ldots & 0 & 0 \\ 0 & \alpha & 1 & \ldots & 0 & 0 \\ \vdots & \vdots & \vdots & & \vdots & \vdots \\ 0 & 0 & 0 & \ldots & \alpha & 1 \\ 0 & 0 & 0 & \ldots & 0 & \alpha \end{pmatrix}.$$

This matrix has α on the diagonal, 1 above the diagonal, and 0 everywhere else. The reader will observe that $(A - \alpha I)^{r-1}v$ is an eigenvector for A, with eigenvalue α.

The basis (*) is called a **Jordan basis for** A.

Suppose that V is expressed as a direct sum of A-invariant subspaces,

$$V = V_1 \oplus \cdots \oplus V_m,$$

and suppose that each V_i is cyclic. If we select a Jordan basis for each V_i, then the sequence of these bases forms a basis for V, again called a **Jordan basis for** A. With respect to this basis, the matrix for A therefore splits into blocks (Fig. 1).

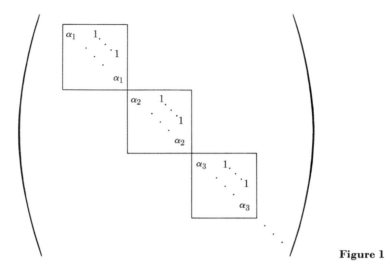

Figure 1

In each block we have an eigenvalue α_i on the diagonal. We have 1 above the diagonal, and 0 everywhere else. This matrix is called the **Jordan normal form for** A. Our main theorem in this section is that this normal form can always be achieved, namely:

Theorem 9. *Let V be a finite dimensional space over the complex numbers, and $V \neq \{O\}$. Let $A: V \to V$ be an operator. Then V can be expressed as a direct sum of A-invariant cyclic subspaces.*

Proof. By Theorem 6, §5 we may assume without loss of generality there exists a number α and an integer $r \geqq 1$ such that $(A - \alpha I)^r = O$. Let $B = A - \alpha I$. Then $B^r = O$. We assume that r is the smallest such integer. Then $B^{r-1} \neq O$. The subspace BV is not equal to V because its dimension is strictly smaller than that of V. (For instance, there exists some $w \in V$ such that $B^{r-1}w \neq 0$. Let $v = B^{r-1}w$. Then $Bv = 0$. Our assertion follows from the dimension relation

$$\dim BV + \dim \text{Ker } B = \dim V.)$$

By induction, we may write BV as a direct sum of A-invariant (or B-invariant) subspaces which are cyclic, say

$$BV = W_1 \oplus \cdots \oplus W_m,$$

such that W_i has a basis consisting of elements $B^k w_i$ for some cyclic vector $w_i \in W_i$ of period r_i. Let $v_i \in V$ be such that $Bv_i = w_i$. Then each v_i

is a cyclic vector, because

$$\text{if } B^{r_i}w_i = 0, \quad \text{then} \quad B^{r_i+1}v_i = 0.$$

Let V_i be the subspace of V generated by the elements $B^k v_i$ for $k = 1, \ldots, r_i + 1$. We contend that the subspace V' equal to the sum

$$V' = V_1 + \cdots + V_m$$

is a direct sum. We have to prove that any element u in this sum can be expressed uniquely in the form

$$u = u_1 + \cdots + u_m, \qquad \text{with } u_i \in V_i.$$

Any element of V_i is of type $f_i(B)v_i$ where f_i is a polynomial, of degree $\leq r_i + 1$. Suppose that

(1) $$f_1(B)v_1 + \cdots + f_m(B)v_m = 0.$$

Applying B and noting that $Bf_i(B) = f_i(B)B$ we get

$$f_1(B)w_1 + \cdots + f_m(B)w_m = 0.$$

But $W_1 + \cdots + W_m$ is a direct sum decomposition of BV, whence

$$f_i(B)w_i = 0, \qquad \text{all } i = 1, \ldots, m.$$

Therefore t^{r_i} divides $f_i(t)$, and in particular t divides $f_i(t)$. We can thus write

$$f_i(t) = g_i(t)t$$

for some polynomial g_i, and hence $f_i(B) = g_i(B)B$. It follows from (1) that

$$g_1(B)w_1 + \cdots + g_m(B)w_m = 0.$$

Again, t^{r_i} divides $g_i(t)$, whence t^{r_i+1} divides $f_i(t)$, and therefore $f_i(B)v_i = 0$. This proves what we wanted, namely that V' is a direct sum of $V_1, \ldots, V_m$.

From the construction of V' we observe that $BV' = BV$, because any element in BV is of the form

$$f_1(B)w_1 + \cdots + f_m(B)w_m$$

with some polynomials f_i, and is therefore the image under B of the element

$$f_1(B)v_1 + \cdots + f_m(B)v_m,$$

which lies in V'. From this we shall conclude that

$$V = V' + \text{Ker } B.$$

Indeed, let $v \in V$. Then $Bv = Bv'$ for some $v' \in V'$, and hence $B(v - v') = 0$. Thus

$$v = v' + (v - v'),$$

thus proving that $V = V' + \operatorname{Ker} B$. Of course this sum is not direct. However, let $\mathfrak{B}'$ be a Jordan basis of V'. We can extend $\mathfrak{B}'$ to a basis of V by using elements of $\operatorname{Ker} B$. Namely, if $\{u_1, \ldots, u_s\}$ is a basis of $\operatorname{Ker} B$, then

$$\{\mathfrak{B}', u_{j_1}, \ldots, u_{j_l}\}$$

is a basis of V for suitable indices $j_1, \ldots, j_l$. Each u_j satisfies $Bu_j = 0$, whence u_j is an eigenvector for A, and the one-dimensional space generated by u_j is A-invariant, and cyclic. We let this subspace be denoted by U_j. Then we have

$$
\begin{aligned}
V &= V' \oplus U_{j_1} \oplus \cdots \oplus U_{j_l} \\
&= V_1 \oplus \cdots \oplus V_m \oplus U_{j_1} \oplus \cdots \oplus U_{j_{l'}}
\end{aligned}
$$

thus giving the desired expression of V as a direct sum of cyclic subspaces. This proves our theorem.

Exercises

In the following exercises, we let V be a finite dimensional vector space over the complex numbers, and we let $A \colon V \to V$ be an operator.

1. Show that A can be written in the form $A = D + N$, where D is a diagonalizable operator, N is a nilpotent operator, and $DN = ND$.

2. Assume that V is cyclic. Show that the subspace of V generated by eigenvectors of A is one-dimensional.

3. Assume that V is cyclic. Let f be a polynomial. What are the eigenvalues of $f(A)$ in terms of those of A? Same question when V is not assumed cyclic.

4. If A is nilpotent and not O, show that A is not diagonalizable.

5. Let P_A be the characteristic polynomial of A, and write it as a product

$$P_A(t) = \prod_{i=1}^{r} (t - \alpha_i)^{m_i},$$

where $\alpha_i, \ldots, \alpha_r$ are distinct. Let f be a polynomial. Express the characteristic polynomial $P_{f(A)}$ as a product of factors of degree 1.

PART THREE

RELATIONS

with

OTHER STRUCTURES

CHAPTER XIII

Multilinear Products

§1. *The tensor product*

Let V, W be vector spaces over a field K. We wish to define a new kind of product between elements of V and W. The value of the product should be in a vector space, and roughly speaking, we wish to have no relations in this product except bilinear relations. In other words, if we denote by $v \otimes w$ the product of elements $v \in V$ and $w \in W$, then we should have only the following relations:

If v_1, $v_2 \in V$ and $w \in W$, then

$$(v_1 + v_2) \otimes w = v_1 \otimes w + v_2 \otimes w.$$

If w_1, $w_2 \in W$ and $v \in V$, then

$$v \otimes (w_1 + w_2) = v \otimes w_1 + v \otimes w_2.$$

If $c \in K$, then

$$(cv) \otimes w = c(v \otimes w) = v \otimes cw.$$

We shall construct such a product, and prove its various properties.

Let U, V, W be vector spaces over K. We recall that a bilinear map

$$g \colon V \times W \to U$$

is a map which to each pair of elements (v, w) with $v \in V$ and $w \in W$ associates an element $g(v, w)$ of U, having the following property:

For each $v \in V$, the map $w \mapsto g(v, w)$ of W into U is linear, and for each $w \in W$, the map $v \mapsto g(v, w)$ of V into U is linear.

Thus a bilinear map is defined in a manner entirely similar to a bilinear form, the only difference being that we allow the values of the map to be in a vector space instead of the field K.

Theorem 1. *Let V, W be finite dimensional vector spaces over the field K. There exists a finite dimensional space T over K, and a bilinear map $V \times W \to T$ denoted by*

$$(v, w) \mapsto v \otimes w,$$

satisfying the following properties.

TP 1. *If U is a vector space over K, and $g\colon V \times W \to U$ is a bilinear map, then there exists a unique linear map*

$$g_*\colon T \to U$$

such that, for all pairs (v, w) with $v \in V$ and $w \in W$ we have

$$g(v, w) = g_*(v \otimes w).$$

TP 2. *If $\{v_1, \ldots, v_n\}$ is a basis of V, and $\{w_1, \ldots, w_m\}$ is a basis of W, then the elements*

$$v_i \otimes w_j \qquad (i = 1, \ldots, n \text{ and } j = 1, \ldots, m)$$

form a basis of T.

Proof. Let $\{v_1, \ldots, v_n\}$ be a basis of V, and let $\{w_1, \ldots, w_m\}$ be a basis of W. For each pair (i, j) with $1 \leq i \leq n$ and $1 \leq j \leq m$ let t_{ij} be a letter. As explained in the appendix of this chapter, we let T be the vector space over K consisting of all formal linear combinations of these elements t_{ij} with coefficients in K, so that these elements form a basis of T over K. Thus elements of T consist of linear combinations

$$\sum_{i=1}^{n} \sum_{j=1}^{m} c_{ij} t_{ij}$$

with $c_{ij} \in K$.

If $v = x_1 v_1 + \cdots + x_n v_n$ and $w = y_1 w_1 + \cdots + y_m w_m$, with x_i, y_j in K, then we define $v \otimes w$ to be the element

$$v \otimes w = \sum_{i=1}^{n} \sum_{j=1}^{m} x_i y_j t_{ij}$$

of T. In particular, $v_i \otimes w_j = t_{ij}$. We now prove that our product $v \otimes w$ has all the required properties.

Proof of TP 1. For simplicity, we abbreviate the sums

$$\sum_{i=1}^{n} \sum_{j=1}^{m} \quad \text{by} \quad \sum_{i} \sum_{j}.$$

We first prove that the map $(v, w) \mapsto v \otimes w$ is bilinear. Let

$$v' = x_1' v_1 + \cdots + x_n' v_n$$

and let v, w be expressed as linear combinations of our bases elements as above. Then

$$v + v' = (x_1 + x_1')v_1 + \cdots + (x_n + x_n')v_n.$$

By definition,

$$(v + v') \otimes w = \sum_i \sum_j (x_i + x_i') y_j t_{ij}$$

$$= \sum_i \sum_j (x_i y_j + x_i' y_j) t_{ij}$$

$$= \sum_i \sum_j (x_i y_j t_{ij} + x_i' y_j t_{ij})$$

$$= \sum_i \sum_j x_i y_j t_{ij} + \sum_i \sum_j x_i' y_j t_{ij}$$

$$= v \otimes w + v' \otimes w.$$

The proof for distributivity on the other side is similar and we omit it. If $c \in K$, then

$$(cv) \otimes w = \sum_i \sum_j (c x_i) y_j t_{ij}$$

$$= \sum_i \sum_j c x_i y_j t_{ij}$$

$$= c \sum_i \sum_j x_i y_j t_{ij}$$

$$= c(v \otimes w).$$

This proves that our product $\otimes$ is bilinear.

Let $g: V \times W \to U$ be a bilinear map. Using the theorem that one can prescribe arbitrarily the values of a linear map on basis elements (Theorem 1 of Chapter IV, §2) we know that there exists a unique linear map

$$g_*: T \to U$$

such that

$$g_*(t_{ij}) = g(v_i, w_j).$$

Then for any v, w expressed as above as linear combinations of our bases elements,

$$g(v, w) = g \left(\sum_i x_i v_i, \sum_j y_j w_j \right)$$

$$= \sum_i \sum_j x_i y_j g(v_i, w_j)$$

$$= g_*(v \otimes w).$$

Thus our required map g_* exists and is uniquely determined.

Proof of TP 2. Let $\{v_1', \ldots, v_n'\}$ be any basis of V, and let $\{w_1', \ldots, w_m'\}$ be any basis of W. We must prove that the elements $v_i' \otimes w_j'$ form a basis of T. Any elements $v \in V$ and $w \in W$ can be expressed as linear combinations

$$v = x_1' v_1' + \cdots + x_n' v_n'$$

and

$$w = y_1' w_1' + \cdots + y_n' w_n'$$

with x_i' and $y_j' \in K$. Then

$$v \otimes w = \sum_i \sum_j x_i' y_j' (v_i' \otimes w_j').$$

Hence the elements

$$v_i' \otimes w_j'$$

generate T over K. There are mn such elements. If they were linearly dependent, the dimension of T would be $< mn$, contradicting the fact that the elements t_{ij} form a basis of T. This proves our theorem.

The space T in Theorem 1 is called the **tensor product** of V and W, and is denoted by $V \otimes W$. We note that its dimension is given by

$$\dim (V \otimes W) = (\dim V)(\dim W).$$

The element $v \otimes w$ associated with the pair (v, w) is also called a **tensor product** of v and w.

EXERCISES

1. Let V, W be finite dimensional spaces over K. Let $F: V \otimes W \to U$ be a linear map. Show that the map

$$(v, w) \mapsto F(v \otimes w)$$

is a bilinear map of $V \times W$ into U.

2. Show that the correspondence $g \mapsto g_*$ of Theorem 1 is an isomorphism between the space of bilinear maps of $V \times W$ into U, and the space of linear maps $\mathcal{L}(V \otimes W, U)$.

3. Let V be a finite dimensional vector space over K. Let $A: V \to V$ be a linear map. Show that there exists a unique linear map $F: V \otimes V \to V \otimes V$ such that

$$F(v \otimes w) = Av \otimes Aw$$

for all $v, w \in V$. This map is denoted by $A \otimes A$.

4. Generalize Exercise 3 to a tensor product $V \otimes W$. Let $A: V \to V$ and $B: W \to W$ be linear maps. Show how to define the linear map

$$A \otimes B: V \otimes W \to V \otimes W.$$

§2. *Isomorphisms of tensor products*

It occurs frequently that we want to take a tensor product of more than two spaces. We have associativity for this product.

Theorem 2. *Let U, V, W be finite dimensional vector spaces over K. Then there is a unique isomorphism*

$$U \otimes (V \otimes W) \to (U \otimes V) \otimes W$$

such that

$$u \otimes (v \otimes w) \mapsto (u \otimes v) \otimes w$$

for all $u \in U$, $v \in V$, and $w \in W$.

Proof. Let $\{u_i\}$, $\{v_j\}$, $\{w_k\}$ be bases for U, V, W respectively. Then the elements

$$(u_i \otimes v_j) \otimes w_k$$

form a basis of $(U \otimes V) \otimes W$, and the elements

$$u_i \otimes (v_j \otimes w_k)$$

form a basis of $U \otimes (V \otimes W)$. By the general theorem on the existence and uniqueness of linear maps, there exists a unique linear map

$$F: U \otimes (V \otimes W) \to (U \otimes V) \otimes W$$

which maps $(u_i \otimes v_j) \otimes w_k$ on $u_i \otimes (v_j \otimes w_k)$. One verifies very easily by the usual linear expansions that for any $u \otimes (v \otimes w)$ in $U \otimes (V \otimes W)$, the map F has the desired effect. Since F maps a basis of $U \otimes (V \otimes W)$ on a basis of $(U \otimes V) \otimes W$, it follows that F is an isomorphism.

Theorem 2 allows us to omit the parentheses in the tensor product of several factors. Thus if $V_1, \ldots, V_r$ are vector spaces over K, we may form their tensor product

$$V_1 \otimes V_2 \otimes \cdots \otimes V_r,$$

and the tensor product

$$v_1 \otimes v_2 \otimes \cdots \otimes v_r$$

of elements v_i in V_i.

Theorems 1 and 2 give the general useful properties of the tensor product. There exist some interesting isomorphisms which can be concocted out of tensor products. We give only one here, frequently used in the calculus of differential geometry.

Theorem 3. *Let V be a finite dimensional vector space over K. Let V^* be the dual space, and $\mathfrak{L}(V, V)$ the space of linear maps of V into itself.*

There exists a unique isomorphism

$$V^* \otimes V \to \mathcal{L}(V, V),$$

which to each element $\varphi \otimes v$ (with $\varphi \in V^*$ and $v \in V$) associates the linear map $L_{\varphi \otimes v}$ such that

$$L_{\varphi \otimes v}(w) = \varphi(w)v.$$

Proof. To each pair (φ, v) in the direct product $V^* \times V$ we associate the linear map $L_{\varphi,v}$ such that

$$L_{\varphi,v}(w) = \varphi(w)v.$$

One verifies at once that this association

$$(\varphi, v) \mapsto L_{\varphi,v}$$

is a bilinear map of $V^* \times V$ into $\mathcal{L}(V, V)$. Consequently, by Theorem 1, there exists a unique linear map of $V^* \otimes V$ into $\mathcal{L}(V, V)$ which to each element $\varphi \otimes v$ associates our linear map $L_{\varphi,v}$. We must now prove that the map

$$\varphi \otimes v \mapsto L_{\varphi,v}$$

gives an isomorphism of $V^* \otimes V$ and $\mathcal{L}(V, V)$. Let $\{v_1, \ldots, v_n\}$ be a basis of V, and let $\{\varphi_1, \ldots, \varphi_n\}$ be the dual basis. Then $\varphi_i(v_k) = 0$ if $i \neq k$ and $= 1$ if $i = k$. Let

$$L_{ij} = L_{\varphi_i, v_j}$$

to simplify the notation. We contend that the elements L_{ij} ($i = 1, \ldots, n$ and $j = 1, \ldots, n$) are linearly independent. Suppose that we have a relation

$$\sum_j \sum_i c_{ij} L_{ij} = 0$$

with $c_{ij} \in K$. Apply the left-hand side to any v_k. We obtain

$$0 = \sum_j \sum_i c_{ij} L_{ij}(v_k).$$

In the sum, $L_{ij}(v_k) = 0$ unless $i = k$, in which case it is equal to v_j. Hence

$$0 = \sum_j c_{kj} v_j.$$

From the linear independence of $v_1, \ldots, v_n$ we conclude that $c_{kj} = 0$ for all j and all k, thereby proving that the linear maps L_{ij} are linearly independent. There are n^2 such maps, and the dimension of $\mathcal{L}(V, V)$ is precisely n^2. Hence these maps L_{ij} form a basis of $\mathcal{L}(V, V)$. Since the map

$$V^* \otimes V \to \mathcal{L}(V, V)$$

sends a basis $\{\varphi_i \otimes v_j\}$ of $V^* \otimes V$ on a basis $\{L_{ij}\}$ of $\mathcal{L}(V, V)$, it follows that the map is an isomorphism, as was to be shown.

EXERCISES

1. Let V, W be finite dimensional vector spaces over K. Show that there is a unique isomorphism of $V \otimes W$ on $W \otimes V$ sending $v \otimes w$ on $w \otimes v$ for all $v \in V$ and $w \in W$.

2. Let V, W be as above. Show that there is a unique isomorphism

$$V^* \otimes W \to \mathcal{L}(V, W)$$

such that

$$\varphi \otimes w \mapsto L_{\varphi,w},$$

where $L_{\varphi,w}$ is the linear map such that $L_{\varphi,w}(v) = \varphi(v)w$.

3. Let V, W be as above. Show that there is a unique isomorphism

$$V^* \otimes W^* \to (V \otimes W)^*$$

which to each tensor product $\varphi \otimes \psi$ ($\varphi \in V^*$ and $\psi \in W^*$) associates a functional $L_{\varphi,\psi}$ of $V \otimes W$ having the property that

$$L_{\varphi,\psi}(v \otimes w) = \varphi(v)\psi(w).$$

Describe this isomorphism in terms of bases and dual bases.

§3. *Alternating products: Special case*

We shall consider another kind of product, used all the time in the theory of differential forms in calculus. Since this product is slightly involved when we consider it in general, we shall spend some time studying a special case which amounts to the cross product of vectors. However, we treat it in a manner which will fit the generalization to arbitrary dimensions.

Let V be a *three*-dimensional vector space over the field K. Let $f: V \times V \to U$ be a bilinear map of V into some vector space U over K. We shall say that f is **alternating** if $f(v, v) = 0$ for all elements v in V. (This is very much like the condition we already met when we studied determinants!) We wish to construct a product of elements of V taking its values in a vector space, and such that the only relations in this product are the bilinear relations, *and* the alternating relation, i.e. if we denote the product of two elements of V by $v \wedge w$, then we should have $v \wedge v = 0$.

Suppose that we have such a product. Then for any v, $w \in V$,

$$(v + w) \wedge (v + w) = O,$$

and by bilinearity, the left-hand side is equal to

$$v \wedge v + w \wedge v + v \wedge w + w \wedge w.$$

Hence the alternating relation implies that

$$(1) \qquad\qquad v \wedge w = -w \wedge v.$$

Let $\{v_1, v_2, v_3\}$ be a basis of V. Any elements v, w in V can be written as linear combinations of the elements of this basis, say

$$v = x_1 v_1 + x_2 v_2 + x_3 v_3,$$

$$w = y_1 v_1 + y_2 v_2 + y_3 v_3.$$

Let $f\colon V \times V \to U$ be a bilinear alternating map. From the bilinear relations, we obtain

$$\begin{aligned}
f(v, w) &= x_1 y_1 f(v_1, v_1) + x_1 y_2 f(v_1, v_2) + x_1 y_3 f(v_1, v_3) \\
&\quad + x_2 y_1 f(v_2, v_1) + x_2 y_2 f(v_2, v_2) + x_2 y_3 f(v_2, v_3) \\
&\quad + x_3 y_1 f(v_3, v_1) + x_3 y_2 f(v_3, v_2) + x_3 y_3 f(v_3, v_3) \\
&= \sum_i \sum_j x_i y_j f(v_i, v_j).
\end{aligned}$$

Using the alternating relations, we see that three terms are equal to 0, and the others can be expressed as linear combinations of $f(v_1, v_2), f(v_1, v_3)$ and $f(v_2, v_3)$. We simply use the fact that

$$f(v_2, v_1) = -f(v_1, v_2), \qquad f(v_3, v_1) = -f(v_1, v_3),$$

and

$$f(v_3, v_2) = -f(v_2, v_3).$$

Hence

$$(2) \qquad f(v, w) = (x_1 y_2 - x_2 y_1) f(v_1, v_2) + (x_1 y_3 - x_3 y_1) f(v_1, v_3)$$

$$+ (x_2 y_3 - x_3 y_2) f(v_2, v_3).$$

Thus, if we have an alternating bilinear map f, the space generated by all values $f(v, w)$ with v, w in V will have dimension at most 3.

We shall now prove that there exists an alternating product of $V \times V$ into a space denoted by $V \wedge V$, generated by all products $v \wedge w$ with v, w in V, and such that $V \wedge V$ has dimension precisely 3.

We select three letters t_{12}, t_{23}, and t_{13} as basis elements for this space. If v, w are elements of V, expressed as above in terms of the basis v_1, v_2, v_3, we define their product $v \wedge w$ to be

$$(x_1 y_2 - x_2 y_1)t_{12} + (x_1 y_3 - x_3 y_1)t_{13} + (x_2 y_3 - x_3 y_2)t_{23}.$$

We note that if $i < j$ then $v_i \wedge v_j = t_{ij}$. It is now easy to verify by brute force that our product is bilinear and alternating. The alternating relation is especially trivial, since if $v = w$, each coefficient is of type

$$x_i x_j - x_j x_i = 0.$$

Let $f: V \times V \to U$ be a bilinear alternating map. Then there exists a unique linear map

$$f_*: V \wedge V \to U$$

such that for all pairs (v, w) of elements of V, we have

$$f(v, w) = f_*(v \wedge w).$$

Proof. By the theorem concerning the existence and uniqueness of linear maps having prescribed values on basis elements, we know that there exists a unique linear map $f_*: V \wedge V \to U$ such that

$$f_*(t_{ij}) = f(v_i, v_j)$$

for each pair of indices i, j with $1 \leq i < j \leq 3$. From (2), we conclude at once that $f(v, w) = f_*(v \wedge w)$ for all v, $w \in V$.

Thus when V has dimension 3, we have proved for alternating products the analogue of Theorem 1, for bilinear alternating maps.

One may ask whether it is not possible to take higher products. The answer is yes, and we leave this as Exercises 1, 2, 3.

Example 1. The theory of alternating products is used a great deal in the calculus of differential forms, and hence we shall select our example from this field.

Let $f: \mathbf{R}^3 \to \mathbf{R}$ be a differentiable function. By definition, for each X in $\mathbf{R}^3$ there exists a linear map denoted by $df(X)$ of $\mathbf{R}^3$ into $\mathbf{R}$ such that for small vectors H,

$$f(X + H) = df(X)H + o(H).$$

(The notation $o(H)$ is borrowed from analysis and we don't explain it here.) Thus df associates with each *point* $X \in \mathbf{R}^3$ a *functional* $df(X)$ in $\mathcal{L}(\mathbf{R}^3, \mathbf{R})$. If we let $\mathbf{R}^3 = V$, then $\mathcal{L}(\mathbf{R}^3, \mathbf{R})$ is none other than the dual space V^*.

Let x, y, z be the coordinates of X. We have three coordinate functions f_1, f_2, f_3 such that

$$f_1(X) = x, \qquad f_2(X) = y, \qquad f_3(X) = z.$$

Then one usually writes

$$df_1(X) = dx, \qquad df_2(X) = dy, \qquad df_3(X) = dz.$$

From the definitions, one verifies at once that dx, dy, dz form a basis of V^*, and in fact form the dual basis of the standard basis of unit vectors $\{e^1, e^2, e^3\}$.

By a **differential form on $\mathbf{R}^3$ of degree 2,** one means a map (not necessarily linear!)

$$\omega: \mathbf{R}^3 \to V^* \wedge V^*$$

from $\mathbf{R}^3$ into the alternating product of the dual space with itself. Since for each X in $\mathbf{R}^3$, dx, dy, dz form a basis of V^*, it follows that $dx \wedge dy$, $dx \wedge dz$, and $dy \wedge dz$ form a basis of $V^* \wedge V^*$. Consequently, there exist *functions*

$$\omega_{ij}: \mathbf{R}^3 \to \mathbf{R} \qquad\qquad (1 \leqq i < j \leqq 3)$$

such that $\omega(X)$ has an expression as a linear combination

$$\omega(X) = \omega_{12}(X)\, dx \wedge dy + \omega_{13}(X)\, dx \wedge dz + \omega_{23}(X)\, dy \wedge dz.$$

These functions ω_{ij} are nothing but the coordinate functions of ω with respect to the stated basis of $V^* \wedge V^*$.

Example 2. Let $V = \mathbf{R}^3$. If $X = (x_1, x_2, x_3)$ and $Y = (y_1, y_2, y_3)$ are elements of $\mathbf{R}^3$, then one defines their cross product

$$X \times Y = (x_1 y_2 - x_2 y_1, x_1 y_3 - x_3 y_1, x_2 y_3 - x_3 y_2).$$

The reader will recognize this as being essentially the alternating product $X \wedge Y$ in terms of coordinates. In the next section, we shall see how to generalize this in higher dimensions by giving the coordinates of the alternating product in terms of higher order determinants.

EXERCISES

1. Let V be a 3-dimensional vector space over K. Define $V \times V \times V$ to be the set of all triples (u, v, w) of elements of V. A **trilinear map**

$$f: V \times V \times V \to U$$

into a vector space U over K is a map which is linear in each component. We say that the trilinear map f is **alternating** if

$$f(u, v, w) = O$$

whenever $u = v$ or $v = w$. If f is alternating, show that $f(u, v, w) = O$ if $u = w$.

2. Let $\{v_1, v_2, v_3\}$ be a basis of V. Let $V \wedge V \wedge V$ be the one-dimensional vector space over K generated by a single letter t_{123}. If X, Y, Z are the coordinate vectors of elements u, v, w of V with respect to the given basis, define the product

$$u \wedge v \wedge w = \text{Det}(X, Y, Z)t_{123}.$$

Prove that this product is trilinear and alternating, using the definition of determinants. Note that $t_{123} = v_1 \wedge v_2 \wedge v_3$.

3. Let $f: V \times V \times V \to U$ be a trilinear alternating map into a vector space U over K. Show that there exists a unique linear map $f_*: V \wedge V \wedge V \to U$ such that

$$f(u, v, w) = f_*(u \wedge v \wedge w)$$

for all u, v, w in V.

4. Let V be a vector space of dimension n over K. Define $V \wedge V$ in a manner analogous to the one used in the 3-dimensional case, and prove the analogue of the properties proved in that special case. [*Hint:* Use all 2×2 determinants $x_i y_j - x_j y_i$ with $1 \leqq i < j \leqq n$.]

§4. *Alternating products: General case*

This section is fairly abstract, and it would be reasonable for some readers to omit it.

In defining the alternating product of an arbitrary number of factors, we take our cue from the alternating product described in the preceding section. We observe that each expression

$$x_i y_j - x_j y_i$$

with $i < j$ is a determinant, and that all such determinants occur as coefficients of $v_i \wedge v_j$. We generalize this in a natural way.

Let V be a vector space over the field K. Let r be an integer $\geqq 1$. We abbreviate by $V^{(r)}$ the set of all r-tuples of elements of V, i.e.

$$V^{(r)} = \overbrace{V \times \cdots \times V}^{r}.$$

An element of $V^{(r)}$ is therefore an r-tuple $(w_1, \ldots, w_r)$ with $w_i \in V$. Each component of the r-tuple is an element of V.

Let U be a vector space over K. By an **r-multilinear map** of V into U one means a map

$$f: V \times \cdots \times V \to U$$

of $V^{(r)}$ into U which is linear in each component. In other words, for each $i = 1, \ldots, r$ we have

$$f(w_1, \ldots, w_i + w_i', \ldots, w_r) = f(w_1, \ldots, w_r) + f(w_1, \ldots, w_i', \ldots, w_r),$$
$$f(w_1, \ldots, cw_i, \ldots, w_r) = cf(w_1, \ldots, w_r)$$

for all $w_i, w_i' \in V$ and $c \in K$. We shall say that a multilinear map f as above is **alternating** if in addition, it satisfies the condition

$$f(w_1, \ldots, w_r) = O$$

whenever two adjacent components are equal, i.e. whenever there exists an index $j < r$ such that $w_j = w_{j+1}$.

We observe that a multilinear alternating map satisfies conditions entirely similar to the first two properties satisfied by determinants. Thus multilinear alternating maps may be viewed as generalizations of determinants. In fact, we may now say that a determinant is a multilinear alternating map on K^n, having the additional property that

$$\mathrm{Det}(e^1, \ldots, e^n) = 1,$$

if $\{e^1, \ldots, e^n\}$ is the standard basis of K^n.

If we recall properties **4, 5, 6** of determinants, we see that the proofs of these properties depended only on **1** and **2**. Hence these proofs are valid in our more general present situation. Thus if we interchange two adjacent components, say w_j and w_{j+1}, then the value of the multilinear alternating map changes by a sign. If any two distinct components w_i and w_j are equal (with $i \neq j$), then

$$f(w_1, \ldots, w_r) = O.$$

These properties are constantly used in computing values of alternating maps.

Our general problem is to define a product between r elements of V, which satisfies the multilinear and alternating relations, and no others. We shall solve this problem in Theorem 6. Before doing that, however, we deduce consequences of these relations.

Theorem 4. *Let V, U be vector spaces over K and let*

$$f \colon V^{(r)} \to U$$

be an r-multilinear alternating map. Let $w_1, \ldots, w_r$ be elements of V, and let $A = (a_{ij})$ be an $r \times r$ matrix in K. Let

$$u_1 = a_{11}w_1 + \cdots + a_{1r}w_r,$$
$$\cdots$$
$$u_r = a_{r1}w_1 + \cdots + a_{rr}w_r.$$

Then

$$f(u_1, \ldots, u_r) = \operatorname{Det}(A)f(w_1, \ldots, w_r).$$

Proof. We have

$$f(u_1, \ldots, u_r) = f(a_{11}w_1 + \cdots + a_{1r}w_r, \ldots, a_{r1}w_1 + \cdots + a_{rr}w_r).$$

We expand this by multilinearity, and obtain a sum of terms

$$\sum_\sigma f(a_{1,\sigma(1)}w_{\sigma(1)}, \ldots, a_{r,\sigma(r)}w_{\sigma(r)})$$

taken over all possible choices $\sigma(1), \ldots, \sigma(r)$, i.e. over all possible maps $\sigma\colon \{1, \ldots, r\} \to \{1, \ldots, r\}$. This sum is equal to

$$\sum_\sigma a_{1,\sigma(1)} \cdots a_{r,\sigma(r)}f(w_{\sigma(1)}, \ldots, w_{\sigma(r)})$$

by taking the scalars out of f. If σ is not a permutation of $\{1, \ldots, r\}$, then two distinct components of the r-tuple

$$(w_{\sigma(1)}, \ldots, w_{\sigma(r)})$$

will be equal, and hence the corresponding term in the sum is equal to 0. Hence we may take the sum only over permutations σ of $\{1, \ldots, r\}$.

If we do this, and shuffle back $(w_{\sigma(1)}, \ldots, w_{\sigma(r)})$ into standard position $(w_1, \ldots, w_r)$, then the sign of each term changes by the sign of the permutation σ. Thus finally

$$f(u_1, \ldots, u_r) = \sum_\sigma \epsilon(\sigma)a_{1,\sigma(1)} \cdots a_{r,\sigma(r)}f(w_1, \ldots, w_r),$$

which is equal to

$$\operatorname{Det}(A)f(w_1, \ldots, w_r)$$

by one of the expressions which we obtained for the determinant. This proves our theorem.

For higher alternating products, we need still a more general expansion formula for alternating maps, namely we need the case when $A = (a_{ij})$ is an $r \times n$ matrix with different r and n. For instance, in the preceding section, $r = 2$ and $n = 3$. We must therefore discuss some notation. We take $1 \leq r \leq n$.

Let S be a subset of the integers $\{1, \ldots, n\}$ consisting precisely of r elements. The number of possible such sets S is equal to the binomial coefficient

$$\binom{n}{r}.$$

The elements of such a set S can be ordered, so that if $i_1, \ldots, i_r$ are these elements, then $i_1 < \cdots < i_r$.

Let
$$\sigma\colon \{1, \dots, r\} \to S$$

be a map, i.e. a rule which to each integer from 1 to r associates an element of S. Assume in addition that $\sigma(i) \neq \sigma(j)$ if $i \neq j$. We may then view σ as a permutation of S. Indeed, if $i_1, \dots, i_r$ are the elements of S, and are ordered so that

$$i_1 < \cdots < i_r,$$

then σ gives rise to the permutation denoted symbolically by

$$\begin{bmatrix} i_1 & \cdots & i_r \\ \sigma(1) & \cdots & \sigma(r) \end{bmatrix}.$$

Thus the permutation is the association

$$i_1 \mapsto \sigma(1), \quad i_2 \mapsto \sigma(2), \quad \dots, \quad i_r \mapsto \sigma(r).$$

The sign of this permutation will be denoted by $\epsilon_S(\sigma)$.

Example. Let $n = 4$ and $r = 3$. Let $S = \{1, 3, 4\}$. Let σ be defined by

$$\sigma(1) = 4, \qquad \sigma(3) = 1, \qquad \sigma(4) = 3.$$

Then σ gives the permutation

$$\begin{bmatrix} 1 & 3 & 4 \\ 4 & 1 & 3 \end{bmatrix}$$

of the set $\{1, 3, 4\}$. Its sign is equal to

$$\epsilon_S(\sigma) = -1.$$

As a matter of notation, we denote by $P(S)$ the set of maps

$$\sigma\colon \{1, \dots, r\} \to S$$

such that $\sigma(i) \neq \sigma(j)$ if $i \neq j$. Thus $P(S)$ is essentially the set of permutations of S.

Let $A = (a_{ij})$ be an $r \times n$ matrix in K. For each subset S of $\{1, \dots, n\}$ consisting of precisely r elements, we can take the $r \times r$ submatrix of A consisting of those elements a_{ij} such that $j \in S$. We denote by

$$\mathrm{Det}_S(A)$$

the determinant of this submatrix. We also call it the subdeterminant of A corresponding to the set S. Then we can write

$$\mathrm{Det}_S(A) = \sum_{\sigma \in P(S)} \epsilon_S(\sigma) a_{1,\sigma(1)} \cdots a_{r,\sigma(r)},$$

where the sum is taken over all maps σ in the set $P(S)$. This is only a rephrasing of a formula for the determinant, taking into account our present notation.

Let $v_1, \ldots, v_n$ be elements of V. For each subset S as above, we denote by v_S the r-tuple

$$v_S = (v_{i_1}, \ldots, v_{i_r}),$$

where $i_1, \ldots, i_r$ are the elements of S so ordered that

$$i_1 < \cdots < i_r.$$

We now have all the necessary notation to state the desired generalization of Theorem 4.

Theorem 5. *Let V, U be vector spaces over K. Let*

$$f\colon V^{(r)} \to U$$

be an r-multilinear alternating map. Let $v_1, \ldots, v_n$ be elements of V, and let $A = (a_{ij})$ be an $r \times n$ matrix in K. Let

$$u_1 = a_{11}v_1 + \cdots + a_{1n}v_n,$$
$$\cdots$$
$$u_r = a_{r1}v_1 + \cdots + a_{rn}v_n.$$

Then

$$f(u_1, \ldots, u_r) = \sum_S \mathrm{Det}_S(A)f(v_S),$$

where the sum is taken over all subsets S of $\{1, \ldots, n\}$ consisting of precisely r elements.

Proof. We have

$$f(u_1, \ldots, u_r) = f(a_{11}v_1 + \cdots + a_{1n}v_n, \ldots, a_{r1}v_1 + \cdots + a_{rn}v_n).$$

Expanding out by multilinearity, we obtain a sum

$$\sum_\sigma a_{1,\sigma(1)} \cdots a_{r,\sigma(r)} f(v_{\sigma(1)}, \ldots, v_{\sigma(r)})$$

over all possible choices σ assigning to each integer from 1 to r and integer from 1 to n. Thus the sum is over all maps

$$\sigma\colon \{1, \ldots, r\} \to \{1, \ldots, n\}.$$

As before, we observe that if $\sigma(i) = \sigma(j)$ for some $i \neq j$, then the corresponding term is 0 because f is alternating. Thus in our sum, we may take only those σ such that $\sigma(i) \neq \sigma(j)$ if $i \neq j$.

Our sum can be decomposed into a double sum, by grouping together all maps σ which send $\{1, \ldots, r\}$ into a given set S, and then taking the sum over all possible such sets S. Thus symbolically, we can write

$$\sum_\sigma = \sum_S \sum_{\sigma \in P(S)}.$$

In each inner sum

$$\sum_{\sigma \in P(S)} a_{1,\sigma(1)} \cdots a_{r,\sigma(r)} f(v_{\sigma(1)}, \ldots, v_{\sigma(r)})$$

we shuffle back the r-tuple $(v_{\sigma(1)}, \ldots, v_{\sigma(r)})$ to the standard position $(v_{i_1}, \ldots, v_{i_r})$, where $i_1, \ldots, i_r$ are the elements of S ordered so that $i_1 < \cdots < i_r$. Then f changes by the sign $\epsilon_S(\sigma)$, and consequently each inner sum is equal to

$$\sum_{\sigma \in P(S)} \epsilon_S(\sigma) a_{1,\sigma(1)} \cdots a_{r,\sigma(r)} f(v_S).$$

Taking the sum over all possible sets S, we obtain exactly the formula stated in the theorem.

The next theorem handles the general case of alternating products.

Theorem 6. *Let V be a finite dimensional vector space over K, of dimension n. Let r be an integer $1 \leq r \leq n$. There exists a finite dimensional space over K, denoted by $\bigwedge^r V$, and an r-multilinear alternating map $V^{(r)} \to \bigwedge^r V$, denoted by*

$$(u_1, \ldots, u_r) \mapsto u_1 \wedge \cdots \wedge u_r,$$

satisfying the following properties.

AP 1. *If U is a vector space over K, and $g: V^{(r)} \to U$ is an r-multilinear alternating map, then there exists a unique linear map*

$$g_*: \bigwedge^r V \to U$$

such that for all $u_1, \ldots, u_r \in V$ we have

$$g(u_1, \ldots, u_r) = g_*(u_1 \wedge \cdots \wedge u_r).$$

AP 2. *If $\{v_1, \ldots, v_n\}$ is a basis of V, then the set of elements*

$$\{v_{i_1} \wedge \cdots \wedge v_{i_r}\} \qquad (1 \leq i_1 < \cdots < i_r \leq n)$$

is a basis of $\bigwedge^r V$.

Proof. For each subset S of $\{1, \ldots, n\}$ consisting of precisely r elements, we select a letter t_S. These letters t_S form a basis of a vector space over K, whose dimension is equal to the binomial coefficient $\binom{n}{r}$. We denote this space by $\bigwedge^r V$. Let $\{v_1, \ldots, v_n\}$ be a basis of V. Let $u_1, \ldots, u_r$ be elements of V. Let $A = (a_{ij})$ be the matrix in K such that

$$u_1 = a_{11}v_1 + \cdots + a_{1n}v_n,$$
$$\cdots$$
$$u_r = a_{r1}v_1 + \cdots + a_{rn}v_n.$$

Define

$$u_1 \wedge \cdots \wedge u_r = \sum_S \mathrm{Det}_S(A)t_S.$$

We contend that this product has the required properties.

We first prove that it is multilinear. This is essentially a routine remark, namely that $\mathrm{Det}_S(A)$ is multilinear as a function of the rows of A. Suppose that

$$u_i' = a_{i1}'v_1 + \cdots + a_{in}'v_n.$$

Let $A_1, \ldots, A_n$ be the rows of A, and $A_i' = (a_{i1}', \ldots, a_{in}')$. Writing the determinant as a function of rows, we have

$$\mathrm{Det}_S(A_1, \ldots, A_i + A_i', \ldots, A_n)$$

$$= \mathrm{Det}_S(A_1, \ldots, A_n) + \mathrm{Det}_S(A_1, \ldots, A_i', \ldots, A_n)$$

and for $c \in K$,

$$\mathrm{Det}_S(A_1, \ldots, cA_i, \ldots, A_n) = c\, \mathrm{Det}_S(A_1, \ldots, A_n).$$

These equations are true directly from the definition of determinants. Consequently

$$u_1 \wedge \cdots \wedge (u_i + u_i') \wedge \cdots \wedge u_r$$

$$= (u_1 \wedge \cdots \wedge u_r) + (u_1 \wedge \cdots \wedge u_i' \wedge \cdots \wedge u_r).$$

Also,

$$u_1 \wedge \cdots \wedge (cu_i) \wedge \cdots \wedge u_r = cu_1 \wedge \cdots \wedge u_r.$$

The product is alternating, because if $u_i = u_{i+1}$ for some i, then two adjacent rows of the matrix A are equal. Hence for each S, two adjacent rows of the submatrix of A corresponding to the set S are equal, and hence $\mathrm{Det}_S(A) = 0$.

We note that

$$t_S = v_{i_1} \wedge \cdots \wedge v_{i_r}$$

if $i_1, \ldots, i_r$ are the elements of S ordered so that

$$i_1 < \cdots < i_r.$$

MULTILINEAR PRODUCTS [XIII, §4]

From the theorem concerning the existence and uniqueness of linear maps having prescribed values on basis elements, we conclude that if $g: V^{(r)} \to U$ is a multilinear alternating map, then there exists a unique linear map

$$g_*: \bigwedge^r V \to U$$

such that for each set S, we have

$$g_*(t_S) = g(v_S) = g(v_{i_1}, \ldots, v_{i_r}),$$

if $i_1, \ldots, i_r$ are as above. By Theorem 5, it follows that

$$g(u_1, \ldots, u_r) = g_*(u_1 \wedge \cdots \wedge u_r)$$

for all elements $u_1, \ldots, u_r$ of V. This proves AP 1.

As for AP 2, let $w_1, \ldots, w_n$ be a basis of V. From the expansion of Theorem 5, it follows that the elements

$$\{w_S\},$$

i.e. the elements

$$\{w_{i_1} \wedge \cdots \wedge w_{i_r}\}$$

with all possible choices of r-tuples $(i_1, \ldots, i_r)$ satisfying

$$i_1 < \cdots < i_r,$$

are generators of $\bigwedge^r V$. The number of such elements is precisely $\binom{n}{r}$. Hence they must be linearly independent, and form a basis of $\bigwedge^r V$, as was to be shown.

The notation v_S was convenient to shorten the expressions appearing above. However, the sum is also frequently written preserving the indices $i_1, \ldots, i_r$. Thus if $\{v_1, \ldots, v_n\}$ is a basis of V, then every element of $\bigwedge^r V$ has a unique expression as a linear combination

$$\sum_{i_1 < \cdots < i_r} c_{i_1 \ldots i_r} v_{i_1} \wedge \cdots \wedge v_{i_r},$$

the sum being taken over all r-tuples $(i_1, \ldots, i_r)$ of integers from 1 to n, satisfying

$$i_1 < \cdots < i_r.$$

One can also shorten this notation, by writing $(i) = (i_1, \ldots, i_r)$. Thus the above sum would be written

$$\sum_{(i)} c_{(i)} v_{i_1} \wedge \cdots \wedge v_{i_r}.$$

Theorem 7. *Let V be a finite dimensional vector space over K. For each pair of integers $r, s \geq 1$ there exists a unique bilinear map*

$$\bigwedge^r V \times \bigwedge^s V \to \bigwedge^{r+s} V$$

such that if $u_1, \ldots, u_r$ and $w_1, \ldots, w_s$ are elements of V, then under this map we have

$$(u_1 \wedge \cdots \wedge u_r) \times (w_1 \wedge \cdots \wedge w_s) \mapsto u_1 \wedge \cdots \wedge u_r \wedge w_1 \wedge \cdots \wedge w_s.$$

Proof. Given $u_1, \ldots, u_r \in V$ we see that the map $V^{(s)} \to \bigwedge^{r+s} V$ given by

$$(w_1, \ldots, w_s) \mapsto u_1 \wedge \cdots \wedge u_r \wedge w_1 \wedge \cdots \wedge w_s$$

is s-multilinear and alternating. Hence there exists a unique linear map

$$L_{(u_1, \ldots, u_r)} : \bigwedge^s V \to \bigwedge^{r+s} V$$

such that $w_1 \wedge \cdots \wedge w_s \mapsto u_1 \wedge \cdots \wedge u_r \wedge w_1 \wedge \cdots \wedge w_s$. Furthermore, the association $(u_1, \ldots, u_r) \mapsto L_{(u_1, \ldots, u_r)}$ is an r-multilinear map

$$V^{(r)} \to \mathfrak{L}(\bigwedge^s V, \bigwedge^{r+s} V),$$

which is clearly alternating, so there exists a unique linear map

$$\bigwedge^r V \to \mathfrak{L}(\bigwedge^s V, \bigwedge^{r+s} V)$$

denoted by $\omega \mapsto L_\omega$ such that $u_1 \wedge \cdots \wedge u_r \mapsto L_{(u_1, \ldots, u_r)}$. It is now clear that if $\omega \in \bigwedge^r V$ and $\eta \in \bigwedge^s V$, then the association

$$(\omega, \eta) \mapsto L_\omega(\eta)$$

is the desired bilinear map.

EXERCISES

1. Let V be a vector space of dimension n over K. Show that $\bigwedge^n V$ has dimension 1 over K.

2. Let V be as in Exercise 1. Let $\{v_1, \ldots, v_n\}$ be a basis of V, and let $A = (a_{ij})$ be an $n \times n$ matrix in K. Write

$$u_1 = a_{11}v_1 + \cdots + a_{1n}v_n,$$
$$\cdots$$
$$u_n = a_{n1}v_1 + \cdots + a_{nn}v_n.$$

Express $u_1 \wedge \cdots \wedge u_n$ in terms of $v_1 \wedge \cdots \wedge v_n$.

3. Let V be a vector space of dimension n over K, and let r be an integer $> n$. Show that any r-multilinear alternating map

$$f: V^{(r)} \to U$$

into a vector space U is the zero map.

4. Let A be an $n \times n$ skew-symmetric matrix in K, i.e. ${}^t A = -A$. Show that the map $(X, Y) \mapsto {}^t X A Y$ defines an alternating form on K^n.

5. Let V be a vector space of dimension n over K. Let $\{v_1, \ldots, v_n\}$ be a basis of V. Let $c \in K$.

(a) Prove that there exists a unique n-multilinear alternating form $f_c \colon V^{(n)} \to K$ such that
$$f_c(v_1, \ldots, v_n) = c.$$

(b) Let f_1 be the unique n-multilinear alternating form of V into K such that
$$f_1(v_1, \ldots, v_n) = 1.$$

If g is an n-multilinear alternating form on V such that $g(v_1, \ldots, v_n) = c \in K$, show that $g = cf_1$.

6. Let V be a vector space of dimension n over K. Let $A \colon V \to V$ be a linear map. Let $f \colon V^{(n)} \to K$ be an n-multilinear alternating form. Let $g \colon V^{(n)} \to K$ be defined by
$$g(w_1, \ldots, w_n) = f(Aw_1, \ldots, Aw_n).$$

Show that g is n-multilinear and alternating.

7. More generally, let V, W be vector spaces over K, and let $A \colon V \to W$ be a linear map. Let $f \colon W^{(n)} \to U$ be an n-multilinear alternating map of W into a space U. Let $g \colon V^{(n)} \to U$ be defined by
$$g(v_1, \ldots, v_n) = f(Av_1, \ldots, Av_n).$$

Show that g is n-multilinear and alternating.

8. Let V be an n-dimensional vector space over K. Let $A \colon V \to V$ be a linear map. Let $w_1, \ldots, w_n$ be elements of V, and let $f \colon V^{(n)} \to U$ be an n-multilinear alternating map. Show that
$$f(Aw_1, \ldots, Aw_n) = \mathrm{Det}(A)f(w_1, \ldots, w_n).$$

Appendix. *The vector space generated by a set*

Let K be a field, and let S be a finite set of objects. For simplicity, we number the elements of S, and thus let
$$s_1, \ldots, s_n$$
be these elements. We wish to define what we mean by the vector space T of "formal" linear combinations
$$c_1 s_1 + \cdots + c_n s_n$$
of elements of S with coefficients c_i in K. If we wish to be quite precise, then we must give first a description of the elements of the vector space T, and then define addition between these elements. Otherwise, the $+$ sign makes no sense. This is not to say that one cannot entirely disregard the

problem, and proceed as if everything were clear. In fact, most people do just this all the time, and are not the worse for it.

However, the purpose of this appendix is precisely to show how one can be precise about this matter. This is in fact quite simple. What do we wish such a "sum" as

$$c_1 s_1 + \cdots + c_n s_n$$

to be like? Well, we wish it to be entirely determined by the "coefficients" $c_1, \ldots, c_n$, and each "coefficient" c_i should be associated with the element s_i of the set S. But an association is nothing but a function. This suggests to us how to define the elements of our space T.

For each $s_i \in S$, and $c \in K$, we define the symbol

$$c s_i$$

to be the function which associates c to s_i, and 0 to s_j if $j \neq i$. If $a \in K$, then obviously,

$$a(c s_i) = (ac)s_i \qquad \text{and} \qquad (c + c')s_i = c s_i + c' s_i.$$

We define T to be the set of all functions of S into K which can be written in the form

$$c_1 s_1 + \cdots + c_n s_n$$

with some $c_i \in K$. Using the obvious preceding properties, we see at once that T is a vector space over K. (Note that we have no problem in taking sums, since we know how to add functions from S into K.)

We contend that the functions

$$1 s_1, \ldots, 1 s_n$$

are linearly independent, and consequently form a basis of T over K.

To prove this, suppose $c_1, \ldots, c_n$ are elements of K such that

$$c_1 s_1 + \cdots + c_n s_n = 0 \quad \text{(the zero function).}$$

Then by definition, the left-hand side takes on the value c_i at s_i, and hence $c_i = 0$. This proves the desired linear independence.

In practice, it is convenient to abbreviate the notation, and to write simply s_i instead of $1 s_i$. The elements of T are now called formal linear combinations of the elements of S, and we have justified precisely this terminology.

CHAPTER XIV

Groups

§1. Groups and examples

We climb one small degree on the scale of abstraction, and define a notion which will include many previous examples as special cases.

A **group** G is a set, together with a rule (called a law of composition) which to each pair of elements x, y in G associates an element denoted by xy in G, having the following properties.

GR 1. *For all x, y, z in G we have associativity, namely*

$$(xy)z = x(yz).$$

GR 2. *There exists an element e of G such that $ex = xe = x$ for all x in G.*

GR 3. *If x is an element of G, then there exists an element y of G such that $xy = yx = e$.*

Strictly speaking, we call G a **multiplicative** group. If we denote the element of G associated with the pair (x, y) by $x + y$, then we write GR 1 in the form

$$(x + y) + z = x + (y + z),$$

GR 2 in the form that there exists an element 0 such that

$$0 + x = x + 0 = x$$

for all x in G, and GR 3 in the form that given $x \in G$, there exists an element y of G such that

$$x + y = y + x = 0.$$

With this notation, we call G an **additive** group. We shall use the $+$ notation only when the group satisfies the additional rule

$$x + y = y + x$$

for all x, y in G. With the multiplicative notation, this is written $xy = yx$ for all x, y in G, and if G has this property, we call G a **commutative,** or **abelian** group.

Example 1. The rational numbers form a group under addition. So do the real numbers, and so do the complex numbers. In fact, for any field K, the elements of K form a group under addition.

Example 2. The non-zero rational numbers form a group under multiplication. So do the non-zero real numbers, so do the non-zero complex numbers, and the non-zero elements of any field K.

Example 3. The complex numbers of absolute value 1 form a group under multiplication.

Example 4. The permutations of $\{1, \ldots, n\}$ form a group under multiplication (i.e. composition of mappings), called the **symmetric group** S_n on n elements.

Example 5. The elements of a vector space form a group under addition.

Example 6. The $m \times n$ matrices over a field K form a group under addition.

Multiplicative groups of matrices

Example 7. (a) The invertible $n \times n$ matrices over a field K form a group under multiplication, denoted by $GL_n(K)$ or $GL(n, K)$. It is called the **general linear group.**

(b) Let V be a vector space over K. The invertible linear maps of V into itself form a group under multiplication (composition of mappings), denoted by $GL(V)$.

Example 8. The real unitary $n \times n$ matrices form a group under multiplication, denoted by $\mathbf{U}_n(\mathbf{R})$ or $\mathbf{U}(n, \mathbf{R})$.

Example 9. The complex unitary $n \times n$ matrices form a group under multiplication, denoted by $\mathbf{U}_n(\mathbf{C})$ or $\mathbf{U}(n, \mathbf{C})$.

Example 10. The $n \times n$ invertible upper triangular matrices over a field K form a group under multiplication.

Example 11. The invertible $n \times n$ matrices over a field K having determinant 1 form a group under multiplication. This group is called the **special linear group.**

Terminology. Additive groups of matrices or linear maps are not interesting. Hence in all mathematics, unless otherwise specified, a group of matrices is *always* understood to be a **multiplicative** group of matrices. The same applies to a group of linear maps, the law of composition being composition of linear maps, written frequently as multiplication.

Note that the various examples of multiplicative groups of matrices given above are non-commutative when $n \geqq 2$. In each case, the verification that the given set is a group is merely a summarized repetition of known properties of the objects involved.

A group consisting of one element is said to be **trivial.** A group in general may have infinitely many elements, or only a finite number. If G has only a finite number of elements, then G is called a **finite group,** and the number of elements in G is called its **order.** The permutation group of Example 4 is a finite group. The determination of its order will be given in an exercise. The group whose elements are $\{1, -1\}$ (and the law of composition is multiplication) has order 2.

Example 12. **The direct product.** Let G, G' be groups. Let $G \times G'$ be the set consisting of all pairs (x, x') with $x \in G$ and $x' \in G'$. If (x, x') and (y, y') are such pairs, define their product to be $(xy, x'y')$. Then $G \times G'$ is a group. Verify in detail that all the conditions are satisfied as an exercise. We call $G \times G'$ the direct product of G and G'.

EXERCISES

1. Show that the order of the symmetric group S_2 is 2. Show that the order of the symmetric group S_3 is 6. In general, prove by induction that the order of the symmetric group S_n is $n!$.

2. In each of the examples given in the text, state explicitly what the unit element of the group is. (The unit element is the element whose existence is asserted in GR 2. We shall prove that it is uniquely determined in the next section.)

3. Show that the set of complex numbers which are roots of the polynomial $f(t) = t^n - 1$ is a group (under multiplication). What is the order of this group?

4. Let S be a set with at least one element. Let G be the set of all maps $f: S \to S$ which are injective and surjective. Show that G is a group, the law of composition being composition of mappings. (Condition GR 1 is already known as the law of associativity of mappings.) This group G is called the group of all **invertible maps** of S into itself. It is a generalization of the notion of permutation group on n elements.

5. Let V be a vector space over the field K, and let $\langle \, , \, \rangle$ be a scalar product on V, i.e. a bilinear symmetric form. By an **automorphism** of the form we shall mean an invertible linear map $A: V \to V$ such that $\langle Av, Aw \rangle = \langle v, w \rangle$ for all $v, w \in V$. Show that the set of automorphisms of the form is a group.

6. Let G be a group, and a, b, c be elements of G. If $ab = ac$, show that $b = c$.

7. Let G, G' be finite groups of orders m, n respectively. What is the order of $G \times G'$?

8. Let G be a finite abelian group of order n, and let $a_1, \ldots, a_n$ be its elements. Show that the product $a_1 \cdots a_n$ is an element whose square is the unit element.

§2. *Simple properties of groups*

We shall now prove various simple statements which hold for all groups.

Let G be a group. *The element e of G whose existence is asserted by* GR 2 *is uniquely determined*, because if e, e' both satisfy this condition, then

$$e' = ee' = e.$$

We call this element the **unit element** of G. We call it the **zero** element in the additive case.

Let $x \in G$. *The element y such that* $yx = xy = e$ *is uniquely determined*, because if z satisfies $zx = xz = e$, then

$$z = ez = (yx)z = y(xz) = ye = y.$$

We call y the **inverse** of x, and denote it by x^{-1}. In the additive notation, we write $y = -x$.

Let G be a group, and H a subset of G. We shall say that H is a **subgroup** if it contains the unit element, and if, whenever $x, y \in H$, then xy and x^{-1} are also elements of H. (Additively, we write $x + y \in H$ and $-x \in H$.) Then H is itself a group in its own right, the law of composition in H being the same as that in G. The unit element of G constitutes a subgroup, and G is a subgroup of itself.

Example 1. A subspace W of a vector space V is in particular a subgroup.

Example 2. The group of complex unitary matrices is a subgroup of the group of all invertible complex matrices (of a given size), etc. ad lib.

There is a general way of obtaining subgroups from a group. Let S be a subset of a group G, having at least one element. Let H be the set of elements of G consisting of all products $x_1 \cdots x_n$ such that x_i or x_i^{-1} is an element of S for each i, and also containing the unit element. Then H is obviously a subgroup of G, called the subgroup **generated** by S. We also say that S is a set of **generators of** H. This notion is analogous to the notion of generators for a vector space, studied earlier in this book. Examples of generators will be given in the exercises.

Let G, G' be groups. A **homomorphism**

$$f: G \to G'$$

of G into G' is a map having the following property: For all $x, y \in G$, we have

$$f(xy) = f(x)f(y)$$

(and in additive notation, $f(x + y) = f(x) + f(y)$).

Example 3.   A linear map is a homomorphism.

Example 4.   Let K be a field, and denote by $K^\times$ its multiplicative group of non-zero elements. Let G be the group of invertible $n \times n$ matrices in K. Then

$$\mathrm{Det}\colon G \to K^\times$$

is a homomorphism. This is nothing but the rule for multiplication of determinants.

Example 5.   The map

$$z \mapsto |z|$$

is a homomorphism of the multiplicative group of complex numbers into the multiplicative group of complex numbers (in fact, into the multiplicative group of positive real numbers).

Example 6.   The map

$$x \mapsto e^x$$

is a homomorphism of the additive group of real numbers into the multiplicative group of positive real numbers. Its inverse map, the logarithm, is also a homomorphism.

Example 7.   Let G be a group. Let x be an element of G. If n is a positive integer, we define x^n to be

$$xx \cdots x$$

the product being taken n times. If $n = 0$, we define $x^0 = e$. If $n = -m$ where m is an integer > 0, we define

$$x^{-m} = (x^{-1})^m.$$

It is then routinely verified that the rule

$$x^{m+n} = x^m x^n$$

holds for all integers m, n. As this verification is slightly tedious, we omit it. But we note that in view of this property, the map

$$n \mapsto x^n$$

is a homomorphism of the additive group of integers $\mathbf{Z}$ into G. When G is written additively, we write nx instead of x^n.

For the sake of brevity, we sometimes say: "Let $f\colon G \to G'$ be a group-homomorphism" instead of saying: "Let G, G' be groups, and let f be a homomorphism of G into G'".

Let $f: G \to G'$ be a group-homomorphism, and let e, e' be the unit elements of G, G' respectively. Then $f(e) = e'$.

Proof. We have $f(e) = f(ee) = f(e)f(e)$. Multiplying by $f(e)^{-1}$ gives the desired result.

Let $f: G \to G'$ be a group-homomorphism. Let $x \in G$. Then

$$f(x^{-1}) = f(x)^{-1}.$$

Proof. We have

$$e' = f(e) = f(xx^{-1}) = f(x)f(x^{-1}).$$

Let $f: G \to G'$ and $g: G' \to G''$ be group-homomorphisms. Then the composite map $g \circ f$ is a group-homomorphism of G into G''.

Proof. We have

$$(g \circ f)(xy) = g\big(f(xy)\big) = g\big(f(x)f(y)\big) = g\big(f(x)\big)g\big(f(y)\big).$$

Let $f: G \to G'$ be a group-homomorphism. We define the **kernel** of f to consist of all elements $x \in G$ such that $f(x) = e'$. *It is trivially verified that the kernel is a subgroup of G.* (It contains e because we proved that $f(e) = e'$. Prove the other properties as a trivial exercise.)

We note that the kernel of a linear map of vector spaces is the same as the kernel of the map when viewed as a group-homomorphism (i.e. additive group-homomorphism).

We recall that a map $f: S \to S'$ of one set into another is said to be **injective** if $f(x) \neq f(y)$ whenever $x \neq y$.

Let $f: G \to G'$ be a group-homomorphism. If the kernel of f consists of e alone, then f is injective.

Proof. Do it yourself, transposing to the present case the argument we gave previously for the analogous statement about linear maps.

Let $f: G \to G'$ be a group-homomorphism. The image of f is a subgroup of G'.

Proof. If $x' = f(x)$ with $x \in G$, and $y' = f(y)$ with $y \in G$, then

$$x'y' = f(xy) = f(x)f(y)$$

is also in the image. Also, e' is in the image, and $x'^{-1} = f(x^{-1})$ is in the image. Hence the image is a subgroup.

Let $f: G \to G'$ be a group-homomorphism. We shall say that f is an **isomorphism** (or more precisely a group-isomorphism) if there exists a homomorphism $g: G' \to G$ such that $f \circ g$ and $g \circ f$ are the identity mappings of G' and G respectively.

Example 8. The function exp is an isomorphism of the additive group of the real numbers onto the multiplicative group of positive real numbers. Its inverse is the log.

Example 9. Two vector spaces which are isomorphic as vector spaces are also isomorphic as additive groups.

A group-homomorphism $f: G \to G'$ which is injective and surjective (i.e. *such that the image of f is G'*) *is an isomorphism.*

Proof. We must define the inverse of f. For each $x' \in G'$, we let $g(x')$ be the unique x such that $f(x) = x'$. It exists because f is surjective, and is unique because f is injective. We must prove that g is a homomorphism. Let x', $y' \in G'$, and let x, $y \in G$ be such that $f(x) = x'$ and $f(y) = y'$. Then $f(xy) = x'y'$. Hence by definition,

$$g(x'y') = xy = g(x')g(y').$$

This proves our assertion.

The proof of the preceding statement is essentially the same as the proof of the analogous statement about linear maps, but in multiplicative notation.

By an **automorphism** of a group one means an isomorphism of the group with itself.

Example 10. Let V be a finite dimensional vector space over the field K, and let $A: V \to V$ be an invertible linear map. Then A can be viewed as an automorphism of the additive group of V.

Example 11. Let G be a commutative group. The map

$$x \mapsto x^{-1}$$

is an automorphism of G. Prove this as an exercise. What does this automorphism look like in additive notation?

EXERCISES

1. Let $\mathbf{R}^\times$ be the multiplicative group of real numbers. Describe explicitly the kernel of the homomorphism absolute value

$$x \mapsto |x|$$

of $\mathbf{R}^\times$ into itself. What is the image of this homomorphism?

2. Let $\mathbf{C}^\times$ be the multiplicative group of complex numbers. What is the kernel of the homomorphism absolute value

$$z \mapsto |z|$$

of $\mathbf{C}^\times$ into $\mathbf{R}^\times$?

3. Let S be the set of all maps of $\mathbf{R}^n$ into itself which are either real unitary maps, or translations. (A **translation** $T: \mathbf{R}^n \to \mathbf{R}^n$ is a map for which there exists a vector B in $\mathbf{R}^n$ such that $T(X) = X + B$ for all $X \in \mathbf{R}^n$.) Let G be the group generated by the elements of S. Then G is called the group of **rigid motions** of $\mathbf{R}^n$. Show that if F is a rigid motion, then F preserves distances, i.e. the distance between $F(X)$ and $F(Y)$ is the same as the distance between X and Y for all X, Y in $\mathbf{R}^n$. The unitary group is a subgroup of G.

4. (a) Let G be the set of all maps of $\mathbf{R}$ into itself of type $x \mapsto ax + b$, where $a \in \mathbf{R}$, $a \neq 0$ and $b \in \mathbf{R}$. Show that G is a group. We denote such a map by $\sigma_{a,b}$. Thus $\sigma_{a,b}(x) = ax + b$.

   (b) To each map $\sigma_{a,b}$ we associate the number a. Show that the association

$$\sigma_{a,b} \mapsto a$$

is a homomorphism of G into $\mathbf{R}^\times$. Describe the kernel.

5. Let G be the set of all maps of $\mathbf{R}^n$ into itself of type

$$\sigma_{A,B}: X \mapsto AX + B,$$

where A is an invertible $n \times n$ matrix, and B is in $\mathbf{R}^n$. Show that G is a group. Show that the map

$$\sigma_{A,B} \mapsto A$$

is a homomorphism of G into the general linear group. Describe the kernel.

6. Let V be a vector space of dimension n over the field K. Show that $GL(n, K)$ is isomorphic to $GL(V)$.

7. Show that the symmetric group S_3 is generated by the permutations

$$\begin{bmatrix} 1 & 2 & 3 \\ 2 & 3 & 1 \end{bmatrix} \quad \text{and} \quad \begin{bmatrix} 1 & 2 & 3 \\ 2 & 1 & 3 \end{bmatrix}.$$

8. Let G be a group. Let a be an element of G. Let

$$\sigma_a: G \to G$$

be the map such that

$$\sigma_a(x) = axa^{-1}.$$

Show that the set of all such maps σ_a with $a \in G$ is a group.

9. Show that the set of automorphisms of a group G is itself a group, denoted by $\text{Aut}(G)$.

10. Let the notation be as in Exercise 8. Show that the association $a \mapsto \sigma_a$ is a homomorphism of G into $\text{Aut}(G)$. The image of this homomorphism is called the group of **inner** automorphisms of G. Thus an inner automorphism of G is one which is equal to some σ_a for some $a \in G$.

11. Let K be a field. Show that the additive group of K is isomorphic to the (multiplicative!) group of matrices of type

$$\begin{pmatrix} 1 & a \\ 0 & 1 \end{pmatrix}$$

with $a \in K$.

12. Let G be the group of all matrices

$$\begin{pmatrix} a & b \\ 0 & d \end{pmatrix}$$

with a, b, d in a field K, and $ad \neq 0$. Show that the map

$$\begin{pmatrix} a & b \\ 0 & d \end{pmatrix} \mapsto (a, d)$$

is a homomorphism of G onto the product $K^\times \times K^\times$ (where $K^\times$ is the multiplicative group of K). Describe the kernel. We could also view our homomorphism as being into the group of diagonal matrices

$$\begin{pmatrix} a & 0 \\ 0 & d \end{pmatrix}$$

which is isomorphic to $K^\times \times K^\times$.

13. (a) Let K be a field, and let $G = G_0$ be the group of 3×3 upper triangular matrices in K, consisting of all invertible matrices

$$\begin{pmatrix} a_{11} & a_{12} & a_{13} \\ 0 & a_{22} & a_{23} \\ 0 & 0 & a_{33} \end{pmatrix}.$$

Let G_1 be the set of matrices

$$\begin{pmatrix} 1 & a_{12} & a_{13} \\ 0 & 1 & a_{23} \\ 0 & 0 & 1 \end{pmatrix}.$$

Show that G_1 is a subgroup of G, and that it is the kernel of the homomorphism which to each triangular matrix T associates the diagonal matrix consisting of the diagonal elements of T.

(b) Let G_2 be the set of matrices

$$\begin{pmatrix} 1 & 0 & a_{13} \\ 0 & 1 & 0 \\ 0 & 0 & 1 \end{pmatrix}.$$

Show that G_2 is a subgroup of G_1.

(c) Show that the map

$$\begin{pmatrix} 1 & a_{12} & a_{13} \\ 0 & 1 & a_{23} \\ 0 & 0 & 1 \end{pmatrix} \mapsto (a_{12}, a_{23})$$

is a homomorphism of the group G_1 onto the direct product of the **additive** group of K with itself. (We denote this group by $K \times K$.) What is the kernel?

(d) Show that the group G_2 is isomorphic to K.

14. Generalize Exercise 13 to the 4×4 case, and then to the $n \times n$ case.

15. (a) Let V be a vector space over a field K, and let v_1 be an element of V. Let G be the set of all invertible linear maps A of V into itself such that $Av_1 = v_1$. Show that G is a group.

(b) More generally, let $\{v_1, \ldots, v_i\}$ be a subset of V. Let G be the set of all invertible operators A of V such that

$$Av_1 = v_1, \quad \ldots, \quad Av_i = v_i.$$

Show that G is a group.

(c) Let S be a set, S' a subset, and let G be the set of all maps f of S into itself such that f is invertible, and such that $f(x) = x$ for all $x \in S'$. Show that G is a group.

16. Let V be a finite dimensional vector space of dimension n over the field K. Let $\{V_1, \ldots, V_n\}$ be a sequence of subspaces, such that dim $V_i = i$, and such that V_i is contained in V_{i+1}. Let G be the set of all invertible operators of V for which $\{V_1, \ldots, V_n\}$ is a fan. Let G_i be the subset of G consisting of all operators A such that $Av = v$ for all $v \in V_i$. Show that $G, G_1, \ldots, G_n$ are groups, and that G_{i+1} is a subgroup of G_i. Compare this geometric description with the groups of matrices of Exercise 14 or 13.

17. Let G be a group, and V a finite dimensional vector space over the field K. By a **representation** of G on V, one means a homomorphism $\rho : G \to GL(V)$ of G into the group of invertible linear maps of V onto itself. The representation is said to be **faithful** if the kernel of ρ is the unit element of G, i.e. if ρ is injective. If we select a basis of V, then ρ amounts to a homomorphism of G into the group of matrices $GL(n, K)$, where $n = \dim V$. Show that a finite group G always admits such a representation, proceeding as follows. Let V be the vector space of formal linear combinations of elements of G, as explained in the appendix of Chapter XIII. Thus the elements of G form a basis for this space, say $\{\sigma_1, \ldots, \sigma_n\}$. For each $\sigma \in G$, let A_σ be the linear map of V into itself such that

$$A_\sigma(\sigma_i) = \sigma\sigma_i.$$

Show that the association $\sigma \mapsto A_\sigma$ is an injective homomorphism of G into $GL(V)$.

18. Work out examples of Exercise 17. (a) Take G to be the group consisting of two elements $\{e, \sigma\}$ with $\sigma^2 = e$. (b) Take G to be the symmetric group S_3. In each case, write down the matrix associated with each element of G, after selecting a definite order for the elements of G.

19. In Exercise 17, if $\sigma \in G$, and $\sigma \neq e$, show that all diagonal elements of A_σ are equal to 0. What is the matrix A_e in Exercise 17?

§3. Cosets and normal subgroups

Let G be a group, and H a subgroup. Let a be an element of G. The set of all elements ax with $x \in H$ is called a **coset** of H in G. We denote it by aH.

In additive notation, a coset of H would be written $a + H$.

Example 1.   Let A be a fixed vector in $\mathbf{R}^n$, viewed as an additive group, and let W be a subspace of $\mathbf{R}^n$. Then the set of all vectors $A + X$ with $X \in W$ is a coset of W in $\mathbf{R}^n$. We may thus view $A + W$ as the translation of W by A. We illustrate this in the next figure when W is a straight line in $\mathbf{R}^2$.

Since a group G may not be commutative, we shall in fact call aH a **left** coset of H. Similarly, we could define **right** cosets, but in the sequel, unless otherwise specified, *coset* will mean left coset.

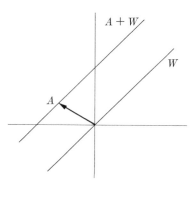

Figure 1

Theorem 1.   *Let aH and bH be cosets of H in the group G. Either these cosets are equal, or they have no element in common.*

Proof.   Suppose that aH and bH have one element in common. We shall prove that they are equal. Let x, y be elements of H such that $ax = by$. Then $a = byx^{-1}$. But yx^{-1} is an element of H. If ax' is an arbitrary element of aH, with x' in H, then

$$ax' = b(yx^{-1})x'.$$

Since $(yx^{-1})x'$ lies in H, we conclude that ax' lies in bH. Hence aH is contained in bH. Similarly, bH is contained in aH, and hence our cosets are equal.

Theorem 2.   *Let G be a group, and H a finite subgroup. Then the number of elements of a coset aH is equal to the number of elements in H.*

Proof.   Let x, x' be distinct elements of H. Then ax and ax' are distinct, for if $ax = ax'$, then multiplying by a^{-1} on the left shows that $x = x'$. Hence if $x_1, \ldots, x_n$ are the distinct elements of H, then $ax_1, \ldots, ax_n$ are the distinct elements of aH, whence our assertion follows.

Let G be a group, and H a subgroup. The number of distinct cosets of H in G is called the **index** of H in G. This index may of course be infinite. If G is a finite group, then the index of any subgroup is finite. The index of a subgroup H is denoted by $(G : H)$.

Corollary.   *Let G be a finite group and H a subgroup. Then*

$$\text{order of } G = (G : H) (\text{order of } H).$$

Proof.   Every element of G lies in some coset (namely, a lies in the coset aH since $a = ae$). By Theorem 1, every element lies in precisely one coset, and by Theorem 2, any two cosets have the same number of elements. The formula of our corollary is therefore clear.

The corollary also shows that the order of a subgroup of a finite group divides the order of the group.

Let G be a group. A subgroup H is said to be **normal** if it is the kernel of some homomorphism of G into some group.

Theorem 3. *Let $f: G \to G'$ be a homomorphism of groups. Let H be its kernel, and let a' be an element of G', which is in the image of f, say $a' = f(a)$ for $a \in G$. Then the set of elements x in G such that $f(x) = a'$ is precisely the coset aH.*

Proof. Let $x \in aH$, so that $x = ah$ with some $h \in H$. Then

$$f(x) = f(a)f(h) = f(a).$$

Conversely, suppose that $x \in G$, and $f(x) = a'$. Then

$$f(a^{-1}x) = f(a)^{-1}f(x) = a'^{-1}a' = e'.$$

Hence $a^{-1}x$ lies in the kernel H, say $a^{-1}x = h$ with some $h \in H$. Then $x = ah$, as was to be shown.

Let $f: S \to S'$ be a map. If x' is an element of S', we denote by $f^{-1}(x')$ the set of all $x \in S$ such that $f(x) = x'$, and call it the **inverse image** of x' under f. It usually consists of more than one element. In Theorem 3, we may say that the inverse image of an element a' of G' is a coset of G.

Example 2. Let A be an $n \times n$ matrix in a field K, and let $L_A: K^n \to K^n$ be the associated linear map. Let $B \in K^n$. Then

$$L_A^{-1}(B)$$

is the set of solutions of the linear equations $AX = B$. Theorem 3 is a generalization of the fact that this set of solutions is a coset of the kernel of L_A, *provided* that there exists at least one solution. Indeed, if X_0 is one solution, and W is the kernel of L_A, then

$$L_A^{-1}(B) = X_0 + W.$$

We had already seen this when we discussed linear equations, and we now have a new name for this phenomenon. The provision that there exists at least one solution amounts to saying that B is in the image of L_A.

We wish now to describe a simple test for a subgroup to be normal. We need some convenient notation. Let S, S' be subsets of a group G. We define SS' to be the set of all elements xx' with $x \in S$ and $x' \in S'$. Then it is easy to verify that if S_1, S_2, S_3 are three subsets of G, then

$$(S_1S_2)S_3 = S_1(S_2S_3).$$

This product simply consists of all elements xyz, with $x \in S_1$, $y \in S_2$ and $z \in S_3$. If H is a subgroup of G, then one verifies easily that $HH = H$.

Theorem 4. *Let G be a group and H a subgroup having the property that $xH = Hx$ for all $x \in G$. If aH and bH are cosets of H, then the product $(aH)(bH)$ is also a coset, and the collection of cosets is a group, the product being defined as above.*

Proof. We have $(aH)(bH) = aHbH = abHH = abH$. Hence the product of two cosets is a coset. Condition GR 1 is satisfied in view of the preceding remarks on multiplication of subsets of G. Condition GR 2 is satisfied, the unit element being the coset $eH = H$ itself. (Verify this in detail.) Condition GR 3 is satisfied, the inverse of aH being $a^{-1}H$. (Again verify this in detail.) Hence Theorem 4 is proved.

The group of cosets in Theorem 4 is called the **factor group** of G by H, and denoted by G/H. We note that it is a group of left or right cosets, there being no difference between these by assumption on H. We emphasize that it is this assumption which allowed us to define multiplication of cosets. If the condition $xH = Hx$ for all $x \in G$ is not satisfied, then we cannot define a group of cosets.

Corollary. *Let G be a group and H a subgroup having the property that $xH = Hx$ for all $x \in G$. Let G/H be the factor group, and let*

$$f: G \to G/H$$

be the map which to each $a \in G$ associates the coset $f(a) = aH$. Then f is a homomorphism, and its kernel is precisely H. Hence H is normal.

Proof. The fact that f is a homomorphism is nothing but a repetition of the definition of the product of cosets. As for its kernel, it is clear that every element of H is in the kernel. Conversely, if $x \in G$, and $f(x) = xH$ is the unit element of G/H, it is the coset H itself, so $xH = H$. This means that $xe = x$ is an element of H, so H is equal to the kernel of f, as desired.

EXERCISES

1. Let $f: G \to G'$ be a homomorphism with kernel H. Assume that G is finite. Show that

order of G = (order of image of f)(order of H).

Compare with the analogous theorem on dimensions of linear maps.

2. (a) Let H be a normal subgroup of a group G. Show that if $x \in H$ and $a \in G$, then axa^{-1} also lies in H.

   (b) Let H be a normal subgroup of G. Show that the left coset aH is equal to the right coset Ha.

3. Let H be a subgroup of G, and assume that $xHx^{-1} = H$ for all $x \in G$. Then $x^{-1}Hx = H$ for all $x \in G$, and $Hx = xH$ for all $x \in G$.

4. Let G be a group and H a subgroup. Show that H is normal if and only if $xHx^{-1} = H$ for all $x \in G$.

5. If G is commutative, show that every subgroup is normal.

6. Let H_1, H_2 be two normal subgroups of G. Show that $H_1 \cap H_2$ is normal.

7. Let $f: G \to G'$ be a homomorphism, and let H' be a subgroup of G'. Show that $f^{-1}(H')$ is a subgroup of G. If H' is normal in G', show that $f^{-1}(H')$ is a normal subgroup of G.

8. Let $f: G \to G'$ be a surjective homomorphism. Let H be a normal subgroup of G. Show that $f(H)$ is a normal subgroup of G'.

9. In each of the following cases, we give a group and a subgroup. Determine whether the subgroup is normal in the given group.

   (a) $G = GL_n(K)$, and $H = $ group of $n \times n$ matrices in K with determinant 1.
   (b) $G = GL_n(\mathbf{R})$ and $H = \mathbf{U}_n(\mathbf{R})$.
   (c) $G = GL_n(K)$, and $H = $ group of diagonal (invertible) matrices in K.
   (d) $G = $ group of upper triangular matrices in K, and $H = $ group of upper triangular matrices in K all of whose diagonal elements are equal to 1.
   (e) $G = $ symmetric group S_n, and $H = $ subgroup of even permutations.
   (f) $G = $ symmetric group S_n, and $H = $ subgroup of permutations leaving the integer n fixed (i.e. such that $\sigma(n) = n$).

10. Let G_0 be the group of all matrices

$$\begin{pmatrix} a & b \\ c & d \end{pmatrix}$$

with *integers* a, b, c, d and having determinant 1. Exhibit three elements in this group.

11. Let G be the group of all matrices

$$\begin{pmatrix} a & b \\ c & d \end{pmatrix}$$

with integers a, b, c, d having determinant 1 or -1. Show that the group of Exercise 10 is a normal subgroup of G. Show that the factor group G/G_0 has order 2.

12. Let G be a group. Define the **center** of G to be the subset of all elements a in G such that $ax = xa$ for all $x \in G$. Show that the center is a subgroup, and that it is a normal subgroup. Show that it is the kernel of the homomorphism in Exercise 10, §2.

13. Let G be a commutative group, and H a subgroup. Show that G/H is commutative.

14. Let G be a finite group with n elements, say $a_1, \ldots, a_n$. For each $x \in G$, show that the elements $xa_1, \ldots, xa_n$ are distinct, and thus constitute a permutation of $a_1, \ldots, a_n$. Thus to each $x \in G$, we can associate a permutation σ_x of $\{1, \ldots, n\}$ such that

$$xa_i = a_{\sigma_x(i)}$$

for $i = 1, \ldots, n$. Show that the map $x \mapsto \sigma_x$ is an injective homomorphism of G into the symmetric group S_n. In this manner we may view G as a subgroup of a permutation group.

15. Let $f: G \to G'$ be a group-homomorphism, and let H be its kernel. Assume that G' is the image of f. Show that G/H is isomorphic to G'.

16. Let G be a group and H a subgroup. Let N_H be the set of all $x \in G$ such that $xHx^{-1} \subset H$. Show that N_H is a group containing H, and that H is normal in N_H.

17. Let G be a group, H a subgroup, N a normal subgroup. Show that NH is a subgroup, and $NH = HN$.

§4. Cyclic groups

The integers $\mathbf{Z}$ form an additive group. We shall determine its subgroups. Let H be a subgroup of $\mathbf{Z}$. If H is not trivial, let a be the smallest positive integer in H. We contend that H consists of all elements na, with $n \in \mathbf{Z}$. To prove this, let $y \in H$, and say $y > 0$. There exist integers n, r with $0 \leq r < a$ such that

$$y = na + r.$$

Since H is a subgroup and $r = y - na$, we have $r \in H$, whence $r = 0$. If $y < 0$, we apply the preceding argument to $-y$ which is in H since H is a subgroup.

Let G be a group. We shall say that G is **cyclic** if there exists an element a of G such that every element x of G can be written in the form a^n for some integer n. (This is equivalent to saying that the map $f: \mathbf{Z} \to G$ such that $f(n) = a^n$ is surjective.) Such an element a of G is then called a **generator** of G.

Let G be a group, and $a \in G$. The subset of all elements a^n ($n \in \mathbf{Z}$) is obviously a cyclic subgroup of G. If m is an integer such that $a^m = e$ and $m > 0$, then we shall say that m is an **exponent** of a.

Let G be a group and a an element of G. Let $f: \mathbf{Z} \to G$ be the homomorphism such that $f(n) = a^n$, and let H be the kernel of f. Two cases arise:

(i) The kernel is trivial. Then f is an isomorphism of $\mathbf{Z}$ onto the cyclic subgroup of G generated by a, because f is injective, and the image of f is precisely equal to this subgroup. Furthermore, this subgroup is infinite cyclic. If a generates G, then G is cyclic. We also say that a has **infinite period.**

Example 1. The number 2 generates an infinite cyclic subgroup of the multiplicative group of complex numbers. Its elements are

$$\ldots, 2^{-5}, 2^{-4}, \tfrac{1}{8}, \tfrac{1}{4}, \tfrac{1}{2}, 1, 2, 4, 8, 2^4, 2^5, \ldots$$

(ii) *The kernel is not trivial.* Let d be the smallest positive integer in the kernel. Then d is called the **period** of a. If m is an integer such that $a^m = e$, then $m = ds$ for some integer s, by what we proved at the beginning of this section. We observe that the elements

$$e, a, \ldots, a^{d-1}$$

are distinct. Indeed, suppose $a^r = a^s$ with $0 \leq r \leq d - 1$ and

$$0 \leq s \leq d - 1,$$

say $r \leq s$. Then $a^{s-r} = e$. Since

$$0 \leq s - r < d,$$

we must have $s - r = 0$, whence $r = s$. We conclude that the cyclic group generated by a in this case has order d.

Example 2.   The multiplicative group $\{1, -1\}$ is cyclic of order 2.

Example 3.   The complex numbers $\{1, i, -1, -i\}$ form a cyclic group of order 4. The number i is a generator.

Example 4.   The matrix

$$\begin{pmatrix} 0 & +1 \\ -1 & 0 \end{pmatrix}$$

is the generator of a cyclic group of order 4 (multiplicative law of composition). Verify this in detail.

Theorem 5.   *Let G be a finite group, and a an element of G. Then the period of a divides the order of G.*

Proof. The order of the subgroup generated by a is equal to d. We can now apply the Corollary of Theorem 2, §3.

Theorem 6.   *Let G be a cyclic group. Then any subgroup of G is cyclic.*

Proof. Let a be a generator of G, so that we have a surjective homomorphism

$$f \colon \mathbf{Z} \to G$$

such that $f(n) = a^n$. Let H be a subgroup of G. Then $f^{-1}(H)$ (the set of $n \in \mathbf{Z}$ such that $f(n) \in H$) is a subgroup A of $\mathbf{Z}$, and hence is cyclic. In fact, we know that there exists a unique positive integer d such that $f^{-1}(H)$ consists of all integers which can be written in the form md with $m \in \mathbf{Z}$. Since f is surjective, it follows that f maps A on all of H, i.e. every element of H is of the form a^{md} with some integer m. It follows that H is cyclic, and in fact a^d is a generator.

EXERCISES

1. A **root of unity** in the complex numbers is a number ω such that $\omega^n = 1$ for some positive integer n. We then say that ω is an n-th root of unity. Describe the set of n-th roots of unity in **C**. Show that this set is a cyclic group of order n.

2. Determine the periods of the following matrices:

(a) $\begin{pmatrix} 0 & 1 & 0 \\ 0 & 0 & 1 \\ 1 & 0 & 0 \end{pmatrix}$
(b) $\begin{pmatrix} 0 & 1 & 0 & 0 \\ 0 & 0 & 1 & 0 \\ 0 & 0 & 0 & 1 \\ 1 & 0 & 0 & 0 \end{pmatrix}$

Generalize to the $n \times n$ case.

3. Let G be a finite group. Show that every element of G has finite period.

4. Let $\omega_1, \ldots, \omega_n$ be roots of unity, and assume that if we let

$$A = \begin{pmatrix} \omega_1 & 0 & \cdots & 0 \\ 0 & \omega_2 & \cdots & 0 \\ \vdots & \ddots & \ddots & \vdots \\ 0 & \cdots & 0 & \omega_n \end{pmatrix}$$

then A has period d. Let B be an invertible $n \times n$ matrix. Show that $B^{-1}AB$ also has period d.

5. In general, let A be any $n \times n$ invertible matrix, and let B be an $n \times n$ invertible matrix. Show that the periods of A and $B^{-1}AB$ are the same.

6. Let $f: G \to G'$ be an isomorphism of groups. Let $a \in G$. Show that the period of a is the same as the period of $f(a)$.

7. Consider the additive group of integers **Z**. Show that it has only two generators, namely 1 and -1. In general, show that an infinite cyclic group has only two generators.

8. Let S_3 be the symmetric group, and let $\epsilon: S_3 \to \{1, -1\}$ be the homomorphism given by the sign of the permutation. What is the order of the kernel of ϵ?

9. Same question applied to S_n instead of S_3.

10. Show that a finite group whose order is a prime number is necessarily cyclic.

11. Show that a group of order 4 is either cyclic, or contains two elements a, b with $a \neq b$ such that $a^2 = b^2 = e$, and $ab = ba$.

12. Show that if A is an $n \times n$ matrix of finite period, then all eigenvalues of A are roots of unity.

13. Let A, B be two finite cyclic groups of orders m and n respectively. Assume that m, n are relatively prime. Show that $A \times B$ is cyclic. What is its order?

14. Let G be a cyclic group, and $f: G \to G'$ a homomorphism. Show that the image of f is cyclic.

15. Let G be a finite cyclic group, of order n. Show that for each positive integer d dividing n, there exists a subgroup of order d.

16. In Exercise 15, show that the subgroup of order d is uniquely determined.

17. Let G be a finite cyclic group of order n. Let a be a generator. Let r be an integer $\neq 0$, and relatively prime to n. Show that a_r is also a generator of G. Show that every generator of G can be written in this form.

18. Let G be cyclic of order p, where p is a prime number. How many generators does G have?

19. Let A, B be abelian groups. Show that the homomorphisms of A into B form a group. (If we write A, B additively, and f, $g: A \to B$ are homomorphisms, define $f + g$ to be the map such that $(f + g)(x) = f(x) + g(x)$. What is the unit element?

20. Suppose that G is a cyclic group of order n, and Z_n is another cyclic group of order n. Show that the group of homomorphisms of G into Z_n is cyclic of order n.

21. Let A be an abelian group, written additively, and let n be a positive integer such that $nx = 0$ for all $x \in A$. Assume that we can write $n = rs$, where r, s are positive relatively prime integers. Let A_r consist of all $x \in A$ such that $rx = 0$, and similarly A_s consist of all $x \in A$ such that $sx = 0$. Show that every element $a \in A$ can be written uniquely in the form $a = b + c$, with $b \in A_r$ and $c \in A_s$. (This result is the analogue of Theorem 5 of Chapter XII, §5.)

22. Let A be an additive abelian group, and let B, C be subgroups. Let $B + C$ consist of all sums $b + c$, with $b \in B$ and $c \in C$. Show that $B + C$ is a subgroup, called the sum of B and C. Define the sum of a finite number of subgroups similarly.

We say that A is the **direct sum** of B and C if every element $x \in A$ can be written uniquely in the form $x = b + c$ with $b \in B$ and $c \in C$, and similarly for several subgroups.

23. Show that the additive abelian group A is the direct sum of subgroups B and C if and only if $A = B + C$ and $B \cap C = \{0\}$.

24. Let A be a finite abelian group of order n, and let

$$n = p_1^{r_1} \cdots p_s^{r_s}$$

be its prime power factorization, the p_i being distinct. Show that A is a direct sum $A = A_1 \oplus \cdots \oplus A_s$ where every element of A_i has period dividing $p_i^{r_i}$.

§5. *Free abelian groups*

We shall deal with commutative groups throughout this section. We wish to analyze under which conditions we can define the analogue of a basis for such groups.

Let A be an abelian group. By a **basis** for A we shall mean a set of elements $v_1, \ldots, v_n$ ($n \geq 1$) of A such that every element of A has a unique expression as a sum

$$c_1 v_1 + \cdots + c_n v_n$$

with integers $c_i \in \mathbf{Z}$. Thus a basis for an abelian group is defined in a manner entirely similar to a basis for vector spaces, except that the coefficients $c_1, \ldots, c_n$ are now required to be integers.

Theorem 7. *Let A be an abelian group with a basis $\{v_1, \ldots, v_n\}$. Let B be an abelian group, and let $w_1, \ldots, w_n$ be elements of B. Then there exists a unique group-homomorphism $f: A \rightarrow B$ such that $f(v_i) = w_i$ for all $i = 1, \ldots, n$.*

Proof. Copy the analogous proof for vector spaces, omitting irrelevant constants, etc.

The theorems concerning the possibility of extending bases from a subgroup are no longer valid for abelian groups. However, one can salvage something from the theory.

To avoid confusion when dealing with bases of abelian groups as above, and vector space bases, we shall call bases of abelian groups **Z-bases.**

Following the geometric spirit of this book, we shall use geometric arguments to prove our result.

Theorem 8. *Let A be a non-zero subgroup of $\mathbf{R}^n$. Assume that in any bounded region of space there exists only a finite number of elements of A. Let m be the maximal number of elements of A which are linearly independent over $\mathbf{R}$. Then we can select m elements of A which are linearly independent over $\mathbf{R}$, and form a Z-basis of A.*

Proof. Let $\{w_1, \ldots, w_m\}$ be a maximal set of elements of A linearly independent over $\mathbf{R}$. Let V be the vector space generated by these elements, and let V_{m-1} be the space generated by $w_1, \ldots, w_{m-1}$. Let A_{m-1} be the intersection of A and V_{m-1}. Then certainly, in any region of space, there exists only a finite number of elements of A_{m-1}. Therefore, if $m > 1$, we may assume inductively that $\{w_1, \ldots, w_{m-1}\}$ is a Z-basis of A.

Now consider the set S of all elements of A which can be written in the form

$$t_1 w_1 + \cdots + t_m w_m$$

with $0 \leqq t_i < 1$ if $i = 1, \ldots, m - 1$ and $0 \leqq t_m \leqq 1$. This set S is certainly bounded, and hence contains only a finite number of elements (among which w_m). We select an element v_m in this set whose last coordinate t_m is the smallest possible > 0. We shall prove that

$$\{w_1, \ldots, w_{m-1}, v_m\}$$

is a **Z**-basis for A. Write v_m as a linear combination of $w_1, \ldots, w_m$ with real coefficients,

$$v_m = c_1 w_1 + \cdots + c_m w_m, \qquad 0 < c_m \leq 1.$$

Let v be an element of A, and write

$$v = x_1 w_1 + \cdots + x_m w_m$$

with $x_i \in \mathbf{R}$. Let q_m be the integer such that

$$q_m c_m \leq x_m < (q_m + 1) c_m.$$

Then the last coordinate of $v - q_m v_m$ with respect to $\{w_1, \ldots, w_m\}$ is equal to $x_m - q_m v_m$, and

$$0 \leq x_m - q_m c_m$$
$$< (q_m + 1) c_m - q_m c_m = c_m \leq 1.$$

Let q_i $(i = 1, \ldots, m - 1)$ be integers such that

$$q_i \leq x_i < q_i + 1.$$

Then

$$(1) \qquad v - q_m v_m - q_1 w_1 - \cdots - q_{m-1} w_{m-1}$$

is an element of S. If its last coordinate is not 0, then it would be an element with last coordinate smaller than c_m, contrary to the construction of v_m. Hence its last coordinate is 0, and hence the element of (1) lies in V_{m-1}. By induction, it can be written as a linear combination of $w_1, \ldots, w_{m-1}$ with integer coefficients, and from this it follows at once that v can be written as a linear combination of $w_1, \ldots, w_{m-1}, v_m$ with integral coefficients. Furthermore, it is clear that $w_1, \ldots, w_{m-1}, v_m$ are linearly independent over **R**, and hence satisfy the requirements of our theorem.

We can now apply our theorem to more general groups. Let A be an additive group, and let $f \colon A \to A'$ be an isomorphism of A with a group A'. If A' admits a basis, say $\{v_1', \ldots, v_n'\}$, and if v_i is the element of A such that $f(v_i) = v_i'$, then it is immediately verified that $\{v_1, \ldots, v_n\}$ is a basis of A.

Theorem 9. *Let A be an additive group, having a basis with n elements. Let B be a subgroup $\neq \{0\}$. Then B has a basis with $\leq n$ elements.*

Proof. Let $\{v_1, \ldots, v_n\}$ be a basis for A. By Theorem 7, there is a homomorphism

$$f \colon A \to \mathbf{R}^n$$

such that $f(v_i) = e^i$ for $i = 1, \ldots, n$, and this homomorphism is obviously injective. Hence it gives an isomorphism of A with its image in $\mathbf{R}^n$. On the other hand, it is trivial to verify that in any bounded region of $\mathbf{R}^n$, there is only a finite number of elements of the image $f(A)$, because in any bounded region, the coefficients of a vector

$$(c_1, \ldots, c_n)$$

are bounded. Hence by Theorem 8 we conclude that $f(B)$ has a $\mathbf{Z}$-basis, whence B has a $\mathbf{Z}$-basis.

Theorem 10. *Let A be an additive group having a basis with n elements. Then all bases of A have this same number of elements n.*

Proof. We look at our same homomorphism $f: A \to \mathbf{R}^n$ as in the proof of Theorem 9. Let $\{w_1, \ldots, w_m\}$ be a basis of A. Each v_i is a linear combination with integer coefficients of $w_1, \ldots, w_m$. Hence $f(v_i) = e^i$ is a linear combination with integer coefficients of $f(w_1), \ldots, f(w_m)$. Hence $e^1, \ldots, e^n$ are in the space generated by $f(w_1), \ldots, f(w_m)$. By the theory of bases for *vector spaces*, we conclude that $m \geqq n$, whence $m = n$.

EXERCISES

1. Let A be an abelian group with a finite number of generators, and assume that A does not contain any element of finite period except the unit element. We write A additively. Let d be a positive integer. Show that the map $x \mapsto dx$ is an injective homomorphism of A into itself, whose image is isomorphic to A.

2. Let the notation be as in Exercise 1. Let $\{a_1, \ldots, a_m\}$ be a set of generators of A. Let $\{a_1, \ldots, a_r\}$ be a maximal subset linearly independent over $\mathbf{Z}$. Let B be the subgroup generated by $a_1, \ldots, a_r$. Show that there exists a positive integer d such that dx lies in B for all x in A. Using Theorem 8 and Exercise 1, conclude that A has a basis.

CHAPTER XV

Rings

In much of the previous work, we have never dealt with division, only with addition and multiplication. Consequently, it is worth while to axiomatize the structure involving only those operations.

Many examples and statements in this chapter are given as very simple exercises which you should carry out in detail.

§1. Rings and ideals

A **ring** R is a set, whose objects can be added and multiplied (i.e. we are given associations $(x, y) \mapsto x + y$ and $(x, y) \mapsto xy$ from pairs of elements of R, into R), satisfying the following conditions:

RI 1. *Under addition, R is an additive (abelian) group.*

RI 2. *For all x, y, $z \in R$ we have*

$$x(y + z) = xy + xz \qquad and \qquad (y + z)x = yx + zx$$

RI 3. *For all x, y, $z \in R$, we have $(xy)z = x(yz)$.*

RI 4. *There exists an element $e \in R$ such that $ex = xe = x$ for all $x \in R$.*

Example 1. Let R be the integers $\mathbf{Z}$. Then R is a ring.

Example 2. Any field is also a ring.

Example 3. Let R be the set of continuous real-valued functions on the interval $[0, 1]$. The sum and product of two functions f, g are defined as usual, namely $(f + g)(t) = f(t) + g(t)$, and $(fg)(t) = f(t)g(t)$. Then R is a ring.

Example 3 can of course be generalized by taking functions on any set, with values in a field, or a ring.

Example 4. If K is a field, then the polynomials of $K[t]$ form a ring.

Example 5. Polynomials in several variables $K[t_1, \ldots, t_n]$ form a ring.

349

Example 6. The $n \times n$ matrices $\text{Mat}_n(K)$ over a field K form a ring. This is simply a brief restatement of some properties concerning addition and multiplication of matrices.

Example 7. Let V be a vector space over the field K. Then the operators of V into itself form a ring $\mathcal{L}(V, V)$. Here the product is composition of mappings. Again, the fact that the ring axioms are satisfied is but a restatement of properties concerning composition of linear maps.

As with groups, we see at once that the element e of a ring is unique. It is often denoted by 1, and is called the **unit element.**

In a ring, the ordinary rules of arithmetic can all be trivially deduced from the axioms. For instance, we have $0x = 0$ and $(-e)x = -x$ for all $x \in R$. We leave the proofs as exercises. We also have $(-e)(-e) = e$. To prove this, note that $e + (-e) = 0$. Multiplying by $-e$, we find

$$-e + (-e)(-e) = 0.$$

Adding e to both sides yields $(-e)(-e) = e$, as desired.

Remark. It is sometimes useful to consider only the first two conditions RI 1 and RI 2, especially in the context when we deal with a vector space. More precisely, let V be a vector space over a field K, and suppose we are given a bilinear map $V \times V \to V$ which we view as a multiplication. We then say that V is a **K-algebra,** to distinguish V from a ring because we have not assumed associativity, or a unit element.

Example 8. Let V be the space of continuous functions, on the real line, periodic of period 2π. Let $f, g \in V$, and define their product $f * g$ by the formula

$$(f * g)(t) = \int_{-\pi}^{\pi} f(t - u)g(u) \, du.$$

Using simple properties of the integral, it is easily verified that conditions RI 1, 2, and 3 are satisfied. The product in this example is called **convolution.**

Example 9. Let G be a finite group. Let K be a field, and let V be the vector space of functions from G into K. If f, g are two such functions, we define their convolution product $f * g$ by the formula

$$(f * g)(x) = \sum_{y \in G} f(xy^{-1})g(y).$$

It is again an exercise to verify that conditions RI 1, 2, 3 are satisfied. This time, however, RI 4 is also satisfied. What is the unit element?

For a non-associative example, cf. Exercise 8.

If a ring satisfies the condition $xy = yx$ for all $x, y \in R$, then the ring is said to be **commutative.**

Let R be a ring. A **left ideal** of R is a subset J of R having the following properties: If $x, y \in J$, then $x + y \in J$ also, the zero element is in J, and if $x \in J$ and $a \in R$, then $ax \in J$.

Using the negative $-e$, we see that if J is a left ideal, and $x \in J$, then $-x \in J$ also, because $-x = (-e)x$. Thus the elements of a left ideal form an additive subgroup of R and we may as well say that a left ideal is an additive subgroup J of R such that, if $x \in J$ and $a \in R$ then $ax \in J$.

We note that R is a left ideal, called the **unit ideal,** and so is the subset of R consisting of 0 alone.

Similarly, we can define a **right ideal** and a **two-sided ideal.** Thus a two-sided ideal J is by definition an additive subgroup of R such that, if $x \in J$ and $a \in R$, then ax and $xa \in J$.

Example 10. Let R be the ring of continuous real-valued functions on the interval $[0, 1]$. Let J be the subset of functions f such that $f(\frac{1}{2}) = 0$. Then J is an ideal (two-sided, since R is commutative).

Example 11. Let R be the ring of integers **Z**. Then the even integers, i.e. the integers of type $2n$ with $n \in$ **Z**, form an ideal. Do the odd integers form an ideal?

Example 12. Let R be a ring, and a an element of R. The set of elements xa, with $x \in R$, is a left ideal, called the **principal left ideal** generated by a. (Verify in detail that it is a left ideal.) We denote it by (a). More generally, let $a_1, \ldots, a_n$ be elements of R. The set of all elements

$$x_1 a_1 + \cdots + x_n a_n$$

with $x_i \in R$, is a left ideal, denoted by $(a_1, \ldots, a_n)$. We call $a_1, \ldots, a_n$ **generators** for this ideal.

Example 13. Let R be a ring. Let L, M be left ideals. We denote by LM the set of all elements $x_1 y_1 + \cdots + x_n y_n$ with $x_i \in L$ and $y_i \in M$. It is an easy exercise for the reader to verify that LM is also a left ideal. Verify also that if L, M, N are left ideals, then $(LM)N = L(MN)$.

Example 14. Let L, M be left ideals. We define $L + M$ to be the subset consisting of all elements $x + y$ with $x \in L$ and $y \in M$. Then $L + M$ is a left ideal. Besides verifying this in detail, also show that if L, M, N are left ideals, then

$$L(M + N) = LM + LN.$$

Also formulate and prove the analogues of Examples 13 and 14 for right, and two-sided ideals.

Example 15. Let L be a left ideal, and denote by LR the set of elements $x_1 y_1 + \cdots + x_n y_n$ with $x_i \in L$ and $y_i \in R$. Then LR is a two-sided ideal. The proof is left as an exercise.

Let R be a ring. By a **subring** R' one means a subset of R such that the unit element of R is in R', and if x, $y \in R'$, then $-x$, $x + y$, and $xy \in R'$. It follows that R' is a ring, the operations of addition and multiplication in R' being the same as those in R.

Example 16. The real-valued differentiable functions on **R** form a subring of the ring of continuous functions.

Example 17. Let V be a vector space over the field K, and let A be an operator of V. The set of all operators of V of type $f(A)$, where f is a polynomial in $K[t]$, is a subring of the ring of linear maps of V into itself.

Remarks on abstract fields. A commutative ring K such that $1 \neq 0$, and such that the set of non-zero elements is a group under multiplication is called an **abstract field.** This second condition may also be expressed by saying that any non-zero element of the ring has a multiplicative inverse. Most of the theorems of linear algebra hold over abstract fields. The only way we ever used special properties of the real and complex numbers are the following:

(1) We used ordering properties in the study of positive definite scalar products.

(2) We used the fact that every polynomial of degree $\geqq 1$ over the complex numbers has a root in the complex numbers. However, what we did in this case would go over just as well over an abstract field having this property, and called **algebraically closed.**

(3) In a very incidental way, for the derivative criterion of multiple roots, we used the fact that our fields contain the rational numbers as a subfield. This was a very minor point in the whole theory.

The student with a liking for more abstract mathematics could therefore read the book interpreting the word field as abstract field, noting only the exceptions listed above. However, this is really a secondary matter at the level of sophistication of the present course, and hence I felt it better to avoid troubling the reader with this additional abstraction.

EXERCISES

1. Show that a field has no two-sided ideals other than the zero and unit ideals.

2. In a ring R, it may happen that a product xy is equal to 0, but $x \neq 0$ and $y \neq 0$. Give an example of this fact in the ring of matrices, and also in the ring of continuous functions on the interval $[0, 1]$.

3. Let R be a commutative ring. If M is an ideal, abbreviate MM by M^2. Let M_1, M_2 be two ideals such that $M_1 + M_2 = R$. Show that $M_1^2 + M_2^2 = R$.

4. Let R be a ring, and J_1, J_2 left ideals. Show that $J_1 \cap J_2$ is a left ideal.

5. Let R be the ring of $n \times n$ matrices over a field K. Show that the set of matrices of type

$$\begin{pmatrix} a_1 & 0 & \cdots & 0 \\ \vdots & \vdots & & \vdots \\ a_n & 0 & \cdots & 0 \end{pmatrix}$$

having components equal to 0 except possibly on the first column, is a left ideal of R. Prove a similar statement for the set of matrices having components 0 except possibly on the j-th column.

6. Let A, B be $n \times n$ matrices over a field K, all of whose components are equal to 0 except possibly those of the first column. Assume $A \neq 0$. Show that there exists an $n \times n$ matrix C in K such that $CA = B$. *Hint:* Consider first a special case where

$$A = \begin{pmatrix} 1 & 0 & \cdots & 0 \\ 0 & 0 & \cdots & 0 \\ \vdots & \vdots & & \vdots \\ 0 & 0 & \cdots & 0 \end{pmatrix}.$$

7. Let V be a finite dimensional vector space over the field K. Let R be the ring of K-linear maps of V into itself. Show that R has no two-sided ideals except $\{O\}$ and R itself. [*Hint:* Let $A \in R$, $A \neq O$. Let $v_1 \in V$, $v_1 \neq O$, and $Av_1 \neq O$. Complete v_1 to a basis $\{v_1, \ldots, v_n\}$ of V. Let $\{w_1, \ldots, w_n\}$ be arbitrary elements of V. For each $i = 1, \ldots, n$ there exists $B_i \in R$ such that

$$B_i v_i = v_1 \quad \text{and} \quad B_i v_j = O \text{ if } j \neq i,$$

and there exists $C_i \in R$ such that $C_i A v_1 = w_i$ (justify these two existence statements in detail). Let $F = C_1 A B_1 + \cdots + C_n A B_n$. Show that $F(v_i) = w_i$ for all $i = 1, \ldots, n$. Conclude that the two-sided ideal generated by A is the whole ring R.]

8. Let R be a commutative ring. A map $D: R \to R$ is called a **derivation** if $D(x + y) = Dx + Dy$, and $D(xy) = (Dx)y + x(Dy)$ for all x, $y \in R$. If D_1, D_2 are derivations, define the bracket product

$$[D_1, D_2] = D_1 \circ D_2 - D_2 \circ D_1.$$

Show that $[D_1, D_2]$ is a derivation.

Example. Let R be the ring of infinitely differentiable real-valued functions of, say, two real variables. Any differential operator

$$f(x, y) \frac{\partial}{\partial x} \quad \text{or} \quad g(x, y) \frac{\partial}{\partial y}$$

with coefficients f, g which are infinitely differentiable functions, is a derivation on R. Hence the set of bracket products, and iterated brackets of such operators is an algebra, which is not associative. Proof?

9. Let R be a ring in which $x^2 = x$ for all $x \in R$. Show that R is commutative.

§2. *Homomorphisms*

Let R, R' be rings. By a **ring-homomorphism** $f \colon R \to R'$, we shall mean a mapping having the following properties: For all x, $y \in R$,

$$f(x + y) = f(x) + f(y), \qquad f(xy) = f(x)f(y), \qquad f(e) = e'$$

(if e, e' are the unit elements of R and R' respectively).

By the **kernel** of a ring-homomorphism $f \colon R \to R'$, we shall mean its kernel viewed as a homomorphism of additive groups, i.e. it is the set of all elements $x \in R$ such that $f(x) = 0$. *Exercise:* Prove that the kernel is a two-sided ideal of R.

Example 1. Let R be the ring of complex-valued functions on the interval $[0, 1]$. The map which to each function $f \in R$ associates its value $f(\frac{1}{2})$ is a ring-homomorphism of R into $\mathbf{C}$.

Example 2. Let R be the ring of real-valued functions on the interval $[0, 1]$. Let R' be the ring of real-valued functions on the interval $[0, \frac{1}{2}]$. Each function $f \in R$ can be viewed as a function on $[0, \frac{1}{2}]$, and when we so view f, we call it the **restriction** of f to $[0, \frac{1}{2}]$. More generally, let S be a set, and S' a subset. Let R be the ring of real-valued functions on S. For each $f \in R$, we denote by $f \mid S'$ the function on S' whose value at an element $x \in S'$ is $f(x)$. Then $f \mid S'$ is called the **restriction** of f to S'. Let R' be the ring of real-valued functions on S'. Then the map

$$f \mapsto f \mid S'$$

is a ring-homomorphism of R into R'.

Example 3. Let K be a field, and $R = K[t]$ the polynomial ring. Let A be a matrix in $\mathrm{Mat}_n(K)$. Then the map

$$f \mapsto f(A)$$

is a ring-homomorphism of R into $\mathrm{Mat}_n (K)$. This is but a restatement of properties of the map $f \mapsto f(A)$ considered previously.

In all the preceding examples, describe explicitly the kernel of the given ring-homomorphism.

Since the kernel of a ring-homomorphism is defined only in terms of the additive groups involved, we know that a ring-homomorphism whose kernel is trivial is injective.

Let $f \colon R \to R'$ be a ring-homomorphism. If there exists a ring-homomorphism $g \colon R' \to R$ such that $g \circ f$ and $f \circ g$ are the respective identity mappings, then we say that f is a **ring-isomorphism.** As with vector spaces and groups, it is also true that if f is a ring-homomorphism which is injective and surjective, then it is a ring-isomorphism. We leave the proof as an exercise.

We shall now define a notion similar to that of factor group, but applied to rings.

Let R be a ring and M a two-sided ideal. If $x, y \in R$, define x **congruent to** y mod M to mean $x - y \in M$. We write this relation in the form

$$x \equiv y \quad (\bmod\ M).$$

It is then very simple to prove the following statements, which will be left to the reader:

(a) We have $x \equiv x \pmod{M}$.

(b) If $x \equiv y$ and $y \equiv z \pmod{M}$, then $x \equiv z \pmod{M}$.

(c) If $x \equiv y$ then $y \equiv x \pmod{M}$.

(d) If $x \equiv y \pmod{M}$, and $z \in R$, then $xz \equiv yz \pmod{M}$, and also $zx \equiv zy \pmod{M}$.

(e) If $x \equiv y$ and $x' \equiv y' \pmod{M}$, then $xx' \equiv yy' \pmod{M}$. Furthermore, $x + x' \equiv y + y' \pmod{M}$.

The proofs of the preceding assertions are all trivial. As an example, we shall give the proof of (e). The hypothesis means that we can write

$$x = y + z \qquad \text{and} \qquad x' = y' + z'$$

with $z, z' \in M$. Then

$$xx' = (y + z)(y' + z') = yy' + zy' + yz' + zz'.$$

Since M is a two-sided ideal, each one of zy', yz', zz' lies in M, and consequently their sum lies in M. Hence $xx' \equiv yy' \pmod{M}$, as was to be shown.

If $x \in R$, we let $\bar{x}$ be the set of all elements of R which are congruent to $x \pmod{M}$. Recalling the definition of a factor group, we see that $\bar{x}$ is none other than the additive coset $x + M$ of x, relative to M. Any element of that coset (also called **congruence class** of x mod M) is called a **representative** of the coset.

We let $\bar{R}$ be the set of all congruence classes of R mod M. In other words, we let $\bar{R} = R/M$ be the additive factor group of R modulo M. Then we already know that $\bar{R}$ is an additive group. We shall now define a multiplication which will make $\bar{R}$ into a ring.

If $\bar{x}$ and $\bar{y}$ are additive cosets of M, we define their product to be the coset of xy, i.e. to be $\overline{xy}$. Using condition (e) above, we see that this coset is independent of the selected representatives x in $\bar{x}$ and y in $\bar{y}$. Thus our multiplication is well defined by the rule

$$(x + M)(y + M) = (xy + M).$$

It is now a triviality to check that the axioms of a ring are satisfied. In particular, the unit element of $\bar{R}$ is $1 + M$, if 1 is the unit element of R.

It is also trivial to verify that the map

$$f\colon R \to \overline{R}$$

such that $f(x) = \overline{x} = x + M$ is a ring-homomorphism of R onto $\overline{R}$, whose kernel is M. We leave this verification to the reader.

EXERCISES

1. Let $f\colon R \to R'$ be a ring-homomorphism. Show that the image of f is a subring of R'.

2. Let V be a finite dimensional vector space over the field K. Let $\mathfrak{B}$ be a basis of V. Show that the map $f \mapsto M_{\mathfrak{B}}^{\mathfrak{B}}(f)$ is a ring-isomorphism of the ring $\mathcal{L}(V, V)$ onto the ring of $n \times n$ matrices (if $n = \dim V$). (This exercise amounts to no more than interpreting past statements concerning $M_{\mathfrak{B}}^{\mathfrak{B}}(f)$ in the present language.)

3. Let R be a ring. Let G be the set of elements $x \in R$ such that there exists an element $y \in R$ for which $xy = yx = e$. Show that G is a group. It is called the group of **units** of R. (If R is the ring of $n \times n$ matrices over a field K, then G is none other than the group of invertible matrices.)

4. Show that a ring-homomorphism of a field K is either the zero map, or an isomorphism of K onto its image.

5. As an example of residue classes let $R = \mathbf{Z}$ be the ring of integers. Let M be an ideal, non-zero, and not the unit ideal. Then we know that M has a unique positive generator n, and thus $M = (n)$. We often write mod n instead of mod (n).

   (a) Show that any integer x is congruent to a unique integer m such that $0 \leq m < n$.

   (b) Show that any integer $x \neq 0$, relatively prime to n, is congruent to a unique integer m relatively prime to n, such that $0 < m < n$.

   (c) Show that if x is an integer $\neq 0$, and relatively prime to n, then $x^{\varphi(n)} \equiv 1 \pmod{n}$, where $\varphi(n)$ is the number of integers m relatively prime to n, such that $0 < m < n$.

   (d) If p is a prime number, what is $\varphi(p)$?

   (e) Determine $\varphi(n)$ for each integer n with $1 \leq n \leq 10$.

6. (a) Let p be a prime number. Show that in the ring $\mathbf{Z}/(p)$, every non-zero element has a multiplicative inverse, and that the non-zero elements form a multiplicative group.   (b) If a is an integer, $a \not\equiv 0 \pmod{p}$, show that

$$a^{p-1} \equiv 1 \pmod{p}.$$

7. Let n, n' be relatively prime positive integers. Let a, b be integers. Show that the congruences

$$x \equiv a \pmod{n},$$
$$x \equiv b \pmod{n'}$$

can be solved simultaneously with some $x \in \mathbf{Z}$.

8. Formulate Exercise 5(a) and (b) for the polynomial ring, over a field X.

9. Let R be a ring, and M, M' two-sided ideals. Assume that M contains M'. If $x \in R$, denote its residue class mod M by $x(M)$. Show that there is a (unique) ring-homomorphism

$$R/M' \rightarrow R/M$$

which maps $x(M')$ on $x(M)$.

10. If n, m are integers $\neq 0$, such that n divides m, apply Exercise 9 to get a ring-homomorphism $\mathbf{Z}/(m) \rightarrow \mathbf{Z}/(n)$.

11. Let R, R' be rings. Let $R \times R'$ be the set of all pairs (x, x') with $x \in R$ and $x' \in R'$. Show how one can make $R \times R'$ into a ring, by defining addition and multiplication componentwise. In particular, what is the unit element of $R \times R'$?

12. Let m, n be relatively prime positive integers. Show that $\mathbf{Z}/(mn)$ is ring-isomorphic to $\mathbf{Z}/(n) \times \mathbf{Z}/(m)$ under the map

$$x \ (\mathrm{mod}\ mn) \longmapsto (x \ \mathrm{mod}\ n, \ x \ \mathrm{mod}\ m).$$

13. Prove that if m, n are positive relatively prime integers, then

$$\varphi(mn) = \varphi(m)\varphi(n).$$

14. Let $f: R \rightarrow R'$ be a ring-homomorphism. Let J' be a two-sided ideal of R', and let J be the set of elements x of R such that $f(x)$ lies in J. Show that J is a two-sided ideal of R.

15. Let R be a commutative ring, and N the set of elements $x \in R$ such that $x^n = 0$ for some positive integer n. Show that N is an ideal.

16. In Exercise 15, if $\bar{x}$ is an element of R/N, and if there exists an integer $n \geqq 1$ such that $\bar{x}^n = 0$, show that $\bar{x} = 0$.

17. Let R be a ring, and Z the set of elements $x \in R$ such that $xy = yx$ for all $y \in R$. Show that Z is a subring, and that Z is commutative.

§3. *Modules*

We may consider a generalization of the notion of vector space over a field, namely module over a ring. Let R be a ring. By a (left) **module** over R, or an R-**module,** one means an additive group M, together with a map $R \times M \rightarrow M$, which to each pair (x, v) with $x \in R$ and $v \in M$, associates an element xv of M, satisfying the following conditions:

MOD 1. *For all x, $y \in R$, and v, $w \in M$, we have*

$$(x + y)v = xv + yv, \qquad x(v + w) = xv + xw.$$

MOD 2. *We have $(xy)v = x(yv)$.*

MOD 3. *If e is the unit element of R, then $ev = v$.*

Example 1. Every left ideal of R is a module.

Example 2. Let M be a module over the ring R. Then M is also a module over any subring R' of R.

Example 3. Let V be a vector space over the field K, and let $R = \mathcal{L}(V, V)$, be the ring of K-linear maps of V into itself. Then V is a module over R, if we define the product of an element $A \in R$ and $v \in V$ to be the element $Av = A(v)$ of V. Properties of linear maps and the definition of the sum of linear maps show that our axioms MOD 1, 2, 3 are satisfied.

Example 4. Let K be a field. Then K^n is a module over the ring of $n \times n$ matrices in K, namely if A is an $n \times n$ matrix in K, and $X \in K^n$, then the ordinary matrix product AX satisfies the conditions MOD 1, 2, 3.

Let R be a ring, and let M, M' be R-modules. By an R-**linear** map (or R-**homomorphism**) $f \colon M \to M'$ one means a map such that for all $x \in R$ and $v, w \in M$ we have

$$f(xv) = xf(v), \qquad f(v + w) = f(v) + f(w).$$

Thus an R-*linear* map is the generalization of a K-linear map when the module is a vector space over a field.

The set of all R-linear maps of M into M' will be denoted by $\mathcal{L}_R(M, M')$.

Example 5. Let M, M', M'' be R-modules. If

$$f \colon M \to M' \qquad \text{and} \qquad g \colon M' \to M''$$

are R-linear maps, then the composite map $g \circ f$ is R-linear. If

$$f_1, f_2 \in \mathcal{L}_R(M, M'),$$

then

$$g \circ (f_1 + f_2) = g \circ f_1 + g \circ f_2.$$

If $g_1, g_2 \in \mathcal{L}_R(M', M'')$, then

$$(g_1 + g_2) \circ f = g_1 \circ f + g_2 \circ f.$$

Prove these relations as exercises.

As with vector spaces, we have to consider very frequently the set of R-linear maps of a module M into itself, and it is convenient to have a name for these maps. They are called R-**endomorphisms** of M. The set of R-endomorphisms of M is denoted by $\mathrm{End}_R(M)$.

Example 6. Let R be a ring, and M a left ideal. Let $y \in M$. The map

$$r_y \colon M \to M$$

such that

$$r_y(x) = xy$$

is an R-linear map of M into itself. Indeed, if $x \in M$, then $xy \in M$ since M is a left ideal, and the conditions for R-linearity are reformulations of definitions (which ones?). We call r_y **right multiplication by** y. Thus r_y is an R-endomorphism of M.

Example 7. Let V be a vector space over a field K, and let A be a K-linear map of V into itself. Let R be the ring consisting of all elements $f(A)$, where f is a polynomial in $K[t]$. Then V is an R-module. Let B be any K-linear map of V into itself. Then B will be an R-endomorphism of V if and only if $AB = BA$, for in that case, as we have seen,

$$f(A)B = Bf(A)$$

for all polynomials f.

Example 8. Let R be a ring and M an R-module. Let $R' = \operatorname{End}_R(M)$. Then R' is a ring. The fact that the ring axioms are satisfied follows from the definitions, and Example 5. *We note that M can be viewed as an R'-module.* Indeed, if $f \in R'$, and $v \in M$, we can associate $f(v)$ with the pair (f, v). It is a routine trivial verification that all the conditions making M into an R'-module are satisfied.

We shall now discuss further the situation of Example 8. With each element $x \in R$, we can associate a map

$$\lambda_x \colon M \to M,$$

namely the map such that

$$\lambda_x(v) = xv.$$

Then for all $v, w \in M$ we have

$$\lambda_x(v + w) = x(v + w) = xv + xw = \lambda_x(v) + \lambda_x(w).$$

Furthermore, if $f \in R' = \operatorname{End}_R(M)$, then by definition,

$$f(xv) = xf(v),$$

and consequently,

$$f \circ \lambda_x(v) = \lambda_x \circ f(v).$$

Hence λ_x is an R'-linear map of M into itself, i.e. an element of $\operatorname{End}_{R'}(M)$. The association

$$\lambda \colon x \mapsto \lambda_x$$

is immediately verified to be a ring-homomorphism of R into $\operatorname{End}_{R'}(M)$. (Do it in detail.)

Theorem 1. *Let R be a ring, and M an R-module. Let J be the set of elements $x \in R$ such that $xv = 0$ for all $v \in M$. Then J is a two-sided ideal of R.*

Proof. If x, $y \in J$, then $(x + y)v = xv + yv = 0$ for all $v \in M$. If $a \in R$, then

$$(ax)v = a(xv) = 0 \qquad \text{and} \qquad (xa)v = x(av) = 0$$

for all $v \in M$. This proves the theorem.

We observe that the two-sided ideal of Theorem 1 is none other than the kernel of the ring-homomorphism

$$x \mapsto \lambda_x$$

described in the preceding discussion.

Theorem 2 (Wedderburn-Rieffel). *Let R be a ring, and L a non-zero left ideal, viewed as R-module. Let $R' = \text{End}_R(L)$, and $R'' = \text{End}_{R'}(L)$. Let*

$$\lambda \colon R \to R''$$

be the ring-homomorphism such that $\lambda_x(y) = xy$ for $x \in R$ and $y \in L$. Assume that R has no two-sided ideals other than 0 and R itself. Then λ is a ring-isomorphism.

Proof. (Rieffel) The fact that λ is injective follows from Theorem 1, and the hypothesis that L is non-zero. Therefore, the only thing to prove is that λ is surjective. By Example 15 of §1, we know that LR is a two-sided ideal, non-zero since R has a unit, and hence equal to R by hypothesis. Then

$$\lambda(LR) = \lambda(L)\lambda(R) = \lambda(R).$$

We now contend that $\lambda(L)$ is a left ideal of R''. To prove this, let $f \in R''$, and let $x \in L$. For all $y \in L$, we know from Example 6 that r_y is in R', and hence that

$$f \circ r_y = r_y \circ f.$$

This means that $f(xy) = f(x)y$. We may rewrite this relation in the form

$$f \circ \lambda_x(y) = \lambda_{f(x)}(y).$$

Hence $f \circ \lambda_x$ is an element of $\lambda(L)$, namely $\lambda_{f(x)}$. This proves that $\lambda(L)$ is a left ideal of R''. But then

$$R''\lambda(R) = R''\lambda(L)\lambda(R) = \lambda(L)\lambda(R) = \lambda(R).$$

Since $\lambda(R)$ contains the identity map, say e, it follows that for every $f \in R''$, the map $f \circ e = f$ is contained in $\lambda(R)$, i.e. R'' is contained in $\lambda(R)$, and therefore $R'' = \lambda(R)$, as was to be proved.

Exercises

1. Let R be a ring, and M an R-module. If $v \in M$, show that $0v = 0$ (the first 0 is the zero of R, and the second is the zero of M).

2. Let V be a vector space over a field K, and let R be a subring of $\mathrm{End}_K(V)$ containing all the scalar maps, i.e. all maps cI with $c \in K$. Let L be a left ideal of R. Let LV be the set of all elements $A_1v_1 + \cdots + A_nv_n$, with $A_i \in L$, and $v_i \in V$. Show that LV is an R-invariant subspace of V.

3. Let R be an algebra over the complex numbers. We assume that the multiplication in R is associative, that R has a unit element (so R is a ring), and that R has no two-sided ideal other than 0 and R. We also assume that R is of finite dimension > 0 over $\mathbf{C}$. Let L be a left ideal of R, of smallest dimension > 0 over $\mathbf{C}$.

   (a) Prove that $\mathrm{End}_R(L) = \mathbf{C}$ (i.e. the only R-linear maps of L consist of multiplication by complex numbers). [*Hint:* Cf. Schur's lemma.]
   (b) Prove that R is ring-isomorphic to the ring of $\mathbf{C}$-linear maps of L into itself.

4. Define the notion of submodule of a module. Define the notion of isomorphism of modules.

5. Let R be a ring. An R-module M is said to be **simple** if $M \neq \{0\}$ and if it has no submodule other than $\{0\}$ or M itself. Let M, M' be simple R-modules, and $f \colon M \to M'$ an R-homomorphism. Show that either $f = 0$ or f is an isomorphism.

6. Let R be a ring, M a module, L a left ideal. Show that LM is a submodule of M. Assume that both L and M are simple. Show that $LM = M$ or $LM = \{0\}$.

§4. Factor modules

We have already studied factor groups, and rings modulo a two-sided ideal. We shall now study the analogous notion for a module.

Let R be a ring, and M an R-module. By a **submodule** N we shall mean an additive subgroup of M which is such that for all $x \in R$ and $v \in N$ we have $xv \in N$. Thus N itself is a module (i.e. R-module).

We already know how to construct the factor group M/N. Since M is an abelian group, N is automatically normal in M, so this is an old story. The elements of the factor group are the cosets $v + N$ with $v \in M$. We shall now define a multiplication of these cosets by elements of R. This we do in the natural way. If $x \in R$, we define $x(v + N)$ to be the coset $xv + N$. If v_1 is another coset representative of $v + M$, then we can write $v_1 = v + w$ with $w \in N$. Hence

$$xv_1 = xv + xw,$$

and $xw \in N$. Consequently $xv_1 + N = xv + N$. Thus our definition is independent of the choice of representative v of the coset $v + N$. It is now trivial to verify that all the axioms of a module are satisfied by this multiplication. We call M/N the **factor module** of M by N, and also M **modulo** N.

We could also use the notation of congruences. If v, v' are elements of M, we write

$$v \equiv v' \pmod{N}$$

to mean that $v - v' \in N$. This amounts to saying that the cosets $v + N$ and $v' + N$ are equal. Thus a coset $v + N$ is nothing but the congruence class of elements of M which are congruent to v mod N. We can rephrase our statement that the multiplication of a coset by x is well defined as follows: If $v \equiv v' \pmod{N}$, then for all $x \in R$, we have $xv \equiv xv' \pmod{N}$.

Example 1. Let V be a vector space over the field K. Let W be a subspace. Then the factor module V/W is called the **factor space** in this case.

Let M be an R-module, and N a submodule. The map

$$f \colon M \to M/N$$

which to each $v \in M$ associates its congruence class $f(v) = v + N$ is obviously an R-homomorphism, because $f(xv) = xv + N = x(v + N)$ by definition. It is called the **canonical** homomorphism. Its kernel is N.

Example 2. Let V be a vector space over the field K. Let W be a subspace. Then the canonical homomorphism $f \colon V \to V/W$ is a linear map, and is obviously surjective. Suppose that V is finite dimensional over K, and let W' be a subspace of V such that V is the direct sum, $V = W \oplus W'$. If $v \in V$, and we write $v = w + w'$ with $w \in W$ and $w' \in W'$, then $f(v) = f(w) + f(w') = f(w')$. Let us just consider the map f on W', and let us denote this map by f'. Thus for all $w' \in W'$ we have $f'(w') = f(w')$ by definition. Then f' maps W' onto V/W, and the kernel of f' is $\{O\}$, because $W \cap W' = \{O\}$. *Hence $f' \colon W' \to V/W$ is an isomorphism between the complementary subspace W' of W and the factor space V/W.* We have such an isomorphism for any choice of complementary subspace W'.

EXERCISES

1. Let V be a finite dimensional vector space over the field K, and let W be a subspace. Let $\{v_1, \ldots, v_r\}$ be a basis of W, and extend it to a basis $\{v_1, \ldots, v_n\}$ of V. Let $f \colon V \to V/W$ be the canonical map. Show that

$$\{f(v_{r+1}), \ldots, f(v_n)\}$$

is a basis of V/W.

2. Let V, W be as in Exercise 1. Let $A: V \to V$ be a linear map, and assume that $AW \subset W$ (i.e. $Aw \in W$ for all $w \in W$). Let $\{v_1, \ldots, v_n\}$ be the basis of V as in Exercise 1. Show that the matrix of A with respect to this basis is of type

$$\begin{pmatrix} M_1 & M_3 \\ O & M_2 \end{pmatrix}$$

where M_1 is a square $r \times r$ matrix, and M_2 is a square $(n - r) \times (n - r)$ matrix.

3. Notation still as in Exercises 1 and 2, show that A can be used to define a linear map $\overline{A}: V/W \to V/W$, by defining

$$\overline{A}(v + W) = Av + W.$$

(In the congruence terminology, if $v \equiv v' \pmod{W}$, then $Av \equiv Av' \pmod{W}$.) Write $\bar{v}$ instead of $f(v)$. Show that the matrix of $\overline{A}$ with respect to $\{\bar{v}_{r+1}, \ldots, \bar{v}_n\}$ is precisely the matrix M_2 of Exercise 2. We call $\overline{A}$ the linear map induced by A on the factor space.

4. Let V be the vector space generated over $\mathbf{R}$ by the functions 1, t, t^2, e^t, te^t, t^2e^t. Let W be the subspace generated by 1, t, t^2, e^t, te^t. Let D be the derivative.
    (a) Show that D maps W into itself.
    (b) What is the linear map $\overline{D}$ induced by D on the factor space V/W?

5. Let V be the vector space over $\mathbf{R}$ consisting of all polynomials of degree $\leq n$ (for some integer $n \geq 1$). Let W be the subspace consisting of all polynomials of degree $\leq n - 1$. What is the linear map $\overline{D}$ induced by the derivative D on the factor space V/W?

APPENDIX 1

Convex Sets

§1. Definitions

Let S be a subset of $\mathbf{R}^m$. We say that S is **convex** if given points P, Q in S, the line segment joining P to Q is also contained in S.

We recall that the line segment joining P to Q is the set of all points $P + t(Q - P)$ with $0 \leqq t \leqq 1$. Thus it is the set of points

$$(1 - t)P + tQ,$$

with $0 \leqq t \leqq 1$.

Theorem 1. *Let $P_1, \ldots, P_n$ be points of $\mathbf{R}^m$. Any convex set which contains $P_1, \ldots, P_n$ also contains all linear combinations*

$$x_1 P_1 + \cdots + x_n P_n,$$

such that $0 \leqq x_i \leqq 1$ for all i, and $x_1 + \cdots + x_n = 1$.

Proof. This is a nice exercise which we won't spoil by working out completely. We merely give a hint: Use induction, and the fact that if $x_n \neq 1$, then the above linear combination is equal to

$$(1 - x_n) \left(\frac{x_1}{1 - x_n} P_1 + \cdots + \frac{x_{n-1}}{1 - x_n} P_{n-1} \right) + x_n P_n.$$

Theorem 2. *Let $P_1, \ldots, P_n$ be points of $\mathbf{R}^m$. The set of all linear combinations*

$$x_1 P_1 + \cdots + x_n P_n$$

with $0 \leqq x_i \leqq 1$ and $x_1 + \cdots + x_n = 1$, is a convex set.

Proof. Very easy exercise.

In view of Theorems 1 and 2, we conclude that the set of linear combinations described in these theorems is the smallest convex set containing all points $P_1, \ldots, P_n$.

The following statements have already occurred as exercises, and we recall them here for the sake of completeness.

(1) *If S and S' are convex sets, then the intersection $S \cap S'$ is convex.*

365

(2) *Let $F: \mathbf{R}^m \to \mathbf{R}^n$ be a linear map. If S is convex in $\mathbf{R}^m$, then $F(S)$ (the image of S under F) is convex in $\mathbf{R}^n$.*

(3) *Let $F: \mathbf{R}^m \to \mathbf{R}^n$ be a linear map. Let S' be a convex set of $\mathbf{R}^m$. Let $S = F^{-1}(S')$ be the set of all $X \in \mathbf{R}^m$ such that $F(X)$ lies in S'. Then S is convex.*

Examples. Let A be a vector in $\mathbf{R}^n$. The map F such that $F(X) = A \cdot X$ is linear. Note that a point $c \in \mathbf{R}$ is a convex set. Hence the hyperplane H consisting of all X such that $A \cdot X = c$ is convex.

Furthermore, the set S' of all $x \in \mathbf{R}$ such that $x > c$ is convex. Hence the set of all $X \in \mathbf{R}^n$ such that $A \cdot X > c$ is convex. It is called an **open half space.** Similarly, the set of points $X \in \mathbf{R}^n$ such that $A \cdot X \geq c$ is called a **closed half space.**

In the following picture, we have illustrated a hyperplane (line) in $\mathbf{R}^2$, and one half space determined by it.

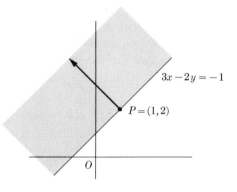

$3x - 2y = -1$

$P = (1, 2)$

O

Figure 1

The line is defined by the equation $3x - 2y = -1$. It passes through the point $P = (1, 2)$, and $N = (3, -2)$ is a vector perpendicular to the line. We have shaded the half space of points X such that $X \cdot N \leq -1$.

We see that a hyperplane whose equation is $X \cdot N = c$ determines two closed half spaces, namely the spaces defined by the equations

$$X \cdot N \geq c \quad \text{and} \quad X \cdot N \leq c,$$

and similarly for the open half spaces.

Since the intersection of convex sets is convex, the intersection of a finite number of half spaces is convex. In the next pictures (Figs. 2 and 3), we have drawn intersections of a finite number of half planes. Such an intersection can be bounded or unbounded. (We recall that a subset S of $\mathbf{R}^n$ is said to be **bounded** if there exists a number $c > 0$ such that $\|X\| \leq c$ for all $X \in S$.)

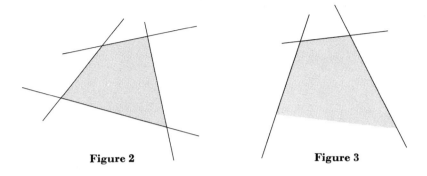

Figure 2   Figure 3

§2. *Separating hyperplanes*

Theorem 3. *Let S be a closed convex set in* $\mathbf{R}^n$. *Let P be a point of* $\mathbf{R}^n$. *Then either P belongs to S, or there exists a hyperplane H which contains P, and such that S is contained in one of the open half spaces determined by H.*

Proof. We use a fact from calculus. Suppose that P does not belong to S. We consider the function for the closed set S given by

$$f(X) = \|X - P\|.$$

It is proved in a course in calculus (with ϵ and δ) that this function has a minimum on S. Let Q be a point of S such that

$$\|Q - P\| \leqq \|X - P\|$$

for all X in S. Let

$$N = Q - P.$$

Since P is not in S, $Q - P \neq O$, and $N \neq O$. We contend that the hyperplane passing through P, perpendicular to N, will satisfy our requirements. Let Q' be any point of S, and say $Q' \neq Q$. Then for every t with $0 < t \leqq 1$ we have

$$\|Q - P\| \leqq \|Q + t(Q' - Q) - P\| = \|(Q - P) + t(Q' - Q)\|.$$

Squaring gives

$$(Q - P)^2 \leqq (Q - P)^2 + 2t(Q - P) \cdot (Q' - Q) + t^2(Q' - Q)^2.$$

Canceling and dividing by $2t$, we obtain

$$0 \leqq 2(Q - P) \cdot (Q' - Q) + t(Q' - Q)^2.$$

Letting t tend to 0 yields

$$0 \leq (Q - P) \cdot (Q' - Q)$$
$$\leq N \cdot (Q' - P) + N \cdot (P - Q)$$
$$\leq N \cdot (Q' - P) - N \cdot N.$$

But $N \cdot N > 0$. Hence

$$Q' \cdot N > P \cdot N.$$

This proves that S is contained in the open half space defined by $X \cdot N > P \cdot N$.

Let S be a convex set in $\mathbf{R}^n$. Then the closure of S (denoted by $\overline{S}$) is convex.

This is easily proved, for if P, Q are points in the closure, we can find points of S, say P_k, Q_k tending to P and Q respectively as a limit. Then for $0 \leq t \leq 1$,

$$tP_k + (1 - t)Q_k$$

tends to $tP + (1 - t)Q$, which therefore lies in the closure of S.

Let S be a convex set in $\mathbf{R}^n$. Let P be a boundary point of S. (This means a point such that for every $\epsilon > 0$, the open ball centered at P, of radius ϵ in $\mathbf{R}^n$ contains points which are in S, and points which are not in S.) A hyperplane H is said to be a **supporting hyperplane** of S at P if P is contained in H, and if S is contained in one of the two closed half spaces determined by H.

Theorem 4. *Let S be a convex set in $\mathbf{R}^n$, and let P be a boundary point of S. Then there exists a supporting hyperplane of S at P.*

Proof. Let $\overline{S}$ be the closure of S. Then we saw that $\overline{S}$ is convex, and P is a boundary point of $\overline{S}$. If we can prove our theorem for $\overline{S}$, then it certainly follows for S. Thus without loss of generality, we may assume that S is closed.

For each integer $k > 2$, we can find a point P_k not in S, but at distance $< 1/k$ from P. By Theorem 3, we find a point Q_k on S whose distance from P_k is minimal, and we let $N_k = Q_k - P_k$. Let N'_k be the vector in the same direction as N_k but of length 1. The sequence of vectors N'_k has a point of accumulation on the sphere of radius 1, say N', because the sphere is compact. We have by Theorem 3, for all $X \in S$,

$$X \cdot N_k > P_k \cdot N_k$$

for every k, whence dividing each side by the length of N_k, we get

$$X \cdot N'_k > P_k \cdot N'_k$$

for every k. Since N' is a point of accumulation of $\{N_k'\}$, and since P is a limit of $\{P_k\}$, it follows by continuity that for each X in S,

$$X \cdot N' \geqq P \cdot N'.$$

This proves our theorem.

Remark. Let S be a convex set, and let H be a hyperplane defined by an equation

$$X \cdot N = a.$$

Assume that for all $X \in S$ we have $X \cdot N \geqq a$. If P is a point of S lying in the hyperplane, then P is a boundary point of S. Otherwise, for $\epsilon > 0$ and ϵ sufficiently small, $P - \epsilon N$ would be a point of S, and thus

$$(P - \epsilon N) \cdot N = P \cdot N - \epsilon N \cdot N = a - \epsilon N \cdot N < a,$$

contrary to hypothesis. We conclude therefore that H is a supporting hyperplane of S at P.

§3. *Extreme points and supporting hyperplanes*

Let S be a convex set and let P be a point of S. We shall say that P is an **extreme point** of S if there do not exist points Q_1, Q_2 of S with $Q_1 \neq Q_2$ such that P can be written in the form

$$P = tQ_1 + (1 - t)Q_2 \qquad \text{with} \qquad 0 < t < 1.$$

In other words, P cannot lie on a line segment contained in S unless it is one of the end-points of the line segment.

We define a set S to be **bounded from below** if there exists a vector $B = (b_1, \ldots, b_n)$ such that for all $X = (x_1, \ldots, x_n)$ in S we have $x_i \geqq b_i$ for $i = 1, \ldots, n$.

Theorem 5. *Let S be a closed convex set which is bounded from below. Then every supporting hyperplane of S contains an extreme point.*

Proof. Let H be a supporting hyperplane, defined by the equation $X \cdot N = P_0 \cdot N$ at a boundary point P_0, and say $X \cdot N \geqq P_0 \cdot N$ for all $X \in S$. Let T be the intersection of S and the hyperplane. Then T is convex, closed, bounded from below. We contend that an extreme point of T will also be an extreme point of S. This will reduce our problem to finding extreme points of T. To prove our contention, let P be an extreme point of T, and suppose that we can write

$$P = tQ_1 + (1 - t)Q_2, \qquad\qquad 0 < t < 1.$$

Dotting with N, and using the fact that P is in the hyperplane, hence $P \cdot N = P_0 \cdot N$, we obtain

(1) $$P_0 \cdot N = tQ_1 \cdot N + (1 - t)Q_2 \cdot N.$$

We have $Q_1 \cdot N$ and $Q_2 \cdot N \geqq P_0 \cdot N$ since Q_1, Q_2 lie in S. If one of these is $> P_0 \cdot N$, say $Q_1 \cdot N > P_0 \cdot N$, then the right-hand side of equation (1) is

$$> tP_0 \cdot N + (1 - t)P_0 \cdot N, = P_0 \cdot N,$$

and this is impossible. Hence both Q_1, Q_2 lie in the hyperplane, thereby contradicting the hypothesis that P is an extreme point of T.

We shall now find an extreme point of T. Among all points of T, there is at least one point whose first coordinate is smallest, because T is closed and bounded from below. (We project on the first coordinate. The image of T under this projection has a greatest lower bound which is taken on by an element of T since T is closed.) Let T_1 be the subset of T consisting of all points whose first coordinate is equal to this smallest one. Then T_1 is closed, and bounded from below. Hence we can find a point of T_1 whose second coordinate is smallest among all points of T_1, and the set T_2 of all points of T_1 having this second coordinate is closed and bounded from below. We may proceed in this way until we find a point P of T having successively smallest first, second, ..., n-th coordinate. We assert that P is an extreme point of T. Let $P = (p_1, \ldots, p_n)$.

Suppose that we can write

$$P = tX + (1 - t)Y, \qquad\qquad 0 < t < 1$$

and points $X = (x_1, \ldots, x_n)$, $Y = (y_1, \ldots, y_n)$ in T. Then x_1 and $y_1 \geqq p_1$, and

$$p_1 = tx_1 + (1 - t)y_1.$$

If x_1 or $y_1 > p_1$, then

$$tx_1 + (1 - t)y_1 > tp_1 + (1 - t)p_1 = p_1,$$

which is impossible. Hence $x_1 = y_1 = p_1$. Proceeding inductively, suppose we have proved $x_i = y_i = p_i$ for $i = 1, \ldots, r$. Then if $r < n$,

$$p_{r+1} = tx_{r+1} + (1 - t)y_{r+1},$$

and we may repeat the preceding argument. It follows that

$$X = Y = P,$$

whence P is an extreme point, and our theorem is proved.

§4. *The Krein-Milman theorem*

Let E be a set of points in $\mathbf{R}^n$ (with at least one point in it). We wish to describe the smallest convex set containing E. We may say that it is the intersection of all convex sets containing E, because this intersection is convex, and is clearly smallest.

We can also describe this smallest convex set in another way. Let E^c be the set of all linear combinations

$$t_1 P_1 + \cdots + t_m P_m$$

of points $P_1, \ldots, P_m$ in E with real coefficients t_i such that

$$0 \leq t_i \leq 1 \quad \text{and} \quad t_1 + \cdots + t_m = 1.$$

Then the set E^c is convex. We leave the trivial verification to the reader. Any convex set containing E must contain E^c, and hence E^c is the smallest convex set containing E. We call E^c the **convex closure** of E.

Let S be a convex set and let E be the set of its extreme points. Then E^c is contained in S. We ask for conditions under which $E^c = S$.

Geometrically speaking, extreme points can be either points like those on the shell of an egg, or like points at the vertices of a polygon, viz.:

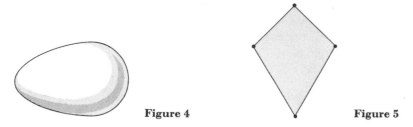

Figure 4   Figure 5

An unbounded convex set need not be the convex closure of its extreme points, for instance the closed upper half plane, which has no extreme points. Also, an open convex set need not be the convex closure of its extreme points (the interior of the egg has no extreme points). The Krein-Milman theorem states that if we eliminate these two possibilities, then no other troubles can occur.

Theorem 6. *Let S be a closed, bounded, convex set. Then S is the convex closure of its extreme points.*

Proof. Let S' be the convex closure of the extreme points of S. We must show that S is contained in S'. Let $P \in S$, and suppose $P \notin S'$. By Theorem 3, there exists a hyperplane H passing through P, defined by an equation

$$X \cdot N = c,$$

such that $X \cdot N > c$ for all $X \in S'$. Let $L \colon \mathbf{R}^n \to \mathbf{R}$ be the linear map such that $L(X) = X \cdot N$. Then $L(P) = c$, and $L(P)$ is not contained in $L(S')$. Since S is closed and bounded, the image $L(S)$ is closed and bounded, and this image is also convex. Hence $L(S)$ is a closed interval, say $[a, b]$, containing c. Thus $a \leq c \leq b$. Let H_a be the hyperplane defined by the equation

$$X \cdot N = a.$$

By the remark following Theorem 4, we know that H_a is a supporting hyperplane of S. By Theorem 5, we conclude that H_a contains an extreme point of S. This extreme point is in S'. We then obtain a contradiction of the fact that $X \cdot N > c \geq a$ for all X in S', and thus prove the Krein-Milman theorem.

EXERCISES

1. Let A be a vector in $\mathbf{R}^n$. Let $F \colon \mathbf{R}^n \to \mathbf{R}^n$ be the translation,

$$F(X) = X + A.$$

Show that if S is convex in $\mathbf{R}^n$ then $F(S)$ is also convex.

2. Let c be a number > 0, and let P be a point in $\mathbf{R}^n$. Let S be the set of points X such that $\|X - P\| < c$. Show that S is convex. Similarly, show that the set of points X such that $\|X - P\| \leq c$ is convex.

3. Sketch the convex closure of the following sets of points.
   (a) $(1, 2)$, $(1, -1)$, $(1, 3)$, $(-1, 1)$
   (b) $(-1, 2)$, $(2, 3)$, $(-1, -1)$, $(1, 0)$

4. Let $L \colon \mathbf{R}^n \to \mathbf{R}^n$ be an invertible linear map. Let S be convex in $\mathbf{R}^n$ and P an extreme point of S. Show that $L(P)$ is an extreme point of $L(S)$. Is the assertion still true if L is not invertible?

5. Prove that the intersection of a finite number of closed half spaces in $\mathbf{R}^n$ can have only a finite number of extreme points.

6. Let B be a column vector in $\mathbf{R}^n$, and A an $n \times n$ matrix. Show that the set of solutions of the linear equations $AX = B$ is a convex set in $\mathbf{R}^n$.

APPENDIX 2

Odds and Ends

In this appendix we recall first what induction is. We have used it many times throughout the book, and most students will know it already, but it may be useful to some to recall precisely what it says. We then prove the algebraic closure of the complex numbers, using only an elementary fact of analysis. Finally, we mention the notion of equivalence relation.

§1. Induction

In proving statements stepwise, we have often used induction. We shall now state precisely the property of integers called induction.

Suppose that for each integer $n \geq 1$ we are given an assertion $A(n)$. We wish to prove that all the assertions $A(n)$ for $n = 1, 2, \ldots$ are true. Suppose that we can prove the following two properties:

(1) The assertion $A(1)$ is true.
(2) For each integer $n \geq 1$, if we assume the assertion $A(n)$, then $A(n + 1)$ is true.

Then **induction** states that all assertions $A(n)$ are true for all integers $n \geq 1$.

Example 1. We wish to prove that for each integer $n \geq 1$, $A(n)$:

$$1 + 2 + \cdots + n = \frac{n(n + 1)}{2}.$$

This is certainly true when $n = 1$, because $1 = 1(1 + 1)/2$. Assume that our equation is true for an integer $n \geq 1$. Then

$$1 + \cdots + n + (n + 1) = \frac{n(n + 1)}{2} + (n + 1) = \frac{n(n + 1) + 2(n + 1)}{2}$$

$$= \frac{n^2 + n + 2n + 2}{2} = \frac{(n + 1)(n + 2)}{2}.$$

Thus we have proved the two properties (1), (2) for the statements denoted by $A(n)$, and we conclude by induction that $A(n)$ is true for all integers $n \geq 1$.

We emphasize that **induction** is an axiom about integers. We assume it as a property of integers. It is, however, a very reasonable property to assume.

§2. *Algebraic closure of the complex numbers*

Using some elementary facts of analysis, we shall now prove that *the complex numbers are algebraically closed, in other words, that every polynomial $f \in \mathbf{C}[t]$ of degree ≥ 1 has a root in $\mathbf{C}$.*

We may write

$$f(t) = a_n t^n + a_{n-1} t^{n-1} + \cdots + a_0$$

with $a_n \neq 0$. For every real $R > 0$, the function $|f|$ such that

$$t \mapsto |f(t)|$$

is continuous on the closed disc of radius R, and hence has a minimum value on this disc. On the other hand, from the expression

$$f(t) = a_n t^n \left(1 + \frac{a_{n-1}}{a_n t} + \cdots + \frac{a_0}{a_n t^n} \right)$$

we see that when $|t|$ becomes large, then $|f(t)|$ also becomes large, i.e. given $C > 0$ there exists $R > 0$ such that if $|t| > R$ then $|f(t)| > C$. Consequently, there exists a positive number R_0 such that, if z_0 is a minimum point of $|f|$ on the closed disc of radius R_0, then

$$|f(t)| \geq |f(z_0)|$$

for all complex numbers t. In other words, z_0 is an absolute minimum for $|f|$. We shall prove that $f(z_0) = 0$.

We express f in the form

$$f(t) = c_0 + c_1(t - z_0) + \cdots + c_n(t - z_0)^n$$

with constants c_i. (We did it in the text, but one also sees it by writing $t = z_0 + (t - z_0)$ and substituting directly in $f(t)$.) If $f(z_0) \neq 0$, then $c_0 = f(z_0) \neq 0$. Let $z = t - z_0$, and let m be the smallest integer > 0 such that $c_m \neq 0$. This integer m exists because f is assumed to have degree ≥ 1. Then we can write

$$f(t) = f_1(z) = c_0 + c_m z^m + z^{m+1} g(z)$$

for some polynomial g, and some polynomial f_1 (obtained from f by changing the variable). Let z_1 be a complex number such that $z_1^m = -c_0/c_m$, and consider values of z of type

$$z = \lambda z_1$$

where λ is real, $0 \leq \lambda \leq 1$. We have

$$f(t) = f_1(\lambda z_1) = c_0 - \lambda^m c_0 + \lambda^{m+1} z_1^{m+1} g(\lambda z_1)$$
$$= c_0[1 - \lambda^m + \lambda^{m+1} z_1^{m+1} c_0^{-1} g(\lambda z_1)].$$

There exists a number $C > 0$ such that for all λ with $0 \leq \lambda \leq 1$ we have $|z_1^{m+1} c_0^{-1} g(\lambda z_1)| \leq C$, and hence

$$|f_1(\lambda z_1)| \leq |c_0|(1 - \lambda^m + C\lambda^{m+1}).$$

If we can now prove that for sufficiently small λ with $0 < \lambda < 1$ we have

$$0 < 1 - \lambda^m + C\lambda^{m+1} < 1,$$

then for such λ we get $|f_1(\lambda z_1)| < |c_0|$, thereby contradicting the hypothesis that $|f(z_0)| \leq |f(t)|$ for all complex numbers t. The left inequality is of course obvious since $0 < \lambda < 1$. The right inequality amounts to $C\lambda^{m+1} < \lambda^m$, or equivalently $C\lambda < 1$, which is certainly satisfied for sufficiently small λ. This concludes the proof.

EXERCISE

1. Assuming the result just proved about the complex numbers, prove that every irreducible polynomial over the real numbers has degree 1 or 2. [*Hint:* Split the polynomial over the complex numbers and pair off complex conjugate roots.]

§3. *Equivalence relations*

Let S be a set. By an **equivalence relation** in S we mean a relation, written $x \sim y$, between certain pairs of elements of S, satisfying the following conditions:

ER 1. *We have $x \sim x$ for all $x \in S$.*
ER 2. *If $x \sim y$ and $y \sim z$, then $x \sim z$.*
ER 3. *If $x \sim y$, then $y \sim x$.*

Suppose we have such an equivalence relation in S. Given an element x of S, let C_x consist of all elements of S which are equivalent to x. Then all elements of C_x are equivalent to one another, as follows at once from our three properties. (Verify this in detail.) Furthermore, you will also verify at once that if x, y are elements of S, then either $C_x = C_y$, or C_x, C_y have no element in common. Each C_x is called an **equivalence class.** We see that our equivalence relation determines a decomposition of S into disjoint equivalence classes. Each element of the class is called a **representative** of the class.

Example 1. Let G be a group and H a subgroup. Define $x \sim y$ to mean that $xH = yH$ for elements x, $y \in G$. One sees at once that this is an equivalence relation. An equivalence class has been called a coset of H (i.e. left coset).

Example 2. Let R be a ring and M a two-sided ideal. Then congruence modulo M is an equivalence relation between elements of R.

Example 3. Let S be the set of all geometric figures in the plane $\mathbf{R}^2$ (i.e. the set of all triangles, squares, rectangles, etc.). Let G be the group generated by all translations and all real unitary maps of $\mathbf{R}^2$. We call G the group of rigid motions of the plane. (Cf. Exercise 3 of Chapter XIV, §2). If α, β are elements of S, we define α to be equivalent to β, and write $\alpha \sim \beta$, if there exists an element $T \in G$ such that $T(\alpha) = \beta$. *Prove that this is an equivalence relation.* It is the equivalence relation of plane geometry. When two figures of the plane are called "equal" in elementary school, this is a fantastic abuse of language. For instance, the following two triangles

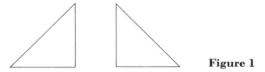

Figure 1

are definitely not "equal", i.e. they are not the same triangle. But they are equivalent in our sense. Thus in plane geometry, the rule about substituting equals for equals is really a rule about equivalent elements, and states nothing more than ER 2.

In mathematics, the word **equal** means **the same.** For instance when we write

$$1 + 2 = 4 - 1$$

we have the same number on each side of this equality, namely the number 3. Of course, the number 3 is represented in two different fashions, but the value of $1 + 2$ is the same as the value $4 - 1$, namely 3.

Of course, equality is a special case of an equivalence relation, when there is precisely one element in each equivalence class.

Example 4. A **rational function** "quotient" of polynomials, f/g. If c is a number such that $g(c) = 0$, then such a quotient is not defined at c. Thus a rational function cannot be viewed as a function of all numbers, and we face the task of defining rational functions rigorously. This is in fact quite easy. Let K be a field. Let (f, g) and (f_1, g_1) be pairs of polynomials in K, such that neither g nor g_1 is equal to 0. We say that such pairs are equivalent if $fg_1 = gf_1$. As an exercise, prove that this is an equivalence relation. The equivalence class of the pair (f, g) is denoted by f/g, and is called a rational function. Observe that our definition of equivalence was adjusted so that it would fit the rule of "cross multiplying". We can now define addition and multiplication of rational functions. If f/g and f_1/g_1 are rational functions, define

$$f/g + f_1/g_1 = (fg_1 + gf_1)/gg_1,$$
$$(f/g)(f_1/g_1) = (ff_1)/(gg_1).$$

Again as an exercise, it is easy to show that this sum and product are independent of the choice of representatives (f, g) and (f_1, g_1) for the rational functions f/g and f_1/g_1 respectively. The rational functions thereby form a ring, and it is again an exercise to prove in detail that all axioms of a ring are satisfied by our addition and multiplication.

Note that according to our definition, if h is a non-zero polynomial, then $fh/gh = f/g$. Indeed, this simply means that $fhg = ghf$, which is certainly true. Thus the ordinary cancellation law holds.

Exercises

1. Let V be a finite dimensional vector space over the field K, and let $\rho: G \to GL(V)$ be a group-homomorphism of a group G into the group of invertible linear maps of V. Given elements $v, w \in V$, define $v \sim w$ if there exists $\sigma \in G$ such that $\rho(\sigma)v = w$. Show that this is an equivalence relation.

2. Let V be a finite dimensional vector space over the field K. If $v, w \in V$, define $v \sim w$ if there exists an invertible linear map $A: V \to V$ such that $Av = w$. Show that there exist precisely two equivalence classes for this relation, one consisting of O alone, and the other consisting of all non-zero elements of V.

3. Let G be a group. Define two elements a, b of G to be **conjugate** and write $a \sim b$, if there exists $x \in G$ such that $xax^{-1} = b$. Show that this is an equivalence relation.

4. Let G be the symmetric group on 3 elements. Using the equivalence relation of Exercise 3, determine the equivalence classes in G. Show that two permutations in the same equivalence class have the same sign.

APPENDIX 3

Angles

For most of this section, we discuss the geometry of 2-space. This discussion is logically independent of calculus, and concerns only linear algebra. At the end we relate the geometry with our sin and cos functions.

Let V be a 2-dimensional vector space (over the real numbers), with a (positive definite) scalar product. By the unit circle in V we shall mean the set of all elements v of V such that $\|v\| = 1$. Thus the unit circle is just the set of unit vectors in V.

Let A be a non-zero element of V. The set of all elements tA, where t is a number ≥ 0, will be called a **half-line,** determined by A. If E is the unit vector in the direction of A, i.e.

$$E = \frac{A}{\|A\|},$$

then one sees at once that E determines the same half-line as A, and is the unique unit vector in V which does so. Thus to determine a half-line it is necessary and sufficient to specify the unit vector having the same direction.

We define an **angle** to be an ordered pair of half-lines $(L_1 L_2)$. If P is the unique point on the unit circle lying on the half-line L_1, and Q is the unique point on the unit circle lying on the half-line L_2, then we denote the angle $(L_1 L_2)$ also by the symbols $\angle PQ$.

Let $\mathcal{B}$ and $\mathcal{B}'$ be two bases of V. If $F: V \to V$ is a linear map, and if we let M be its associated matrix relative to $\mathcal{B}$, $\mathcal{B}$ (or as we also say, relative to $\mathcal{B}$), and let M' be the associated matrix of F relative to $\mathcal{B}'$, then we know that there exists a matrix N such that $M' = NMN^{-1}$. Using the rule concerning the product of determinants, we conclude that the determinant of M is equal to the determinant of M'. Hence the determinant does not depend on the choice of bases. We call it the determinant of F.

We recall that an orthogonal map is a linear map which preserves lengths (or scalar products).

Proposition 1. *The determinant of an orthogonal map F is equal to 1 or -1.*

Proof. Let $\{v_1, v_2\}$ be an orthonormal basis of V. Let a, b, c, d be numbers such that

$$F(v_1) = av_1 + bv_2,$$
$$F(v_2) = cv_1 + dv_2.$$

Since F is orthogonal, the lengths of $F(v_1)$ and $F(v_2)$ are equal to 1, and these two elements are perpendicular. This means that

$$a^2 + b^2 = 1, \quad c^2 + d^2 = 1, \quad ac + bd = 0.$$

Hence

$$1 = (a^2 + b^2)(c^2 + d^2) = a^2c^2 + b^2c^2 + a^2d^2 + b^2d^2,$$
$$0 = (ac + bd)^2 = a^2c^2 + 2abcd + b^2d^2.$$

From these we obtain

$$(ad - bc)^2 = 1,$$

thereby proving that the determinant squared is equal to 1. Hence the determinant itself is 1 or -1.

We define a **rotation** to be an orthogonal map whose determinant is equal to 1.

Proposition 2. *Let $\mathfrak{B}$ be an orthonormal basis of V, and let F be a linear map of V into itself. Then F is a rotation if and only if there exist numbers a, b such that $a^2 + b^2 = 1$, and such that the matrix of F relative to $\mathfrak{B}$ is*

$$\begin{pmatrix} a & -b \\ b & a \end{pmatrix}.$$

If F is a rotation, a, b are as above, and $\mathfrak{B}'$ is another orthonormal basis of V such that the linear map sending $\mathfrak{B}$ on $\mathfrak{B}'$ is a rotation, then

$$M_{\mathfrak{B}'}^{\mathfrak{B}'}(F) = M_{\mathfrak{B}}^{\mathfrak{B}}(F).$$

Proof. Assume first that F is a rotation, and let us keep the notation of Proposition 1. We have $ad - bc = 1$. Hence

$$-bc = 1 - ad, \quad ac = -bd.$$

Multiplying the first of these equations by a, the second by b and adding yields

$$0 = a - a^2d - b^2d.$$

Since $a^2 + b^2 = 1$, we get $a = d$. From this it follows at once that $c = -b$, and our first assertion is proved. Conversely, it is trivially verified that a linear map represented by a matrix of the given type is a rotation.

Let now $\mathfrak{B}' = \{w_1, w_2\}$ be another orthonormal basis of V, and assume that it differs from $\{v_1, v_2\}$ by a rotation. By what we have just proved, there exist numbers x, y such that $x^2 + y^2 = 1$, and

$$v_1 = xw_1 + yw_2,$$
$$v_2 = -yw_1 + xw_2.$$

Thus the matrix

$$N = \begin{pmatrix} x & -y \\ y & x \end{pmatrix}$$

is equal to $M_{\mathfrak{B}}^{\mathfrak{B}'}(id)$ by definition. Since $N^{-1} = \begin{pmatrix} x & y \\ -y & x \end{pmatrix}$ (as one sees by a direct computation), it follows that

$$M_{\mathfrak{B}}^{\mathfrak{B}'}(F) = \begin{pmatrix} x & y \\ -y & x \end{pmatrix} \begin{pmatrix} a & -b \\ b & a \end{pmatrix} \begin{pmatrix} x & -y \\ y & x \end{pmatrix},$$

and a direct computation shows that this is the same matrix as

$$\begin{pmatrix} a & -b \\ b & a \end{pmatrix},$$

thereby proving our proposition.

Proposition 3. *Let F, G be two rotations. Then $F \circ G$ is a rotation. There exists an inverse F^{-1} for F, and F^{-1} is a rotation.*

Proof. The first assertion follows directly from the product rule for determinants. The second follows from the equations

$$1 = D(I) = D(FF^{-1}) = D(F)D(F^{-1}),$$

together with the assumption that $D(F) = 1$, provided we know that the inverse exists. The fact that an orthogonal linear map has an inverse, and that this inverse is orthogonal will be left as an exercise.

Let E_1 be a unit vector in V. The subspace of V which is perpendicular to E_1 has dimension 1 (because V has dimension 2). If E_2 is a unit vector generating this subspace, then any other vector perpendicular to E_1 can be written tE_2 for some number t. Hence there exist exactly two unit vectors in V perpendicular to E_1, and these are E_2, $-E_2$.

Proposition 4. *Let P, A be unit vectors in V. Then there exists a unique rotation F such that $F(P) = A$.*

Proof. Let F_1, F_2 be rotations mapping P on A. Then

$$F_1^{-1}(F_2(P)) = P.$$

Hence $F_1^{-1}F_2$ is a rotation which leaves P fixed. If we can prove that such a rotation is the identity map, then we conclude that $F_1^{-1}F_2 = I$, and $F_2 = F_1$, as desired. Let G be a rotation leaving P fixed. Let E be a unit vector perpendicular to P. Then $\{P, E\}$ is a basis for V. Since G is orthogonal, it follows that $G(E)$ is perpendicular to P, hence is equal to E or $-E$. If $G(E)$ were equal to $-E$, then the determinant of G would be equal to -1, which is impossible. Hence $G(E) = E$. Hence G leaves both P, E fixed, and since G is linear, it must be the identity map. We have therefore proved our uniqueness statement.

As for existence, let E be as above, and let a, b be numbers such that

$$A = aP + bE.$$

There exists a unique linear map F such that $F(P) = A$ and $F(E) = -bP + aE$. Since A is a unit vector, we have $a^2 + b^2 = 1$, and hence the determinant of F is 1. Furthermore, $F(P)$ and $F(E)$ are perpendicular (their scalar product is obviously 0). Hence F is a rotation, and has the desired effect.

Our next task is to define the sine and cosine of an angle. For this we must consider an additional structure on the vector space, that of orientation.

Two orthonormal bases $\mathcal{B}$ and $\mathcal{B}'$ of V will be said to have the **same orientation** if the (unique) orthogonal map F sending $\mathcal{B}$ into $\mathcal{B}'$ is a rotation. If this orthogonal map is not a rotation, then we say that $\mathcal{B}$ and $\mathcal{B}'$ have **opposite orientation.**

Remark. If $\mathcal{B}$ and $\mathcal{B}'$ have the same orientation, and if $\mathcal{B}'$, $\mathcal{B}''$ have the same orientation, then $\mathcal{B}$ and $\mathcal{B}''$ have the same orientation. Furthermore, $\mathcal{B}$ has the same orientation as itself. If $\mathcal{B}$ and $\mathcal{B}'$ have the same orientation, then $\mathcal{B}'$ and $\mathcal{B}$ have the same orientation. These statements are easily proved, and the arguments will be left to the reader.

The set of all orthonormal bases of V having a given orientation will be said to determine an **orientation** of V. There exist exactly two orientations of V. (Trivial proof, left as an exercise.)

Let us now assume given an orientation on V. Let $\angle PQ$ be an angle. Of the two unit vectors which are perpendicular to P, exactly one of them, say E, will be such that $\{P, E\}$ has the given orientation (because $\{P, E\}$ and $\{P, -E\}$ have opposite orientations).

There exist numbers a, b such that

$$Q = aP + bE.$$

Since Q has length 1, we see that $Q \cdot Q = 1 = a^2 + b^2$. Thus relative to the basis $\{P, E\}$, we see that the point having coordinates (a, b) lies on the unit circle. We define the **cosine** of the angle $\angle PQ$ to be the number a, and the **sine** of the angle $\angle PQ$ to be the number b. We abbreviate these by cos and sin.

Let $\angle PQ$ and $\angle AB$ be two angles, and let F be the rotation such that $F(P) = A$. If $F(Q) = B$, then we shall say that $\angle PQ$ is **congruent to** $\angle AB$. It is easily proved that in that case, $\angle AB$ is congruent to $\angle PQ$. Trivially, $\angle PQ$ is congruent to itself. It is also easily proved that if $\angle PQ$ is congruent to $\angle AB$ and $\angle AB$ is congruent to $\angle CD$, then $\angle PQ$ is congruent to $\angle CD$. We shall leave these easy proofs as exercises.

Proposition 5. *Two angles $\angle PQ$ and $\angle AB$ are congruent if and only if*

$$\cos \angle PQ = \cos \angle AB,$$
$$\sin \angle PQ = \sin \angle AB.$$

Proof. Assume first that the two angles are congruent, and let F be the rotation such that $F(P) = A$, $F(Q) = B$. Let E be the unit vector such that $\{P, E\}$ is the orthonormal basis having the given orientation. By definition, $\{F(P), F(E)\}$ has the same orientation. Let a, b be numbers such that

$$Q = aP + bE.$$

Since F is linear, we get

$$F(Q) = aF(P) + bF(E).$$

Since $F(P) = A$, it follows by definition that the cosines of our two angles are equal, and so are their sines.

The converse will be left as an exercise.

Let $\angle PQ$ be an angle. We define **minus** $\angle PQ$ to be the angle $\angle QP$, write it $-\angle PQ$, and also call it the **negative** of $\angle PQ$. We leave it as an exercise to prove that if two angles are congruent, then their negatives are congruent.

Let $\angle PQ$ and $\angle QR$ be two angles. We define their **sum** to be the angle $\angle PR$.

Let $\{P, E\}$ be an orthonormal basis having the given orientation. We call the angle $\angle PE$ a **positive right angle**. We call $\angle PQ$ a **flat** angle if $Q = -P$.

It is then possible to prove entirely within the context of linear algebra, directly from our definitions, all the properties of sines and cosines of angles which have been proved in the *First Course in Calculus* for the sin and cos functions. All the relevant definitions have now been made. In fact, we note that the addition formula for the cosine function was proved in our *First Course* by a method which applies verbatim, since all the concepts involved in it have now received an analytic definition.

It is a good exercise for anyone interested to carry out these proofs.

It is also possible to carry out the proofs by first relating directly our sines and cosines of angles with the sin and cos functions as defined analytically in an appendix to our *First Course*, say by power series, and satisfying the basic properties $f' = g$, $g' = -f$, $f(0) = 0$, $g(0) = 1$, from which all the other analytic properties were derived. This is done as follows.

Proposition 6. *Assume that an orientation of V has been fixed. Given a number θ, let F_θ be the rotation whose associated matrix with respect to any orthonormal basis having the given orientation is*

$$\begin{pmatrix} \cos\theta & -\sin\theta \\ \sin\theta & \cos\theta \end{pmatrix}.$$

If θ, φ are numbers, then $F_{\theta+\varphi} = F_\theta F_\varphi = F_\varphi F_\theta$. Also, $F_{-\theta} = F_\theta^{-1}$. We have $F_\theta = F_\varphi$ if and only if θ and φ differ by a period $2n\pi$.

Proof. The fact that the matrix of a rotation is the same for two orthonormal bases having the same orientation was proved in Proposition 2. A direct multiplication of matrices will show that our assertions are true, using the addition formulas for sine and cosine.

Given an angle $\angle PQ$, we observe that we can find its sine and cosine as follows. We let F be the rotation such that $F(P) = Q$. By Proposition 2 and properties of sine and cosine, there exists a number θ such that $F = F_\theta$. Then

$$\cos \angle PQ = \cos\theta \qquad \text{and} \qquad \sin \angle PQ = \sin\theta.$$

To each angle, we have associated a rotation, and hence a set of numbers of type $\theta + 2n\pi$. Conversely, given a rotation F and a point P on the unit circle, we can associate to these the angle $\angle PQ$ where $Q = F(P)$.

Let $\angle PQ$ be an angle and θ a number. We define the expression "$\angle PQ$ *has θ radians*" to mean that F_θ is the rotation associated with the angle $\angle PQ$. If $\varphi = \theta + 2n\pi$, and if $\angle PQ$ has θ radians, then $\angle PQ$ also has φ radians.

Using Proposition 5, it now follows trivially that the cosine of the sum of two angles satisfies the usual addition formula, if we use the analogous formula for the cos function. We give the proof as an example.

Let $\angle PQ$ have θ radians, and $\angle QR$ have φ radians. Then $F_\theta(P) = Q$ and $F_\varphi(Q) = R$. Hence

$$F_{\theta+\varphi}(P) = F_\varphi(F_\theta(P)) = R.$$

Hence $\angle PR$ has $\theta + \varphi$ radians. Applying the formula

$$\cos(\theta + \varphi) = \cos\theta\cos\varphi - \sin\theta\sin\varphi,$$

and the definitions, we get the addition formula for the cosine of the sum of two angles.

The addition formula for the sine is proved in the same way.

Answers to Exercises

Answers to Exercises

Chapter I, §1

	$A + B$	$A - B$	$3A$	$-2B$
1.	$(1, 0)$	$(3, -2)$	$(6, -3)$	$(2, -2)$
2.	$(-1, 7)$	$(-1, -1)$	$(-3, 9)$	$(0, -8)$
3.	$(1, 0, 6)$	$(3, -2, 4)$	$(6, -3, 15)$	$(2, -2, -2)$
4.	$(-2, 1, -1)$	$(0, -5, 7)$	$(-3, -6, 9)$	$(2, -6, 8)$
5.	$(3\pi, 0, 6)$	$(-\pi, 6, -8)$	$(3\pi, 9, -3)$	$(-4\pi, 6, -14)$
6.	$(15 + \pi, 1, 3)$	$(15 - \pi, -5, 5)$	$(45, -6, 12)$	$(-2\pi, -6, 2)$

Chapter I, §2

1. No **2.** Yes **3.** No **4.** Yes **5.** No **6.** Yes **7.** Yes **8.** Yes

Chapter I, §3

1. $5, 10, 30, 14, 10 + \pi^2, 245$ **2.** $-3, 12, 2, -17, 2\pi^2 - 16, 15\pi - 10$
4. (b) and (d)   **6.** $\frac{2}{3}, \frac{2}{5}, 0$

Chapter I, §4

1. $\sqrt{5}, \sqrt{10}, \sqrt{30}, \sqrt{14}, \sqrt{10 + \pi^2}, \sqrt{245}$
2. $\sqrt{2}, 4, \sqrt{3}, \sqrt{26}, \sqrt{4\pi^2 + 58}, \sqrt{\pi^2 + 10}$
3. $(\frac{3}{2}, -\frac{3}{2}), (0, 3), \frac{2}{3}(-1, 1, 1), \frac{17}{26}(1, -3, 4),$

$$\frac{\pi^2 - 8}{2\pi^2 + 29} (2\pi, -3, 7), \qquad \frac{15\pi - 10}{\pi^2 + 10} (\pi, 3, -1)$$

4. $\frac{3}{5}(-2, 1), \frac{6}{5}(-1, 3), \frac{1}{15}(2, -1, 5), \frac{17}{14}(1, 2, -3),$

$$\frac{2\pi^2 - 16}{\pi^2 + 10} (\pi, 3, -1), \qquad \frac{3\pi - 2}{49} (15, -2, 4)$$

5. $0, 0$ **6.** $\sqrt{\pi}, \sqrt{\pi}$ **7.** $\sqrt{2\pi}$ **8.** $\sqrt{2}$

13. (a) $\dfrac{35}{\sqrt{41 \cdot 35}}, \dfrac{6}{\sqrt{41 \cdot 6}}, 0$

(b) $\dfrac{1}{\sqrt{17 \cdot 26}}, \dfrac{16 \cdot}{\sqrt{17 \cdot 41}}, \dfrac{25}{\sqrt{26 \cdot 41}}$

Chapter I, §5

1. $X = (1, 1, -1) + t(3, 0, -4)$ **2.** $X = (-1, 5, 2) + t(-4, 9, 1)$

3. $y = x + 8$ **4.** $4y = 5x - 7$ **6.** (c) and (d)

7. (a) $x - y + 3z = -1$ (b) $3x + 2y - 4z = 2\pi + 26$
(c) $x - 5z = -33$

8. (a) $2x + y + 2z = 7$ (b) $7x - 8y - 9z = -29$
(c) $y + z = 1$

9. $(3, -9, -5)$, $(1, 5, -7)$ (Others would be constant multiples of these.)

10. (a) $2(t^2 + 5)^{1/2}$ **11.** $(15t^2 + 26t + 21)^{1/2}$, $\sqrt{146/15}$

12. $(-2, 1, 5)$ **13.** $(11, 13, -7)$

14. (a) $X = (1, 0, -1) + t(-2, 1, 5)$ (b) $X = (1, 0, 0) + t(11, 13, -7)$

15. (a) $-\frac{1}{3}$ (b) $-2/\sqrt{42}$ (c) $4/\sqrt{66}$ (d) $-\sqrt{2}/3$

16. $t = \dfrac{(P - Q) \cdot N}{N \cdot N}$ **17.** $(1, 3, -2)$ **18.** $2/\sqrt{3}$ **19.** $(-4, \frac{11}{2}, \frac{15}{2})$

20. $\dfrac{8}{\sqrt{35}}$ **21.** (a) $\frac{1}{2}(-3, 8, 1)$ (b) $(-\frac{2}{3}, \frac{11}{3}, 0)$, $(-\frac{7}{3}, \frac{13}{3}, 1)$ **22.** $\dfrac{P + Q}{2}$

Chapter I, §6

1. $(-4, -3, 1)$ **2.** $(-1, 1, -1)$ **3.** $(-9, 6, -1)$

4. 0 **5.** E_3, E_1, E_2 in that order.

7. $(0, 0, 0)$ and $(0, -1, 0)$, no

Chapter I, §7

1. (a) $-\dfrac{1}{10} - \dfrac{3i}{10}$ (b) 2 (c) $-1 + 3i$ (d) $-1 + 3i$

(e) $6\pi + (7 + \pi^2)i$ (f) $-2\pi + \pi i$ (g) $\pi\sqrt{2} - 3 + (\pi + 3\sqrt{2})i$

(h) $-8 - 6i$

2. (a) $\frac{1}{2} + \frac{1}{2}i$ (b) $\frac{3}{10} - \frac{1}{10}i$ (c) $\frac{3}{5} + \frac{2}{5}i$ (d) $\frac{2}{5} + \frac{1}{5}i$

Chapter II, §2

2. (a) $A - B$, $(1, -1)$ (b) $\frac{1}{2}A + \frac{3}{2}B$, $(\frac{1}{2}, \frac{3}{2})$
(c) $A + B$, $(1, 1)$ (d) $3A + 2B$, $(3, 2)$

3. (a) $(\frac{1}{3}, -\frac{1}{3}, \frac{1}{3})$ (b) $(1, 0, 1)$ (c) $(\frac{1}{3}, -\frac{1}{3}, -\frac{2}{3})$

7. $(3, 5)$ **8.** $(-5, 3)$

Chapter III, §1   On Matrices

1. $A + B = \begin{pmatrix} 0 & 7 & 1 \\ 0 & 1 & 1 \end{pmatrix}$, $3B = \begin{pmatrix} -3 & 15 & -6 \\ 3 & 3 & -3 \end{pmatrix}$

$-2B = \begin{pmatrix} 2 & -10 & 4 \\ -2 & -2 & 2 \end{pmatrix}$, $A + 2B = \begin{pmatrix} -1 & 12 & -1 \\ 1 & 2 & 0 \end{pmatrix}$

$$2A + B = \begin{pmatrix} 1 & 9 & 4 \\ -1 & 1 & 3 \end{pmatrix}, \qquad A - B = \begin{pmatrix} 2 & -3 & 5 \\ -2 & -1 & 3 \end{pmatrix}$$

$$A - 2B = \begin{pmatrix} 3 & -8 & 7 \\ -3 & -2 & 4 \end{pmatrix}, \qquad B - A = \begin{pmatrix} -2 & 3 & -5 \\ 2 & 1 & -3 \end{pmatrix}$$

2. $A + B = \begin{pmatrix} 0 & 0 \\ 2 & -2 \end{pmatrix}, \qquad 3B = \begin{pmatrix} -3 & 3 \\ 0 & -9 \end{pmatrix} \qquad -2B = \begin{pmatrix} 2 & -2 \\ 0 & 6 \end{pmatrix},$

$A + 2B = \begin{pmatrix} -1 & 1 \\ 2 & -5 \end{pmatrix} \qquad A - B = \begin{pmatrix} 2 & -2 \\ 2 & 4 \end{pmatrix}, \qquad B - A = \begin{pmatrix} -2 & 2 \\ -2 & -4 \end{pmatrix}$

3. ${}^t A = \begin{pmatrix} 1 & -1 \\ 2 & 0 \\ 3 & 2 \end{pmatrix}, \qquad {}^t B = \begin{pmatrix} -1 & 1 \\ 5 & 1 \\ -2 & -1 \end{pmatrix}$

4. ${}^t A = \begin{pmatrix} 1 & 2 \\ -1 & 1 \end{pmatrix}, \qquad {}^t B = \begin{pmatrix} -1 & 0 \\ 1 & -3 \end{pmatrix}$

7. Same **8.** $\begin{pmatrix} 0 & 2 \\ 0 & -2 \end{pmatrix}$, same

9. $A + {}^t A = \begin{pmatrix} 2 & 1 \\ 1 & 2 \end{pmatrix}, \qquad B + {}^t B = \begin{pmatrix} -2 & 1 \\ 1 & -6 \end{pmatrix}$

11. Rows of A: $(1, 2, 3), (-1, 0, 2)$

Columns of A: $\begin{pmatrix} 1 \\ -1 \end{pmatrix}, \begin{pmatrix} 2 \\ 0 \end{pmatrix}, \begin{pmatrix} 3 \\ 2 \end{pmatrix}$

Rows of B: $(-1, 5, -2), (1, 1, -1)$

Columns of B: $\begin{pmatrix} -1 \\ 1 \end{pmatrix}, \begin{pmatrix} 5 \\ 1 \end{pmatrix}, \begin{pmatrix} -2 \\ -1 \end{pmatrix}$

12. Rows of A: $(1, -1), (2, 1)$ Columns of A: $\begin{pmatrix} 1 \\ 2 \end{pmatrix}, \begin{pmatrix} 2 \\ 1 \end{pmatrix}$

Rows of B: $(-1, 1), (0, -3)$ Columns of B: $\begin{pmatrix} -1 \\ 0 \end{pmatrix}, \begin{pmatrix} 1 \\ -3 \end{pmatrix}$

Chapter III, §1 On Dimensions

1. 4. Possible basis: $\begin{pmatrix} 1 & 0 \\ 0 & 0 \end{pmatrix}, \begin{pmatrix} 0 & 1 \\ 0 & 0 \end{pmatrix}, \begin{pmatrix} 0 & 0 \\ 1 & 0 \end{pmatrix}, \begin{pmatrix} 0 & 0 \\ 0 & 1 \end{pmatrix}$

2. mn; $\{E_{ij}\}$ where E_{ij} has component 1 at the (i, j) place and 0 otherwise

3. n **4.** $n(n + 1)/2$

5. $\begin{pmatrix} 0 & 1 \\ 1 & 0 \end{pmatrix}, \begin{pmatrix} 1 & 0 \\ 0 & 0 \end{pmatrix}, \begin{pmatrix} 0 & 0 \\ 0 & 1 \end{pmatrix}$

6. $n(n + 1)/2$

7. n; E_i where E_i is the $n \times n$ matrix whose ii-th term is 1 and all other terms are 0.

8. 0, 1, or 2 **9.** 0, 1, 2, or 3

Chapter III, §3

1. $IA = AI = A$ **2.** 0

3. (a) $\begin{pmatrix} 3 & 2 \\ 4 & 1 \end{pmatrix}$ (b) $\begin{pmatrix} 1 & 0 \\ 1 & 4 \end{pmatrix}$ (c) $\begin{pmatrix} 33 & 37 \\ 11 & -18 \end{pmatrix}$

5. $AB = \begin{pmatrix} 4 & 2 \\ 5 & -1 \end{pmatrix},\qquad BA = \begin{pmatrix} 2 & 4 \\ 4 & 1 \end{pmatrix}$

6. $AC = CA = \begin{pmatrix} 7 & 14 \\ 21 & -7 \end{pmatrix},\qquad BC = CB = \begin{pmatrix} 14 & 0 \\ 7 & 7 \end{pmatrix}$

If $C = xI$, where x is a number, then $AC = CA = xA$.

7. $(3, 1, 5)$, first row   **8.** Second row, third row, i-th row

10. A possible M is $\begin{pmatrix} -1 & 0 \\ 0 & -1 \end{pmatrix}$.

11. (a) $A^2 = \begin{pmatrix} 0 & 0 & 1 \\ 0 & 0 & 0 \\ 0 & 0 & 0 \end{pmatrix}$, $A^3 = O$ matrix.   If $B = \begin{pmatrix} 0 & 1 & 1 & 1 \\ 0 & 0 & 1 & 1 \\ 0 & 0 & 0 & 1 \\ 0 & 0 & 0 & 0 \end{pmatrix}$ then

$B^2 = \begin{pmatrix} 0 & 0 & 1 & 2 \\ 0 & 0 & 0 & 1 \\ 0 & 0 & 0 & 0 \\ 0 & 0 & 0 & 0 \end{pmatrix}$, $B^3 = \begin{pmatrix} 0 & 0 & 0 & 1 \\ 0 & 0 & 0 & 0 \\ 0 & 0 & 0 & 0 \\ 0 & 0 & 0 & 0 \end{pmatrix}$ and $B^4 = O$.

(b) $A^2 = \begin{pmatrix} 1 & 2 & 3 \\ 0 & 1 & 2 \\ 0 & 0 & 1 \end{pmatrix}$, $A^3 = \begin{pmatrix} 1 & 3 & 6 \\ 0 & 1 & 3 \\ 0 & 0 & 1 \end{pmatrix}$, $A^4 = \begin{pmatrix} 1 & 4 & 10 \\ 0 & 1 & 4 \\ 0 & 0 & 1 \end{pmatrix}$

12. (a) $\begin{pmatrix} 4 \\ 9 \\ 5 \end{pmatrix}$ (b) $\begin{pmatrix} 3 \\ 1 \end{pmatrix}$ (c) $\begin{pmatrix} x_2 \\ 0 \end{pmatrix}$ (d) $\begin{pmatrix} 0 \\ x_1 \end{pmatrix}$

13. (a) $\begin{pmatrix} 2 \\ 4 \end{pmatrix}$ (b) $\begin{pmatrix} 4 \\ 6 \end{pmatrix}$ (c) $\begin{pmatrix} 3 \\ 5 \end{pmatrix}$

14. (a) $\begin{pmatrix} 3 \\ 1 \\ 2 \end{pmatrix}$ (b) $\begin{pmatrix} 12 \\ 3 \\ 9 \end{pmatrix}$ (c) $\begin{pmatrix} 5 \\ 4 \\ 8 \end{pmatrix}$

15. Second column of A **16.** i-th column of A

18. $\begin{pmatrix} 1 & a+b \\ 0 & 1 \end{pmatrix}, \begin{pmatrix} 1 & na \\ 0 & 1 \end{pmatrix}$

20. $\begin{pmatrix} 1 & -a \\ 0 & 1 \end{pmatrix}$

22. $\begin{pmatrix} a & b \\ \dfrac{-a^2}{b} & -a \end{pmatrix}$ for any $a, b \neq 0$; if $b = 0$, then $a = 0$.

24. $\begin{pmatrix} 0 & 1 \\ -1 & 0 \end{pmatrix}$

25. (a) 2   (b) 4   (c) 8

29. $\begin{pmatrix} 1 & 0 & 0 \\ 0 & 4 & 0 \\ 0 & 0 & 9 \end{pmatrix}, \begin{pmatrix} 1 & 0 & 0 \\ 0 & 8 & 0 \\ 0 & 0 & 27 \end{pmatrix}, \begin{pmatrix} 1 & 0 & 0 \\ 0 & 16 & 0 \\ 0 & 0 & 81 \end{pmatrix}$

30. Diagonal matrix with diagonal $a_1{}^k$, $a_2{}^k$, ... $a_n{}^k$

31. $0, 0$

Chapter IV, §1

1. (a) $\cos x$ (b) e^x (c) $1/x$

3. (a) 11 (b) 13 (c) 6

4. (a) $(e, 1)$ (b) $(1, 0)$ (c) $(1/e, -1)$

5. (a) $(e + 1, 3)$ (b) $(e^2 + 2, 6)$ (c) $(1, 0)$

6. (a) $(2, 0)$ (b) $(\pi e, \pi)$

7. (a) 1 (b) 11

8. Ellipse $9x^2 + 4y^2 = 36$ **9.** Line $x = 2y$

10. Circle $x^2 + y^2 = e^2$, circle $x^2 + y^2 = e^{2c}$

11. Cylinder, radius 1, z-axis $=$ axis of cylinder   **12.** Circle $x^2 + y^2 = 1$

Chapter IV, §2

1. All except (c), (g)

4. If u is one element such that $Tu = w$, then the set of all such elements is the set of elements $u + v$ where $Tv = 0$.

8. Only Ex. 8.

9. If $F(A) = 0$, image $=$ point $F(P)$. If $F(A) \neq 0$, image is the line $F(P) + tF(A)$.

12. Parallelogram whose vertices are B, $3A$, $3A + B$, 0

13. Parallelogram whose vertices are 0, $2B$, $5A$, $5A + 2B$

14. 0   **18.** (a) $(-1, -1)$ (b) $(-2/3, 1)$ (c) $(-2, -1)$

19. (a) $(4, 5)$ (b) $(11/3, -3)$ (c) $(4, 2)$

Chapter IV, §3

6. Constant functions

7. Ker $D^2 =$ polynomials of deg ≤ 1, Ker $D^n =$ polynomials of deg $\leq n - 1$

9. (a) Constant multiples of e^x (b) Constant multiples of e^{ax}

10. (a) $n - 1$ (b) $n^2 - 1$

12. $n(n + 1)/2$

Basis $n = 2$

$$\left\{ \begin{pmatrix} 0 & 1 \\ 1 & 0 \end{pmatrix} \begin{pmatrix} 1 & 0 \\ 0 & 0 \end{pmatrix} \begin{pmatrix} 0 & 0 \\ 0 & 1 \end{pmatrix} \right\}$$

Basis $n = 3$

$$\left\{ \begin{pmatrix} 1 & 0 & 0 \\ 0 & 0 & 0 \\ 0 & 0 & 0 \end{pmatrix} \begin{pmatrix} 0 & 0 & 0 \\ 0 & 1 & 0 \\ 0 & 0 & 0 \end{pmatrix} \begin{pmatrix} 0 & 0 & 0 \\ 0 & 0 & 0 \\ 0 & 0 & 1 \end{pmatrix} \begin{pmatrix} 0 & 1 & 0 \\ 1 & 0 & 0 \\ 0 & 0 & 0 \end{pmatrix} \begin{pmatrix} 0 & 0 & 1 \\ 0 & 0 & 0 \\ 1 & 0 & 0 \end{pmatrix} \begin{pmatrix} 0 & 0 & 0 \\ 0 & 0 & 1 \\ 0 & 1 & 0 \end{pmatrix} \right\}$$

15. (c) $n(n-1)/2$ **16.** $n(n+1)/2$

17. (a) 0   (b) $m+n$, $\{(u_i, 0), (0, w_j)\}$; $i = 1, \ldots, m$; $j = 1, \ldots, n$. If $\{u_i\}$ is a basis of U and $\{w_j\}$ is a basis of W.

Chapter V, §1

1. (a) $(5, 3)$ (b) $(5, 0)$ (c) $(5, 1)$ (d) $(0, -3)$

Chapter V, §2

1. (a) $\begin{pmatrix} 1 & 0 & 0 & 0 \\ 0 & 1 & 0 & 0 \end{pmatrix}$ (b) $\begin{pmatrix} 1 & 0 & 0 & 0 \\ 0 & 1 & 0 & 0 \\ 0 & 0 & 1 & 0 \end{pmatrix}$

(c) $3I$ (d) $7I$ (e) $-I$ (f) $\begin{pmatrix} 1 & 0 & 0 & 0 \\ 0 & 1 & 0 & 0 \\ 0 & 0 & 0 & 0 \\ 0 & 0 & 0 & 0 \end{pmatrix}$

2. (a) $\begin{pmatrix} 0 & -1 \\ 1 & 0 \end{pmatrix}$ (b) $\dfrac{1}{\sqrt{2}}\begin{pmatrix} 1 & -1 \\ 1 & 1 \end{pmatrix}$ (c) $\begin{pmatrix} -1 & 0 \\ 0 & -1 \end{pmatrix}$ (d) $\begin{pmatrix} -1 & 0 \\ 0 & -1 \end{pmatrix}$

(e) $\dfrac{1}{2}\begin{pmatrix} 1 & \sqrt{3} \\ -\sqrt{3} & 1 \end{pmatrix}$ (f) $\dfrac{1}{2}\begin{pmatrix} \sqrt{3} & -1 \\ 1 & \sqrt{3} \end{pmatrix}$ (g) $\dfrac{1}{\sqrt{2}}\begin{pmatrix} -1 & 1 \\ -1 & -1 \end{pmatrix}$

3. $\begin{pmatrix} \cos\theta & \sin\theta \\ -\sin\theta & \cos\theta \end{pmatrix}$ **4.** $\dfrac{1}{\sqrt{2}}(-1, 3)$ **5.** $(-3, -1)$ **8.** cI

9. $\begin{pmatrix} \cos\theta\cos\varphi - \sin\theta\sin\varphi & -(\cos\theta\sin\varphi + \cos\theta\sin\varphi) \\ \cos\theta\sin\varphi + \cos\theta\sin\varphi & \cos\theta\cos\varphi - \sin\theta\sin\varphi \end{pmatrix}$

Chapter VI, §2

1. dim 4

2. (a) $\dfrac{1}{\sqrt{3}}(1, 1, -1)$ and $\dfrac{1}{\sqrt{2}}(1, 0, 1)$

(b) $\dfrac{1}{\sqrt{6}}(2, 1, 1)$, $\dfrac{1}{5\sqrt{3}}(-1, 7, -5)$

3. $\dfrac{1}{\sqrt{6}}(1, 2, 1, 0)$ and $\dfrac{1}{\sqrt{39}}(-1, -2, 5, 3)$

4. $\dfrac{1}{\sqrt{2}}(1, 1, 0, 0)$, $\tfrac{1}{2}(1, -1, 1, 1)$, $\dfrac{1}{\sqrt{18}}(-2, 2, 3, 1)$

5. $\sqrt{80}\,(t^2 - 3t/4)$, $\sqrt{3}\,t$

6. $\sqrt{80}\,(t^2 - 3t/4)$, $\sqrt{3}\,t$, $10t^2 - 12t + 3$

Chapter VI, §3

1. (a) 2   (b) 2   (c) 2   (d) 1   (e) 2   (f) 3   (g) 3   (h) 2

3. n

4. (a) dim. = 1   basis = $(1, -1, 1)$

(b) dim. = 2   basis = $(1, 1, 0)(0, 1, 1)$

(c) dim. = 1   basis = $\left(\dfrac{\pi - 3}{10}, \dfrac{\pi + 2}{5}, 1 \right)$

(d) dim. = 0

5. (a) 1   (b) 1   (c) 0   (d) 2   **6.** $n - 1$

Chapter VI, §4

5. (a) $2x_1y_1 - 3x_1y_2 + 4x_2y_1 + x_2y_2$

(b) $4x_1y_1 + x_1y_2 - 2x_2y_1 + 5x_2y_2$

(c) $5x_1y_1 + 2x_1y_2 + \pi x_2y_1 + 7x_2y_2$

(d) $x_1y_1 + 2x_1y_2 - x_1y_3 - 3x_2y_1 + x_2y_2 + 4x_2y_3 + 2x_3y_1$
$+ 5x_3y_2 - x_3y_3$

(e) $-4x_1y_1 + 2x_1y_2 + x_1y_3 + 3x_2y_1 + x_2y_2 + x_2y_3 + 2x_3y_1$
$+ 5x_3y_2 + 7x_3y_3$

(f) $-\dfrac{1}{2}x_1y_1 + 2x_1y_2 - 5x_1y_3 + x_2y_1 + \dfrac{2}{3}x_2y_2 + 4x_2y_3 - x_3y_1 + 3x_3y_3$

Chapter VII, 3§

1. (a) -20 (b) 5   (c) 4   (d) 5   (e) -76 (f) -14

2. (a) -18 (b) 45   (c) 0   (d) 0   (e) 4   (f) 14   (g) 108   (h) 135   (i) 10

3. $a_{11}a_{22} \cdots a_{nn}$ **4.** 1

6. (a) 3   (b) -24 (c) 16   (d) 14   (e) 0   (f) 8   (g) 40   (h) -10 (i) $\displaystyle\prod_{i=1}^{N} a_{ii}$

7. 1   **8.** $t^2 + 8t + 5$

Chapter VII, §4

1. (a) $x = -\frac{1}{3}, y = \frac{2}{3}, z = -\frac{1}{3}$ (b) $x = \frac{5}{12}, y = -\frac{1}{12}, z = \frac{1}{12}$

(c) $x = -\frac{5}{24}, y = \frac{97}{48}, z = \frac{1}{3}, w = -\frac{25}{48}$

(d) $x = \frac{11}{2}, y = \frac{38}{5}, z = \frac{1}{10}, w = 2$

Chapter VII, §5

1. (a) 1   (b) 1   (c) -1 (d) 1   (e) 1   (f) 1   (g) 1   (h) -1 (i) -1

2. (a) $\begin{bmatrix} 1 & 2 & 3 \\ 3 & 1 & 2 \end{bmatrix}$ (b) $\begin{bmatrix} 1 & 2 & 3 \\ 2 & 3 & 1 \end{bmatrix}$ (c) $\begin{bmatrix} 1 & 2 & 3 \\ 3 & 2 & 1 \end{bmatrix}$ (d) $\begin{bmatrix} 1 & 2 & 3 & 4 \\ 3 & 1 & 2 & 4 \end{bmatrix}$

(e) $\begin{bmatrix} 1 & 2 & 3 & 4 \\ 2 & 1 & 4 & 3 \end{bmatrix}$ (f) $\begin{bmatrix} 1 & 2 & 3 & 4 \\ 4 & 2 & 1 & 3 \end{bmatrix}$ (g) $\begin{bmatrix} 1 & 2 & 3 & 4 \\ 3 & 2 & 4 & 1 \end{bmatrix}$

(h) $\begin{bmatrix} 1 & 2 & 3 & 4 \\ 2 & 4 & 1 & 3 \end{bmatrix}$ (i) $\begin{bmatrix} 1 & 2 & 3 & 4 \\ 3 & 1 & 4 & 2 \end{bmatrix}$

Chapter VII, §9

1. (a) $-\dfrac{1}{20}\begin{pmatrix} 4 & 1 & -7 \\ -4 & -6 & 2 \\ 12 & 2 & 6 \end{pmatrix}$ (b) $\dfrac{1}{5}\begin{pmatrix} 2 & 23 & -11 \\ 1 & 19 & -8 \\ 0 & -10 & 5 \end{pmatrix}$

(c) $\dfrac{1}{4}\begin{pmatrix} 3 & 2 & -9 \\ 1 & 2 & -3 \\ -2 & -4 & 10 \end{pmatrix}$ (d) $\dfrac{1}{5}\begin{pmatrix} 5 & -16 & 3 \\ 0 & 7 & -1 \\ 0 & -2 & 1 \end{pmatrix}$

(e) $-\dfrac{1}{76}\begin{pmatrix} 0 & -19 & 0 \\ -32 & -14 & 12 \\ 28 & 17 & -20 \end{pmatrix}$

3. (c) $\dfrac{1}{ad-bc}\begin{pmatrix} d & -b \\ -c & a \end{pmatrix}$

Chapter VII, §10

1. 2   **2.** 2   **3.** 2   **4.** 3   **5.** 4   **6.** 3   **7.** 2   **8.** 3

Chapter VII, §11

2. (a) 14   (b) 1
3. (a) 11   (b) 38   (c) 8   (d) 1
4. (a) 10   (b) 22   (c) 11   (d) 0

Index

Index